917.304 WITHDRAWN 1996

The
EARLY
AMERICA
K

A Traveler's
Guide

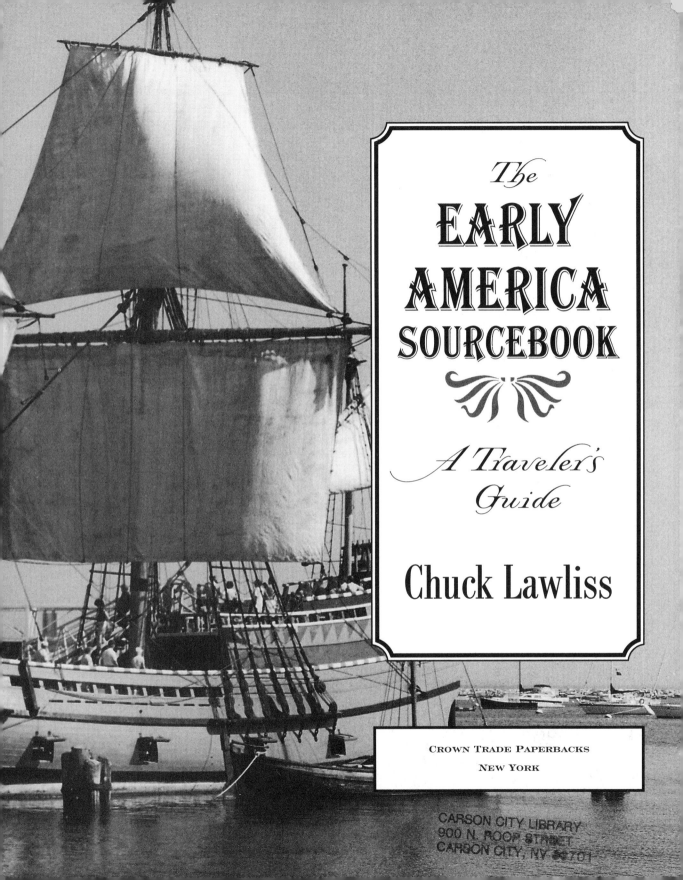

The
EARLY AMERICA SOURCEBOOK

A Traveler's Guide

Chuck Lawliss

CROWN TRADE PAPERBACKS
NEW YORK

©1996 Maps Copyright Fodor's Travel Publications
Maps adapted by Bob Roman
Copyright © 1996 by Chuck Lawliss

Published by Crown Trade Paperbacks, Inc., 201 East 50th Street, New York, New York 10022. Member of the Crown Publishing Group.

Random House, Inc. New York, Toronto, London, Sydney, Auckland

CROWN TRADE PAPERBACKS and colophon are trademarks of Crown Publishers, Inc.

Manufactured in the United States of America

Design by Lauren Dong / Lenny Henderson

Library of Congress Cataloging-in Publication Data
Lawliss, Chuck.
The early America sourcebook : a traveler's guide / Chuck Lawliss.
    p.   cm.
Includes index.
1. Historic sites—United States—Guidebooks. 2. United States—Guidebooks. I. Title.
            E159.L38   1996
917.304'929—dc20   96-4302
                                                  CIP

ISBN 0-517-88391-0

10 9 8 7 6 5 4 3 2 1

First Edition

CONTENTS

INTRODUCTION

I once lived in a tiny house on a lovely courtyard in the Society Hill section of Philadelphia. The house was built around 1760, and in the early days was rented to sea captains and others who came on business to the largest city in the British colonies. When I registered to vote, I was pleased to learn that I was a resident of the First Ward of the First Congressional District in the country. Philadelphia was the capital of the country when the first districts were drawn up, and Independence Hall, then the capitol building, was only a short walk from my house.

To live in Society Hill it is well to have a sense of the past. I have that, perhaps in extremis. The past has always been with me. An ancestor of mine, Captain John Stanhope, arrived in the Massachusetts Bay Colony in 1640. Some of his descendants headed north to settle in the New Hampshire Grants. Two were members of Ethan Allen's Green Mountain Boys. My cousin still works a farm that was in the family when Vermont was an independent republic.

When I was young, these stories nourished me. My grandmother, who lived with us, was a member of the Daughters of the American Revolution. Her sister was the family historian and knew all the good stuff about our relatives, even third cousins twice removed. None had ever lived in great houses or won great battles, but that didn't trouble me. They had been part of history, and that was enough.

I am a second-generation antique nut. My mother spent her spare time in auctions and antique shops, her spare cash on her collections of clocks and glassware, quilts and hooked rugs. She called her obsession "antiquing." I became her willing co-conspirator. Hereditary, you say, but neither of my sisters nor my brother showed any symptoms of the disease.

My personal obsession includes architecture. I have four favorite styles: the true New England Colonial saltbox, like the 1637 Hoxie House in Sandwich, on Cape Cod; Federal, like the Harrison Gray Otis House in Boston; Georgian, like the Hammond-Harwood House in Annapolis; and Greek Revival—it takes a cold heart indeed to resist Stanton Hall in Natchez.

It isn't simply the artifacts of Early America that fascinate. It is a great saga. Think of the "starving time" at Jamestown, when the settlers simply tried to endure. Or the massacre at Deerfield, when western Massachusetts was the frontier. Or the young George Washington, losing his first battle to his future allies, the French, in what turned out to be the beginning of the French and Indian War.

All this was a prelude to the Revolution, the War for Independence. I have always been amazed that a group of colonists, farmers mostly, cared enough for their rights to stand up to the most powerful empire on earth. Experience a bit of the Revolution for yourself. Go to Lexington, stand where the Minutemen watched the Redcoats approach, and think about what their leader, Captain John Parker, told them just before the British began shooting: "Stand your ground. Don't fire unless fired upon. But if they mean to have a war, let it begin here."

Or visit Valley Forge, preferably on a cold, dreary winter's day. Imagine yourself dressed in rags, sleeping in a hut, achingly hungry. You are at the nadir of the Revolution's seven long years, "the times," wrote Thomas Paine, "that try men's souls." It is one thing to be brave when your adrenaline is pumping in the heat of battle, quite another to endure extreme hardship and deprivation, day after day, when you know that you can desert, simply walk away and go home.

Or go to Yorktown, the scene of the final battle. Imagine that you are an aide, waiting with Washington and the French officers for the surrender. The Redcoats come on the field to stack arms. The British band is playing "The World Turned Upside Down." Cornwallis is absent, pleading illness. His stand-in attempts to give his sword in surrender to the senior French officer, who refuses, indicating that it rightfully belongs to Washington.

This book is full of such events and such places. Its purpose is to introduce—or reintroduce—you to Early America and the places and events that shaped it, from the beginning to the eve of the Civil War. It covers all the states east of the Mississippi River, and concentrates primarily on English settlements and English colonies. This was done, in part, for reasons of space, and because the early Spanish settlements in California and the Southwest formed a major part of an earlier book, *The Old West Sourcebook, A Traveler's Guide.*

You will find in these pages all the major sites of Early America and a number of less well known sites that also, individually and collectively, help illuminate their time. A chronology traces the important dates in our early history. Short essays expand on various aspects of our heritage, from the Great Awakening and the clothing worn by the colonists to a guide to architectural styles and a summary of the almost forgotten Colonial wars that led up to the Revolution. Heroes and a few villains are profiled in short biographies. Sprinkled throughout are quotes from a wide range of sources, and many historical photographs and early prints and engravings.

May you enjoy your journey to our country's past. It's a wonderful experience. I know, I've been there.

VISITING NATIONAL PARKS
AND MONUMENTS

Much of the significant history of Early America is preserved on properties managed by the National Park Service. They usually offer a wide range of services: ranger-led tours, orientation, films, exhibits, and living-history programs. Rangers know the properties intimately, and visitors should feel free to ask questions.

It is prudent to phone ahead, particularly if you are coming from a distance. Find out what programs will be offered while you are there. Maybe make reservations if necessary.

Few properties have food facilities, but most have picnic areas. Picnicking while surrounded by history is a delight.

Do not disturb a historic site. Everything on the site, even the stones on the ground, is part of the historical environment, a precious national resource being preserved for future generations. And don't litter. The golden rule is "Take only pictures, leave only footprints."

Many properties charge admission. If you plan to visit several properties, you will save money by obtaining one of the three types of passes offered by the Park Service. All admit the holder and the people in his or her car, or the immediate family if arriving by bus.

Golden Eagle Passport. Available for $25 to people under sixty-two years of age. Valid for one year, from January 1 to December 31. May be purchased at any of the properties that charge entrance fees, or by mail from the Park Service.

Golden Age Passport. Free lifetime pass for people aged sixty-two or older. Also provides a 50-percent discount on fees for camping, boat launching, and parking. Golden Age Passports must be picked up in person at a national park or at a National Park Service Office, and require proof of age.

Golden Access Passport. Carries the same privileges as the Golden Age Passport. Available to handicapped persons who are eligible for federal benefits as a result of disability.

For further information, write the National Park Service, Washington, D.C. 20240, or telephone 202/343-4747.

PART I

SETTING THE SCENE

1

A CHRONOLOGY OF EARLY AMERICA

1000 Leif Eriksson settles Vinland.

1492 Christopher Columbus's first voyage.

1497 John Cabot reaches Newfoundland.

1513 Juan Ponce de León lands in Florida.
Vasco Núñez de Balboa sees the Pacific.

1519 Hernando Cortés lands in Mexico.

1520 Disease kills most of Mexico's Aztecs.

1525 Giovanni da Verrazzano discovers the Hudson River.

1532 Francisco Pizarro destroys the Inca Empire in South America.

1534 Jacques Cartier sails up the St. Lawrence River and claims the territory for France.

1536 Esteban and Fray Marcos search for Cíbola in North America's Southwest.

1539 Hernando de Soto's expedition explores the area between Florida and the Mississippi.

1540 Francisco Coronado sets out for Cíbola.

1542 Juan Rodriguez Cabrillo reaches California.

1562 Jean Ribaut starts a French colony on the coast of what now is South Carolina.

1564 The French establish Fort Caroline.

1565 The Spanish destroy Fort Caroline.

1568 The French destroy San Mateo in Florida.

1585 English captain Francis Drake reaches San Francisco Bay on his way around the world.

1585 Francis Drake destroys St. Augustine and takes surviving Roanoke colonists back to England.

1587 John White leads a second expedition to Roanoke—the Lost Colony.

1588 The English fleet defeats the Spanish Armada.

1598 Juan de Oñate settles New Mexico.

1607 Three ships sent by the London Company land at Cape Henry, Virginia. Captain John Smith and others found Jamestown.

1608 Champlain founds Quebec.

1609 Henry Hudson sails up the Hudson River.

1610 All but sixty of the 500 settlers in Jamestown die during the "starving time."

1610 Santa Fe founded.

1612 Settlers plant tobacco in Virginia for the first time.

1614 Pocahontas, daughter of Powhatan, marries John Rolfe in Jamestown.

1619 The first African slaves arrive in Virginia. The first representative government in the European colonies begins with Virginia's House of Burgesses.

1620 The Pilgrims sail from England to Cape Cod on the *Mayflower*. They make a plan of government called the Mayflower Compact. Virginia settlers organize the first public library in the colonies.

1621 Massasoit, leader of the Wampanoag Indians, establishes peace with the Pilgrims.

1622 Opechancanough leads a great Indian massacre of settlers around Jamestown.

1626 The Dutch buy Manhattan Island from the Indians.

1628 Massachusetts colonists at Merrymount celebrate May Day with a May pole, dancing, and drinking. The revival of this pagan festival horrifies the Plymouth Pilgrims.

1632 Lord Calvert founds Maryland.

1633 The first school in the North American colonies is founded in New Amsterdam.

1636 Robert Williams founds Rhode Island.
Harvard College is founded.

1638 Peter Minuit leads a group of Swedish settlers to the Delaware River.

1648 Massachusetts grants a charter to the shoemakers of Boston, the first labor organization in America.

1661 John Eliot publishes his translation of the Bible into the Algonquin language, which is also the first Bible ever to be printed in the colonies.

1664 The British capture New Amsterdam and rename it New York.

1669 Charleston is founded in South Carolina.

1675 Massasoit's son Metacomet fights New England colonists in King Philip's War.

1677 North Carolinians rebel against English taxes.

1680 Pueblo Indians led by Popé attack the Spaniards and drive them out of New Mexico.

1681 William Penn founds Pennsylvania.

1682 La Salle reaches the mouth of the Mississippi River and claims possession of the surrounding territory, which he names Louisiana, for King Louis XIV.

1686 King James II sends Sir Edmund Andros to control the New England colonists.

1692 Witchcraft trials are held in Salem, Massachusetts.

1699 Williamsburg becomes capital of Virginia.

1704 The first regularly issued newspaper in the colonies, the *Boston News-Letter,* begins publication.

1733 James Oglethorpe settles Savannah, Georgia.

1735 In Charleston, the first opera in the colonies is produced.

1737 In Boston, the Charitable Irish Society holds the first celebration of St. Patrick's Day. It is first celebrated in Philadelphia in 1780 and in New York in 1784.

1737 John Higley mints the first Colonial copper coins. They bear the words "I am good copper" and "Value me as you will."

1741 Panic sweeps through New York City after a series of fires. Rumors spread that blacks and poor whites are plotting to seize power. Although little evidence is produced, 101 blacks are convicted; eighteen blacks and four whites are hanged, thirteen blacks are burned alive, and seventy are banished.

1749 The first American repertory acting company is established in Philadelphia.

1758 A school for blacks is founded in Philadelphia by an Anglican missionary group.

1760 George III becomes king of England.
The population of the thirteen American colonies is estimated at 1,600,000.
The South Carolina legislature completely bans the slave trade in the colony, but the British crown disallows the policy.

1763 The Treaty of Paris ends the Seven Years War.
The Proclamation of 1763 forbids American colonists to settle west of the Appalachians.
The four-year task of surveying the boundary line between Pennsylvania and Maryland is begun by Jeremiah Dixon and Charles Mason.

1765 The Stamp Act forces the colonies to pay taxes on printed matter.

1766 Parliament repeals the Stamp Act.

1767 Parliament adopts the Townshend Acts, taxing tea and other goods.

1770 Five Americans are killed in the Boston Massacre.

1773 In the Boston Tea Party, fifty rebels throw chests of tea into Boston Harbor to protest the tea tax.

1773 Britain blockades Boston Harbor.

1774 The First Continental Congress meets in Philadelphia to protest and petition George III.

1775 At the Virginia convention in Richmond, Patrick Henry opposes the arbitrary rule of Britain with a speech that closes, "Give me liberty or give me death."
Battles of Lexington and Concord.
Ethan Allen captures the strategic British garrison of Fort Ticonderoga and its arsenal of military supplies.
The Second Continental Congress meets in Philadelphia and names George Washington commander in chief of the American forces.
Britain declares war on America.
Battle of Bunker Hill in Boston.
Wilderness Road opens to pioneers.

1776 Thomas Paine publishes *Common Sense*.
The Declaration of Independence is proclaimed.
The British capture New York City, and American troops retreat to Pennsylvania.

American troops defeat the British at Fort Sullivan at Charleston, South Carolina.
Washington crosses the Delaware, captures Trenton and Princeton, New Jersey.

1777 Americans under General Gates defeat General Burgoyne at Saratoga.
The Marquis de Lafayette arrives in Philadelphia to volunteer his services for the American cause.
Fearing a British invasion, the Continental Congress flees Philadelphia.
In the Second Battle of Saratoga, Americans defeat General Burgoyne's Redcoats.
Renaming itself Vermont, the "republic" adopts a constitution mandating male suffrage and banning slavery.
Washington and his army winter at Valley Forge.

1778 George Rogers Clark captures forts at Cahokia, Kaskaskia, and Vincennes in the Ohio Valley.
France comes to the aid of America.
After taking two British prizes, John Paul Jones raids the fort at Whitehall, England, and burns a ship in the harbor.
Benjamin Franklin is appointed the American diplomatic representative to France.
The British launch a vigorous southern campaign with the capture of Savannah, Georgia.

1779 George Rogers Clark forces the surrender of the British fort at Vincennes, Indiana.
Commanding the *Bonhomme Richard* and three other ships, John Paul Jones engages the British frigate *Serapis* off the coast of England, capturing the *Serapis* but losing his own ship.
The British end the occupation of Newport, Rhode Island, to concentrate on the southern campaign.
Washington leads the Continental Army into winter quarters at Monmouth, New Jersey.
Low morale and supplies, desertions, and attempts at mutiny plague the army.

1780 In the worst defeat of the Revolution, General Benjamin Lincoln surrenders Charleston and

5,800 troops to the British.

British Major John André is captured near Tarrytown, New York, carrying the plans for Benedict Arnold's surrender of West Point. He is convicted and hanged. Arnold escapes and becomes a general in the British Army.

1781 The Continental Congress adopts its first constitution, the Articles of Confederation.

Congress issues an additional $191 million in Continental paper currency. By spring of this year, this money will have no value, and the American economy will be close to collapse.

General Daniel Morgan decisively defeats British forces at Cowpens, South Carolina.

Cornwallis, now with an army of 7,500, begins a campaign to conquer Virginia.

After a series of raids in Virginia, Cornwallis arrives at Yorktown to establish a base to maintain communication by sea with Clinton's New York forces.

French ships sail up Chesapeake Bay to transport the combined forces of Washington and Rochambeau to Virginia. There the army of 9,000 Americans and 9,000 French troops begins the siege of Yorktown.

Cornwallis surrenders. This event marks the end of British hopes of victory in America.

1782 The Loyalists begin to leave America, mainly for Nova Scotia and New Brunswick. If they stay, they face charges of treason or collaboration, and property confiscation.

Peace talks begin between Britain and America, and a preliminary treaty is signed in Paris that is favorable to the United States.

1783 Great Britain officially declares an end to the hostilities in America.

The Continental Army disbands.

The Treaty of Paris is signed, formally ending the war.

1785 Thomas Jefferson is appointed minister to France, succeeding Benjamin Franklin.

1786 The postwar depression reaches a low point, caused by currency shortage, and high taxes lead to individual states issuing unstable currency.

1787 The Constitutional Convention gathers in Philadelphia in May. The Constitution is adopted and published in September.

The Federalist is published in New York newspapers.

The Northwest Ordinance divides the Northwest Territory (the area north of the Ohio River) among several states. It forbids slavery in the area.

1788   The Constitution is ratified by three quarters of the states and becomes law.

1789   George Washington is elected first president of the United States.
The first national Thanksgiving Day is established by Congress.

1790   The national capitol is fixed at a Potomac River site from 1800; it will remain at Philadelphia until then.
Benjamin Franklin dies.
The first United States census shows a total U.S. population of 3,929,625; Philadelphia is the largest city, with 42,000 inhabitants.

1791   The first ten amendments to the Constitution, the Bill of Rights, is passed by Congress.
Vermont becomes the fourteenth state.

1792   Kentucky becomes the fifteenth state.

1793   Eli Whitney invents the cotton gin.

1796   John Adams is elected second President.
Tennessee becomes the sixteenth state.

1798   Congress passes the Alien and Sedition Acts.

1799   George Washington dies.

1800   Thomas Jefferson is elected third President.
The Library of Congress is established. The 1815 purchase of Jefferson's 7,000-volume library will form the nucleus of the collection.
Pennsylvania horticulturist John Chapman, better known as Johnny Appleseed, begins distributing seed and young apple trees to settlers bound for Ohio.

1801   John Marshall is appointed chief justice of the Supreme Court.

1803   Ohio becomes the seventeenth state.
The Supreme Court case of *Marbury v. Madison* establishes the process of judicial review.

1804   Lewis and Clark begin their expedition.
Alexander Hamilton is killed in a duel with Aaron Burr.

1807   Robert Fulton's steamship *Clermont* travels up the Hudson River from New York to Albany.

1808   James Madison is elected fourth President.
John Jacob Astor founds the American Fur Company.

1811   William Henry Harrison defeats the Shawnee at Tippecanoe.

1812   Louisiana becomes the eighteenth state.

1812   In the War of 1812, America eventually defeats Britain once and for all.

1814   Andrew Jackson defeats the Creek Indians at Horseshoe Bend.
Francis Scott Key writes "The Star-Spangled Banner" to celebrate the American victory over the British at Baltimore.

1816   James Monroe is elected fifth President.
Indiana becomes the nineteenth state.
The first steamboat operates on the Mississippi River.

1817   Construction begins on the Erie Canal.
Mississippi becomes the twentieth state.

1818   Illinois becomes the twenty-first state.

1819   Alabama becomes the twenty-second state.

1820   The Missouri Compromise is enacted, permitting Missouri to be admitted as a slave state, Maine as a free state.

1821   Florida is purchased from Spain for $15 million.

1823   President Monroe proclaims the Monroe Doctrine.

1824   The Erie Canal is completed.
John Quincy Adams is elected sixth President.

1826   Thomas Jefferson and John Adams both die on July 4.

1828   Andrew Jackson is elected seventh President.

1830   The Indian Removal Act clears the way for forcing Indians to move west of the Mississippi.
Peter Cooper builds a steam-powered train, the *Tom Thumb,* for the Baltimore & Ohio Railroad.

How to Recognize Architectural Styles

New England Colonial (1620–1740). The Puritans built boxlike houses in the familiar way they had known in England—two rooms wide and one or two rooms deep, with two stories. A lean-to in the back of the house, with the roof lowered to cover it, formed a "saltbox" shape. Some houses had a second-story overhang, or "jetty," to create more space upstairs. These houses were admirably suited to the New England environment. Heavy timber frames were covered with unpainted shingles or clapboards for protection against winter winds. Pitched, shingled roofs shed heavy snows, and a large central chimney warmed the house. Heavy doors and small, high, leaded casement windows guarded against Indian attack. Ornament was frowned upon, except for carved pendants, or "pendills," hanging from the corners over the second-story overhangs.

Dutch Colonial (1625–1840). The Huguenot settlers who came through Holland from France in the early 1600s settled in the valleys of the Hudson and Delaware rivers. They built their Dutch-style stone, wood, or brick houses with steeply pitched gambrel roofs (a roof with two slopes, the lower one steeper and sometimes flared—the familiar "barn" shape). These roofs sometimes reached down beyond the building to provide shelter for the porch. Flared eaves were sometimes used to protect the walls from rain. Dutch Colonial town houses were usually four or five stories tall, with the owner living above his ground-floor shop. The front door often was divided into two parts—the "Dutch door"—to admit air and light but not roving animals.

German Colonial (1680–1800). German colonists seeking religious freedom arrived in William Penn's colony about 1680. They created orderly settlements, building solid rectangular houses in the German medieval tradition—often with central chimneys, steep, shingled roofs with dormers, and thick stone walls, using fieldstone or limestone from nearby quarries. The windows had many panes, and a pent roof to shelter the first floor was common. These handsome buildings can be found in Pennsylvania and western Maryland. Later German Colonial buildings took on Georgian features as the influence of English styles spread through the colonies.

Georgian (1700–76). The first Georgian building constructed in America was the Wren Building at the College of William and Mary in Williamsburg, Virginia. The Georgian style, developed in England by Christopher Wren, Inigo Jones, and James Gibbs, was based on the vision of order, balance, and dignity that characterized the Italian Renaissance, particularly the works of the Italian architect Palladio. As the colonies became more prosperous, the leading planters and merchants used English architectural building manuals and pattern books to construct stately and elegant Georgian houses.

In the Northeast, Georgians were usually built of narrow clapboard, often painted blue-green, salmon, or yellow. In rural Pennsylvania and in the Hudson River Valley, Georgians were of fieldstone. In the mid-Atlantic and the Southern colonies, brick Georgians were common. In the North, central chimneys warmed the house, but in the South, end chimneys heated the many rooms in the winter and allowed the heat of cooking to escape in the sultry summer. Characteristics of Georgians include hipped roofs, elaborate entrances, decorative railings or balustrades, Palladian central windows, keystone lintels, and sash windows with heavy dividers or "muntins."

Federal or Adam (1780–1820). The Federal or Adam style was based on the work of the Scottish architect Robert Adam, who was prominent in England in the 1760s and 1770s. He had traveled in Italy to see Roman ruins, and he was inspired by the variety of room shapes and colorful interiors. Roman decorative motifs of urns, garlands, and sheaves of wheat embellished his reserved exteriors and classical fireplaces. American builders learned about the Adam style from pattern books. The first use of the style was the dining-room ceiling at Mount Vernon. Wealthy Americans in Eastern port cities soon built Adam houses. Elliptical fanlights over the front door, slender, curved wrought-iron stair railings, and Palladian windows provided decorative contrasts to the simple but elegant square or rectangular exterior.

The Adam style has been called the Federal style because it was favored by the leaders of the new nation. It was more refined and lighter in feeling than the early Georgians. Windowpanes were larger, but their dividers were more slender; roofs were lower and often hidden behind balustrades; rounded and oval shapes were more freely used. Like Georgian houses, Federal houses were built of frame and clapboard with central chimneys in the North, and of brick with end chimneys in the South. Characteristics of the style include a boxlike shape with a low-pitched, side-gabled roof; a Palladian window on the second floor over the main entrance; a balustrade; stone lintels; arched windows in dormers; slender sidelights and elliptical fan-shaped windows over the front door; and graceful wrought-iron handrails.

The architects who perfected the style were Samuel McIntire in Salem, Massachusetts; Charles Bulfinch in Boston; Alexander Parris in Maine; John McComb in New York City; Dr. William Thornton and Benjamin Latrobe in Washington, D.C.; William Jay in Savannah; and Gabriel Manigault in Charleston, South Carolina.

Roman Revival (1800–50). Thomas Jefferson popularized Roman architecture in America by using the Roman style for his residence, Monticello, and for the buildings on the grounds of the University of Virginia in Charlottesville. He rejected Colonial styles because of their association with England. As minister to France, Jefferson traveled in Italy and became familiar with the work of the Renaissance architect Andrea Palladio, and he looked to Palladio for inspiration for his own architectural work.

The Roman style, more monumental than the Greek style, was considered appropriate for major public buildings. The first U.S. Capitol, designed by William Thornton, typified the style with a projecting central pediment and classical portico, a symmetrical façade, and a shallow dome. Statehouses and courthouses across the country followed the example. Characteristics of the style include arch and dome construction, round windows, Corinthian column capitals, arched openings, roof balustrades, and a classical pediment or portico.

Greek Revival (1820–50). The "discovery" in 1804 by Lord Elgin of the Parthenon in Athens, the most important building of classical Greece, sparked a Greek Revival movement in England. Twenty years later it reached the United States. Greek ideals of democracy, beauty, and simplicity were fitting for the proud new republic. The founding fathers chose Greek Revival for many buildings in the new capital at Washington. The most familiar example of the style, however, is the antebellum Southern mansion.

Characteristics of the style include a gabled portico or temple façade with Doric or Ionic columns, often in relief; roof slopes are low and often are hidden behind parapets and heavy cornices; construction is post-and-beam. The early-nineteenth-century architects Benjamin Latrobe and Robert Mills promoted the style. In 1829, Minard LeFebre published a builders' handbook for Greek Revival architecture.

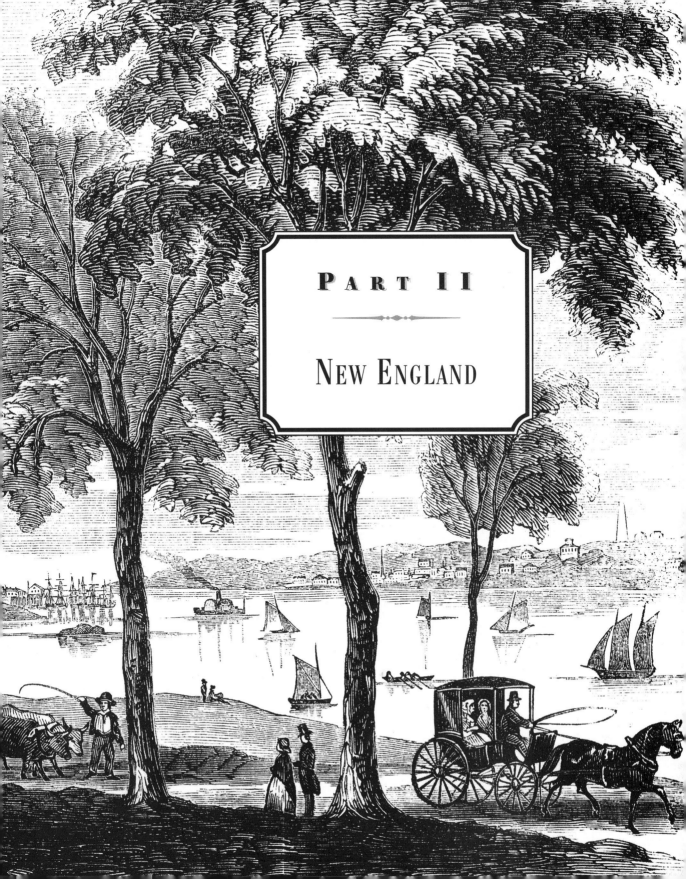

PART II

NEW ENGLAND

MAINE

Portland

VERMONT

Rutland

Lebanon

NEW
HAMPSHIRE

91

89

NEW
YORK

7

Brattleboro

Keene

Manchester

Kittery

Dover

Portsmouth

Haverhill

Amesbury

Newburyport

95

Concord

MASSACHUSETTS

Deerfield

91

Pittsfield

Lenox

Amherst

Northampton

Stockbridge

90

Great Barrington

Springfield

Sturbridge

Andover

Ipswich

Gloucester

Danvers

Beverly

Lexington

Waltham

Salem

Marblehead

Concord

Cambridge

Saugus

Newton

Boston

Quincy

Worcester

Sudbury
Center

Braintree

Dedham

3

84

495

Provincetown

Cape
Cod

Plymouth

Eastham

Sandwich

Lakeville

Enfield

Riverton

Windsor

Putnam

Storrs

Pawtucket
Providence

R.I.

Den
Chatha

South
Yarmou

6

New Bedford

Centerville

Windsor
Locks

Hartford

Manchester

Bristol

Wethersfield

Plainfield

395

Warwick

East Greenwich

North Kingston

Jamestown

Little Compton

Kent

CONNECTICUT

Litchfield

Meriden

East
Haddam

Norwich

Newport

Kingston

Woodbury

Waterbury

84

Danbury

New Haven

Westerly

Martha's
Vineyard

Nantucket

Ridgefield

95

Milford

Stratford

Branford

Guilford

Madison

Clinton

Old Saybrook

Old Lyme

New London

Groton

Mystic

Stonington

Fairfield

Norwalk

New Canaan

Greenwich

Long Island
Sound

ATLANTIC OCEAN

495

Long Island

N

0   100 miles

0   150 km

2

CONNECTICUT

The Dutch came first, building a trading post in the Connecticut River Valley in 1623. Ten years later a party of Pilgrims from Massachusetts settled at the site of present-day Windsor. Soon the rich land of eastern Connecticut was attracting "squatters" from Massachusetts. Thomas Hooker came with a hundred followers in May 1836, and settled at Hartford. Other groups settled at Windsor and Wethersfield. In 1639, at the urging of Hooker, the settlers met and adopted the Fundamental Orders of Connecticut.

At first the settlers got along with the Indians. Then the Pequots arrived from the Hudson River Valley and began killing isolated settlers. In 1637 the militia made a surprise raid on the Pequots at Mystic, killing all they could find. They tracked the rest to a swamp in Fairfield, slaughtered most of them, and took the survivors as slaves.

John Davenport and a group of Puritans arrived in New Haven in 1638, traded the Indians goods for land, and settled in. They believed that "the word of God shall be the only rule," and allowed only church members to vote. The first governor, Theophilus Eaton, announced that the Commandments of Moses would be the model for the colony. Jury trials were not allowed because there was no mention of them in the Bible. Towns were settled nearby—Stamford, Fairfield, Greenwich, Milford—and were part of the New Haven Colony. Friction developed between the Puritans in New Haven and the more liberal citizens of Hartford, and New Haven attempted to have the English Crown declare it a separate colony.

Governor John Winthrop Jr. went to London in 1661 and persuaded Charles II to allow Connecticut to govern itself. In 1667, however, James II decided to take all of New England under his personal control. The English governor, Sir Edmund Andros, declared all charters void, and ordered the charter returned. When Andros arrived to claim the charter, the story goes, it was placed in the hollow of a great oak tree. When William and Mary came to the throne, the colony's rights were restored, and the charter brought out of hiding.

The British attacked Connecticut four times in the Revolution. In 1777, General William Tryon, the royal governor of New York, burned the Continental Army's

Preceding spread: View of New London, Connecticut, from the Shore Road. Courtesy Library of Congress, Prints and Photographs Division.

tents and food at Danube. Two years later the British ravaged New Haven, Fairfield, and Norfolk. Benedict Arnold led the British attack, and he returned in 1781 to invade Groton and New London, which had become a major port for privateers who continually harassed British shipping.

BRANFORD

Harrison House (124 Main St.; 203/488-4828). J. Frederick Kelly, a twentieth-century architect, restored this circa-1725 saltbox. Period furnishings. Herb garden. Open Wednesday though Saturday afternoons, June through September.

BRISTOL

American Clock and Watch Museum (100 Maple St.; 203/583-6070). More than 3,000 timepieces are displayed in a historic 1801 house. There is a video on the history of clock and watch manufacturing. Garden.

Bookshop. Open daily, March through November.

New England Carousel Museum (95 Riverside Ave.; 203/585-5411). More than three hundred carved, wooden antique carousel figures, including two chariots. Restoration workshop. Open daily, April through October; Wednesday through Saturday the rest of the year.

Lock Museum of America (3½ miles northwest on CT 72, then west ¾ mile on U.S. 6 to 130 Main St. in Terryville; 203/589-6359). Antique locks, displays of lock history and design. Open daily, May through October.

CLINTON

Stanton House (63 East Main St.; 203/669-2132). The original site of the first classroom of Yale University. A 1789 thirteen-room house is connected to a general store. Period furnishings. Staffordshire dinnerware. Weapons collection. Bed used by Marquis de

The Nathan Hale Schoolhouse in East Haddam.

Lafayette during an 1824 visit. Open daily, June through September.

DANBURY

Scott-Fanton Museum (43 Main St.; 203/743-5200). The buildings here include the 1790 Dodd Shop, which has a historic display of the hat industry; the 1785 Rider House, with period furnishings; and Huntington Hall, which houses a research library. Open afternoons, Wednesday through Sunday.

EAST HADDAM

This Connecticut Valley town is the location of the Goodspeed Opera House, which is the home of the American Musical Theatre, and the Gillette Castle.

    Amasa Day House (4 miles southeast via local roads to 67 River Rd.; 203/873-8144 or 203/247-8996). The period furnishings in this 1816 house include some pieces owned by three generations of the Day family. Stenciled floors and stairs. Open Wednesday through Sunday, August through Labor Day; weekends in June and

July and from Labor Day through early October.

    Nathan Hale Schoolhouse (Main St. at rear of St. Stephen's Church; 203/873-9547). In this one-room schoolhouse, the Revolutionary War patriot taught during the winter of 1773. Period furnishings, memorabilia. Open weekends, Memorial Day through Labor Day.

    Accommodations: *Bishopsgate* (7 Norwich Rd.; 203/873-1677). An 1818 Federal house near the Connecticut River offers six guest rooms furnished with period pieces. Full breakfast. Afternoon tea or sherry. Moderate. Open year-round.

ENFIELD

Martha A. Parsons House (1387 Enfield St.; 203/745-6064). On display are antiques collected by the Parsons family over 180 years. George Washington memorial wallpaper. Open Sundays, May through October.

FAIRFIELD

Ogden House (1520 Bronson Rd.; 203/259-1598). This restored 1750 saltbox farmhouse

Don't Tread On Me.

—MOTTO ON THE FLAG OF THE USS *RATTLESNAKE*

THE HARTFORD CONVENTION

The New England states opposed the War of 1812 because the British navy blockaded their ports and depressed their mercantile economy. Leaders of the conservative Federal Party met in Hartford in 1814 to discuss strategy. Some wanted to secede from the Union and form a New England Confederacy, but the convention contented itself with resolving that a state had a right "to interpose its authority" to correct "infractions" of the Constitution of the federal government. The end of the war changed the political climate in New England, putting an end to all talk of secession.

by Leon Volkmar. Open Tuesday through Friday and Sunday.

Accommodations: *Homestead Inn* (420 Field Point Rd.; 203/869-7500). Built in 1799 for a gentleman, this house was sold in 1859 to innkeepers, who converted it to an Italianate Victorian, adding a cupola and a wraparound porch. Twenty-three guest rooms, all with private bath. Continental breakfast. Well-known three-star restaurant on the premises. Expensive. Open year-round.

GROTON

Fort Griswold Battlefield State Park (1½ miles south of U.S. 1 on Monument St. and Park Ave.; 203/449-6877). A 135-foot monument to the eighty-eight soldiers slain here in 1781 by British troops under the command of Benedict Arnold. Museum open daily, Memorial Day through Labor Day; weekends Labor Day through Columbus Day.

GUILFORD

Hyland House (84 Boston St.; 203/453-9477). A restored 1660 house with period furnishings. Herb garden, tours. Daily except Monday, Labor Day through Columbus Day; weekends only, Labor Day through Columbus Day.

Henry Whitfield State Museum (½ mile south on Whitfield St.; 203/453-2457). One of the oldest stone houses in New England, this 1639 house has been restored with 17th- and 18th-century furnishings. Exhibits. Herb garden, gift shop. Open Wednesday through Sunday, except mid-December through mid-January.

Thomas Griswald House Museum (171 Boston St.; 203/453-3176). This fine 1775 saltbox displays costumes of the 1800s. Period gardens. Blacksmith shop. Open daily except Monday, early June through mid-September.

has period furnishings and an authentic kitchen garden. Open Thursday and Sunday, mid-May through mid-October.

Fairfield Historical Society (636 Old Post Rd.; 203/259-1598). A museum displays furniture, paintings, maritime artifacts, dolls, toys, clocks, and farm implements. Open daily except Saturday.

GREENWICH

Putnam Cottage/Knapp Tavern (243 East Putnam Ave.; 203/869-9697). Near this 1690 tavern, General Israel Putnam made a daring escape from the Redcoats in 1779. Rare scalloped shingles. Exhibits. Restored barn. Herb garden. Open Sunday, Wednesday, and Friday.

Bush Holley House (South off U.S. 1, at 39 Strickland Rd. in Cos Cob; 203/869-6899). This 1732 residence of a successful farmer now contains an important art collection, including paintings by Childe Hassam, Elmer Livingston MacRae, and John Henry Twachman; sculptures by John Rogers; and pottery

The Henry Whitfield House in Guilford. Courtesy Henry Whitfield State Museum.

HARTFORD

This city, now the state capital, was made virtually independent in 1662 by Charles II, but an attempt was made by Sir Edmund Andros, governor of New England, to seize its charter. The document was hidden by Joseph Wadsworth in a hollow tree since known as the Charter Oak; a plaque on Charter Oak Avenue marks where the tree once stood.

Raymond E. Baldwin Museum of Connecticut History (State Library, 231 Capitol Ave.; 203/566-3056). Exhibits include the Colt Collection of Firearms, as well as Connecticut artifacts, including the 1662 Royal Charter. Open weekdays.

Butler-McCook Homestead (396 Main St.; 203/522-1806, or 203/247-8996). A preserved 1782 house, occupied until 1971 by four generations of one family. Family antiques, Victorian toys, Victorian garden. Open Tuesday, Thursday, and Sunday, mid-May through mid-October.

Wadsworth Atheneum (600 Main St.; 203/278-2670, or 203/247-9111). One of the nation's oldest continuously operated art museums, with more than 40,000 works including important early American paintings. English and American silver. Open daily except Monday.

Old State House (800 Main St.; 203/522-6766). The oldest state house in the nation, designed by Charles Bulfinch. The restored Senate chamber has a Gilbert Stuart portrait of George Washington. Displays and exhibits. Open daily.

Connecticut Historical Society (1 Elizabeth St.; 203/236-5621). Permanent and changing exhibits on state history in nine galleries. More than 2 million books and manuscripts. Open Tuesday through Friday and Sunday, Memorial Day through Labor Day; Tuesday through Sunday the rest of the year.

Noah Webster Foundation and Historical Society (227 South Main St. in West Hartford; 203/521-5362). This 18th-century homestead was the birthplace of

The Holley-Williams House in Lakeville.

America's first lexicographer, compiler of the *Blue-Backed Speller* (1783) and the *American Dictionary* (1828). Memorabilia, period furniture, costumed guides. Open daily except Wednesday.

Center Church and Ancient Burying Ground (Main and Gold streets; 800/249-5631). This 1807 church is patterned after London's St. Martins-in-the-Fields, with Tiffany stained-glass windows. Its cemetery contains markers dating from 1640.

KENT

Sloane-Stanley Museum and Kent Furnace (1 mile north on U.S. 7; 203/927-3849 or 203/566-3055). A New England barn houses Eric Sloan's collection of Early American tools, and a re-creation of his studio. Located on the site of the 1826 furnace. Video presentation. Open Wednesday through Sunday, mid-May through October.

LAKEVILLE

Holley-Williams House Museum (Main St.; 203/735-2848). Virtually unchanged since it was built for iron master John Milton Holley in 1808, the Federal-style house with portico overlooks the site of Furnace Village Forge. The house was occupied by Holley's descendants until 1971. Period furniture, portraits by noted itinerant painters. Gardens, outbuildings, a carriage house with a model of an iron forge. Tours. Open weekends, July through early October.

LITCHFIELD

Tapping Reeve House and Law School (South St.; 203/567-4501). This 1773 house was used as America's first law school. Graduates included Aaron Burr and John C. Calhoun. Period furnishings, garden. Open Wednesday through Sunday, mid-May through mid-October.

MADISON

Allis-Bushness House and Museum (853 Boston Post Rd.; 203/245-4567). This 1785 house has four-corner fireplaces, doctor's office and equipment, exhibits of costumes and dolls. Herb garden. Open Wednesday, Friday, and Saturday, early June through Labor Day.

    Deacon John Grave House (Academy and School streets; 203/245-4798). A 1685 frame garrison Colonial house. Open daily except Monday, Memorial Day through Labor Day; weekends only in spring and fall.

MANCHESTER

Cheney Homestead (106 Hartford Rd.; 203/643-5588). Built in 1780 by Timothy Cheney, clockmaker, this was the birthplace of brothers who launched the once-promising silk industry. Period furniture, paintings and etchings. Open Thursday and Sunday.

MERIDEN

Solomon Goffe House (677 North Colony St.; 203/634-9088). This gambrel-roofed 1711 house has period furnishings, artifacts, tours led by costumed guides. Open Saturday and Sunday, July through August; first Sunday of the month the rest of the year.

MILFORD

Milford Historical Society Wharf Lane Complex (34 High St.; 203/874-2664). Three historic houses, including Eells-Stow House (circa 1700), believed to be the oldest house in town and featuring an unusual "dog sled" stairway; Stockade House (circa 1780), an early stockade; and Bryan-Downs House (circa 1785), a two-story structure that houses more than 400 Indian artifacts. Open Sunday, Memorial Day through Columbus Day.

MYSTIC

Mystic Seaport (50 Greenmanville Ave., 1 mile south of I-95, exit 90; 203/572-5315). A re-created 19th-century seaport on 170 acres comprising the nation's largest maritime museum, dedicated to preserving 19th-century maritime history. Visitors board the 1841 whaler *Charles W. Morgan* (which made thirty-seven voyages from the South Seas to the Arctic), the square-rigged *Joseph Conrad,* and the fishing schooner *L.A. Dunton.* Among the scores of exhibits are a ropewalk, a rigging loft, a hoop shop, a printing press, a drugstore, a bank, a cooperage, a smithy, and a sail loft. Children's museum, cruises on a 1908 steamboat, special events. Restaurants, shops. Open daily, May through October.

    Dennison Homestead (2 miles east of I-95, exit 90, on Pequotsepos Rd.; 203/536-9248). Restored and furnished with the heirlooms of eleven generations of one family. Tours. Open every afternoon except Tuesday, mid-May through mid-October.

NEW CANAAN

New Canaan Historical Society (13 Oenoke Ridge Rd.; 203/966-1776). The First Town House (once the town hall) has a costume museum, a library, and the 1845 Cody Drugstore, a reproduction of the town's first pharmacy. On the grounds of the *Hanford-Silliman House Museum* (circa 1755) are a tool museum, a hand press, a one-room schoolhouse, and sculptor John Rogers' studio and museum. Town House open Tuesday through Saturday, other buildings Wednesday, Thursday, and Sunday.

NEW HAVEN

Yale University (center of city; 203/432-2300). Founded by ten Connecticut ministers and named for Elihu Yale, an early donor. On the Old Campus is Connecticut Hall, where Nathan Hale (class of 1773) roomed. Guided walking tours (Visitor Information Office, Phelps Gateway, 344 College St.; 203/432-2300). The Yale Art Gallery (1111 Chapel St. at York) has an excellent collection of American paintings.

The Green. These sixteen acres were laid out in 1636, making New Haven the first planned city in America. On the two common are three churches: *United* (1813), *Trinity Episcopal* (1814), and *Center Congregational* (1813), which is a masterpiece of Georgian architecture.

Grove Street Cemetery (Grove and Prospect Streets). The first cemetery in the country divided into family plots. Buried here are Noah Webster, Eli Whitney, Charles Goodyear, and many early settlers.

Pardee-Morris House (325 Lighthouse Rd., south of I-95, exit 50; 203/562-4183). Built in 1850, burned by the British in 1779, then rebuilt in 1780, the house has period furnishings and a kitchen garden. Open weekends, June through August.

Fort Hale Park and Restoration (4 miles southeast on Woodward Ave.; 203-787-8790). Federal guns here kept British warships out of the harbor in 1812. Old Black Rock Fort, from Colonial days, has been reconstructed, and Fort Nathan, from the Civil War era, has been restored. Both offer spectacular views of the harbor. Picnicking. Tours daily, Memorial Day through Labor Day.

Accommodations: *Inn at Chapel West* (1201 Chapel St.; 203/777-1201). The ten guest rooms in this restored 1860 Victorian mansion are individually furnished with antiques, and many have fireplaces. Continental breakfast, afternoon tea or wine, concierge. Expensive. Open year-round.

NEW LONDON

Ye Olde Towne Mill (Mill St. and State Pier Rd., under Gold Star Bridge; 203/443-8331 or 203/447-5250). Built for John Winthrop Jr., New London's founder and the state's sixth governor, the mill has recently been restored. Open daily, June through mid-September.

Shaw Mansion (305 Bank St.; 203/443-1209). Naval headquarters for the state during the Revolution, this 1758 building now houses a historical and genealogical library. The museum is open irregularly; phone for information.

Joshua Hempstead House (11 Hempstead St.; 203/443-8331, or 203/247-8996). Built in 1678, this restored house with period furnishings is the oldest in the city. Next door is the Nathaniel Hempstead House, one of two surviving examples in the state of mid-18th-century cut-stone architecture. Seven rooms with period furnishings. Both houses are open Tuesday through Saturday afternoons, mid-May through mid-October.

NORWALK

Mill Hill Historic Park (Wall St. and East Ave.; 203/846-0525). A complex of historic buildings includes the Town House Museum (circa 1835), **Fitch House Law Office** (circa 1740), and an 1826 schoolhouse. Old cemetery. Open Sundays, May through October.

Historic South Norwalk (1 mile southeast via I-95, exit 14/N15S, bounded by Washington, Water, and North and South

Main streets). This 19th-century waterfront neighborhood is listed on the National Registry of Historic Places.

NORWICH

Leffingwell Inn (348 Washington St.; 203/889-9440). Sons of Liberty meetings were held here, and once Washington stopped by. The owner, Christopher Leffingwell, helped finance Ethan Allen's attack on Fort Ticonderoga. Museum, period rooms. Open daily except Monday, mid-May through Labor Day.

Tantaquidgeon Indian Museum (5 miles south on CT 32, at 1819 Norwich–New London Turnpike in Uncasville; 203/848-9145). Works of Mohegan and other New England tribes. Open daily except Monday, May through October.

Indian Burial Grounds (Sachem St. off CT 32). Buried here is Uncas, chief of the Mohegan, who gave the original land for the settlement of Norwich. (Uncas was the title character in James Fenimore Cooper's novel *The Last of the Mohicans.*)

Colonial Cemetery (entrance on East Town St.). This is the burial place of many Revolutionary War soldiers and Samuel Huntington, signer of the Declaration of Independence.

OLD LYME

Florence Griswold Museum (98 Lyme St., one block west off I-95, exit 70; 203/434-5542). The daughter of a sea captain, Mrs. Griswold turned her stately late-Georgian 1817 mansion into the most celebrated art colony at the turn of the 20th century. The museum houses paintings by Willard Metcalf, Childe Hassam, and other artists of the colony, as well as early New England furnishings and decorative arts. Open Tuesday

BENEDICT ARNOLD

Benedict Arnold was a patriot hero. He also was proud, ambitious and acquisitive—a dangerous combination that would make his name synonymous in his country with betrayal and treason. Born the son of a Connecticut merchant, Arnold married into the aristocracy, failed in business, took to drink, and was unable to support his family. The Revolution proved a mixed blessing for him. It tapped his capacities for leadership and gave him the fame he craved, but it also provided an outlet for his selfishness and greed.

He participated in the capture of Fort Ticonderoga, but it was Ethan Allen and his Green Mountain Boys who took the fort and the glory. Arnold then led part of the force sent to invade Canada. He took a thousand men through the Maine wilderness, hampered by driving rainstorms, flooding rivers, and nearly impassable forests. He joined in an unsuccessful assault on Quebec, but was wounded and forced to retire.

Promoted to brigadier general, Arnold fought with distinction at Lake Champlain, Ridgefield, and Saratoga. Though greatly admired by Washington, he had made influential enemies, and his acquisitiveness had led to corruption in his command. He was court-martialed and cleared of most of the charges, though not all. An official reprimand from Washington angered Arnold, and probably played a part in his decision to sell himself to the enemy.

A widower, Arnold married nineteen-year-old Peggy Shippen, daughter of an important Philadelphia family. She took part in the conspiracy to betray West Point, where he had taken command. The British agreed to pay Arnold £20,000 if his betrayal led to the capture of West Point and the 3,000 troops there. Major John André, the British go-between, was seized carrying incriminating papers returning from a meeting with Arnold.

Arnold fled to New York City, expecting to be given a high command in the British army, but was disappointed. His new masters did not trust him. He went to England in 1791, where he died ten years later.

through Sunday, June through September; Wednesday through Sunday the rest of the year.

First Congregational Church (96 Lyme St.; 203/434-5542), built in 1817 and rebuilt in 1907 after a fire, is a classic New England church, with slender Ionic columns and a graceful steeple and spire. It was designed by Samuel Belcher, the architect of the Griswold house.

Accommodations: *Griswold Inn* (36 Main St., Essex; 203/767-1776). This inn has been open for business every day since it opened June 7, 1776. The main building was the first three-story structure built in Connecticut. The inn now includes a 1738 taproom and several dining rooms. One has a collection of steamboat prints, another a collection of vintage firearms. The twenty-five guest rooms all have private bath and period furnishings. Continental breakfast. Moderate. Open year-round.

OLD SAYBROOK

General William Hart House (350 Main St.; 203/388-2622). The 1767 Georgian residence of a rich merchant and politician, featuring eight corner fireplaces, one of which is decorated with Sadler & Green transfer-print tiles illustrating Aesop's Fables. Original wainscoting, period furnishings, Colonial gardens. Open Friday through Sunday, mid-June through mid-September.

PLAINFIELD

Prudence Crandall House (west on CT 14A to junction of CT 169 in Canterbury; 203/546-9916). New England's first academy for black girls (1833-34) was in this two-story frame building. Period furnish-

ings, exhibits, research library, gift shop. Open Wednesday through Sunday; closed mid-December through mid-January.

PUTNAM

Roseland Cottage (7 miles northwest via CT 171 and 169 in Woodstock; 203/928-4074). Built in 1846, this is one of the most important surviving examples of a Gothic Revival "cottage," complete with period furnishings. It was the summer home of the influential abolitionist and publisher Henry C. Bowen. Surrounded by original outbuildings, including one of the first indoor bowling alleys in the country. Large parterre garden, edged by 1,800 dwarf boxwood. Presidents Grant, Hayes, Harrison, and McKinley attended Bowen's Fourth of July parties here. Open Wednesday through Sunday, Memorial Day through Labor Day.

RIDGEFIELD

Keeler Tavern (132 Main St.; 203/438-5485). A British cannonball is still embedded in the wall of the tavern, which was once the headquarters of Revolutionary War patriots. It was also the summer home of architect Cass Gilbert. Period furnishings, gardens, tours, museum shop. Open Wednesdays and weekends. Closed in January.

RIVERTON

Hitchcock Museum (CT 20, center of village; 203/738-4950). A historic church displays a collection of 18th-century furnishings by Hitchcock and others. Phone for schedule.

Solomon Rockwell House (3 miles southwest on CT 20, 2 miles south on CT 8, at 225 Prospect St. in Winsted; 203/379-8433). An 1813 house built for an early industrialist. Hitchcock chairs, vintage clocks, Revolutionary and Civil War memorabilia. Open Thursday through Sunday, June through mid-September.

Accommodations: *Old Riverton Inn* (436 East River Rd.; 203/379-1006). This three-story Federal structure was opened for business by Jesse Ives in 1796 and was known on the post road between Hartford and Albany as the Ives Tavern. It offers guests twelve rooms with private bath and a full breakfast. Bar and restaurant on premises. Moderate to expensive. Open year-round.

STONINGTON

Old Lighthouse Museum (7 Water St.; 203/535-1440). Built in 1823, this was the first government-operated lighthouse in the state. Exhibits include Stonington-made firearms and stoneware, ship models, whaling gear, China trade objects, folk art. Children's gallery. Open daily except Monday, May through October.

STORRS

Nathan Hale Homestead (8 miles southwest via U.S. 44 to 2299 South St. in Coventry; 203/742-6917, or 203/247-8996). A country-Georgian house built by Nathan's father, Richard, restored with many original furnishings. Open mid-May through mid-October.

Windham Textile and History Museum (8 miles south on CT 195 to 157 Union St. in Willimantic; 203/456-2178). This museum documents the evolution of the textile industry. Antique machinery, 19th-century architectural drawings, demonstrations, tours. Open Thursday through Sunday afternoons.

STRATFORD

Captain David Judson House (967 Academy Rd.; 203/378-0630). Built around 1723, the house has been restored to its original appearance. A museum behind the house displays artifacts relating to local history. Open Wednesdays and weekends, mid-April through October.

WATERBURY

Mattatuck Museum (144 West Main; 203/753-0381). Exhibits of industrial history, decorative arts, period rooms. Paintings and prints by Connecticut artists. Open Tuesday through Saturday, July through August. Daily except Monday the rest of the year.

WETHERSFIELD

Buttolph-Williams House (249 Broad St. at Marsh; 203/529-0460 or 203/247-8996). Fine collections of pewter, delft, fabrics, and period furniture are displayed in a circa 1700 restored building. Open daily except Tuesday, May through October.

Webb-Deane-Stevens Museum (211 Main St.; 203/529-0612). The museum comprises three houses that stand in the center of old Wethersfield: the Joseph Webb house (1752), the Silas Deane house (1766), and the Isaac Stevens house (1788). All are restored and furnished to reflect the different lifestyles of their owners—a merchant, a diplomat, and a tradesman. Flower and herb gardens. Open daily except Tuesday, May through October, Friday through Sunday the rest of the year.

First Church of Christ, Congregational United Church of Christ (Main and Marsh streets; 203/529-1575). This church was established in 1635, the meetinghouse built in 1761 and restored in 1973. Open Monday through Friday.

WINDSOR

Oliver Ellsworth Homestead (778 Palisado Ave.; 203/688-8717). The restored 1781 home of one of the five men who drafted the Constitution; Ellsworth later served as a diplomat. Washington and Adams were visitors here. Many original furnishings. Open Tuesday through Saturday, April through October.

United Church of Christ Congregational (75 Palisado Ave.; 203/688-7229). This, the first church in Windsor, is a classic Georgian, built in 1794. The cemetery dates from 1644. Open daily. (Request key at church office, 107 Palisado Ave.)

WINDSOR LOCKS

Noden Reed House and Barn (58 West St.; 203/627-9212). In the 1840 house and 1825 barn are collections of furnishings, clothing, quilts, kitchen utensils, and old newspapers and periodicals. Open Wednes-day and Sunday afternoons, May through October.

Old New-Gate Prison (8 miles west of I-91 at exit 40; in East Granby at junction of Newgate Rd. and CT 20; 203/653-3563, or 203/566-3005). The site of a 1707 copper mine that was converted to a Revolutionary War prison for Tories (1775-82) and used as a state prison until 1827. Self-guided tour of underground caverns where prisoners lived. Open Wednesday through Sunday, mid-May through October.

WOODBURY

Glebe House and Gertrude Jekyll Garden (on Hollow Rd. off U.S. 6; 203/263-2855). A circa-1770 farmhouse (or "glebe") where Samuel Seabury lived when elected America's first Episcopal bishop in 1783. Period furnishings. Garden designed by noted English landscape architect Gertrude Jekyll. Open Wednesday through Sunday afternoons, April through November.

3

MASSACHUSETTS

The Pilgrims were looking for the Hudson River when they found Cape Cod. They wanted to continue their search for the Hudson, but "dangerous shoals and roaring breakers" changed their mind. After exploring the cape for a month, the leaders chose Plymouth as the site for their colony, and the *Mayflower* landed there on December 21, 1620.

The first winter was hell—the "starving time," in the words of Governor William Bradford—and half of the original hundred were dead by spring. Probably all would have perished if the friendly Indians hadn't taught them how to survive in the wilderness. The Pilgrims expressed their gratitude at a celebration of thanksgiving that fall.

The Massachusetts Bay Company, though not as well known, was a much larger operation. In 1630, John Winthrop and the first of 2,000 Puritans arrived on the *Arabella* at a site on the Charles River that they named Boston. Better financed than the Pilgrims, the Puritans arrived with tools, livestock, and adequate provisions.

From the start, Boston's economy depended on the sea. The land was poor for farming, but the waters were rich with cod. Soon ships laden with dried cod were sailing to the Catholic Mediterranean and returning with molasses, sugar, wine, and gold. By 1700, Boston was the third-busiest port in the British Empire.

The seeds of revolution were sown early. From 1660 on, England saddled the colonies with a flow of unpopular laws and taxes. Boston became the center of resistance to England's attempts to curtail the rights of the colonists, to control their trade, and to tax them without allowing them representation in Parliament.

Riots in 1768 forced the British to send troops to Boston, and friction between the town and the troops resulted in the deaths of five men in the Boston Massacre of 1770. Three years later, two hundred men dressed as Indians threw three shiploads of tea into the harbor to protest the tea tax. An angry King George III closed the port and sent more troops. Throughout New England, militia units drilled and piled up supplies. The stage was set for a military confrontation.

The Revolution began in and around Boston. The first shots were fired in April 1775 at Lexington and Concord, and for the first year Boston was the focus of the war. George Washington took command of the troops in July, and a ring of militia units kept the British penned in the city. After a costly victory at Bunker Hill, the British were ready to quit Boston. When Washington fortified Dorchester Heights in a single night, the British realized their position was untenable, and evacuated the city on March 17, 1776, never to return.

The British realized that they had to drive the Americans from their positions across the water, or evacuate Boston. They drove the Americans out but at a price—more than 1,000 British casualties to 400 for the sharpshooting Americans. Courtesy Library of Congress, Prints and Photographs Division.

AMESBURY

John Greenleaf Whittier House (86 Friend St.; 508/388-1337). The poet lived here from 1836 until his death in 1892. The six-room house contains books, manuscripts, pictures and furniture. The Garden Room, where he wrote *Snow-Bound* and many other works, is unchanged. Open Tuesday through Saturday, May through October.

    Bartlett Museum (270 Main St.; 508/388-4528). Memorabilia of the town, dating from the 1654 settlement. The Indian artifact collection is considered one of the finest in the state. Open Wednesday through Sunday afternoons, late May through Labor Day.

AMHERST

Emily Dickinson Homestead (280 Main St.; 413/542-8161). The birthplace and home of the poet. Selected rooms are open to tours by appointment. Open daily, June through August; Wednesday through Saturday the rest of the year.

    Amherst History Museum (67 Amity St.; 413/256-0678). In the 18th-century Strong House, exhibits reflect changing tastes in local architecture and interior decoration. Collection of textiles and artifacts. Open Wednesdays and Saturdays, mid-May to mid-October.

ANDOVER

Addison Gallery of American Art (Phillips Academy, Main St.; 508/749-4016). More than 7,000 paintings, sculpture, prints, and photographs. A ship model collection traces the era of sail. Open daily except Mondays, September through July.

    Amos Blanchard House and Barn Museum (97 Main St.; 514/475-2236). This 1819 house features period rooms, local history exhibits. The barn has farm equipment, household items, and an old fire wagon. Tours by appointment. Open weekdays.

BEVERLY

Hale House (39 Hale St.; 508-922-1186). The house was built in 1694 by the Rev.

SAMUEL ADAMS

"We cannot make events," Samuel Adams once said. "Our business is to improve them." The revolutionary leader was a man of great self-discipline and patience who reminded his contemporaries of John Calvin, "cool, abstemious, polished, refined." He was uniformly respected, if not always liked.

Adams, the son of a Boston merchant, graduated from Harvard in 1740, where he publicly defended the thesis that "it is lawful to resist the Supreme Magistrate, if the Commonwealth cannot be otherwise preserved." This credo became a hallmark of his career.

After failing as a brewer and newspaper publisher, Adams found that politics was his true calling. He rose to prominence in the Massachusetts Assembly during the opposition to the Stamp Act in 1765. An organizer of Boston's Sons of Liberty, he believed there was a British plot to destroy constitutional liberty, and played a key political role in the Revolution until its end.

Adams recruited talented younger men to the cause, including his second cousin John Adams. He planned and coordinated Boston's resistance to the Tea Act, which climaxed in the famous Tea Party, and he worked diligently for the creation of the Continental Congress, and represented Massachusetts in it from 1774 to 1781. He served three terms as governor before retiring in 1797. On his death, in 1803, John Adams described him as "born and tempered a wedge of steel to split the knot of *lignum vitae*" that bound America to Britain.

John Hale, whose wife was accused of witchcraft. Rare wallpaper and furnishings. Open Friday through Sunday, mid-June through Labor Day.

Cabot House (117 Cabot St.; 508-922-1186). The brick mansion of a Revolutionary War privateer, the house was built in 1871 after it was written that "the Cabots of Beverly are now said to be by far the most wealthy in New England." Continental Navy exhibit, period rooms, art. Open Wednesday through Saturday.

Balch House (448 Cabot St.; 508/922-1186). John Balch came to America in 1623 as one of the first permanent settlers of Massachusetts Bay. Built in 1636, this is one of the two oldest wood frame houses in America. Open Wednesday through Sunday, mid-May to mid-October.

BOSTON

John Winthrop and 800 colonists first settled in Charleston, just north of the Charles River, and moved to Boston in 1630. They arrived too late to plant crops, and one in four died the first winter, mostly of starvation. A ship arrived with provisions in the spring, and the new Puritan commonwealth began to thrive. The Revolution began here in 1770, when Redcoats fired on an angry mob, killing five in what is now called the Boston Massacre. In 1773 the Boston Tea Party dumped East Indian tea into the bay in a protest against restriction of colonial trade by British governors. In retaliation, Britain closed the port. In April 1775, British general Thomas Gage decided to march on Concord to capture military supplies. During the night of April 18–19, Paul Revere spread the news to Lexington and Concord in a ride immortalized by Henry Wadsworth Longfellow. The Revolution had begun. The Battle of Bunker Hill followed the battles of Lexington and Concord. On May 17, 1776, General William Howe and his troops evacuated the city.

THE FREEDOM TRAIL

A walking tour through downtown Boston leads to 16 points of historic interest, in addition to monuments, shrines, and exhibits just off the trail, most of which are part of the *Boston National Historical Park.* (The trail is marked by signs and a red sidewalk line. Brochures are available from Visitors Bureau information centers at Prudential Plaza and Boston Common.)

'TWAS THE LAW

Many Colonial ordinances were petty, and penalties were cruel by today's standards. For example, it was an offense to declare a minister's sermon uninspiring, or to walk in the garden on Sunday. For more serious crimes, ears were cut off, noses were slit, and holes were bored in tongues. Adultery was a capital offense. In the Massachusetts Bay Colony, the code of law adopted in 1641 included the medieval trial by ordeal, including the bizarre ordeal by touch, based on the belief that if a murderer touched his victim's body it would begin to bleed.

State House (Beacon St. at head of Park St.; 617/727-3676). Since it was completed in 1795, wings have been added to both sides. The original design by Charles Bulfinch, America's first professional architect. Tours. Open Monday through Friday.

Park Street Church (1 Park St.; 617/523-3383). The church is called "Brimstone Corner" because brimstone for gunpowder was stored here during the War of 1812. Noted abolitionist William Garrison delivered his first antislavery address here in 1829. Tours. Open Tuesday through Saturday, July and August.

Granary Burying Ground (Tremont St. opposite end of Bromfield St.). Paul Revere, John Hancock, Samuel Adams, victims of the Boston Massacre, and some signers of the Declaration of Independence are among those buried here, on what was once the site of the town granary. Open daily.

King's Chapel (Tremont at School St.). The first Anglican church in America (1686) became, in 1786, the first Unitarian church in America. Adjacent to this 1754 church is the King's Chapel Burying Ground. Open Monday through Saturday.

Site of first free public school (School St. opposite Old City Hall). Here, in 1635, was built the Boston Public Latin School, the country's first free school. Across the street is sculptor Richard S. Greenough's *statue of Benjamin Franklin.*

Globe Corner Book Store Building (corner of School and Washington streets: 617/523-6658). A meeting place of Longfellow, Emerson, Hawthorne, Harriet Beecher Stowe, and other local literati. The restored 1712 building is one of the city's oldest. Open daily.

Old South Meeting House (310 Washington St.; 617/482-6438). The site of many important revolutionary town meetings, including those that sparked the Boston

The Henry Wadsworth Longfellow House in Cambridge. Courtesy National Park Service, Longfellow National Historic Site.

Tea Party. Multimedia exhibits. Open daily.

Old State House (206 Washington at State St.; 617/720-3290). Boston's oldest public building (1729) once served as the seat of the Royal Governor and the Colonial Legislature. The *Site of the Boston Massacre* is marked by a circle of cobblestones in the pavement outside. From the balcony, the Declaration of Independence was first proclaimed to the citizens of Boston. Exhibits. Open Monday through Friday.

Faneuil Hall Marketplace (Merchants Row; 617/523-1300). Peter Faneuil (pronounced *Fan'l*) bequeathed this two-story building to the city in 1742 as a public meeting hall and marketplace. It is called the "Cradle of Liberty" because it was the scene of mass meetings in the years just before the Revolution. Today it is a bustling marketplace of shops and restaurants, pushcarts and food stalls. Open daily. Adjacent is the *Ancient and Honorable Artillery Company Museum* (817/227-1638), chartered in 1638 as a school for officers. Open Monday through Friday.

Paul Revere House (19 North Sq.; 617/523-2338). This is the only 17th-century structure left in downtown Boston. From this circa-1680 house, the silversmith left for his historic ride on April 18, 1775. Revere artifacts and memorabilia. Open daily, April through December; daily except Mondays, the rest of the year.

Old North Church (193 Salem St. at foot of Hull St.; 617/523-6676). From the steeple's highest window were hung two lanterns, sending Revere to warn the Minutemen in Lexington that the British were coming. The oldest (1723) church building in the city. Open daily April through December; daily except Monday,the rest of the year.

Copp's Hill Burying Ground (Hull and Snowhill streets). During the Revolution, British cannon placed here were trained on Charlestown and Bunker Hill across the Charles River. Rev. Cotton Mather and Edmund Hart (builder of the USS *Constitution*) are buried here. Open daily.

Bunker Hill Monument (Monument

A hurry of hoofs in
a village street,
A shape in the
moonlight, a bulk in
the dark,
And beneath, from
the pebbles, in pass-
ing, a spark
Struck out from a
steed flying fearless
and fleet:
That was all! And
yet, through the
gloom and the light,
The fate of a nation
was riding that
night.

—HENRY
WADSWORTH
LONGFELLOW,
"PAUL REVERE'S
RIDE," *1861*

Square, Charlestown, near the USS
Constitution; 617/242-5641). A 221-foot
granite obelisk commemorates the Battle of
Bunker Hill, June 17, 1775. A 294-step spiral staircase leads to the top of the monument, with its view of the Boston area.
Ranger-led tours are available from mid-
April to early November. Demonstrations of
musket firing are given from mid-June
through Labor Day. Open daily.

U.S.S. Constitution (Charleston Navy
Yard, from I-93 north, exit 25, follow signs
across Charlestown bridge; from I-93 south,
exit 28 to Sullivan Sq., follow signs;
617/426-1812). "Old Ironsides," launched in
1797, was engaged in more than forty battles
without defeat. Museum displays ship artifacts. Open daily.

**Other historic sites include: Harrison
Gray Otis House** (141 Cambridge St., enter
from Lynde St.; 617/266-3956). Otis, a
statesman and lawyer, built this first of three
houses designed for him by Charles Bulfinch
in 1796. It became a rooming house for a
century after Otis moved to Beacon Hill. It
has been restored to its former elegance.
Tours. Open Tuesday through Friday afternoons and Saturdays.

**Frederick Law Olmsted National
Historic Site** (99 Warren St. in Brookline;
617/566-1689). Former home and office of
the founder of landscape architecture in
America, the site's landscaped grounds were
designed by Olmsted. Tours. Open Friday
through Sunday.

Isaac Royall House (³/₄ mile south off
I-93, at 15 George St. in Medford; 617/396-
9032). Built in 1637 as a four-room farmhouse by John Winthrop, first governor of
the Bay Colony, and enlarged in 1732 by
Royall. Chippendale and Hepplewhite furnishings. Open Tuesday through Sunday,
May through October.

Shirley-Eustis House (33 Shirley St.;

617/442-2275). The house was built in 1747
for William Shirley, the royal governor, and
restored to Federal style when Governor
William Eustis lived here from 1818 to 1825.
Open Thursday through Sunday afternoons,
June through September; Wednesday and
Sunday afternoons, March through May and
October through December.

African Meeting House (Smith Ct., off
Joy St. on Beacon Hill; 617/742-5415). Built
by free blacks in 1806, this building was an
educational and religious center and the site
of the founding of the New England Anti-
Slavery Society in 1832. Today it is part of
the Museum of Afro-American History.
Tours are available. Open weekdays.

Boston Tea Party Ship and Museum
(Congress St. Bridge on Harborwalk;
617/338-1773). The atmosphere of the 1773
Boston Tea Party is re-created aboard a full-
sized working replica of the tea party ship.
Visitors come aboard and help costumed
guides throw the tea chests into the harbor.
The museum has an audiovisual presentation, exhibits, and artifacts. Open daily, year-
round.

Black Heritage Trail (starts at Museum
of Afro-American History). Tours, available
by appointment, led by National Park
Service guides, go to sites in the Beacon Hill
section relating to the history of 19th-century
black Boston. Brochures and maps are available at the visitor center, 46 Joy St., second
floor (617/742-5415).

Boston by Foot (contact 77 North
Washington St., Boston, MA 02114; 617/
367-2345). Architectural walking tours are
conducted from May through October; these
include the Heart of Freedom Trail (daily);
Beacon Hill (daily); Copley Square (Fridays
and Saturdays); North End (Saturdays);
Children's Tour (Saturdays and Sundays);
Downtown Skyline (Sundays).

Accommodations: *Newbury   Guest*

House (261 Newbury St. in Back Bay; 617/262-4243 or 800/437-7668). A restored 1882 Victorian town house offers fifteen guest rooms and continental breakfast. Moderate to expensive. Open year-round.

BRAINTREE

General Sylvanus Thayer Birthplace (786 Washington St.; 617/848-1640). The soldier, educator, and superintendent of West Point from 1817 to 1833 was born in the 1720 house, furnished in the style of the period. Military and local historic displays. An adjacent 18th-century barn houses farm equipment and tools. Open weekend afternoons, mid-April through mid-October.

Abigail Adams House (North and Norton streets, 2 miles east in Weymouth; 617/335-1849). The daughter of a local clergyman, Abigail became the wife of President John Adams and the mother of President John Quincy Adams. The 1774 house has period furnishings. Open daily except Monday, July through Labor Day.

MEET THE PRESS

In 1639, Stephen Daye began operating a printing press in Cambridge, Massachusetts, and a year later he published Cotton Mather's *Whole Book of Psalms*—the first book published in America. Presses were costly to import, however, and printing got off to a slow start, but by 1700 Boston had about a dozen presses. In 1738, Christopher Sower published a German-language newspaper near Philadelphia. Benjamin Franklin, the most notable of the early printers, learned his trade from his brother, who was publisher of *The New England Courant*.

CAMBRIDGE

Harvard University (Harvard Square). America's oldest university was founded in 1638, and now includes Harvard and Radcliffe colleges, as well as ten graduate and professional schools. Massachusetts Hall, on Harvard Yard, the oldest building still standing, was built in 1720, and was the architectural inspiration for the campus. Student-

The Reverend Jonathan Ashley House in Historic Deerfield. Photo by Amanda Merullo, 1994.

JOHN WINTHROP

A third-generation son of English landed gentry, John Winthrop migrated to America to avoid "corruptions" in English society at a time when Puritans were being persecuted. He was the founding governor of the Massachusetts Bay Colony and served in that capacity from 1630 to 1649, becoming the embodiment of the Puritan concept of the "nursing father." He wanted the colony to become "a Citty upon a hill, the eyes of all people. . . ."

Winthrop regarded the governorship as his lifetime position, but many were opposed to his arbitrary methods. He consistently defended discretionary rule and the magisterial veto, over the resistance of the town deputies. To achieve a Puritan utopia, Winthrop and his colleagues committed themselves to a policy of intolerance. Dissenters were invariably punished.

By the 1640s, the final decade of his life, the growth of the colony and Boston's development as a port had made Winthrop's policies seem outdated. Ironically, it was this transformation that made his imagery of a "Citty upon a hill" an emblem of America.

guided tours may be arranged through the Information Center (1350 Massachusetts Ave; 617/495-1573). It is open daily, June through August, and daily except Sunday the rest of the year.

Christ Church (Zero Garden St. at the Common; 617/876-0200). This 1759 Episcopal church, a fine Georgian structure designed by Peter Harrison, is the oldest in Cambridge. It was used as a barracks during the Revolution. Open daily.

Longfellow National Historic Site (105 Brattle St., ½ mile from Harvard University; 617/876-4491). A 1759 Georgian house on the site was Washington's headquarters during the 1775–76 siege of Boston, and Longfellow's home from 1837 until his death in 1882. Longfellow taught at Harvard, and his books are here. Open daily.

The Blacksmith House (56 Brattle St.; 617/354-3036). The 1808 home of the blacksmith made famous by Longfellow. Currently it is a coffee shop and bakery. Open daily.

CENTERVILLE

Centerville Historical Society Museum (513 Main St.; 508/775-0331). The museum houses exhibits interpreting Cape Cod's history, art, industry, and domestic life. Early American furniture, housewares, quilts, costumes, dolls, Sandwich glass, Marine Room. Open Wednesday through Sunday, June to mid-September.

Osterville Historic Society Museum (3 miles southwest at junction of West Bay and Parker roads in Osterville; 508/428-5861). A sea captain's house with period furnishings, Sandwich glass, Chinese porcelain, majolica and Staffordshire pottery. Boatbuilding museum, ship models. The restored Cammett House (circa 1730) is on the grounds. Open Tuesday, Thursday, and Sunday afternoons, mid-June through September.

Accommodations: *Inn at Fernbrook* (481 Main St.; 508/775-4334). A handsome 1881 three-story home, designed so that no two rooms share the same wall, offers seven rooms and three suites. Breakfast and afternoon tea or sherry, concierge, lawn games. The heart-shaped rose garden was designed by Frederick Law Olmsted. Gazebo, pond with ducks and geese. Expensive. Open year-round.

CHATHAM

Old Atwood House (Stage Harbor Rd. ½ mile off MA 28; 508/945-2493). A 1752 house displays memorabilia of Joseph C. Lincoln, a Cape Cod novelist, and a mural by Alice Stalknecht: *Portrait of a New England*

Town. Open Wednesday through Saturday afternoons, mid-June through September.

CONCORD

Minute Man National Historic Park (North Bridge Unit, Monument St.; 508/369-6993). The park includes the famous Minuteman statue by Daniel Chester French and the reconstructed North Bridge over the Concord River. The visitor center (174 Liberty St.) has exhibits and a movie. Open daily.

The Old Manse (Monument St. at North Bridge; 508/369-3909). The 1770 parsonage of Concord's early ministers, including Rev. William Emerson, Ralph Waldo Emerson's grandfather. Nathaniel Hawthorne lived here for a time, and made it the setting for his *Mosses from an Old Manse.* Original furnishings. Open daily except Tuesdays, mid-April through October.

Sleepy Hollow Cemetery (Bedford St. northeast of square). The final resting place of Ralph Waldo Emerson, Nathaniel Hawthorne, Margaret Sidney, Daniel Chester French, and Henry David Thoreau.

The Wayside (455 Lexington Rd.; 508/369-6975). At various times, Nathaniel Hawthorne, and Margaret Sidney, author of the *Five Little Peppers* books, lived here. Orientation program, tours. Open May through October.

Orchard House and School of Philosophy (399 Lexington Rd.; 508/369-4118). Louisa May Alcott wrote *Little Women* here. Tours available. Open daily, April through December, weekends only in March.

Concord Museum (200 Lexington Rd.; 508/369-9609). Emerson's study, Thoreau's belongings used at Walden Pond, Revere's signal lantern. Open daily.

Thoreau Lyceum (156 Belknap St.; 508/369-5912). Concord history and Thoreau memorabilia. A replica of Thoreau's Walden house is on the grounds. Open daily.

Codman House (Codman Rd., 5 miles south off MA 2, via Bedford Rd. in Lincoln; 617/259-8843). Originally a circa-1740 two-story, L-shaped Georgian mansion, in 1797–98 it was more than doubled in size by merchant John Codman to imitate an English country house. Family furnishings, formal Italian garden. Open Wednesday through Sunday afternoons, June to mid-October.

Fruitlands Museums (15 miles west on MA 2 in Harvard; 508/456-9028). Bronson Alcott conducted his experiment in community life here. Four museums, including the Fruitlands Farmhouse, which contains furniture, books, and memorabilia of the Alcott family and the Transcendentalists. The Shaker Museum houses furniture and handicrafts of the sect. The Picture Gallery has primitive portraits and works of Hudson River School artists. There is also an American Indian Museum. Tearoom, gift shop. Open Tuesday through Sunday, mid-May to mid-October.

Accommodations: *Hawthorne* (462 Lexington Rd.; 508/369-5610). An inn with seven guest rooms, antiques, and a library with a fireplace. Continental breakfast and afternoon tea. No smoking. Moderate to expensive. Open year-round.

DANVERS

Rebecca Nurse Homestead (149 Pine St.; 508/774-8799). The circa-1680 saltbox home of a saintly woman accused of and executed for witchcraft in 1692. Restored rooms with period furnishings. Outbuildings. A reproduction of the Salem Village Meetinghouse. Open daily except Mondays, mid-June to mid-September; weekends mid-September through October.

Glen Magna Farms (2 miles north on U.S. 1, then ¼ mile east via Centre St. to

Ingersoll; 508/774-9165). A furnished 20-room mansion with exceptional gardens. The Derby summer house was built in 1794 by Samuel McIntire. On the roof are life-size carvings of a reaper and a milkmaid. Open Tuesday and Thursday, June through September.

DEDHAM

Fairbanks House (511 East St. at Eastern Ave., off U.S. 1; 617/326-1170). Built in 1636, this is one of the oldest frame houses still standing. Family heirlooms. Tours. Open daily except Mondays, May through October.

DEERFIELD

Historic Deerfield, Inc. (Information Center, Hall Tavern, The Street; 413-774-5581). Thirteen historic houses with period furnishings, silver, ceramics, textiles. Daily walking tours, except on major holidays.

Memorial Hall Museum (Deerfield Academy, Memorial St.; 413/774-7476). The oldest academy building (1798) houses Indian relics and colonial furnishings. Open daily, May through October.

Accommodations: *The Deerfield Inn* (The Street, 413/774-5587). This 1884 two-story inn, furnished with antiques, has twenty-three guest rooms and afternoon tea. Library, excellent restaurant. Expensive. Open year-round.

DENNIS

Josiah Dennis Manse (77 Nobscusset Rd.; no phone). The restored 1736 home of the minister for whom the town was named. Antiques, a spinning and weaving exhibit, and a Marine Wing. An old schoolhouse is on the grounds. Open Tuesdays and Thurs-

days, July through late August.

Jericho House and Historical Center (Old Main St. and Trotting Park Rd. in West Dennis). Period furniture in an 1801 house. Also a barn museum with old tools, a model of a salt works, vintage photographs. Open Monday, Wednesday, and Friday, July through late August.

For further information on the historic properties in Dennis, call the Chamber of Commerce (800/243-9920), or visit the information booth at the junction of MA 28 and 134.

EASTHAM

Eastham Windmill (Windmill Green). This restored windmill (1680) is the oldest on Cape Cod. Open daily, late June through Labor Day.

Swift-Daley House (on U.S. 6; 508/255-1766). Period furniture in a 1741 house. Open Monday through Friday, July and August.

GLOUCESTER

Cape Ann Historical Museum (27 Pleasant St.; 508/283-0455). A Federal-style circa-1805 house displays decorative arts and furnishings, paintings by Fitz Hugh Lane. Extensive material on the Gloucester fishing industry and Cape Ann history. Open Tuesday through Saturday.

Sargent House Museum (49 Middle St.; 508/281-0133). A late-18th-century Georgian house built for Judith Sargent, feminist writer and sister of Governor Winthrop Sargent. Also the home of her second husband, John Murry, leader of Universalism. Period furnishings, glass, china, silver, needlework. Portraits by John Singer Sargent. Open Friday through Sunday, June to mid-October.

GREAT BARRINGTON

Colonel Ashley House (9 miles south via MA 7 to Ashley Falls, then ½ mile on Rannapo Rd. to Cooper Hill Rd.; 413/229-8600). This is the elegant 1735 home of social leader Ashley. A political meeting he held here produced the Sheffield Declaration, forerunner to the Declaration of Independence. Period furnishings. Open Wednesday through Sunday, July and August; weekends, Memorial Day through June and September through Columbus Day.

Accommodations: *Seekonk Pines Inn* (142 Seekonk Cross Rd. at Rte. 23; 413/528-4192 or 800/292-4192). This inn dates from 1832, when Horace Church bought 200 acres and built a frame farmhouse. Now restored, the inn has six guest rooms with antiques, quilts, and private bath, a library, and a living room with piano. Garden, pool, country breakfast. Moderate. Open year-round.

HAVERHILL

John Greenleaf Whittier Birthplace (305 Whittier Rd., I-495 to exit 52, 1 mile east on MA 110; 508/373-3979). The Whittier family homestead since the late 1600s, this was the setting for his best-known poems, including "Snow-bound" and "Barefoot Boy." His writing desk and mother's bedroom are here. Original furnishings. Open daily except Monday.

Haverhill Historical Society (240 Water St.; 508/374-4626). Located in The Buttonwoods, an early-1800s house that displays period furnishings, glass, china, Hannah Dustin relics, memorabilia from early theaters. On the grounds is the John Ward House (1641) and an early shoe factory with displays. Tours available. Open Wednesdays and Thursdays and Saturday and Sunday afternoons.

IPSWICH

John Whipple House (53 Main St. on MA 1A; 508/356-2811). This 1640 house with a garden contains 17- and 18th-century furniture. Open Wednesday through Sunday, May to mid-October.

John Heard House (40 South Main; 508/356-2811). A 1795 house with furnishings from the China trade. Operated in conjunction with the Whipple House, with the same schedule.

LENOX

Hawthorne Cottage (at Tanglewood, on West St., 1½ miles southwest of town center on MA 183; festival phone: 413/637-1940 during summer, 617/266-1492 the rest of the year). Replica of the "Little Red House" where Hawthorne lived in 1850–51 now contains music studios, Hawthorne memorabilia. Tanglewood is the home of the famous Tanglewood Music Festival, held each summer. The house is open before each festival concert.

Accommodations: *Village Inn* (16 Church St.; 413/637-0020 or 800/253-0917). The Whitlock family built a large home and two nearby barns in 1771, and four years later connected the barns to the house, adapting them to accommodate guests. The Village Inn has been in operation ever since. Some of the thirty-two guest rooms (with private bath) have four-poster canopied beds and working fireplaces. A restaurant on the premises serves breakfast, tea, and dinner. Moderate. Open year-round.

LEXINGTON

On Lexington Green, April 19, 1775, eight Minutemen were killed in what is considered the first organized fight of the Revolutionary

*When 700 Redcoats
arrived in Lexington
on April 18, 1775,
Captain John Parker
told his 77 Minutemen:
"if they mean to have
a war, let it begin
here." In the first bat-
tle of the Revolution,
the British were sent
back reeling to Boston.
Courtesy Library of
Congress, Prints and
Photographs Division.*

War. Down the street came the British, 700 strong. To the right of the green is the tavern the militia used as headquarters. Here, seventy-seven Minutemen lined up near the west end of the green, facing down the road. Nearby is a boulder with a plaque bearing Captain John Parker's words: "Stand your ground. Don't fire unless fired upon. But if they mean to have a war, let it begin here!"

Battle Green (center of town). The Old Monument and the Boulder mark the line of Minutemen, seven of whom are buried under the monument.

Hancock-Clarke House (36 Hancock St.; 617/862-1703). In this 1698 house (one of three operated by the Lexington Historical Society), John Hancock and Samuel Adams were awakened by Paul Revere's alarm. Period furniture, utensils, portraits, a small museum. Open daily, mid-April through October.

Buckman Tavern (1 Bedford St., facing Battle Green; 617/862-1703). Minutemen assembled in this 1709 tavern before the battle. Period furnishings and portraits. Open daily, mid-April through October; weekends in November.

Munroe Tavern (1332 Massachusetts Ave.; 617/862-1703). The 1695 tavern served as a British hospital after the battle. George Washington dined here in 1769. Period furnishings and artifacts. Open Friday through Sunday, mid-April through October.

Museum of Our National Heritage (33 Marrett Rd. at Massachusetts Ave.; 617/861-6559). Exhibits on Lexington and the Revolution. Open daily.

LOWELL

Whistler House Museum of Art (243 Worthen St.; 508/452-7641). Birthplace of the painter James Abbott McNeill Whistler. Exhibits include several of his etchings, as well as other 19th- and early-20th-century art. Open daily except Mondays, June through August; Wednesday through Sunday, March through May and September through December.

Lowell National History Park. (Downtown Visitor Center, 246 Market St.; 508/970-5000). The park commemorates Lowell's legacy as the most important planned industrial city in America. The first large-scale center for production of cotton cloth, the city became a model of industrial development. The park includes mill build-ings, a 5.6-mile industrial canal system. Tours by barge and trolley, July through Columbus Day. Visitor center open daily.

MARBLEHEAD

Abbott Hall (Town Hall, Washington Rd.; 617/631-0528). The original "Spirit of '76" painting is displayed here, as well as the 1684 deed to the town from the Manepashemet Indians. Museum with marine room. Gift shop. Open daily, from the last weekend in May through October.

Jeremiah Lee Mansion (161 Wash-ington St.; 617/631-1069). Generals Glover, Lafayette, and Washington were entertained in this 1768 Georgian mansion, which has period antiques and furnishings. Open daily, mid-May to mid-October.

King Hooper Mansion (8 Hooper St.; 617/631-2608). A restored 1728 mansion with garden. Open Monday through Friday, weekend afternoons.

Accommodations: *Harbor Light Inn* (58 Washington St.; 616/631-2186, or 617/631-7407). Built in 1712, this building was trans-formed into a Federal mansion in 1820. Completely restored, the elegant inn, fur-nished in the period, offers twenty guest rooms with private bath, continental break-fast. Moderate to expensive. Open year-round.

MARTHA'S VINEYARD

There was a whaling fleet here before the island became a summer resort. Many inhab-itants are of Indian descent. Edgartown was the first settlement, and has been the county seat since 1642. Oak Bluffs was the site of annual summer camp meetings for church groups in the 1830s, and the "Gingerbread Cottages of the Campground" are still in evi-dence. *Vincent House* (Main St., Edgartown; 508/627-8017), built in 1672, is the oldest on the island and has been lovingly restored. Open daily, June through August. *The Old Whaling Church* (1843), a fine example of Greek Revival architecture, is now a per-forming-arts center.

Accommodations: *Edgartown Inn* (56 North Water St.; 508/627-4794). Thomas Worth, a whaling captain, built this Federal house in 1798. (Fort Worth, Texas, was named after his son, a hero of the Mexican War.) Among the luminaries who have stayed here are Daniel Webster, Nathaniel Hawthorne, and John F. Kennedy. The house, which hasn't been changed much, offers twenty guest rooms (sixteen with private bath), full breakfast. Moderate to expensive. Open April through November.

NANTUCKET

From the late 1600s until the early 1800s, this island, thirty miles south of Cape Cod, was the greatest whaling port in the world. The Nantucket Historical Association main-tains the following properties, which are open daily, June through October:

Jethro Coffin House (north on North Water to West Chester, left to Sunset Hill), built in 1686, is Nantucket's oldest house.

Whaling Museum (Broad St. near Steamboat Wharf) has relics of whaling days. Tryworks, scrimshaw, candle press, whale skeleton.

Research Center (next to museum on Broad St.) has ships' logs, diaries, charts, old photographs, library.

Old Windmill (Mill Hill, off Prospect St.) was built in 1746 of wood from wrecked ships.

Hadwen House (Main and Pleasant streets) is an 1845 Greek Revival mansion with period furnishings and garden.

THE GREAT AWAKENING

In the 1740s, a wave of fundamental, orthodox Protestantism swept the colonies. It was called the Great Awakening, and was created by two charismatic evangelists, Jonathan Edwards and George Whitefield. Edwards became famous for his fire-and-brimstone sermons, which provoked near hysteria in his listeners. Influenced by Edwards, Whitefield was an orator of legendary ability who attracted thousands to his outdoor meetings. Even Benjamin Franklin was moved by Whitefield. The Awakening eventually ran its course, but it had a long-term influence on the country. It contributed to a new spirit of secularism and loosened the hold the old-guard Puritans had on church and political matters.

1800 House (Miss St. off Pleasant St.) was the home of the sheriff, and has period furnishings and a kitchen garden.

Old Gaol (Vestal St.) is an unusual two-story 1805 building.

Folger-Franklin Seat and Memorial Boulder (1 mile from west end of Main St.) was the birthplace of Abiah Folger, the mother of Benjamin Franklin.

Museum of Nantucket History (Straight Wharf) has exhibits of Nantucket history and craft demonstrations in the old Macy Warehouse.

Information about the historical properties open to the public may be obtained at the Information Bureau (25 Federal St.; 508/228-0925).

Accommodations: *Cobblestone Inn* (5 Ash St.; 508/228-1987). Tristram Coffin built a simple, two-story house here in 1725, which later was expanded into a six-bedroom guest house. It has retained the four original fireplaces, wide floorboards, and curved corner support posts from a ship's frame. Guest rooms (all with private bath) have period furnishings, and some have fireplaces and canopy beds. Brick patio and garden, continental breakfast. Moderate. Open year-round.

NEW BEDFORD

New Bedford Whaling Museum (18 Johnny Cake Hill; 508/997-0046). The main attraction here is an 89-foot half-scale model of the whaler *Lagoda*. Scrimshaw, murals of whales, and whale skeleton. Period rooms, collections of toys, dolls, prints, ship models. Film shown July and August. Open daily.

Seaman's Bethel (15 Johnny Cake Hill; 508/992-3295). The "Whaleman's Chapel," referred to by Herman Melville in *Moby-Dick,* has a pulpit shaped like a ship's prow. Many cenotaphs are dedicated to sailors lost at sea. Open Monday through Saturday, May through Columbus Day; Sunday afternoons the rest of the year.

NEWBURYPORT

Coffin House (16 High Rd.; 508/463-2057). This house, built in 1654, was enlarged several times, and contains furnishings of eight generations of Coffins. Tours available. Open Wednesday through Sunday, June to mid-October.

Cushing House Museum (98 High Rd.; 508/462-2681). This 1810 Federal mansion was the home of Caleb Cushing, the first U.S. envoy to China. Collections of needlework, paperweights, toys, paintings, silver, clocks, china, furnishings. Garden. Open Tuesday through Saturday, May through October.

NEWTON

Jackson Homestead (527 North Washington St.; 617/552-7238). Once a stop on the Underground Railroad, this 1809 house

The Round Stone Barn at Hancock Shaker Village in Pittsfield.

has exhibits of Newton history, collections of toys, textiles, and tools. Open Monday through Thursday, July and August.

NORTHAMPTON

Museum Houses (413/584-6011), all open Wednesday through Sunday, March through December, include the 1813 *Damon House,* notable for its formal parlor exhibit; the 1798 *Shepherd House,* focusing on the lifestyle at the turn of the 19th century; and the 1730 *Parsons House,* with exhibits on local architecture.

PITTSFIELD

Arrowhead (760 Holmes Rd.; 413/442-1793). Herman Melville wrote *Moby-Dick* while living in this 1780 house. Historic displays. Headquarters of Berkshire County Historical Society. Open daily, June through Labor Day; Thursday through Monday, Labor Day through October.

THE MAYFLOWER COMPACT

The first written framework of government in what now is the United States was the Mayflower Compact, signed by the Pilgrims and other colonists on the ship *Mayflower* in November 1620. Storms had driven the ship to Cape Cod, several hundred miles north of the planned destination in Virginia, placing the Pilgrims outside the bounds of the government authority they had contracted with in England.

William Bradford, the leader of the Pilgrims, was alarmed to learn that some of the others felt no obligation to respect the rules of the Pilgrims. In his words, they wanted to "use their owne libertie." The male heads of Pilgrim and non-Pilgrim families therefore drew up a compact that bound all signers to accept whatever form of government was established after they went ashore. The compact created a "Civil Body Politic" to enact "Just and equal Laws, Ordinances, Acts, Constitutions and Offices." Every adult male had to sign the agreement before leaving the ship. The compact remained in effect until Plymouth was incorporated into the short-lived Dominion of New England in 1686 and subsequently absorbed into the Massachusetts Bay Colony In 1691.

The Mayflower II *at Plimouth Plantation. Photo by Ted Curtin.*

◆━I━◆

Being thus arrived in a good harbor, and brought safe to land, they [the Pilgrims] fell upon their knees and blessed the God in Heaven who had brought them over the vast and furious ocean . . . again to set their feet on the firm and stable earth, their proper element.

—WILLIAM BRADFORD, OF PLIMOUTH PLANTATION, CIRCA 1630

Hancock Shaker Village (5 miles west on U.S. 20 at junction of MA 41; 413/443-0188). This village, a Shaker settlement from 1790–1960, now is a 1,200-acre living-history museum of Shaker life and crafts. Shaker furniture is housed in twenty restored buildings, including the Round Stone Barn. Craft demonstrations, farm animals, gardens, picnicking, gift shop. Open daily, April through November.

PLYMOUTH

The first permanent settlement north of Virginia began here on December. 21, 1620, when 102 men, women, and children arrived on the *Mayflower*. Although plagued by exposure, cold, hunger, and disease during the first terrible winter, the colony was firmly established by the following year.

Plimoth Plantation (3 miles south on MA 3A; 508/746-1622). A year-round living-history museum re-creating life in Plymouth. *Visitor Center* has multi-image orientation program, exhibits, gift shop, restaurant. *Pilgrim Village* has fourteen houses and the

Fort-Meetinghouse. Costumed interpreters portray Pilgrims. *Hobbemock's (Wampanoag Indian) Homesite* is a large, bark-covered house with tools and artifacts. *Mayflower II* (State Pier, on Water St.), a ninety-foot bark, is a full-sized reproduction of the ship that carried the Pilgrims here. Costumed interpreters portray crew and passengers.

Plymouth Rock (Water St., on the harbor). The traditional site of the landing.

Cole's Hill (south of Plymouth Rock). Here the Pilgrims who perished during the first winter were secretly buried. *Burial Hill* is just west of the town square; Governor Bradford is among those buried here.

Howland House (33 Sandwich St.; 508/746-9590). A restored 1666 Pilgrim house with period furnishings. Open Monday through Saturday, Memorial Day to mid-October.

Harlow Old Fort House (119 Sandwich St.; 508/746-0012). Demonstrations of spinning, weaving, and candle-dipping in a 1677 house with an herb garden. Open Wednesday through Saturday, July through October.

Richard Sparrow House (42 Summer St.; 508/747-1240). The oldest (1640) restored home in Plymouth. Craft gallery. Open daily except Wednesdays, Memorial Day to mid-October.

Mayflower Society House Museum (4 Winslow St. off North St.; 508/746-2590). Nine rooms with period furnishings in a 1754 house with a formal garden. Open daily, July through Labor Day; Friday through Sunday, Memorial Day through June and early September.

Pilgrim Hall Museum (75 Court St.; 508/746-1620). Possessions of the first Pilgrims, including furniture, household items, ceramics, decorative arts. Open daily.

Spooner House (27 North St.; 508/746-0012). The Spooner family occupied this 1747 house for five generations. It is furnished with their heirlooms, and contains a collection of Oriental export wares. Open Wednesday through Saturday, June through October.

National Monument to the Forefathers (Allerton St.; 508/746-1620). At eighty-one feet tall, the monument, which depicts the virtues of the Pilgrims, is the largest solid-granite monument in the country. Open daily, May through October.

QUINCY

The Adams National Historic Site (135 Adams St., off Furnace Brook Pkwy.). John Adams bought this 1731 house in 1787. Original furnishings. *John and John Quincy Adams Birthplaces* (133 and 147 Franklin streets). Two 17th-century saltboxes. The elder Adams was born and reared at 133 Franklin Street; his son in the other house. While living here, Abigail Adams wrote many of her famous letters to her husband, John Adams. Tours available at the *Adams Historic Sites Visitor Center* (1250 Hancock St.; 617/773-1177, administered by the National Park Service. Visitor center and sites open daily.

Quincy Homestead (1010 Hancock St. at Butler Rd.; 617/472-5117). Four generations of Quincys lived here, including Dorothy Quincy, the wife of John Hancock. Two rooms were built in 1686, the rest of the house in the early 18th century. Period furnishings, herb garden. Open Wednesday through Sunday, May through October.

United First Parish Church (1306 Hancock St. at Washington; 617/773-1290). John Adams and John Quincy Adams and their wives are entombed in this 1828 church. Tours daily, late April to mid-November.

Josiah Quincy House (20 Muirhead St. in Wollaston; 617/227-3966). This fine 1770

Georgian mansion, furnished with family heirlooms, was the home of this branch of the Quincy family. Tours available. Open Tuesdays, Thursdays, and weekends, June through mid-October.

SALEM

Panic swept this charming town in 1692, and nineteen persons charged with witchcraft were hanged on Gallows Hill, another "pressed" to death, and at least two others died in jail. Nathaniel Hawthorne lived here in the early 1800s, and the people and events of the seaport found their way into his novels.

Salem Maritime National Historic Site (9 acres on waterfront; 508/745-1470). Historic buildings include *Derby Wharf* (off Derby St.), a center of Salem shipping from 1760 to 1810; the 1819 *Custom House* has restored offices; the *Scale House* and the *Bonded Warehouse* were the sites of early customs operations; the 1762 *Derby House* was the home of merchant Elias Hasket Derby, the country's first millionaire; *Narbonne House* contains archaeological exhibits; and the 1800 *West India Good Store* has coffee, teas, spices, and other goods for sale. *Visitor Information* (Central Wharf Warehouse; 508/745-1470) is open daily.

House of the Seven Gables (54 Turner St. off Derby St.; 508/744-0991). This 1668 house was the setting for Hawthorne's classic novel. Audiovisual introduction, tours of the house and Hawthorne's birthplace. On the grounds are the 1682 Hathaway House and the 1655 *Becket House*. Garden café. Open daily except the first two weeks in January.

Peabody Museum and Essex Institute (East India Sq.; 508/745-9500). This museum, founded by sea captains in 1799,

And we have now with Horror seen the Discovery of such a Witchcraft! An Army of Devils is horribly broke in upon . . . our English Settlements: and the Houses of the Good People there are fill'd with the doleful Shrieks of their Children and Servants.

—*COTTON MATHER*

THE ADAMSES: FATHER, ABIGAIL, AND SON

The son of a Massachusetts farmer, John Adams excelled at Harvard and became one of the most respected lawyers in Boston. In the belief that the accused always has the right to a vigorous defense, he defended the British soldiers accused of killing civilians in the 1770 Boston Massacre. His Colonial sympathies, though, soon came to the fore.

Adams led the protest against the Stamp Tax, and in 1774 he was sent as a delegate to the First Continental Congress. He proposed the election of Washington as commander-in-chief, and was the "colossus of the debate" on the Declaration of Independence. By 1778 he had served on more committees than any other member, simultaneously acting as a one-man war department.

For a decade Adams served as a diplomat. He secured Dutch loans and chaired the commission that concluded the peace treaty with England, ending as ambassador to the English court, where he was received by George III, the king against whom he had helped lead a revolution.

Adams served as Washington's Vice President, then was elected President. His presidency was marred by the threat of war with France, and after a single term he was defeated by Jefferson. Deeply hurt by the rejection of the voters, he returned to Massachusetts and refused all further public involvement.

Adams was reconciled with Jefferson, who had been a friend in Europe, and they began a correspondence that is considered a monument of the American Enlightenment. He and Jefferson died on the same day, July 4, 1826, the fiftieth anniversary of independence.

ABIGAIL ADAMS

Descended from well-known New England families, Abigail (Smith) Adams was self-educated, reading widely and studying French. When she was nineteen, she married John Adams, a young lawyer, and moved to his home in Braintree, Massachusetts, where she stayed through the Revolution. There she raised four children, Abigail, John Quincy, Charles, and Thomas Boylston. A fifth child died in infancy.

When John was away on revolutionary political matters, Abigail ran the household and the family farm, engaged in business enterprises, purchased land, and dealt with tenants. In 1784 she joined her husband

has five world-famous collections in thirty galleries, including marine art and Asian export art. The Essex Institute features historical interpretations of the area. Museum open daily; Institute daily, June through October; daily except Mondays the rest of the year. The museum manages three historic houses: the 1804 *Gardner-Pingree House* (128 Essex St.), a beautiful example of the work of master builder Samuel McIntire; 1684 *John Ward House* (behind Essex Institute); and the 1772 *Crowinshield-Bentley House* (Essex St. and Hawthorne Blvd.). All open daily, June through October.

Ropes Mansion and Garden (318 Essex St.; 508/745-9500). This late-1720s gambrel-roofed Georgian mansion has been

in Europe, where he was the minister to Great Britain. During his terms as Vice-President and President, she lived in New York, Philadelphia, and Washington, before they retired to Quincy, Massachusetts.

Abigail Adams found her true calling as a correspondent. For more than four decades she wrote letters to her husband and children, relatives, and friends. Despite her lack of training, she perfected her style and excelled at her craft. "My pen is always freer than my tongue," she wrote to John in 1775. "I have wrote many things to you that I suppose I never could have talked."

Her letters provide a window on eighteenth-century life, private and public. They also convey her zeal for politics, her intense interest in national affairs, and her avid patriotism. In March 1776 she vented a complaint about the legal subjection of married women: "I desire you would Remember the ladies, and be more generous and favorable to them than your ancestors," she wrote. "Do not put unlimited powers into the hands of the Husbands."

JOHN QUINCY ADAMS

The eldest and most gifted son of John Adams, John Quincy Adams followed almost precisely in his father's footsteps as diplomat, congressman, senator, secretary of state, and President of the United States.

In 1802, he was elected a U.S. senator from Massachusetts, as a Federalist, but he was too independent to follow the party line. His support of the Jefferson Administration cost him his Senate seat. He was one of the commissioners who arranged for the Treaty of Ghent, which ended the War of 1812. As secretary of state, he drafted the Monroe Doctrine and acquired Florida from Spain.

In 1824 he was the New England candidate for President, but neither he nor the other candidates commanded an electoral majority. In the House of Representatives, Henry Clay threw his support to Adams, who was then elected over Andrew Jackson. Adams then made Clay his secretary of state. Adams was the target of partisan abuse throughout his administration.

He was brilliant, but his ideas were ahead of their time. He was an advocate of national planning. He wanted a protective tariff, federal funding for roads and canals, a national university, and government support for scientific investigation. He got none of them. Savagely attacked as an aristocrat and a quasi-Federalist, he lost his 1828 reelection bid to Jackson.

Three years later, Adams was elected to Congress, where he battled almost singlehandedly against a Southern-dominated House for the right of antislavery groups to be heard. Subjected to a gag rule and threatened with censure and expulsion, he persisted in defending a constitutional right. Many see his congressional record as his crowning achievement.

restored and furnished in the style of the period. The garden is nationally famous for its beauty and variety.

Witch House (310½ Essex St.; 508/744-0180). The 1642 home of witchcraft trial judge Jonathan Corwin. Open daily, mid-March through November.

Stephen Phillips Memorial Trust House (34 Chesnut St.; 508/744-0440). A Federal-style 1804 mansion with McIntire touches. Rugs and porcelains reflect the seafaring past of the family. Open daily, late May to mid-October.

Accommodations: *The Salem Inn* (7 Summer St.; 508/741-0680, or 800/446-2995). In 1834, sea captain Nathaniel West built this Federal mansion on what is now the Salem Heritage Trail. It offers twenty-

The House of the Seven Gables in Salem.

two guest rooms with private bath on four floors, some with whirlpool baths and fireplaces. Patio, rose garden, antiques, continental breakfast. Moderate.

SANDWICH

Sandwich Glass Museum (129 Main St.; 508/888-0251). The museum's collection of Sandwich glass is internationally famous. Open daily, April through October.

Heritage Plantation (Grove and Pine Sts.; 508/888-3300). The site's Military Museum houses the Lilly collection of miniature soldiers and antique firearms. The Art Museum has an Early American collection of scrimshaw, weathervanes, grade signs, primitive paintings, and Currier & Ives collection. Antique autos, rides, carousel, café, picnic area. Open daily, mid-May through late October.

Hoxie House and Dexter Gristmill (Water St.; 508/888-1173). A restored mid-17th-century house and operating mill. Open daily, mid-June through mid-October.

SAUGUS

Saugus Iron Works National Historic Site (244 Central St.; 617/233-0050). The birthplace of the American steel industry, the site includes a reconstructed furnace, a forge, and the mill of the country's first successful integrated ironworks. A furnished 17th-century house is on the site, as well as a working blacksmith shop and seven working waterwheels. Open daily, April through October.

SOUTH YARMOUTH

Winslow Crocker House (Old King's Hwy., U.S. 6A, in Yarmouth Port; 508/362-4385). A Georgian house, circa 1780, with furnishings from the 17th through 19th centuries. Open Tuesdays, Thursdays, and weekends, June to mid-October.

Captain Bangs Hallet House (off MA 6A, near Yarmouth Port Post Office; 508/362-3021). An early-19th-century sea captain's home and gate house. Open Wednesday, Friday, and Sunday afternoons, June through September.

STOCKBRIDGE

Mission House (Main and Sergeant streets; 413/298-3239). Built in 1739 for missionary John Sergeant, the house is now a museum of colonial life that includes an Indian museum. Gardens. Tours available. Open daily except Mondays, Memorial Day through Columbus Day.

Merwin House "Tranquillity" (14 Main St.; 413/298-4703). This 1825 brick house in late Federal period, later enlarged with a "shingle" style wing, contains European and American furniture and decorative arts. Open Tuesdays, Thursdays, and weekends, June to mid-October.

Accommodations: *The Red Lion* (Main St.; 413/298-5545). Established in 1773, this inn has eighty-two guest rooms, colonial decor, and a collection of antiques. It has full hotel services and a restaurant with a traditional New England menu. Moderate to expensive. Open year-round.

Guides in period costumes outside the Fitch House in Old Sturbridge Village. Photo by Thomas Neill.

STURBRIDGE

Old Sturbridge Village (on U.S. 20W, 2 miles west of I-84 exit 2 and I-90 exit 9; 508/347-3362). An authentic re-creation of a rural New England community of the early 18th century, the village encompasses forty historical buildings, moved here from other locations in New England. The 1707 *Fenno House,* the 1735 *Stephen Fitch House,* and the 1832 Greek Revival *Baptist Church* are of particular interest. Artisans' shops with demonstrations include blacksmith, printer, tinner, cooper, and potter. Law office, bank, and school. Galleries exhibit antique time-pieces, glass, and guns. At the edge of the village is the *Pliny Freeman Farm,* where 19th-century agriculture is practiced today. The *Mill Neighborhood* has a water-powered saw, grist and carding mills. Costumed interpreters. Open daily.

   Accommodations: *Publick House* (on Rte. 131, 1½ miles south of jct. U.S. 20, I-84 exit 3, off I-90 exit 9; 508-347-3313). Once a tavern built in 1771, this inn, on historic Sturbridge Common, offers seventeen guest rooms, colonial decor, antiques, tennis, restaurant on premises. Moderate. Open all year.

SUDBURY CENTER

Accommodations: *Longfellow's Wayside Inn* (Wayside Inn Rd., 3 miles southwest, just off U.S. 20; 508/443-1776). Originally restored and once owned by Henry Ford, this 1702 inn was the setting for Longfellow's *Tales of a Wayside Inn.* Period furniture. Also on the property is the 1798 *Redstone School,* immortalized in "Mary Had a Little Lamb." Open daily as an operating inn with ten guest rooms, period furnishings, restaurant on premises. Moderate. Open year-round.

WALTHAM

Gore Place (U.S. 20 at Waltham-Watertown line; 617/894-2798). The twenty-two-room mansion, designed in Paris and built in 1805, is one of New England's finest examples of Federal architecture, housing Early American, European, and Oriental antiques. There is a living-history farm. Open daily except Monday, mid-April through mid-November.

   Lyman Estate "The Vale" (185 Lyman St.; 617/891-7232). Designed for Boston merchant Theodore Lyman by Samuel McIntire, and remodeled in the 1880s, the ballroom and parlor of this 1793 mansion retain Federal style. Five operating greenhouses, landscaped grounds. Greenhouses open weekdays and Sunday afternoons. House open only for groups, by appointment.

WORCESTER

Salisbury Mansion (40 Highland St.; 508/753-8278). The 1772 home of businessman and philanthropist Stephen Salisbury, now restored to its 1830s appearance. Tours. Open Thursday through Sunday afternoons.

   American Antiquarian Society (185 Salisbury St.; 508/755-5221). This research library has the largest collection of source materials pertaining to the first 250 years of American history. Tours available. Open weekdays.

4

RHODE ISLAND

Florentine navigator in the service of France, Giovanni da Verrazzano, visited Narragansett Bay in Rhode Island in 1524, but it wasn't until 1636 that the first permanent settlement was founded. Roger Williams, a religious refugee from Massachusetts, obtained land at Providence from his friends, the Narragansett Indians. ("It was not price nor money that could have purchased Rhode Island," he wrote. "Rhode Island was purchased by love.")

From the beginning, his settlement was known for its policy of religious and political freedom. Similar communities were settled nearby, and in 1623 King Charles II granted them a royal charter, officially creating the "State of Rhode Island and Providence Plantations."

By the 1650s, fine harbors at Providence, Newport, Bristol, Warren, and other towns made Rhode Island competitive with Massachusetts for maritime commerce. During the wars between England and France, Rhode Island captains were privateers who preyed upon French shipping.

When British commercial policies began to affect the maritime trade, Rhode Island was a leader in the resistance. In 1765 the first violent act against Britain took place when a Newport mob destroyed a British warship to protest the impressment of seamen. Four years later a British revenue ship was destroyed in Newport; another, the *Gaspee,* was later burned in a raid.

In 1776, Rhode Island was the first colony to proclaim independence from Great Britain, two months before the Declaration of Independence was signed. The British occupied Newport during the Revolution, and nearly destroyed its economy. The only major battle in Rhode Island was an abortive attempt to dislodge British troops from the town.

EAST GREENWICH

Kent County Court House (Main St. on U.S. 1; 401/885-0020). Built in 1750 and last remodeled in 1909, this structure is an interesting example of colonial civic architecture. Open weekdays.

General James Mitchell Varnum House and Museum (57 Pierce St.; 401/884-4110). The home of a Revolutionary War officer and lawyer is furnished in the style of the period. Colonial garden. Open Tuesday through Saturday, June through August.

Varnum Armory and Military Museum (6 Main St.; 401/884-4110). Collections of artifacts and memorabilia from all the nation's wars. Open by appointment.

JAMESTOWN

Sidney L. Wright Museum (26 North Rd., located in the library; 401/423-7280). Exhibits of Indian and early colonial artifacts from Conanicut Island. Open daily except Sundays.

Old Watermill ($1\frac{1}{2}$ miles north on North Rd., south of RI 138; 401/423-1798). This 1787 mill has been restored to working order. Open weekends, mid-June to mid-September.

Watson Farm (North Rd. south of RI 138; 401/423-0005). A 280-acre farm, dating from 1796, is being worked as a typical farm of the period. Self-guided tour. Open Tuesdays, Thursdays, and Sundays, June to mid-October.

KINGSTON

Kingston Library (Kingstown Rd.; 401/783-8254). George Washington and Benjamin Franklin visited this 1776 library, which housed the Rhode Island General Assembly at the time the British were occupying Newport. Open daily except Sundays.

LITTLE COMPTON

Wilbur House (1 mile south on RI 77 at West Rd.; no phone). The local historical society restored this 1680 house and its 18th- and 19th-century additions. Period furnishings. Carriages and sleighs in an 1860 barn. Artist's studio and one-room schoolhouse. Open daily except Mondays, June to mid-September.

Gray's Store (4 Main St. in Adamsville, 7 miles northeast on local road; 401/635-4566). Built in 1788, this store became the area's first post office in 1804. Antique soda fountain, candy and tobacco cases. Open daily.

NEWPORT

The first Quakers to emigrate from England to America settled here in 1657. Newport became a famous resort after the Civil War,

when many wealthy families built magnificent summer palaces along Cliff Walk, many of which are now open to the public.

Redwood Library and Athenaeum (50 Bellevue Ave.; 401/847-0292). Built by master colonial architect Peter Harrison in 1750 and used as a club for English officers during the occupation, it now is the oldest library building in continuous use in the country. Collections of early books and portraits. Open daily except Sundays.

Newport Historical Society Museum (82 Touro St.; 401/846-0813). Collections of Colonial art, Newport silver, pewter, Early American glass, china, and furniture. Tours of Colonial Newport. Open Tuesday through Saturday, mid-June through September.

Friends Meeting House (Farewell and Marlborough streets; 401/846-0813). Built in 1699, expanded in 1729 and 1807, this building spans three centuries of architecture and construction. Quaker costume display. Tours by appointment.

Trinity Church (Queen Anne Square; 401/846-0660). The church has been in continuous use since it was built in 1726. George Washington attended services here. The interior has Tiffany windows and an organ personally tested by Handel before it was shipped from London. Tours by appointment.

Seventh Day Baptist Meeting House (82 Touro St.; 401/846-0813). A historic 1729 church built by master builder Richard Munday. Open Tuesday through Saturday.

Touro Synagogue National Historic Site (72 Touro St.; 401/847-4794). The oldest synagogue (housing the oldest torah) in America, built in 1763 by Peter Harrison, America's first architect. Services follow the Sephardic Orthodox ritual of the synagogue's founders. Open daily except Saturdays, late June through Labor Day; Sunday afternoons the rest of the year.

Samuel Whitehorne House (416 Thames

Boats crowd the waters off Newport, Rhode Island, in the mid-1800s. Courtesy Library of Congress, Prints and Photographs Division.

St.; 401/849-7300). This 1811 house has exquisite 18th-century furniture, silver, and pewter, Chinese porcelain, Irish crystal, and Pilgrim-era furniture. Garden. Open Friday through Monday, May through October.

Wanton-Lyman-Hazard House (17 Broadway; 401/846-0813). Built around 1645, this is the oldest house in Newport, and one of the finest Jacobean houses in New England. The site of the 1765 Stamp Act riot. Eighteenth-century garden, tours. Open Tuesday through Saturday, mid-June through late August.

Whitehall Museum House (3 miles northeast on Berkeley Ave. in Middletown; 401/846-3316). This restored hip-roofed country house was built in 1729 for Bishop George Berkeley, philosopher and educator. Open daily, June through August.

Hammersmith Farm (Ocean Dr.; 401/846-0420 or 401/846-7346). The farm dates from 1640, but became famous as the unofficial summer White House during the Kennedy Administration. In 1887, a twenty-eight-room, shingle-style summer cottage was added, and was the site of the wedding reception of John and Jacqueline Kennedy. The gardens were designed by Frederick Law

Olmsted. Tours. Gift shop. Open daily, April through early December.

Accommodations: *Melville House* (39 Clarke St.; 401/847-0640). Officers of the French army were once quartered in this 1750 shingled house, and it was later owned by the Melville family (no relation to the author) and is on the National Registry of Historic Places. Seven guest rooms, five with private bath. Furnished with antiques. Continental breakfast. Moderate. Open March through January.

NORTH KINGSTOWN

Gilbert Stuart Birthplace (5 miles south off RI 1A to 815 Gilbert Stuart Rd., northwest of Saunderstown; 401/294-3001). Birthplace of portraitist Gilbert Stuart (1755–1828). Period furnishings. Snuff mill powered by wooden waterwheel. Partly restored gristmill. Tours available. Open daily except Fridays, April through October.

Smith's Castle (1½ miles south on U.S. 1; 401/294-3521). The blockhouse, circa 1638, destroyed by fire in 1676 and rebuilt in 1678, is one of the oldest plantation houses in the country and the only known existing house where Roger Williams preached. Period furnishings and garden. Open Thursday through Monday, June through August; Friday through Sunday in May and September.

Casey Farm (3½ miles south on RI 1A, past Jamestown Bridge, on Boston Neck Rd. in Saunderstown; 401/294-2868). The site of Revolutionary War activities, this farmhouse was built circa 1750, and continuously occupied by the Casey family for 200 years. Restored farm with animals, gardens. Family furnishings and paintings. Open Saturdays June through October.

PAWTUCKET

Pawtucket, where Samuel Slater founded the nation's first cotton mill, is regarded by historians as the birthplace of the Industrial Revolution in America.

Slater Mill National Historic Site (Roosevelt Ave. at Main; 401/725-8638). The first water-powered cotton mill was built here in 1793 by Samuel Slater. Also on the site are the 1810 Wilkinson Mill and the 1758 Sylvanus Brown House. The Slater mill has an operating restored water-power system,

The Wilbur House in Little Compton.

including raceways and eight-ton wheel. Spinning and weaving demonstrations are given. Open daily except Mondays, June through Labor Day; weekends, March through May and September through October.

PROVIDENCE

Rhode Island State House (Smith St.; 401/277-2357). In this 1901 McKim, Mead & White capitol is a full-length portrait of George Washington by Gilbert Stuart, and the original charter granted to Rhode Island by Charles II in 1663. Tours available. Open weekdays.

Old State House (150 Benefit St.; 401/277-2678). The General Assembly met here between 1762 and 1900. Independence was proclaimed in this building, two months before the Declaration was signed in Philadelphia. Open weekdays.

First Baptist Church in America (75 North Main; 401/454-3418). The oldest Baptist congregation in America, established in 1638, built the present church in 1775. Open weekdays. Tours after Sunday services.

First Unitarian Church (Benefit and Benevolent streets; 401/421-7970). Organized as the First Congregational Church in 1720, the church, built in 1816, was designed by John Holden Greene and has the largest bell ever cast by Paul Revere. Open weekdays, September through June.

John Brown House (52 Power St.; 401/331-8575). This Georgian masterpiece, one of the finest 18th-century houses in the country, was designed by John's brother Joseph. Built in 1786, the house rises three stories, and a balustrade surrounds the roof. The fourteen-room interior is elegantly decorated. John Quincy Adams visited here, and proclaimed it the most magnificent house he had ever seen. Fine Rhode Island furniture, silver, and china. Tours available. Open daily, March through December; daily except Mondays the rest of the year.

Governor Stephen Hopkins House (Benefit and Hopkins streets; 401/421-0694). The 1707 house of a signer of the Declaration of Independence and ten-time governor of the state. Period furnishings and garden. Open Wednesday and Saturday afternoons, April through December.

Walking tours. The Providence Preservation Society offers ninety-minute tape tours and walking-tour booklets of several historic neighborhoods. Both available weekdays at 21 Meeting St.; 401/831-7440.

Accommodations: *Old Court Inn* (144 Benefit St.; 401/751-2002 or 401/351-0747). Built in 1863 as a church rectory, Old Court is next to the historic Rhode Island Courthouse and overlooks the Old State House. Listed on the National Registry of Historic Places, the Italianate inn has twelve-foot ceilings, elaborate moldings, and chandeliers. Eleven guest rooms, breakfast. Moderate to expensive. Open all year.

WARWICK

General Nathanael Green Homestead (13 miles west via RI 117, in Coventry, at 50 Taft St.; 401/821-8630). This 1770 homestead was the residence of Washington's second-in-command during the Revolutionary War. Restored cannon. Open Wednesdays and weekends, March through November.

Walking tour of Historic Apponaug Village. More than thirty structures of historic interest are noted on a walking-tour brochure from the Department of Economic Development, 3275 Post Rd.; 401/738-2000.

WESTERLY

Babcock-Smith House (124 Granite St.; 401/596-4424, or 401/596-5704). This two-story, gambrel-roofed, circa-1732 Georgian mansion was the residence of Dr. Joshua Babcock, the town's first physician and a friend of Benjamin Franklin. Later the house was home to Orlando Smith, who discovered granite on the grounds. A furniture collection covers two centuries. Colonial garden. Open Wednesdays and Sundays, July to mid-September; Sundays only, May and June and mid-September to mid-October.

Touro Synagogue in Newport. Photo by John T. Hopf.

CANADA

St. Lawrence River

NEW BRUNSWICK

QUÉBEC

MAINE

95

Moosehead Lake

15

Penobscot River

16

Eastport

1

Bangor

95

1

Machi

St. Albans

VERMONT

91

Waterville

Searsport

Ellsworth

Buckport

Burlington

St. Johnsbury

95

Augusta

Camden

ACADIA NAT'L. PARK

Shelburne

Montpelier

1

Vergennes

Androscoggin

Damariscotta

Lake Champlain

89

Poland Spring

R.

Wiscasset

Middlebury

Connecticut River

93

NEW HAMPSHIRE

Bath

Boothbay Harbor

Brandon

Hanover

Sebago Lake (Standish)

95

Freeport

Windsor

Wolfeboro

Portland

91

Franklin

Weston

89

Kennebunk

Springfield

Newport

Grafton

Bellows Falls

Concord

Dover

York

Kittery

ATLANTIC OCEAN

N

7

Manchester

Portsmouth

Brattleboro

Keene

Exeter

Bennington

Jaffrey

Salem

95

MASSACHUSETTS

91

495

Boston

0   100 miles

0   150 km

5

MAINE

Sometime around A.D. 1000, the Vikings became the first white men to come to what is now Maine, but they didn't stay long enough to leave much to remember them by. By the beginning of the seventeenth century, fishermen were camping on the coast to repair their boats, dry their fish, and trade with the Algonquins. The first English settlement was established in 1607 at the mouth of the Kennebec River by Sir George Popham and a group of colonists, many of whom were fresh from English jails. They built the first ship to be constructed in America, but returned to England after their first Maine winter.

Captain John Smith explored the Maine coast in 1614 and wrote glowingly of lobsters, crabs, and "such excellent fish as many as the net can hold." In 1641 the English Crown charted its first city in America, to be built on the site of present-day York. Over the ensuing years, the English here had to fight off the French, who also had claims on Maine. The area was made part of the Massachusetts colony in 1652, where it would stay until Maine became a state in 1820.

Battles with the Indians racked Southern Maine from the 1670s until 1713. Entire settlements were abandoned, and refugees fled to Massachusetts. During the thirty years of peace that followed the end of Queen Anne's War, the coast was resettled. The French surrendered their claims in the area in 1759, and Maine became resolutely English.

Maine, with only fifteen incorporated towns and a population of about 20,000, was the least developed part of New England. The interior was settled only to a distance of some twenty miles from the shore. A primitive road ran parallel to the coast as far as the Kennebec River. John Adams traveled the road in 1771, a trip he described as "vastly disagreeable."

During the Revolution, the only fighting in Maine was the British raid on Falmouth in 1775, which destroyed the town. It was rebuilt after independence, and renamed Portland.

AUGUSTA

Men from the Plymouth Colony established a trading post in 1628 on the site of Chushnoc, an Indian village, but they abandoned it around 1700. Settlers returned decades later, and Fort Western was built in 1754 to protect them against Indian raid. The town developed on both sides of the Kennebec River. Augusta became an active port, shipping timber, furs, and other goods downriver forty-five miles to the sea.

Fort Western (Center City Plaza, 16 Cony St.; 207/626-2385). Built in 1754, the fort later was a store and a settlement for factory workers. The 100-by-32-foot main building, made of hewn logs covered in shingles, and topped by four chimneys, is one of the finest remnants of Colonial America. Open daily, mid-June to Labor Day; weekends, Labor Day to Columbus Day.

Maine State Museum (Capitol Park, State, and Capitol streets; 207/287-2301). Exhibits depict the state's environment, prehistory, social history, and manufacturing heritage. Military, political, and geographical artifacts. Open daily.

BATH

Maine Maritime Museum and Shipyard (243 Washington, 2 miles south of U.S. 1; 207/443-1316). Exhibits of navigational instruments, models, and scrimshaw. Demonstrations of seafaring techniques in the summer. Tours. Open daily.

Popham Colony (16 miles south on ME 209, on Sabino Head; no phone). Sir George Popham did not survive his first winter, and the colonists returned to England, but not before completing the first ship to be built in the colonies, the thirty-ton *Virginia.* In 1775, Benedict Arnold set off from here to invade Canada, and markers chart the 194-mile *Arnold Trail* to Coburn Gore, on the Canadian border. A seventy-foot tower at the site offers a panoramic view of the coast. Open daily.

BOOTHBAY HARBOR

English settlers arrived here after Captain John Smith sailed up from Jamestown in 1614 and proclaimed it an ideal fishing station. Later it was a seaport, then a shipbuilding center.

Boothbay Railway Village (1 mile north on ME 27; 207/633-4727). Historical exhibits of railroads, rural life. Steam-train rides. On eight acres are a general store, a one-room schoolhouse, and two restored railroad stations. Open daily, mid-June through mid-October.

Accommodations: *Harbour Towne Inn* (71 Townsend Ave.; 207/633-4300, or for reservations 800/722-4240). A rambling Queen Anne on the harbor. Six guest rooms in house and carriage house, all with private bath and some with deck. Penthouse suite, continental breakfast, no smoking, moderate to expensive. Open all year.

BUCKSPORT

Jed Prouty Tavern (52–54 Main St.; 207/469-3113 or 203/469-7972). A 1782 stagecoach inn whose guests included Martin Van Buren, Andrew Jackson, William Henry Harrison, and John Tyler. Restaurant. Open daily.

Accursed Tombstone (Buck Cemetery, Main and Hicks). A granite obelisk on the grave of town founder Jonathan Buck bears an indelible mark in the shape of a woman's leg, said to have been put there by a witch whom he had hanged.

CAMDEN

Old Historical Conway House Complex (on U.S. 1 at edge of town; 207/236-2257). The Mary Meeker Cramer Museum contains paintings, ship models, quilts, and other memorabilia. The complex also includes a restored 18th-century farmhouse, and a collection of carriages and sleighs in an old barn, as well as a blacksmith shop. Open Tuesday through Friday, July and August.

Accommodations: *Whitehall* (52 High St.; 207/236-3391) is a spacious, fifty-room 1834 resort inn. Edna St. Vincent Millay was a guest here in 1912. Valet service, garden with patio, tennis, lawn games, bar and restaurant. American plan available. Moderate. Open from Memorial Day to mid-October.

DAMARISCOTTA

Chapman-Hall House (Main and Church; no phone). This restored 1754 house has an original whitewashed kitchen and period furniture. Open daily except Sundays, Memorial Day through Labor Day.

St. Patrick's Church (west to Newcastle, then 2 miles north off U.S. 1; 207/563-3240). The bell in the steeple of this 1804 church, one of the oldest surviving Catholic churches in New England, was made by Paul Revere.

Colonial Pemaquid State Memorial (14 miles south via ME 130 in New Harbor;

207/677-2423). Archaeologists have found foundations of a jail, a tavern, and private homes at this site. Also here is the Fort William Henry State Memorial, a reconstructed 1692 fort tower with a museum containing portraits, relics, maps, and copies of Indian deeds. Open daily, Memorial Day through Labor Day.

Pemaquid Point Lighthouse Park (18 miles south at end of ME 130; 207/677-2494). An 1827 lighthouse that towers above the surf. *Fisherman's Museum* in old lightkeeper's house. Museum open daily, Memorial Day through Labor Day.

EASTPORT

Settled in 1772, Eastport, at the tip of Passsamaquoddy Bay on Moose Island, is the easternmost city in the country. British soldiers, smugglers, sea captains, and shipwreck victims are buried in *Hillside Cemetery* on High Street. On the mainland is the *Passamaquoddy Indian Reservation* (5 miles north on ME 190 at Pleasant Point; 207/853-2551). In 1604, Samuel de Champlain was the first European to encounter members of this Algonquin tribe, some 700 descendents of whom live here today. Open daily. The *Waponahki Museum* on the reservation presents a pictorial history of the tribe and displays artifacts.

Barracks Museum (74 Washington St.; no phone). In this building, which once served as the officers' barracks for a nearby fort, is a small museum. Open Tuesday through Saturday, Memorial Day through Labor Day.

ELLSWORTH

Judd Black Mansion (West Main St.; 207/667-8671). An early Georgian dwelling, built by a local landowner. Antiques, garden,

There was a time
before our time,
It will not come
again,
When the best ships
still were wooden
ships
But the men were
iron men.
From Stonington to
Kennebunk
The Yankee hammers plied
To build clippers of
the wave
That were New
England's pride.
The Flying Cloud,
and the Northern
Light,
The Sovereign of the
Seas
—There was salt
music in the blood
That thought of
names lie these.

—STEPHEN
VINCENT BENÉT
"AMERICAN NAMES"

THE EUROPEANS COME TO AMERICA

The Vikings were first. Around A.D. 1000, they sailed from the British Isles to Greenland, where they established a colony, then moved on to Labrador, the Baffin Islands, and finally to Newfoundland. There they established a colony named Vineland, and from that base explored along the coast of North America. Inexplicably, after a few years the Vikings abandoned Vineland. Stories of their discovery of a "new world" circulated through Europe, but five centuries would pass before anyone followed their paths of exploration.

The stimulus to exploration was trade. Marco Polo's journey to Cathay was Europe's "discovery" of the wealth of the Islamic world and the Orient. The newly unified states of Portugal, Spain, France, and England were envious of the Italian princes and merchants who dominated the land routes to the East. And in the latter half of the fifteenth century, war between European states and the Ottoman Empire severely impaired trade. None of this would matter if there were a sea route to the East.

Portugal led the way. Portuguese seamen, encouraged by Prince Henry the Navigator, sailed southward along the African coast. They didn't sail to the Orient during the prince's lifetime, but they developed the compass and the quadrant, made advances in cartography, and designed and built highly maneuverable little ships known as caravels.

Things began happening after John II ascended to the throne of Portugal. In 1487 he commissioned Bartolomeu Dias to find a water route to India. He made it around the tip of Africa and into the Indian Ocean before his frightened crew forced him to turn back. A year later Vasco da Gama reached India and returned to Portugal laden with jewels and spices. In 1500, Pedro Alvares Cabral discovered and claimed Brazil for Portugal. Other Portuguese captains established trading posts in the South China Sea, the Bay of Bengal, and the Arabian Sea. These water routes made Lisbon Europe's new trade capital.

Spain's imperial ambitions were launched by Christopher Columbus. Finding a sponsor in Ferdinand and Isabella, the Italian-born navigator sailed west in August 1492 with three ships, the *Niña*, the *Pinta*, and the *Santa María*. After ten weeks he sighted an island in the Bahamas, which he named San Salvador. Thinking he had found islands near Japan, he sailed on until he reached Cuba, which he thought was China.

Columbus returned to Spain with many products unknown to Europe (coconuts, tobacco, sweet corn, potatoes), and with tales of dark-skinned natives whom he called Indians, because he assumed he had been sailing in the Indian Ocean. He had found no gold, but he was hailed as the discoverer of the western route to the East. He made three more voyages to America, exploring Puerto Rico, the Virgin Islands, Jamaica, and Trinidad. Each time he returned home more convinced that he had reach the East.

Not everyone agreed with him. King John II believed Columbus had discovered islands in the Atlantic already claimed by Portugal, and petitioned the Pope to support his claim. Subsequent explorations persuaded most Europeans that Columbus had discovered a "New World." Ironically, a German geographer, Martin Waldseemuller, accepted the claim of Amerigo Vespucci that he had landed on the American mainland before Columbus, and in 1507 Waldseemuller published a book in which he named the new land "America."

More Spanish explorers came in the wake of Columbus. In 1513 Juan Ponce de León explored the coast of Florida. The same year, Vasco Nuñez de Balboa crossed the Isthmus of Panama and discovered the Pacific Ocean. Between 1519 and 1522, Ferdinand Magellan's expedition (he was killed along the way) sailed around the tip of South America, across the Pacific to the Philippines, through the Indian Ocean, and back to Europe around the southern tip of Africa.

Two expeditions made Spain the wealthiest nation in Europe. In the first, in 1519, Hernando Cortés led a small army of Spaniards against the Aztec Empire of Mexico. Completing the conquest in 1521, Cortés took control of the Aztecs' fabulous gold and silver mines. Ten years later an expedition led by Francisco Pizarro overwhelmed the Inca Empire of Peru, securing for Spain the great Inca silver mines of Potosí.

In 1535 and 1536 Cabeza de Vaca explored the American Southwest, adding that region to Spain's New World empire. At the same time, Pedro de Mendoza founded a colony near present-day Buenos Aires in Argentina. From 1539 to 1542 Francisco Vásquez de Coronado journeyed through much of the Southwest looking for gold and the legendary Seven Cities of Cíbola. At about the same time, Hernando de Soto explored from Florida to the Mississippi. By 1650 Spain's empire was complete, and fleets of ships were carrying the plunder back to Spain.

To plunder was acceptable because the New World was populated by pagans. To Christianize the pagans was necessary because it was part of God's plan. To kill them was also right because they were Satan's warriors. Killing Indians and destroying their culture was viewed as the fulfillment of the European secular and religious vision of the New World.

France was also exploring the Americas. In 1524, Giovanni da Verrazzano was commissioned to find a northwest passage around North America to India. He was followed in 1534 by Jacques Cartier, who explored the St. Lawrence River as far as present-day Montreal. In 1562, Jean Ribault headed an expedition that explored the St. Johns River in Florida. The Spanish soon pushed the French out of Florida, and the French then directed their efforts north and west. In 1608, Samuel de Champlain built a fort at Quebec and explored the area north to Nova Scotia and south to Cape Cod.

New France produced no gold or silver. The French traded furs with inland tribes, and fished off the coast. New France was sparsely populated by trappers and missionaries, and dotted with forts and trading posts. France policy hampered growth. Charters were given to fur-trading companies, then revoked, and colonization was put under the government's Company of New France, which failed. In 1663 the king took direct control of New France. New France never was able to match the wealth of New Spain or the growth of the British colonies to the south.

The Dutch also explored America. Formerly a Protestant province of Spain, the Netherlands was determined to become a commercial power in its own right. Exploration was a means to that end. In 1609, Henry Hudson led an expedition to America for the Dutch East India Company, and laid claim to the area along the Hudson River as far north as present-day Albany. In 1614 the Dutch government gave the New Netherland Company the territory between New France and Virginia. Ten years later the West India Company settled groups of colonists on Manhattan Island and at Fort Orange.

In 1497, Henry VII of England sponsored an expedition headed by John Cabot, who explored a part of Newfoundland. But until the reign of Queen Elizabeth, the English were preoccupied with establishing control over the British Isles and with their European trade. By the mid-1500s, though, England had recognized the advantages of trade with the East. In 1560, English merchants hired Martin Frobisher to search for a northwest passage, and between 1576 and 1578 he and John Davis explored along the Atlantic coast.

Queen Elizabeth granted charters to Sir Humphrey Gilbert and Sir Walter Raleigh to colonize America. Gilbert landed on Newfoundland, but failed to establish military posts. A year later, Raleigh sent a company to explore territory that he named Virginia after Elizabeth, the "virgin queen," and in 1585 he sponsored a second voyage, this time to explore the Chesapeake Bay region. By the seventeenth century the English had taken the lead in colonizing North America, establishing settlements all along the Atlantic coast.

The Wadsworth-Longfellow House in Portland. Courtesy Maine Historical Society.

carriage house. Open daily except Sunday, June to mid-October.

FREEPORT

Pettengill Farm (Pettengill Rd.; 207/865-3170). Built circa 1800 as a homestead on a saltwater farm, the saltbox house has never been modernized. Three fireplaces warm the first floor, and on the second floor, pictures of 19th-century sailing vessels have been etched into the plaster. The house, a half-mile down a dirt road not suitable for vehicles, is open by appointment only.

KENNEBUNK

Brick Store Museum (117 Main St.; 207/985-4802). In a block of restored 18th-century commercial buildings is William

Lord's 1825 Brick Store, which displays historical and maritime collections. The museum offers tours of the historic district. Open daily, mid-April to mid-December; Tuesday through Saturday the rest of the year.

Taylor-Berry House (24 Summer St.; 207/985-4802). A handsome, five-bayed Federal house built in 1803 for William Taylor, a sea captain. Stenciling by Moses Eaton was discovered when wallpaper was removed in the 1940s. The furnishings are mostly family heirlooms. Open Tuesday through Friday, June through September.

Accommodations: *Captain Fairfield* (Pleasant and Green streets at Village Green; 207/967-4454, or 800/322-1928). In the historic district, mere steps from the village green and harbor, this 1813 sea captain's Federal mansion offers nine guest rooms with period furnishings and canopy beds. Garden, full breakfast, afternoon tea, evening snacks. No smoking. Expensive.

KITTERY

Ships sailed the Piscataqua River here almost from the town's founding in 1647. A Continental Navy ship, the *Raleigh,* was built here in 1776, and a year later John Paul Jones took command of the Kittery-built *Ranger* and sailed to France to bring news of Burgoyne's surrender, where she received the first official salute given the American flag by a foreign warship. Today a statue of John Paul Jones stands in the center of Kittery.

Fort McClary Memorial (3 miles east of U.S. 1 in Kittery Point; 207/439-7545). This rise of land was fortified in the early 18th century to protect ships against pirates and the French. Originally called Fort William, it was garrisoned during the Revolution and renamed Fort McClary in honor of Major Andrew McClary, who was killed at Bunker Hill. Today the surviving structures, some of which were built after the Revolution, include the hexagonal blockhouse, the brick magazine, the foundation of the barracks, and part of the surrounding wall. Interpretive displays. Open daily, Memorial Day through Labor Day.

William Pepperrell House (Pepperrell Road, private). Built in 1720 as the residence of a Welsh shipper and lumber magnate, the house has been extensively remodeled by subsequent generations. A year after his death in 1760, his widow built a fashionable Georgian mansion, the *Lady Pepperrell House* (Pepperrell Road, private), with a commanding view of the river and harbor. Also on Pepperrell Road are the *First Congregational Church* and *Old Parsonage.* The church, built in 1730, is the oldest in the state.

Kittery Historical and Naval Museum (Rogers Rd. off U.S. 1 by rotary at ME 236; 207/439-3080). Exhibits show the history of the U.S. Navy and southern Maine's maritime heritage. Open Monday through Friday, June through October, Friday the rest of the year.

Sarah Orne Jewett House (north on I-95 to ME 236, then 10 miles northwest to 5 Portland St. in South Berwick; 603/436-3205). Built in 1774, this house belonged to the sea-captain grandfather of the noted author. It is elaborately appointed with imported furniture and tapestries. Jewett spent most of her life in this Georgian residence, which has been beautifully restored. Open Tuesdays, Thursdays, and weekends, June to mid-October.

Hamilton House (north on I-95 to ME 236, then 10 miles northwest to Vaughan's Lane in South Berwick; 207/436-3205). A 1785 Georgian on the Salmon Falls River, with period furnishings, garden, tours. Open Tuesday, Thursday, and weekends, June through August.

MACHIAS

Fort O'Brien Memorial (5 miles east on ME 92). The remains of a fort commanding the harbor, commissioned by Washington in 1775.

Burnham Tavern Museum (Main St. just off U.S. 1 on ME 192; 207/255-4432). A 1770 stagecoach stop displaying memorabilia from 1770 to 1830. Open Monday through Friday, June to mid-October.

Ruggles House (20 miles south on U.S. 1, then ¼ mile off U.S. 1 in Columbia Falls; 207/483-4637, or 207/546-7903). This 1820 Adam-style house has an unusual "flying" staircase, elaborate woodcarving, and period furnishings. Open daily, June to mid-October.

*The Sayward-Wheeler
House in York Harbor.
Photo by Stephen
Ganem.*

POLAND SPRING

Shaker Museum (1 mile south on ME 26 in New Gloucester; 207/926-4527). The remains of the Shaker community founded here in 1783, consisting of thirteen buildings, all typify the Shaker ideal of uncluttered, functional beauty. The 1794 Meetinghouse is considered one of the best surviving examples of Shaker architecture. Other buildings include a store, a boys' shop, and the ministry's shop. The museum displays furniture, textiles, and farm tools. Open June to mid-October.

PORTLAND

From 1623, the fishing and trapping in the area has attracted settlers to this Casco Bay peninsula. The French and English fought over it, and the English won out and built the town of Falmouth. White pines from the nearby forests became masts for the ships of the Royal Navy. During the Revolution, British ships opened fire on the town and leveled it. After the war, the town was gradually rebuilt, and on July 4, 1786, it was renamed Portland. It grew into one of the Atlantic seaboard's great commercial centers.

The Wadsworth-Longfellow House (487 Congress St.; 207/772-1807, or 207/774-1822). The childhood home of the poet Henry Wadsworth Longfellow. His grandfather, General Peleg Wadsworth, built the house in 1785 after fighting in the Revolution. This was the first private residence in the city to be built entirely of brick. Period furniture and family possessions. Open Tuesday through Saturday, June to mid-October.

Tate House (1270 Westbrook St.; 207/774-9781). A Georgian structure built in 1755 by an agent of the Royal Navy, and beautifully furnished in the style of the period. Herb gardens. Open daily except Monday, July to mid-September.

Museum at Portland Headlight (1000 Shore Rd. in Fort Williams Park, Cape Elizabeth; 207/799-2661). This is the oldest lighthouse in continuous use in the country, erected on orders from George Washington. Open daily, June through October, weekends November and December and April and May.

Accommodations: *Inn on Carleton* (46 Carleton St.; 207/775-1910 or 800/639-1779). An 1869 Victorian town in the city's historic West End. Seven guest rooms, three with private bath. Period furnishings, clock collection, breakfast. No smoking. Open all year. Moderate.

SEARSPORT

Penobscot Marine Museum (Church St. off U.S. 1; 207/548-2529). There are several old houses here: *Old Town Hall* (1845), *Merithew House* (circa 1860), and the *Fowler-True-Ross House* (1825); the last typifies the post-and-beam construction of the early 19th century. The *Philips Library and Carver Memorial Gallery* displays ship models, marine paintings, and vintage furnishings. Open daily, Memorial Day to mid-October.

STANDISH

Marrett House (ME 25; 207/642-3032). Daniel Marrett bought this fine 1789 Georgian house when he moved here in 1796 to be the town parson, and it remained in the family for 150 years. Family furnishings, handsome garden. Open Tuesdays, Thursdays, and weekends, mid-May through September. Reverend Marrett's 1804 *Old Red Church* (Oak Hill Road), currently

---

A FISHERMAN'S PARADISE

In 1497, when John Cabot first made landfall in America, somewhere north of Newfoundland, he found Indian fishing nets and evidence of vast schools of cod. Like Columbus, he was searching for a western passage to the Orient, new territories for the English crown and, of course, gold. But the cod, whose firm flesh could be preserved better than that of other fish, also stimulated European interest. Within a few years, English, French, and Portuguese vessels were fishing off the Grand Banks and curing their catches on America's northern shores. With the founding of the Massachusetts Bay Colony in 1630, cod fishing became an established industry and cod a major item of trade. The Reverend Hugh Peter established the first fisheries at Marblehead, and by 1665, about 1,300 fishing boats were working the rich waters of Cape Sable Island, at the southern tip of Nova Scotia.

---

owned by the town, holds services in the summer. On the second floor is the museum of the Standish Historical Society.

WATERVILLE

Redington Museum (64 Silver St.; 207/872-9439). Waterville Historical Society collections include 18th- and 19th-century furnishings, manuscripts, and Indian relics. Apothecary museum. Open Tuesday through Saturday, mid-May through September.

Two-Cent Footbridge (Front St.). One of the few remaining former toll footbridges in the country.

Old Fort Halifax (1 mile east on U.S. 201, on Bay St. in Winslow; no phone). This 1754 blockhouse is near the bridge over the Kennebec River, which gives a view of the Ticonic Falls. Open daily, Memorial Day through Labor Day.

WISCASSET

Nickels-Sortwell House (Main and Federal; 207/882-6218). This classic 1807 Federal house was built for a shipmaster in the lumber trade. From 1820 to 1900, it was used as a hotel, then restored as a private home. Family furnishings, restored garden. Open Wednesday through Sunday, June through September.

Lincoln County Museum and Old Jail (Federal St.; 207/882-6817). The first penitentiary in Maine, built in 1809, displays local artifacts in the jailer's house. Open daily except Mondays, July through Labor Day.

YORK

Settled in the 1630s, York was repeatedly attacked by Indians. A series of garrison houses were built at strategic points, and the *MacIntire Garrison* (ME 91, not open to the public) is a surviving example. Its has sawn walls, nearly eight feet thick, and a second-story overhang.

Sayward-Wheeler House (79 Barrell Lane, 2 miles south in York Harbor; 603/436-3205). York merchant Jonathan Sayward bought a 1718 Georgian house, enlarged it, and filled it with fine Chippendale furniture.

With its original furnishings, the house now belongs to the Society for the Preservation of New England Antiquities. Tours. Open Wednesday through Sunday, June to mid-October.

Old York Historical Society (York St. and Lindsay Rd.; 207/363-4974). The society offers guided tours of seven buildings dating from the 1700s. Open Tuesday through Saturday, mid-June through September. The buildings include the 1750 *Jefferds Tavern and Schoolhouse,* furnished as a tavern and now used as an orientation center. The schoolhouse next door is probably the state's oldest. The 1742 *Emerson-Wilcox House* served at various times as a general store, tavern, and post office, as well as a private home. The 1719 *Old Gaol* (on U.S. 1A), used as a jail until 1860, is one of the oldest English public buildings remaining in the country. The circa-1760 *John Hancock Warehouse* (Lindsay Rd. at York River) is one of the earliest surviving customs houses in the state, now used to interpret the maritime history of the area. The *Elizabeth Perkins House* is a late-1800s summer cottage on the banks of the York River, at Sewall's Bridge, and the *George Marshall Store,* a mid–19th-century general store, is now being used as the office of the society.

6

NEW HAMPSHIRE

The first Europeans to settle here were Englishmen seeking not religious freedom but a profitable trade in fish and furs. In 1623 David Thomson led a dozen or so men to Odiorne's Point on the Piscataqua River, where they found life was harder than they had imagined. Thomson stayed four years, then moved on to Boston.

In 1629 John Mason was given permission to develop the land between the Piscataqua and Merrimack rivers. He stayed in England, but he named the area New Hampshire after his home county of Hampshire. Several settlements were founded, but all failed except the one at Strawbery Banke, the future Portsmouth.

In 1641 the Massachusetts Bay Colony took control of New Hampshire, which consisted of only four towns—Portsmouth, Dover, Exeter, and Hampton. It remained part of Massachusetts until 1679, when it became a separate royal province.

Indian attacks slowed New Hampshire's growth. In 1689, Abenaki and Pennacook Indians killed many settlers along the Cocheco River and at Salmon Falls and Exeter. Portsmouth and Dover were raided repeatedly in the 1690s. A treaty in 1713 ended the fighting, but it broke out again in "Governor Dummer's War" in the 1720s. The government finally solved the problem by giving high bounties to Indian hunters.

With the Indians gone, the colony was prospering by the mid-1700s. Agriculture flourished. Several hundred Scotch-Irish settled in the Merrimack Valley and began producing high-quality linen. Portsmouth merchants grew rich in the lumber trade.

No Revolutionary War battles were fought in New Hampshire, but the colony produced two important military leaders. John Sullivan led a raid on Fort William and Mary, near Portsmouth, and made off with a large quantity of supplies. He later commanded troops in battles in Rhode Island and Pennsylvania. John Stark played a key role in the Battle of Bunker Hill in Boston, although he is best remembered for a remark he made before the Battle of Bennington. He pointed to the Redcoats and told his men, "There, my boys, are your enemies. We'll beat them before night, or Molly Stark will be a widow."

After the war, New Hampshire was the ninth state to vote in favor of the Constitution, providing, on June 21, 1788, the two-thirds majority needed for ratification.

The harbor at Portsmouth, New Hampshire. Courtesy Library of Congress, Prints and Photographs Division.

CONCORD

State House (Main St.; 603/271-2154). The original structure, of Federal design, a central pavilion with two wings and a tower, was enlarged and remodeled in the 1860s, and enlarged again in 1910. Open weekdays.

Pierce Manse (14 Penacook St.; 603/224-0094 or 603/225-2068). Home of President Franklin Pierce from 1842 to 1848, the house has been reconstructed and moved to the present site. Many original furnishings. Open Monday through Friday, mid-June to mid-September.

Canterbury Shaker Village (15 miles north to I-93 exit 18, follow signs; 603/783-9511). In 1774, two Shakers established a thriving community here, one of two still in operation in the country. Today twenty-two buildings remain of the hundred that once graced the 4,000-acre community. There are tours of six buildings and a museum. Restaurant and gift shop. Open daily, May through October; Friday through Sunday, April and November and December.

Accommodations: *Colby Hall* (17 miles west on U.S. 202 to Henniker, ½ mile west on Western Ave; 603/428-3281). A historic circa-1800 farmhouse that has been a tavern, church, meetinghouse, and private school, offers sixteen guest rooms. Pool, lawn games, ice skating, complimentary breakfast. Restaurant serves dinner. Open year-round. Expensive.

DOVER

Woodman Institute (182-190 Central Ave., ½ mile south on NH 108; 603/742-1038). Established in 1915 to study the history, art, and natural history of the region, the institute has three historic houses on the site: the 1645 Garrison House, the only garrison in the state still in its original form; the 1818 Woodman house, the residence of the institute's donor; and the 1813 John P. Hale House, with articles of local history and antique furniture. Open afternoons, Tuesday through Saturday, except February and March.

EXETER

Gilman Garrison House (12 Water St.; 603/436-3025). Built with hewn logs between 1676 and 1690 as a fortified tower, the house still has a pulley arrangement to raise and lower the door. Remodeled in the mid-18th century. Period furnishings. Open Tuesdays, Thursdays, and weekends, June to mid-October.

FRANKLIN

Daniel Webster Birthplace State Historical Site (4 miles southwest on NH 127; 603/934-5057). A replica of the two-room farmhouse in which Webster was born in 1782 while his father was fighting in Washington's army. The house contains family books and furniture. Open irregularly. Phone for information.

Congregational Christian Church (47 South Main St. on U.S. 3; 603/934-4242). Daniel Webster attended this 1820 church. A bust of Webster by Daniel Chester French is outside. Open Sundays.

HANOVER

Webster Cottage (32 North Main; 603/643-5782). Daniel Webster lived here during his last year as a Dartmouth College student. Period and Shaker furniture, Webster memorabilia. Open Wednesdays and weekends, June to mid-October.

Saint-Gaudens National Historic Site (5 miles south on NH 10, then 12 miles south off NH 12A, in Cornish; 603/675-2175). *Aspet,* built about 1800 and once a tavern, was the residence and studio of sculptor Augustus Saint-Gaudens. *The Puritan, Adams Memorial* and *Shaw* are among the 100 works on display. Formal gardens. Sculptor in residence. Interpretive programs. Open daily, Memorial Day through October.

DANIEL WEBSTER

Flexibility and compelling oratory were the key to Daniel Webster's political success. As a congressman from New Hampshire, he was a strong advocate of states' rights, opposing the War of 1812 and hinting at nullification. Then, as a congressman and later as a senator from Massachusetts, he supported federal action to stimulate the economy. He won fame by denouncing nullification when South Carolina advocated it. He opposed the expansion of slavery, then insisted that no law was needed to prevent it when he promoted the Compromise of 1850.

Webster was secretary of state twice, in 1841–43 and 1850–52, and is considered one of the greatest ever to hold the office. He negotiated the Webster-Ashburton Treaty, which settled the dispute over the Maine–New Brunswick border, ending a threat of war between Britain and the United States. The most highly paid attorney of his time, he exerted considerable influence on constitutional law, arguing for several decisions that strengthened the federal government against the state governments, and the judiciary against the legislative and executive branches.

As an orator, Webster had no equal. He moved judges and juries, colleagues in Congress, and vast audiences. An example came in his reply in Congress to a Southern nullification, which concluded with the words, "Liberty and Union, now and forever, one and inseparable!"

Webster, Henry Clay, and John C. Calhoun formed what was called the "great triumvirate," though they rarely combined except in opposition to President Andrew Jackson. All had presidential ambitions; none received their party's nomination.

Although identified with the Boston aristocracy, Webster came from a New England farm. An education at Dartmouth helped him rise in the world. Despite a large income, he was in constant debt as a result of high living, unfortunate land speculation, and the expense of being a gentleman farmer.

JAFFREY

Barrett House "Forest Hall" (10 miles southeast on NH 124, then ¼ mile south on NH 123A in New Ipswich on Main St.;

The Webster Cottage in Hanover.

603/878-2517). Industrialist Charles Barrett gave his son this hilltop estate in 1820 as a wedding present. It includes a Federal house with a ballroom, a summer house, and extensive grounds. Twelve museum rooms contain many original furnishings, including portraits and musical instruments. Tours available. Open Thursday through Sunday, June to mid-October.

Accommodations: *Benjamin Prescott Inn* (Route 124 east; 603/532-0637). Colonel Benjamin Prescott, a governor of New Hampshire, built his house here in 1775. In 1852, two of his sons razed the original and built this two-family Greek Revival house on its foundations. Each of the nine guest rooms (with private bath) is individually furnished with antiques. Working dairy farm, breakfast. Moderate. Open year-round.

KEENE

Wyman Tavern (339 Main; 603/352-1895). The first meeting of Dartmouth College trustees was held here in 1770. Now furnished in the style of the 1820s. Open Thursday through Saturday, June through September.

MANCHESTER

Currier Gallery of Art (192 Orange St.; 603/669-6144). American and European paintings and sculpture. New England decorative art. One of New England's leading small museums. Open daily except Mondays.

Manchester Historic Association (129 Amherst St.; 603/662-7531). Museum and library with collections and exhibits illustrating life in Manchester from its settlement in 1722 to the present. Firefighting equipment, decorative arts, costumes, paintings. Open Tuesday through Saturday.

Accommodations: *Bedford Village Inn* (8 miles southwest via NH 101; 5 miles west of I-293, Bedford exit, at 2 Old Bedford Rd.; 603/472-2602). In a converted early 1800s barn are twelve suites individually decorated and furnished with antiques. Excellent restaurant. Open year-round. Expensive.

NEWPORT

Fort at No. 4 (10 miles west on NH 11/103, then 11 miles south on NH 11/12, near Charlestown; 603/826-5700). Reconstructed French and Indian Wars log fort, complete with stockade, great hall, cow barns, and living quarters. Indian artifacts, demonstrations. Open daily except Tuesdays, Memorial Day through Labor Day; weekends Labor Day through Columbus Day.

PORTSMOUTH

Portsmouth Trail is a tour of houses from 1684 into the 19th century. Walking-tour maps are available at the Chamber of Commerce (500 Market St.;603/436-1118). Houses include the *Moffatt-Ladd House* (154 Market St.; 603/436-8221), built by Captain John Moffatt in 1763, and later the home of his son-in-law General William Whipple, a signer of the Declaration of Independence. Many original furnishings, formal gardens. Open daily, mid-June to mid-October. *Warner House* (150 Daniel St. at Chapel St.; 603/436-5909) is one of New England's finest Georgian houses. Scagliola in the dining room, restored mural paintings on the stairway walls, exquisite paneling.

Period furnishings. Benjamin Franklin is said to have installed the lightning rod on the west wall. Open Tuesday through Sunday, June to mid-October. *John Paul Jones House* (43 Middle St. at State St.; 603/436-8420). While his ship *America* was being readied in the fall of 1782, John Paul Jones stayed in the commodious house of Sarah Purcell, a widow who was operating it as an inn. The carpenter who built the house in 1758 may have been the African American Hopestill March, renowned for his fine gambrel-roofed houses. Period furniture. Collections of costumes, china, glass, documents, and weapons. Tours available. Open daily, mid-May to mid-October. *Governor John Langdon House* (143 Pleasant St.; 603/ 436-3205). Langdon made his fortune during the Revolution in shipbuilding and privateering, served three terms as governor, and later was president *pro tem* of the U.S. Senate. This monumental house was built in the 1780s, and was admired by George Washington when he was a guest. Architect

The Clark House in Wolfeboro.

BRITAIN AND FRANCE BATTLE FOR SUPREMACY

For a century, Britain and France fought for supremacy, and America became one of many theaters of war in a global struggle, They were formally at war four times, and each time the war in America was given a different name,

King William's War (1689–97) was the American expansion of the War of the League of Augsburg in Europe between William of Orange and Louis XIV of France. New England became involved in fierce frontier fighting against Indians who were allied with the French.

Queen Anne's War (1701–13) was the expansion of the War of the Spanish Succession. Fighting in America ranged from the Gulf of Mexico to the St. Lawrence River. When it was over, the British claimed Arcadia (Nova Scotia), Newfoundland, and the region around the Hudson, and the powerful Iroquois were their allies.

King George's War (1745–48), called in Europe the War of the Austrian Succession, was bloody but indecisive in America. Britain returned to the French the fortress of Louisbourg in Nova Scotia, which had been taken by New England troops. No one thought the peace would last.

The French and Indian War (1754–61), also called the Seven Years War, was the American extension of the Great War for Empire, It started when the governor of Virginia sent George Washington, a militia officer, to warn the French away from the present site of Pittsburgh. They refused to go, and there were two skirmishes. Major fighting erupted on the northeastern boundary of New England, along the Lake Champlain corridor, at the headwaters of the Ohio River, and in the West Indies. It became a world conflict, and it went badly for the British everywhere except in India. Britain suffered one defeat after another. In America, the defeat of Braddock's army left the frontier in turmoil.

The situation was turned around largely because of the efforts of William Pitt, who came into the British government in 1715, He assumed direct control of the war effort, establishing a unity of command. His plans, his policies, and his hand-picked generals and admirals brought a series of brilliant victories. In America the triumph of Wolfe over Montcalm at Quebec destroyed the French Empire in North America forever. The Treaty of Paris in 1763 confirmed British supremacy. France vacated North America. The lands east of the Mississippi went to Britain, and the lands west of the Mississippi went to Spain, to compensate for the loss of Florida. The British Empire was the leading power in the world.

Stanford White added the large wing at the rear. Landscaped grounds with gazebo, rose and grape arbor, and perennial garden beds. Tours available. Open Wednesday through Sunday, June to mid-October. *Rundlet-May House* (364 Middle St.; 603/436-3205). A farmboy moved here in the 1790s, became a rich merchant, and built this three-story Federal-style mansion, which sits on an artificial terrace eight feet above street level. Family furnishings and accessories, a fine collection of Portsmouth Federal furniture. Open Wednesday through Sunday, June to mid-October.

Strawbery Banke Museum (Hancock and Marcy streets; 603/433-1100). This ten-acre site, settled in 1630, was a plantation compound. Named for the abundance of wild berries growing along the shores of the Piscataqua River, it was renamed Portsmouth in 1653 and became a thriving waterfront neighborhood during the 17th and 18th centuries. The restored area is now an outdoor museum with forty-two buildings dating from 1695. Seven of the houses are furnished to illustrate different periods in the area's history. Tours, shops. Exhibits, crafts demonstrations, picnicking. Open daily, May through October.

Fort Constitution (4 miles east on NH 1B in New Castle; no phone). News of the British order to prohibit the importation of gunpowder into the colonies was carried to the Sons of Liberty in the Portsmouth area, and they stormed this fort and seized its five tons of gunpowder. Much of the powder was used by the patriots at Bunker Hill. Today only the base of the original fort's walls remains. Open daily, mid-June through early September; weekends from late May to mid-June and late September to mid-October.

Fort Stark State Historic Site (Wild Rose Lane, 5 miles east off NH 1B in New Castle; 603/433-8583). Once part of the coastal defense system, which dates from 1746, the fort is on Jerry's Point, overlooking the Piscataqua River, Little Harbor, and the Atlantic. Open weekends, late May to mid-October.

Accommodations: *Inn at Christian Shore* (335 Maplewood Ave.; 603-431-6770). A Federal house offers six guest rooms, four with private bath. Antiques, oil paintings, continental breakfast. Inexpensive.

SALEM

America's Stonehenge (5 miles east of I-93, just off NH 111 in North Salem; 603/893-8300). This thirty-acre archaeological site, once known as Mystery Hill, dates from 1000 B.C., and consists of stone slabs, chambers, and tunnels that seem to have been arranged as a great outdoor astronomical facility for observing stars and charting the seasons. Shaped monoliths indicate the rising and setting of the sun at the solstice and equinox and other astronomical alignments. One five-ton slab, standing on stone legs, is called the Sacrificial Table; it is etched with channels that might have conveyed blood into stone receptacles. The builders may have been Indians, Celts, Greeks, Phoenicians, medieval explorers, or extraterrestrials. Open daily, May through October; weekends April and November.

WOLFEBORO

Clark House (South Main; 603/569-4997). The Wolfboro Historical Society is housed in this 1778 family homestead with period furnishings. On the premises are a one-room schoolhouse and a firehouse with restored equipment dating from 1842. Open daily except Sundays in July and August.

THE SECOND WAR OF INDEPENDENCE

Independence didn't end America's problems with Britain, and they took a turn for the worse during the war that broke out between Britain and France in 1793. To prevent the United States from supplying the French, Britain blockaded European ports and began seizing American ships. This brought demands for retaliation, but Presidents George Washington and John Adams successfully avoided a confrontation.

The situation grew worse after Napoleon came to power. The British began imposing much stricter blockades, and began a policy of impressment. They claimed the right to stop neutral ships on the high seas to look for "deserters," and, in the course of searching American ships, wrongfully took many American seamen and forced them into service in the British navy.

From 1807 to 1811, both Presidents Thomas Jefferson and James Madison attempted to force Britain to change its policies by restricting trade. When neither economic coercion nor negotiation brought an easement, war sentiment built. Young "War Hawks" from the West and South argued that the right to freely export American products must be defended.

In spite of bitter opposition from New England Federalists, the United States declared war on June 18, 1812. The army planned to invade Canada on three fronts—up Lake Champlain toward Montreal, across the Niagara frontier, and from Detroit into upper Canada. All three campaigns were disasters. On the Lake Champlain front, American forces withdrew before the campaign began; the forces on the Niagara frontier were thrown back at the Battle of Queenston Heights; the invasion of Upper Canada ended with the British capturing Detroit.

In contrast was the performance of the small American navy. In quick succession, the *Constitution* defeated the *Guerriere*, the *United States* captured the *Macedonian* and brought her into port as a prize of war, and the *Constitution* defeated the *Java* off the coast of Brazil. Despite those victories, the British navy effectively blockaded the American coast and laid it open to attack.

In 1813, attempts to invade Canada failed again, although Captain Oliver Perry's ships won the Battle of Lake Erie, and General William Henry Harrison defeated the British and the Indians in Canada at the Battle of the Thames.

With France collapsing the following year, the British launched major campaigns. Americans resisted gallantly at the battles of Chippawa and Lundy's Lane on the Niagara frontier, but suffered a severe blow when British troops occupied Washington. President Madison and Congress were forced to flee, and the White House and other public buildings were burned. Morale was at a low ebb, and the Federalists were in open revolt.

American fortunes took a turn for the better. The British army that had captured Washington failed to take Baltimore, and Thomas Macdonough's naval force won a decisive victory at the Battle of Plattsburg Bay on Lake Champlain, driving the invading British army back into Canada. When Parliament heard of the defeat at Plattsburg, it lost interest in the war. The day before Christmas in 1814, the Treaty of Ghent was signed, ending the war.

A final battle was still to be fought. The British army proceeding against the Gulf Coast could not be informed of the peace in time. On January 8, 1815, Andrew Jackson and his troops inflicted a crushing defeat on the British at New Orleans. Called the "Second War of Independence," the War of 1812 had vindicated American independence, and a surge of national self-confidence swept the country.

7

VERMONT

The first white man to come to the hunting grounds of the Algonquin and Iroquois was Samuel de Champlain, who sailed down the 120-mile long lake in 1609, and gave it his name. In 1666 the French attempted a settlement on the lake at Isle la Motte, but the first permanent settlement in Vermont would be made by the English at Fort Dummer, near present-day Brattleboro, in 1724.

In 1764 the governor of New Hampshire, taking a liberal view of his powers, began granting town charters west of the Connecticut River, and the area between the Connecticut and Lake Champlain became known as the New Hampshire Grants. Not to be outdone, New York claimed the area and also began issuing grants.

Trouble came in 1770. The king decreed that New York's claim was valid, and settlers who had obtained land from New Hampshire were forced to buy it again from New York proprietors or be evicted. A vigilante group called the Green Mountain Boys was formed to resist New Yorkers attempting to evict a Vermonter. New York sheriffs were prevented from serving eviction notices, and settlers from New York were beaten and their houses burned.

The Green Mountain Boys, led by Ethan Allen, captured Fort Ticonderoga from the British in May 1775, in the first offensive of the Revolution. The only battle fought in Vermont, however, was a rearguard action at Hubbardton. Although the 1777 Battle of Bennington is named for a Vermont town, the fighting took place just across the border in New York.

After the war, Vermont, still concerned that New York's land claims might be held valid, declared itself an independent republic, and remained one for fourteen years, running its own postal service, coining its own money, naturalizing citizens of other states and countries, and negotiating with other states and nations. Its constitution prohibited slavery, mandated free public education, and guaranteed suffrage to males whether they owned property or not.

In 1781, Ethan Allen made Vermont's position clear in a letter to Congress: "I am as resolutely determined to defend the independence of Vermont as Congress [is] that of the United States, and rather than fail will retire with the hardy Green Mountain Boys into the desolate caverns of the mountains and wage war with human nature at large." The problem was solved in 1791, when Vermont entered the Union as the fourteenth state.

BELLOWS FALLS

Rockingham Meetinghouse (5 miles north on VT 103, 1 mile west of I-91 exit 6, on Old Rockingham Rd. in Rockingham; 802/463-3964). Built in 1787 and restored in 1907, this building has antique glass windows. There is an old burying ground with quaint epitaphs. Open daily, mid-June through Labor Day.

The State Capitol in Montpelier, Vermont. Courtesy Library of Congress, Prints and Photographs Division.

BENNINGTON

Ethan Allen's Green Mountain Boys, who made their headquarters here, were known to neighboring New Yorkers as "the Bennington Mob." On August 16, 1777, that "mob" won a decisive battle of the Revolutionary War.

Old First Church (Monument Ave. in Old Bennington; 802/447-1223). Built in 1805, this church, with its original box pews and Asher Benjamin steeple, is an excellent example of early Colonial architecture. Tours available. Old Burying Ground has the graves of those who fell in the Battle of Bennington, and poet Robert Frost. Church open daily, Memorial Day to mid-October.

Bennington Battle Monument (15 Monument Circle in Old Bennington; 802/447-1571). A 306-foot limestone obelisk commemorating the decisive battle (which was fought just across the border in New York, see Greenwich, New York). An elevator takes visitors to an observation platform.

Open daily, mid-April through October.

Bennington Museum (1 mile west on West Main; 802/447-1571). Exhibits of early Vermont and New England artifacts. Paintings (including some by Grandma Moses), sculpture, Bennington pottery. The schoolhouse museum includes Moses family memorabilia, Revolutionary War collections. Open daily.

Accommodations: *Four Chimneys* (21 West Rd, 1 mile west on VT 9; 802/447-3500). A restored Georgian Revival mansion, furnished with antiques, has seven guest rooms and an excellent restaurant. Moderate. Open year-round.

BRANDON

Stephen A. Douglas Birthplace (2 Grove St. on U.S. 7; 802/247-6401). The cottage where the "Little Giant" was born in 1813. Douglas attended Brandon Academy before moving to Illinois in 1833. Open by appointment.

BURLINGTON

Ethan Allen Homestead (2 miles north off VT 127; 802/865-4556). The leader of the Green Mountain Boys lived in this 1787 farmhouse. Museum, tours, audiovisual presentation. Open Tuesday through Sunday, early May through late October. Also open Mondays in summer.

GRAFTON

Old Tavern at Grafton (Main St. and Townshend Rd.; 802/843-2231). The tavern has been visited by many famous guests since it opened for business in 1801, and their names are inscribed over the desk. Today it is a country inn and restaurant with antique furnishings. Open daily, May to March. Dining by reservation.

MIDDLEBURY

Sheldon Museum (1 Park St.; 802/388-2117). In an 1829 brick house is a comprehensive collection of 19th-century Vermontiana. Authentic furnishings, portraits, pewter, Staffordshire, clocks, pianos, toys, dolls, and local relics. Tours. Open Monday through Friday, June through October; Wednesdays and Fridays the rest of the year.

Congregational Church (on Common; 802/388-7634). Although built in 1809 after a plan in the *Country Builder's Assistant,* as modified by architect Lavius Fillmore, this is, architecturally, one of the finest churches in the state. Open Fridays and Saturdays, June through August.

Middlebury College (west of town on VT 125; 802/388-3711). Two buildings are of historical importance: *Painter Hall,* (1815) is the oldest college building in the state; the *Emma Willard House* (1814) was

the location of the first female seminary. Open weekdays.

Old Stone House (11 miles southwest via U.S. 5S or I-91 south to Orleans, then 2 miles northeast on an unnumbered road to Brownington Village). A museum in a four-story 1836 granite building, built by the Reverend Alexander Twilight, one of the first black college graduates in the country. Period furniture, early farm, household and military items. Open daily, July and August, Friday through Tuesday, mid-May and June and September to mid-October.

Accommodations: *Swift House* (25 Stewart Lane; 802/388-9925). An 1815 house with twenty-one guest rooms in two buildings, some with private whirlpool and fireplace. Four-poster beds, quilts, complimentary breakfast, restaurant. Moderate to expensive.

RUTLAND

Hubbardston Battlefield and Museum (7 miles west via U.S. 4 exit 5; 802/759-2412). On July 7, 1777, the Green Mountain Boys and troops from Massachusetts and New Hampshire stopped British forces pursuing the American army from Fort Ticonderoga. This was the only battle fought on Vermont soil, and the first in a series that led to the capitulation of Burgoyne at Saratoga. Battle monument, picnicking, visitor center. Open Wednesday through Sunday, Memorial Day through Columbus Day.

ST. ALBANS

Chester A. Arthur Historic Site (10 miles west via VT 36 to Fairfield, then on an unpaved road to the site; 802/828-3226). A replica of the house of the twenty-first President. Nearby is the 1830 brick church where Arthur's father was preacher. Exhibit of Arthur's life and career. Picnicking. Open Wednesday through Sunday, June to mid-October.

St. Albans Historical Museum (Church St.; 802/527-7933). Collections of railroad memorabilia, farm implements, clothing, toys and dolls. Re-created doctor's office. Open Tuesday through Saturday, May through September.

ST. JOHNSBURY

St. Johnsbury Athenaeum (30 Main; 802/748-8291). A public library and art gallery displaying works by Albert Bierstadt and other artists of the Hudson River School. Open Monday through Friday, year-round.

Fairbanks Museum and Planetarium (Main and Prospect; 802/748-2372). Exhibits on natural science, regional history, archaeology, anthropology, and the arts, including more than 4,500 mounted birds and mammals. Antique farm. Open daily, year-round. Planetarium open daily, July and August; weekends the rest of the year.

The birthplace of Chester A. Arthur near St. Albans.

SHELBURNE

Shelburne Museum (7 miles south on U.S. 7; I-89 exit 13; 802/985-3346). On display here is one of the finest collections of American folk art in the world. The museum is a complex of thirty-seven buildings, many of them historic structures moved here from other sites in New England. They include seven houses, a one-room schoolhouse, a general store, and a railroad station. Some are furnished in period style; others are used to display the immense art and Americana collection of Electra Havemeyer Webb, who, together with her husband, J. Watson Webb, founded the museum in 1947. A huge, horseshoe-shaped barn (constructed from pieces of eleven older barns and two gristmills) was used to house the family's collection of carriages and sleighs. Also on the site are a jail, a blacksmith shop, a covered bridge, and the lake steamer SS *Ticonderoga*.

There are outstanding collections of quilts, coverlets, and other textiles, as well as of weathervanes, cigar-store Indians, and other folk-art objects; there is a miniature circus train, and a gallery of ship figureheads

The lake steamer Ticonderoga *at the Shelburne Museum.*

and maritime art. Two modern buildings hold excellent collections of paintings and antique furniture. Open daily, mid-May to mid-October.

Shelburne Farms (Harbor and Bay roads; 802/985-8666). The former estate of railroad magnate William Seward Webb, who married Lila Vanderbilt. The 110-room English cottage-style manor house was on 4,000 acres, 1,000 now. The visitor center is in the Gate House, a cottage-style building. The formal gardens, overlooking Lake Champlain, are being restored to their original design. The five-story-high Farm Barn, which surrounds a central courtyard, currently houses a bread bakery, a furniture shop, and offices. Also of note is the brick Queen Anne Revival Coach Barn. The complex includes a working dairy. Open daily, June through mid-October.

Accommodations: *Inn at Shelburne Farms* (Bay and Harbor Rds.; 802/985-8498). This was the 1899 country manor house of William Seward and Lila Vanderbilt

Webb. The twenty-four guest rooms have original decor and furnishings. There are walking trails on grounds designed by Frederick Law Olmsted. Tennis, croquet, rowing, lake fishing, restaurant on premises. Open mid-May to mid-October.

SPRINGFIELD

Springfield Art and Historical Society (9 Elm St.; 802/885-2415). Collections of 19th-century American art and artifacts, Richard Lee pewter, Bennington pottery, local historic relics. Open Tuesday through Friday.

Eureka Schoolhouse (on VT 11, Charleston Rd.; 802/672-3773). Built in 1790, this is the oldest surviving schoolhouse in the state. Nearby is a century-old lattice-truss covered bridge. Open daily, Memorial Day through Columbus Day.

Reverend Dan Foster House and Old Forge (6 miles north on Valley St. to Weathersfield Center Rd. in Weathersfield; 802/885-2779). A historic 1790 parsonage contains period furniture and textiles. The forge has working machinery and bellows. Tours available. Open Thursday through Monday, late June through September.

VERGENNES

John Strong Mansion (6 miles southwest via VT 22A, on VT 17, in West Addison; 802/759-2309). A 1785 Federal house, restored and furnished in the style of the period. Open Friday through Monday, mid-May through October.

Rokeby (2 miles north on U.S. 7, 6 miles south of ferry route on U.S. 7, Ferrisburg; 802/877-3406). Built in 1785, this was the ancestral home of abolitionist Rowland T. Robinson, and was a station on the Underground Railroad. It contains artifacts and archives of four generations. The eighty-five-acre farm includes an icehouse, a creamery, and a stone smokehouse. Tours available.

Open Thursday through Sunday, June through October.

Accommodations: *Strong House Inn* (82 West Main St.; 802/877-3337). This Federal–Greek Revival hybrid house, built in 1834 by Samuel Paddock Strong, situated on a ridge with fine views of the Green Mountains to the east and the Adirondacks to the west, is on the National Registry of Historic Places. Free-standing staircase, elegant moldings and doors, seven guest rooms, five with private bath. Full breakfast, dinner available. No smoking. Open year-round. Moderate.

WESTON

Old Mill Museum (on VT 100, center of village). Old-time tools. Tinsmith in residence. Tours in July and August. Open daily, Memorial Day through Columbus Day.

Constitution House in Windsor.

Farrar-Mansur House Museum (north side of common; no phone). A restored 1797 house and tavern with nine rooms. Period furnishings and paintings. Open Monday through Friday, Memorial Day through Columbus Day.

Vermont Country Store (on VT 100, south of Village Green; 802/824-3184). A reminder of what shopping was once like. Penny candy and other old-fashioned foodstuffs and merchandise. Open daily.

WINDSOR

Constitution House (16 North Main St., on U.S. 5; 802/672-3773). The 18th-century tavern where the constitution of the Republic of Vermont was signed on July 8, 1777. Museum. Open Wednesday through Sunday, mid-May to mid-October.

Covered bridge. Crossing the Connecticut River, this is the longest covered bridge in the country.

In the early 1800s Fort Delaware guarded the river approach to Wilmington. Courtesy Library of Congress, Prints and Photographs Division.

PART III

THE MID-ATLANTIC

Montréal

ONTARIO

Ottawa ☆

Massena

Lake Champlain

Canton   Potsdam   Plattsburgh

11   Saranac Lake   Lake Placid

Watertown   ADIRONDACK FOREST PRESERVE   Crown Point

Sackets Harbor   Ticonderoga

87

Toronto   *Lake Ontario*   Oswego   NEW YORK   Lake George Village

81   Boonville

Rochester   Rome   Saratoga Springs   Greenwich

Niagra Falls   90   Palmyra   90   Herkimer   Johnstown   Amsterdam

Buffalo   Batavia   Auburn   **Syracuse**   *Mohawk R.*   Schenectady

East Aurora   Canandaigua   Geneva   Cazenovia   Howes Cave   **Albany** ☆

Lake Erie   *Five Fingers Lakes*   Cooperstown

90   Ithaca   81   CATSKILL FOREST PRESERVE   Coxsackie

17   Corning   Elmira   88   Hudson

Jamestown   17   Binghamton   Kingston   Rhinebeck

New Paltz   Hyde Park

PENNSYLVANIA   Poughkeepsie

17   87

0 ———— 100 miles   Manticello   Newburgh   Fishkill

0 ———— 150 km   Scranton   Barryville   West Point   Garrison   84

Monroe   Mt. Ki

Stony Point   Tarrytown

White Plains   **New Rochelle**

Yonkers

NEW JERSEY   **New York City**   495

Long Island

Sag Harbor   Amagansett

Port Jefferson   East Hampton

Huntington   495   Southampton

New York City   Bethpage   Sayville

Bay Shore   0 ———— 30 miles

0 ———— 50 km

N

8

N E W   Y O R K

Giovanni da Verrazzano entered New York Harbor in 1524, and in 1609, Samuel de Champlain explored the valley of the lake that bears his name, and Henry Hudson sailed up the river that bears his. There was a trading post at Fort Nassau (Albany) in 1614. New Amsterdam was founded in 1625 on the southern tip of Manhattan Island.

In a series of swaps, the English took Manhattan from the Dutch in 1664, ceded it back to them in 1673, and took it back again the following year. The British made New York less of a trading post and more of a permanent settlement. New York was cosmopolitan almost from the beginning; in1644 a priest noted eighteen languages spoken in the city.

New Yorkers, the British learned, were hard to govern. In 1689, Jacob Leisler, who was later hanged for treason, overthrew the Crown representative, assumed leadership of the settlement, and launched an attack on the French in Canada. John Peter Zenger was jailed on a charge of "seditious libel" for having criticized the British rulers, but won his case, establishing the principle of a free press.

Wars with the Indians and the French kept the area in turmoil until 1763. New York was a center of Tory sentiment, but grievances against Britain grew. The Stamp Act Congress met in New York in 1765 to protest taxation by a Parliament in London and assert their rights, as "Englishmen," to be taxed by their own representatives. New York staged its own Tea Party in 1774, and on July 9, 1776, rioters toppled the statue of George II in Bowling Green. It was melted down into bullets that, according to

legend, killed an estimated four hundred Redcoats.

Following the Battle of Long Island in 1776, the British occupied the city until 1785, when Washington and his army paraded triumphantly down Bowery Lane. On the balcony of Federal Hall at Wall Street, on April 30, 1789, George Washington was inaugurated as first President of the United States. New York City was the state capital until 1797, the capital of the Confederation from the year 1785, and for a year after Washington was sworn in as president, it was the capital of the new republic.

ALBANY

Schuyler Mansion State Historic Site (32 Catherine St.; 518/434-0834). This 1761 Georgian mansion was the home of Philip Schuyler, Revolutionary War general and U.S. senator. Alexander Hamilton married Schuyler's daughter here. Tours available. Open Wednesday through Sunday, Mid-April through October.

Arbour Hill (9 Ten Broeck Place; 518/436-9826). This 1798 brick Federal house with Greek Revival additions was built by General Abraham Ten Broeck, and later became the home of the prominent Alcott family. Period furniture, paintings, changing exhibits. Open Wednesday through Sunday, March through December.

Historic Cherry Hill (523½ South Pearl St.; 518/434-4791). Built in 1787 for Philip Van Rensselaer, a prominent merchant farmer, and lived in by four generations until 1963. Gardens, nine period rooms with family furnishings. Tours available. Open daily except in January.

Schuyler Mansion in Albany.

Shaker Heritage Society (Albany-Shaker Rd.; 518/456-7890). Located on the site of the first Shaker settlement in America are an 1848 meetinghouse, an orchard, and the cemetery where Shaker founder Mother Ann Lee is buried. Tours by appointment. Open daily.

Albany Institute of History and Art (125 Washington Ave.; 518/463-4478). Regional silver, pewter, and furniture. Hudson-Mohawk paintings and sculpture. Regional history. Tours available. Luncheon gallery. Open daily except Mondays.

Crailo State Historic Site (9½ Riverside Ave. in Rensselaer, 1½ blks south of U.S. 9 and 20; 518/463-8738). An 18th-century Dutch house, now a museum of Dutch culture in the Hudson Valley. Audiovisual presentation. Open Wednesday through Sunday, mid-April through October.

Rensselaerville (27 miles southwest via NY 443 to end of NY 85; 518/797-3783). This village, settled in 1787, has restored homes, inns, churches, and a gristmill. Open daily.

Accommodations: *Mansion Hill Inn* (115

Philip St. at Park Ave.; 518/465-2038). A Victorian with eight guest rooms on the top two floors and a restaurant on the street level. The inn is in the historic district just around the corner from the Governor's Executive Mansion. Full breakfast. Dinner. Inexpensive to moderate.

AMAGANSETT (LONG ISLAND)

Miss Amelia Cottage Museum (Main St. and Windmill Lane; 516/267-3020). Built in 1725 by Jacob Schelinger, the cottage is furnished to show how people lived from the earliest Colonial times through the early 18th century. Open Saturday afternoons, June through September.

AMSTERDAM

Guy Park State Historic Site (366 West Main St.; 518/842-8200). Former 1773 home of Guy Johnson, Superintendent of Indian Affairs, who remained loyal to King George III. Later served as a tavern. Exhibits on Erie Canal. Phone for schedule.

Old Fort Johnson (Route 5; 518/843-0300). This two-story 1749 Georgian residence was built by Sir William Johnson, land baron, soldier, and Indian agent. Johnson was knighted after his victory at the battle of Lake George and made superintendent of Indian Affairs. As many as a thousand Indians camped here during the Indian councils held at the fort. The home is furnished in the period and contains items of local history. Open daily, May through October.

National Shrine of the North American Martyrs (6 miles west on NY 5S in Auriesville, Dewey Hwy., exit 27; 518/853-

3033). Site of Ossernenon, the early Mohawk settlement where Father Isaac Jogues and companions, the first canonized martyrs in America, were put to death. Birthplace of Blessed Kateri Tekakwitha. Chapel, museum, cafeteria. Open daily, early May through October.

Erie Canal (6 miles west on NY 5S at Fort Hunter). The site of the last remaining section of the original 1822 canal.

Scholarie Crossing State Historic Site (5 miles west just off NY 5S, in Fort Hunter; 518/829-7516). Seven arches of the Scholarie Aqueduct, remains of original canal locks. Picnicking, wagon rides, tours. Open Wednesday through Sunday, mid-May through October.

AUBURN

Seward House (33 South St.; 315/252-1283). Home, circa 1816, of William Henry Seward, New York governor, U.S. Senator, Secretary of State under Lincoln and Andrew Johnson, and the man responsible for the purchase of Alaska. Civil War and Alaskan artifacts, period furnishings. Open Tuesday through Saturday, April through December.

Owasco Teyetasta Native American Museum (Emerson Park; 315/253-8051). Exhibits on traditional Northeast Woodlands Indian arts and culture. Open Wednesday through Sunday, Memorial Day through Labor Day.

Harriet Tubman Home (180 South St.; 315/252-2081). Born a slave, Harriet Tubman escaped in 1849 and later rescued more than 300 other slaves via the Underground Railroad. Settling here after the Civil War, she continued to pursue humanitarian endeavors. Open Tuesday through Thursday and weekends; closed January.

BARRYVILLE

Fort Delaware Museum of Colonial History (on NY 97 in Narrowburg; 914/252-6660). A replica of a 1755 stockade, blockhouses, cabins, and gardens. Exhibits. Film. Demonstrations depict life of early settlers. Colonial military encampments during summer. Picnicking. Open daily, June through Labor Day; weekends Memorial Day through late June.

BATAVIA

Holland Land Office Museum (131 West Main St.; 716/343-4727). Here, deeds to the lands in the Holland Purchase were issued. The stone office was built in 1815 by Joseph Ellicott, land agent. Indian and pioneer artifacts, period furniture. Open Monday through Thursday.

Le Roy House (½ mile east of jct. of NY 19 and NY 5, at 23 East Main St. in El Roy; 716/768-7433). An early-19th-century house with period furnishings. Open Tuesday through Friday and Sunday afternoons in the summer.

BAY SHORE (LONG ISLAND)

Sagtikos Manor (3 miles west on NY 27A; 516/661-8348). Apple Tree Wicke, built in 1692, served as General Henry Clinton's headquarters. Original parlor and kitchen, antiques. Open Wednesday through Thursday and Sundays, July and August; Sundays only in June.

BETHPAGE (LONG ISLAND)

Old Bethpage Village Restoration (Round Swamp Rd., 1 mile south of L.I. Expwy., exit 48; 516/572-8401). More than twenty-five pre–Civil War buildings include blacksmith, carpentry, and hat shops, general store, tavern, schoolhouse, church, homes, and working farm. Craftsmen depict life in the mid-1800s. Film, picnic area. Open Wednesday through Sunday.

BOONVILLE

Constable Hall (7 miles northwest via NY 120, unnumbered road; 315/397-2323). A limestone Georgian built in 1820 by William Constable, son of one of New York's most powerful merchants, who joined Alexander MaComb and William McCornick in the MaComb Purchase, which consisted of one-tenth of the state. Family memorabilia. Open daily except Mondays, June to mid-October.

CANANDAIGUA

Granger Homestead (295 North Main; 716/394-1492). The 1816 home of Gideon Granger, Postmaster General under Jefferson and Madison. Nine restored rooms, original furnishings, carriage museum. Open daily except Mondays, June through August; Tuesday through Saturday, mid-May through June and September.

Accommodations: *The Acorn Inn* (4508 Rte. 64S; 716/229-2834). This 1796 stagecoach inn now serves guests afternoon tea by the fire. The four guest rooms are furnished with antiques and canopy beds. Full breakfast. Moderate.

CANTON

Silas Wright House and Museum (3 East Main; 315/386-8133). The Greek Revival home, circa 1832, of a U.S. senator and gov-

ernor. First floor restored, second-floor gallery. Open Tuesday through Friday.

CAZENOVIA

Lorenzo State Historic Site (¾ mile south on NY 13; 315/655-3200). Elegant 1807 Federal mansion built by John Lincklaen. Original furnishings, garden, arboretum. Open Wednesday through Sunday, May through October.

COOPERSTOWN

Farmers' Museum and Village Cross-roads (1 mile north on NY 80; 607/547-

2533). Outdoor museum of rural life in early 1800s. Craftsmen present printing, weaving, and blacksmithing demonstrations. Village has historic buildings and barn with exhibits. Special events occur throughout the year. Open daily, May through October; daily except Mondays, April and November through December.

National Baseball Hall of Fame and Museum (Main St.; 607/547-9988). Dedicated to the game and its players. Plaques honoring the game's all-time greats. Displays on baseball's greatest moments. Complete history of the game. A theater presents a special multimedia show. Gift shop. Open daily.

The Bronck Museum in Coxsackie.

Boscobel, near Garrison.

Fenimore House (1 mile north on NY 80; 607/547-2533). Large American folk art collection. Indian art and artifacts. James Fenimore Cooper memorabilia. Academic and decorative art of 1800–50. Open daily, May through October; daily except Mondays, November and December.

CORNING

Benjamin Patterson Inn Museum Complex (59 West Pulteney St.; 607/937-5281). Restored and furnished 1796 inn, built to encourage settlement in Genesee County. Also here is the De Monstoy Log Cabin, circa 1785, as well as a one-room school. The Starr Barn has agricultural exhibits and a blacksmith shop. Open daily except Sundays.

COXSACKIE

Bronck Museum (4 miles south of Coxsackie Thruway, exit 21B, on U.S. 9W, then right on Peter Bronck Rd.; 518/731-8862). Built in 1663 by Pieter, brother of Jonas Bronck, whose 500-acre "bouwerie" became New York City's Bronx. A complex of early Dutch houses with outbuildings, including a 13-sided barn. Open daily except Mondays, late June through August.

CROWN POINT

Crown Point State Historic Site (north on NY 9N/22, 4 miles east at Champlain Bridge; 518/597-3661). Preserved ruins of fortifications occupied by French, British, and American forces during the French and

Indian and Revolutionary wars—Fort St. Frederick (1734) and Fort Crown Point (1759). Visitor center, audiovisual presentation, exhibits, self-guided tours. Open Wednesday through Saturday and Sunday afternoons, May through October.

EAST AURORA

Millard Fillmore Museum (24 Shearer Ave.; 716/652-4228). This 1825 house that Fillmore built for his wife contains original furnishings and memorabilia. The circa-1830 carriage house is built of lumber from the former Nathaniel Fillmore farm, and houses the Fillmore sleigh. Open Wednesdays and weekends, June to mid-October.

EAST HAMPTON (LONG ISLAND)

"Home, Sweet Home" House and Windmill (14 James Lane; 516/324-0713). Childhood home of John Howard Payne, who wrote "Home, Sweet Home." The house, built circa 1680, has period furniture, English china, mementos, exhibits. Windmill in rear. Tours available. Open daily except February.

Historic Mulford Farm (James Lane, adjacent to Payne House; 516/324-6850). A living-history 1680 farm museum. New England architecture, period rooms, costumed interpreters. Open daily, afternoons in July and August; weekends, June and September.

Clermont, near the town of Hudson.

Historic Clinton Academy (151 Main; 516/324-6850). The first preparatory school in New York (1784) is a museum with historic artifacts of Eastern Long Island. Same schedule as Mulford Farm (see above).

Hook Mill (36 North Main, on Montauk Hwy.). A completely equipped 1806 windmill. Tours available. Open late June through early September.

Accommodations: *Maidstone Arms* (207 Main St.; 516/324-5006). Overlooking the village green, this 1860 colonial has nineteen elegant rooms, all individually decorated with fireplace, private bath, and refrigerator. Full breakfast. Excellent restaurant. Expensive.

FISHKILL

Madam Brett Homestead (southwest on I-84, exit NY 52, then west 3 miles at 50 Van Nydeck Ave. in Beacon; 914/831-6533). The oldest standing structure in Dutchess County, occupied by the same family from 1709 to 1954, contains furnishings of seven genera-

OFF TO THE RACES

Horse racing was popular throughout the colonies. Boston, New York, and Philadelphia had racetracks. Hempstead, on Long Island, had a racecourse that was sixteen miles long and four miles wide, and annual races were held there as early as 1670. In 1750, English thoroughbreds were brought to the colonies. This revolutionized racing, and most famous American racehorses were descended from them. The quarter horse, an American breed adapted to sprinting, is believed to have begun with horses bred to race the quarter-mile stretch between Virginia governor Sir William Berkeley's plantation and Jamestown. The governor and his friends would race the quarter mile every Sunday after church.

tions. Open the first Sunday of every month.

Van Wyck Homestead Museum (south of town, at jct. of U.S. 9 and I-84; 914/896-9560). A headquarters of the Continental Army, the site of the court-martial of Enoch Crosby, a spy for the Continental Army. Washington, Lafayette, and von Steuben visited here. Collection of Hudson Valley folk art. Open weekends, Memorial Day through Labor Day.

Mount Gulian Historic Site (145 Sterling St., off NY 9D at Chelsea Ridge Park, in Beacon; 914/831-8172). Headquarters of Baron von Steuben during the final period of the Revolution. Birthplace of the Order of the Society of the Cincinnati, the first veterans' organization. Open Wednesday and Sunday afternoons, April through December.

GARRISON

Boscobel (4 miles north on NY 9D; 914/265-3638). A fine example of New York Federal architecture, this mansion was built by States Morris Dyckman in 1806. Period furnishings, formal gardens, view of the Hudson River. Tours available. Open daily except Tuesdays, March through December.

Foundry School Museum (4 miles north on NY 9D, at 63 Chestnut St. in Cold Spring; 914/265-4010). West Point foundry memorabilia, an old-fashioned schoolroom, Indian artifacts, antiques. Open Tuesday through Thursday and Sundays, March through December.

Accommodations: *The Bird and Bottle Inn* (Rte. 9, Old Albany Post Rd.; 914/424-3000). Built in 1761 as Warren's Tavern, this yellow farmhouse is now a National Historic Landmark. Timbered ceilings, old paneling in the inn's restaurant provide a Colonial ambiance. The four guest rooms have canopied or four-poster beds and fireplaces. Full breakfast. Expensive.

GENEVA

Rose Hill Mansion (3 miles east on the northeast shore of Seneca Lake, on NY 96A, just south of U.S. 20; 315/789-3848). An 1839 Greek Revival country estate with Empire furnishings. Tours available. Open daily, May through October.

GREENWICH

Bennington Battlefield State Historic Site (7 miles southeast via NY 372, 6 miles south on NY 22, and 2 miles east on NY 67, east of North Hoosick, in the town of Waloomsac; 518/279-1155). Militiamen under General John Stark stopped a British force here in August 1777. Picnicking. Open daily, Memorial Day through Labor Day.

HERKIMER

Herkimer House State Historic Site (8 miles east on NY 169, off NY 5S; 315/823-0398). General Nicholas Herkimer of the Continental Army lived in this 1752 house. Period furnishings, family cemetery, monument, picnicking, visitor center. Phone for schedule.

Herkimer County Historical Society (400 North Main St. at Court St.; 315/866-6413). A mansion on the site of Fort Dayton contains exhibits of county history. Tours of the 1834 County Jail available. Open weekdays.

HOWES CAVE

Old Stone Fort Museum Complex (8 miles southeast via NY 7, 30 in Schoharie; 518/295-7192). A church built here in 1772 was fortified against raids by Tories and Indians and became known as the Lower Fort. A major attack came in 1780. The building was restored as a house of worship in 1785. Exhibits of the Revolution, Indian, and Schoharie Valley artifacts. Badgley Museum and Carriage House. Open daily except Mondays, May through October.

HUDSON

Clermont State Historic Site (16 miles south on NY 9G, then west on County Rte. 6; 518/537-4240). The ancestral home of Robert R. Livingston, a drafter of the Declaration of Independence, who later administered the oath of office to George Washington. Lived in by seven generations of the family. Period furnishings, gardens, tour, museum store, visitor center. Open Wednesday through Sunday, mid-April through October.

Shaker Museum and Library (149 Shaker Museum Rd., 18 miles northeast via NY 66, County Rte. 13; 518/794-9100). A large collection of Shaker culture, displayed in twenty-six galleries in three buildings. Furniture, crafts, basketry, tools. Picnicking, gift shop, café. Open daily, May through October.

Martin Van Buren National Historic Site (9 miles north, on NY 9H; 518/758-9689). The retirement home of the eighth President. Van Buren purchased Lindenwald in 1839 from General William Paulding. The thirty-six-room house is on twenty acres. Tours available. Open daily, May through October.

James Vanderpoel House (11 miles north on U.S. 9 in Kinderhook; 518/758-9265). The Columbia County Historical Society maintains a museum in this circa-1820 Federal house, featuring period furnishings and art. The society also maintains the 1737 *Luykas Van Alen House* (4 miles northeast on NY 66, then 6 miles north on NY 9H; no phone) as a museum of Dutch

PETER STUYVESANT

There was more to Peter Stuyvesant than a wooden leg. From 1647 to 1664, as director general of New Netherland, he was responsible for exploiting the commercial potential of the New World for the Dutch West India Company. His administration resulted in a strong influx of colonists, two cities, thirteen villages, two forts, and three colonies, and a promising transatlantic trade.

Stuyvesant, the son of a minister, was noted for his inflexible nature. In 1639 he was the company's commissary of stores on the island of Curaçao. When the director suddenly died, Stuyvesant took his place. In 1644 he attacked St. Martin, an island lost by the Dutch to the Spanish, and sustained a severe wound resulting in the amputation of his right leg. To recover his health, he returned home.

Appointed director general of New Netherland, he arrived on Manhattan Island in 1646 to find that the colony had seriously deteriorated. The factious colonists were unconcerned for the prosperity of the settlement. Stuyvesant attacked the problem vigorously, but it took him six years to restore confidence. He also inherited unstable relations with the Indians in the area. He restored order by treating the Indians pragmatically, trading with them when he could, and using force when he had to.

In 1651, ordered to eliminate competition from the Swedes trading along the Delaware River, Stuyvesant captured New Sweden and incorporated its population into New Netherland. One problem proved insoluble: his English neighbors to the north. They continually pressed upon Dutch lands and disregarded intercolonial agreements. In 1666 a British squadron forced him to surrended New Netherland.

Stuyvesant went home to defend his decision to surrender, then returned to the colony he had once governed, now renamed New York, to live quietly on his farm until his death.

18th-century domestic culture. Both open Wednesday through Sunday, Memorial Day through Labor Day.

HUNTINGTON (LONG ISLAND)

Walt Whitman Birthplace State Historic Site (246 Old Walt Whitman Rd.: 516/427-5240). Boyhood home of the poet, with period furnishings, a museum, and an audiovisual presentation. Tours, picnicking. Open Wednesday through Sunday year-round.

David Conklin Farmhouse (2 High St. at New York Ave.; 516/427-7045). Four generations of Conklins lived in this 1750 house, which features period rooms. Other properties maintained by the Huntington Historical Society include the 1795 *Kissam House* (434 Park Ave.), a Federal house, barn, and other outbuildings, and the *Huntington Trade School* (209 Main), the headquarters of the society.

Whaling Museum (2 miles west on NY 25A in Cold Spring Harbor; 516/367-3418). The museum features a fully equipped whaleboat, marine paintings, scrimshaw, and ship models. Open daily, Memorial Day through Labor Day; daily except Mondays, the rest of the year.

Joseph Lloyd Manor House (3 miles north on Lloyd Lane in Lloyd Harbor; 516-941-9444). A 1767 manor house, elegantly furnished, with a period garden. Open weekend afternoons, Memorial Day through mid-October.

HYDE PARK

Mills Mansion State Historic Site (4 miles north on U.S. 9 in Miles-Norris State Park, Staatsburg; 914/889-8851). Built in 1832, this Greek Revival mansion was enlarged in

1895 by architects McKim, Mead & White into a sixty-five-room, neoclassical country residence for Ogden Mills. Furnished in Louis XIV, Louis XV, and Louis XVI styles, with tapestries, art objects. The park overlooks the Hudson. Open Wednesday through Sunday, mid-April through October.

JOHNSTOWN

Johnson Hall State Historic Site (Hall Ave.; 518/762-8712). The 1763 home of General Sir William Johnson, first baronet of New York Colony, includes a hall with period furnishings, a stone blockhouse, an interpretation center, tours. Open Wednesday through Sunday afternoons, mid-May through October.

KINGSTON

Senate House State Historic Site (312 Fair St. in Stockade District; 914/338-2786). A 1676 stone residence in which the first state senate met in 1777, furnished in 18th-century Dutch style. Paintings by John Vanderlyn and others are displayed in a museum. Boxwood garden. Open Wednesday through Sunday, mid-April through October.

Old Dutch Church (Main and Wall streets; 914/338-6759). George Clinton, first governor of New York and vice-president under Jefferson and Madison, is buried on the grounds of this 19th-century church. Church and museum tours by appointment, Monday through Friday.

Hurley Patentee Manor (4 miles southwest, NY Thruway exit 19, then south to Old NY 209, then County Rte. 29; 914/331-5414). A 1696 Dutch cottage expanded in 1745 to a two-story English country mansion. Original furnishings and woodwork. Open daily except Mondays, July through Labor Day.

Delaware and Hudson Canal Museum (15 miles south, NY Thruway exit 19, then south on NY 209, left on NY 213 in High Falls; 914/687-9311). Canal-boat models, dioramas, memorabilia, tours. Open Thursday through Monday, May through October.

LAKE GEORGE VILLAGE

Fort William Henry Museum (Canada St., south end of village on U.S. 9; 518/668-5471). A rebuilt 1755 fort featuring French and Indian War relics, military drills, musket and cannon firings, demonstrations of bullet molding. Tours in July and August. Open daily, May through October.

MONROE

Museum Village in Orange County (Museum Village Rd., west on NY 17M, U.S. 6, NY 17 exit 129; 914-782-8247). A living-history museum of more than twenty-five buildings depicting the crafts of 19th-century America. Print shop, log cabin, drugstore, general store, schoolhouse. Broom maker, candlemaker, blacksmith, weaver. Farm animals, gardens, shops, food service, picnicking. Open Wednesday through Saturday, May to early December.

MOUNT KISCO

John Jay Homestead State Historic Site (I-684 exit 6, left on NY 35, east to Jay St., between Katonah and Bedford Village; 914/232-5651). The estate of the first Chief Justice of the United States and four generations of his descendants. American portrait collection, period furnishings, gardens, farm buildings, tours. Open Wednesday through Sunday, May through Labor Day.

NEWBURGH

Washington's Headquarters State Historic Site (84 Liberty St.; 914/562-1195). The 1750 Jonathan Hasbrouck house was Washington's headquarters for more than sixteen months. The Dutch vernacular fieldstone house is furnished as his headquarters. Museum, audiovisual program, tours. Open Wednesday through Sunday, mid-April through October.

NEW PALTZ

Huguenot Street Old Stone Houses (Visitor Center, 6 Broadhead Ave.; 914/255-1660). Six stone dwellings, 1692–1712, a 1717 reconstructed French church, and the 1694 Jean Hasbrouck House of medieval Flemish stone, all furnished with heirlooms. Open Wednesday through Sunday, early June through Labor Day.

Locust Lawn (4 miles south on NY 32; 914/255-1660). The 1814 Federal mansion of Josiah Hasbrouck has a smokehouse and a farmers' museum. On site is the 1738 Terwilliger Homestead. Open Wednesday through Sunday, early June through Labor Day.

NEW ROCHELLE

Thomas Paine Cottage (20 Sicard St.; 914/632-5376). The house where Paine, the author of *Common Sense,* lived after his return from Europe, now a museum of Paine artifacts and memorabilia. Open Friday through Sunday; closed in winter.

NEW YORK CITY

Castle Clinton National Monument (Battery Park; 212/264-4456). Built in 1811 as a fort, this later was a place of public entertainment called Castle Garden, where Jenny Lind sang in 1850. In 1855 it was taken over for an immigrant-receiving station by the state, and more than 7 million people entered the country here before the opening of Ellis Island in 1892. Open daily.

Bowling Green (Broadway, east of the Battery). Originally a Dutch market, the city's oldest park is said to be the place where Peter Minuit purchased Manhattan for twenty-four dollars' worth of trinkets. The park fence dates from 1771. Open daily.

The George Gustav Heye Center of the National Museum of the American Indian (1 Bowling Green St.; 212/283-2420). The world's largest collection of materials of the native peoples of North, Central, and South America. Open daily.

Fraunces Tavern and Museum (54 Pearl St.; 212/425-1778). A museum, housed in the 1719 tavern and four adjacent 19th-century buildings, interprets the history and culture of Early America through paintings, prints, decorative arts, and artifacts. The Long Room is the site of Washington's farewell to his officers at the end of the Revolution in 1783. Tours available. Restaurant open daily, museum open Monday through Saturday.

Locust Grove in Poughkeepsie. Photo by D. Szeba.

A canal boat ride at the Erie Canal Village in Rome.

Trinity Church (Broadway at Wall St.; 212/602-0800). The church, built in 1846, is the third to occupy this site. Robert Fulton and Alexander Hamilton are buried in its famous graveyard. Museum, parish center with dining room open to the public. Open daily.

Federal Hall National Memorial (Wall and Nassau streets; 212/264-4456). This 1842 Greek Revival building is on the site of the original Federal Hall, where the Stamp Act congress met (1765). Washington was inaugurated here on April 30, 1789, and the first Congress met here in 1789–90. Originally a custom house, the building was for many years the subtreasury of the United States. The J. Q. A. Ward statue of Washington is on the Wall Street steps. Open weekdays.

St. Paul's Chapel (Fulton St. and Broadway; 212/602-0874). A Georgian chapel of Trinity Church, built in 1766, this is the oldest public building in continuous use in Manhattan. Washington's pew is in the north aisle. Chancel ornaments by L'Enfant, Waterford chandeliers, concerts Mondays and Thursdays at noon. Open daily.

South Street Seaport Museum (South and Fulton streets at East River; 212/669-9424). The city's maritime history is displayed in an eleven-block restored area. The emphasis is on South Street in the days of sailing ships. Moored here are the *Ambrose* lightship; the *Lettie G. Howard,* a fishing schooner; the square rigged *Wavertree;* the four-masted bark *Peking;* and the schooner *Pioneer.* Exhibits of models, prints, photos, and artifacts. Tours available. Open daily.

The Church of the Ascension (10th St. and Fifth Ave.; 212/254-8620). This 1840 Episcopal English Gothic church was built in 1840 and redecorated in 1885–89 under the direction of Stanford White. It houses John La Farge's mural *The Ascension of Our Lord,* and sculptured angels by Louis Saint-Gaudens. Open daily.

The New York Historical Society (170 Central Park West, between 76th and 77th streets; 212/873-3400). Exhibits on American history, with an emphasis on New York. Open Wednesday through Friday.

Museum of the City of New York (1220 Fifth Ave., between 103rd and 104th streets; 212/534-1672). Paintings, prints, photographs, ship models, and theatrical memorabilia dating from 1769 onward. Dutch Gallery. Walking tours of the city (Sundays in spring and fall). Open Wednesday through Sunday.

Hamilton Grange National Memorial (287 Convent St. at West 141st St.; 212/ 283-5154). The 1802 Federal residence of Alexander Hamilton. Open Wednesday through Sunday.

Dyckman House Park and Museum (4881 Broadway at 204th St.; 212/304-9422). The only remaining 18th-century Dutch farmhouse on Manhattan Island, built circa 1783 by William Dyckman. Period furnishings. A replica of a British officers' hut is on the grounds. Smokehouse, garden. Open daily except Mondays.

Morris-Jumel Mansion (Jumel Terrace, West 160th St., ½ block east of St. Nicholas Ave.; 212/923-8008). Built in 1765 by Colonel Roger and Mary Philipse Morris, this was Washington's headquarters in 1776. Later it became a British command post and Hessian headquarters. Purchased by French merchant Stephen Jumel in 1810, the house was the scene of the marriage of his widow, Madame Eliza Jumel, to Aaron Burr in 1833. The mansion is the only remaining Colonial residence in Manhattan. Period furnishings. Open daily except Mondays.

OSWEGO

Fort Ontario State Historic Site (foot of East 7th St.; 315/343-4711). The original fort was built by the British in 1755, and used as an army installation from 1840 to 1946. The fort commanded the route from the Hudson and Mohawk valleys to the Great Lakes. The restored site re-creates life at a military installation during the 1860s. Tours, special programs, drills. Open daily, Memorial Day through Labor Day.

PALMYRA

Mormon Historic Sites and Bureau of Information (Hill Cumorah, 4 miles south on NY 21, near I-90 exit 43; 315/597-5851). Guides give daily tours to the following sites, all open daily: *Mill Cumorah,* where the golden plates from which Joseph Smith translated the *Book of Mormon* were delivered to him. A monument to the Angel Moroni now stands on the hill. Visitor center. *Joseph Smith House* (Stafford Rd.; 315/597-4383), where Smith lived as a young man. Nearby is the Sacred Grove where he had his first vision. *E. B. Grandin Print Shop* (217 East Main; 315/597-0019). Between June 1829 and March 1930, the first edition of 5,000 copies of the *Book of Mormon* was printed here.

Ailing Coverlet Museum (122 William St.; 315/597-6737). The largest collection of American jacquard and hand-woven coverlets in the country. Open weekend afternoons, June through mid-October.

PLATTSBURGH

Macdonough Monument (City Hall Place). An obelisk commemorates the 1814 naval victory at the Battle of Plattsburgh.

Kent-Delord House Museum (17 Cumberland Ave.; 518/561-1035). This historic

1797 house served as British officers' quarters during the Battle of Plattsburgh. Period furnishings, tours. Open Tuesday through Saturday, March through December.

PORT JEFFERSON (LONG ISLAND)

Thompson House (4 miles west on NY 25A, on North Country Rd. in Setauket; 516/941-9444). Historian Benjamin F. Thompson was born in this circa-1700 saltbox in 1784. It has been furnished to depict 18th-century life on Long Island. Herb garden. Open weekends, Memorial Day to mid-October.

POUGHKEEPSIE

Locust Grove (2 miles south of Mid-Hudson Bridge at 370 South Rd.; 914/454-4500). This circa-1830 house, the home of Samuel F. B. Morse, inventor of the telegraph, was remodeled by him into a Tuscan villa in 1847. The Morse Room displays telegraph equipment and memorabilia. Exhibits of dolls, fans, and books owned by the Morse family. Paintings, tours. Open Wednesday through Sunday, Memorial Day through September; weekends in October.

RHINEBECK

Montgomery Place (North on NY 9G to Annandale-on-Hudson, estate along Hudson River; 914/758-5461). This 1805 mansion was remodeled in the mid-1800s in the Classic Revival style. Coach house, greenhouse, museum, garden shop., visitor center. Open daily except Tuesdays, April through October; weekends in March and November and December.

Accommodations: *Beekman Arms* (4 Mill St. on U.S. 9; 914/876-7077). Opened in 1776 as a stagecoach inn, it offers fifty-nine rooms and an excellent restaurant, the Beekman 1766 Tavern. Guests may also choose to stay in the Delameter Guest House (an 1844 Carpenter Gothic), the Delameter Carriage House, or the Courtyard, all excellent. Breakfast. Moderate.

ROCHESTER

Susan B. Anthony House (17 Madison St.; 716/235-6124). The pioneering suffragist lived here for forty years. Mementos of the women's suffrage movement. Open Thursday through Saturday.

Stone-Tolan House (2370 East Ave., 4 miles southeast of I-490 in Brighton; 716/442-4606). A restored 1792 pioneer homestead and tavern, with gardens and orchards. Open Friday through Sunday.

The Landmark Center (133 South Fitzhugh St. at Troup St.; 716/546-7029). The Campbell-Whittlesey House Museum is a Greek Revival house with Empire furnishings. Also here is the Hoyt-Potter House. Gift shop, tours. Open weekends.

Strong Museum (1 Manhattan Sq.; 716/263-2700). More than a half-million objects are on display, including toys, furnishings, decorative arts, and advertisements that chronicle American life since 1820. Café, museum shop. Open daily.

ROME

Fort Stanwix National Monument (122 East Park St.; 315/336-2090). A reconstructed earth-and-log fort on the location of a 1758 fort. Here the Iroquois signed a treaty opening territory east of the Ohio River to colonial expansion. British troops besieged the fort in 1777, until General Benedict Arnold forced their retreat. Costumed guides, film, museum. Open daily, April through November.

Tomb of the Unknown Soldier of the American Revolution (201 West James St.). The tomb was designed by Lorimar Rich, who also designed the Tomb of the Unknown Soldier at Arlington National Cemetery.

Erie Canal Village (2½ miles west on NY 49; 315/337-3999). The buildings of this 1840s canal village include church, blacksmith shop, train station, schoolhouse, manor home, stable, and settlers' cabin. Orientation center, trips on the horse-drawn 1840 canal packet boat *Chief Engineer*. Picnicking. Open daily, mid-May through Labor Day.

SACKETS HARBOR

Sackets Harbor Battlefield State Historic Site (505 West Washington St., overlooking the lake; 315/646-3634). On the battlefield are the Union Hotel (1818), Commandant's House (1850), and the U.S. Navy Yard (1812–1955). Exhibits, demonstrations, tours, visitor center. Open daily, mid-May through late October.

SAG HARBOR (LONG ISLAND)

Sag Harbor Whaling and Historical Museum (Garden and Main; 516/725-0770). Relics of whaling days and historical artifacts are on display in the former home of local ship owner Benjamin Hunting. Open daily, mid-May through September.

Customs House (Garden St.; 516/941-9444). A customs house and post office dating from the late 18th and early 19th

The Battle of Saratoga. Courtesy Library of Congress, Prints and Photographs Division.

Ethan Allen demands the surrender of Fort Ticonderoga. Courtesy Library of Congress, Prints and Photographs Division.

centuries, with antique furnishings. Open daily except Mondays, July and August; weekends, May and June, September and October.

SARANAC LAKE

Six Nations Indian Museum (on Buck Pond Rd., off NY 3 in Onchiota; 518/891-2299). Exhibits portray Native American life. Council ground, artifacts, lectures on Indian culture and history. Open daily, July and August.

SARATOGA

Saratoga National Historical Park (30 miles north of Albany on U.S. 4, NY 32; 518/664-9821). In two 1777 engagements, September 19 and October 7, Americans under Horatio Gates defeated General Burgoyne in the battles of Saratoga, the turning point of the war because they brought France into the war on the side of the colonies. The park features reconstructed earthwork defenses and one historic house, the one-room *John Neilson House,* which was occupied by a few American officers. A nine-mile auto tour has ten stops. Also here is the *Boot Monument,* dedicated to Benedict Arnold, who rallied American troops to victory (Arnold lost his leg during the battle). The 155-foot *Surrender Monument* is closed for restoration. In the area is the 1777 General Philip Schuyler House (8 miles north on U.S. 4 in Schuylerville.) The visitor center shows a film, "Checkmate on the Hudson." Open daily.

Accommodations: *Six Sisters* (149 Union Ave.; Saratoga Springs; 518/583-1173). An unusual Victorian house, with a large second-story bay window, is decorated with élan. Near the race track. Four guest rooms, full breakfast. Inexpensive to moderate.

SAYVILLE (LONG ISLAND)

Suffolk Marine Museum (1 mile west on Montauk Hwy., Suffolk County Park in West Sayville; 516/854-4974). Oyster cull house. Boat shop. Tugboat *Charlotte,* oyster vessel *Priscilla,* oyster sloop *Modesty.* Open daily except Mondays.

SOUTHAMPTON (LONG ISLAND)

Southampton Historical Museum (17 Meeting House Lane, off Main; 516/283-1612). The museum is housed in an 1843 whaling captain's home with period rooms, displaying a large collection of Indian artifacts. On the grounds are a one-room schoolhouse, a carriage house, and an 18th-century village street with various shops. A barn has been converted to a country store. Open daily except Mondays, mid-June to mid-September.

Old Halsey House (South Main St.; 516/283-1612). Built in 1648, this is the old-est English frame house in the state. Period furnishings, Colonial herb garden. Open daily except Mondays, mid-June to mid-September.

Water Mill Museum (northeast on Old Mill Rd. in Water Mill; 516/726-4625). A restored 1644 gristmill houses old tools, other exhibits. Craft demonstrations. Open daily except Tuesdays, Memorial Day through Labor Day.

SOUTHOLD (LONG ISLAND)

The Old House (on NY 25, on Village Green in Cutchogue; 516/734-7122). This 1649 house is a good example of early English Colonial architecture. Period furnishings. Also on the Village Green are the early-18th-century *Wickham Farmhouse* and the *Old School Museum* (1840). Open daily except Mondays, July through Labor Day; weekends in June and September.

STONY POINT

Stony Point Battlefield State Historic Site (2 miles north of town, off U.S. 9W, on Park Rd.; 914/786-2521). The site of the Revolutionary battle in which General "Mad Anthony" Wayne successfully stormed British fortifications on July 15–16, 1779. This ended the last serious threat to Washington's forces in the North. The 1826 lighthouse here is the oldest on the river. A museum has an audiovisual program. Musket demonstrations, tour, picnic area. Open Wednesday through Sunday, mid-April through October.

SYRACUSE

Erie Canal Museum (Weighlock Bldg., Erie Blvd. East and Montgomery St.; 315/471-0593). Exhibits seen from sixty-three-foot reconstructed canal boat detail the

. . . I ordered him to deliver the fort instantly. [When] he asked by what authority I demanded it, I answered him, "In the name of the great Jehovah, and the Continental Congress."

—ETHAN ALLEN, *REPORT ON THE CAPTURE OF FORT TICONDEROGA, 1775*

construction and operation of the canal. Open daily. The museum also maintains the *Canal Center* (Lyndon Rd., 4 miles east at jct. of NY 5 and 92, in Erie Canal State Park; 315/471-0593). Exhibits describe canal structures, aqueducts, and bowstring bridges. Open daily except Mondays, Memorial Day through Labor Day.

New York State Canal Cruises (800/ 545-4318 or 315/685-8500). Excursions of various lengths depart Albany, Syracuse, and Buffalo, June through October. Phone for schedule.

TARRYTOWN

Sunnyside (on West Sunnyside Lane, west of U.S. 9, 1 mile south of NY Thruway, exit 9; 914/631-8200). Washington Irving's Hudson River estate (1835–59). Irving's furnishings, library and personal property. Gift shop, picnicking. Open daily except Tuesdays, March through December; weekends the rest of the year.

Philipsburg Manor (in North Tarrytown, on U.S. 9, 2 miles north of NY Thruway exit 9; 914/631-8200, ext. 904). A colonial farm and trading site (1720–50), including manor house, barn, restored operating gristmill, and wooden millpond bridge across the Pocantico River. Film, tours, exhibition center, gift shop. Open daily except Tuesdays, March through December; weekends the rest of the year.

Van Courtland Manor (in Croton-on-Hudson, at Croton Point Ave., exit on U.S. 9, 10 miles north of NY Thruway exit 9; 914/ 638-8200, ext. 904). The post–Revolutionary War estate of a prominent Colonial family, an elegantly furnished manor house, ferry-house inn, and kitchen building. The "Long Walk" has flanking gardens. Demonstrations of open-hearth cooking, brickmaking, weaving. Gift shop. Open daily, March through December.

Lyndhurst (635 South Broadway, ½ mile south of Tappan Zee Bridge, on U.S. 9; 914/631-0046). Perhaps the finest example of the Gothic Revival style in the country, Lyndhurst was the summer home of the financier Jay Gould. When it was built in 1838, Alexander Jackson Davis, the architect, strove to create a mansion with an atmosphere of romance and rural ease. Some sixty-seven landscaped acres overlook the Hudson. Family furnishings, art, and books. A National Trust property. Tours available. Open daily except Mondays, May through October; weekends the rest of the year.

Old Dutch Church of Sleepy Hollow (Broadway and Pierson St.; 914/631-1123). A restored 1685 church of Dutch origins, with a replica of its original pulpit. The adjacent cemetery has graves of Washington Irving and Andrew Carnegie. Open daily.

TICONDEROGA

Fort Ticonderoga (2 miles east on NY 74; 518/585-2821). Built in 1755 by the French, who called it Carillon, the fort was successfully defended by the Marquis de Montcalm against a greater British force in 1758. It was captured by the British in 1759, and by Ethan Allen and his Green Mountain Boys in 1775, the first American victory. The stone fort was restored in 1909. It has a large collection of cannon. A museum displays collections of weapons, paintings, and personal articles of soldiers garrisoned here. Tours are led by costumed guides. Cannon and musket firing daily. Fife-and-drum corps parade daily in July and August. Special events, museum shop, restaurant, picnicking. Open daily, early May to mid-October.

Hancock House Replica (3 Wicker St., at Moses Circle: 518/585-7868). A replica of the house built for John Hancock in Boston, maintained as a museum and research library with period furnishings. Open daily, June through September, daily except Sundays the rest of the year.

WHITE PLAINS

Washington's Headquarters (Virginia Rd. in North White Plains; 914/949-1236). Washington operated out of this 1776 house when he outfoxed General Lord Howe. Howe, commanding a stronger, fresher force, permitted Washington to retreat to an impregnable position. Revolutionary War artifacts, demonstrations. Open Wednesday through Sunday.

Miller Hill Restoration (North White Plains; no phone). Restored earthworks built by Washington's troops and used in the Battle of White Plains, October 28, 1776. Open daily, year-round.

YONKERS

Hudson River Museum of Westchester (511 Warburton Ave.; 914/963-4550). The museum includes Glenview Mansion, an Eastlake-inspired Hudson River house overlooking the Palisades. Regional art and history exhibits. Open Wednesday through Sunday.

St. Paul's Church National Historic Site (897 South Columbus Ave. in Mount Vernon, 10 miles southeast via Hutchinson River Pkwy., exit 8; 914/667-4116). This 1763 church was the setting for the Great Election of 1733, which led to a free press in Colonial America. The church was a hospital for British and Hessian troops during the Revolution. It was completed after the war, and served not only as a church but also as a meeting house and courtroom where Aaron Burr once practiced law.

9

PENNSYLVANIA

Henry Hudson, an Englishman employed by the Dutch, sailed into Delaware Bay in 1609, but the first settlers in Pennsylvania were Swedes who came in 1643. Twelve years later they ceded their settlement on Tinicum Island near the mouth of Schuylkill River to the Dutch, and in 1664 the English took over.

Charles II made the Quaker William Penn proprietor of the lands west of the Delaware River. In the colony that bore his name, Penn laid "the foundation of a free colony for all mankind," guaranteeing civil liberty, religious freedom, and economic opportunity. Soon the colony was the most prosperous in America, attracting settlers from other colonies and abroad.

Penn stayed in America only two years, from 1682 to 1684, and returned in 1699 for another two years. When he first arrived, his representatives were laying out the city of Philadelphia, and shortly after his arrival he executed a "treaty of purchase and amity" with the Indians. On his second visit, Penn established a legislature and guaranteed freedom of worship to those believing in "One almighty God."

Pennsylvania began to industrialize early. Iron ore was discovered in 1684, and the first forge was built in 1716; there were fifty forges and furnaces in the colony by the eve of the revolution. By then the colonies, led by Pennsylvania, were producing one seventh of the world's iron.

As problems with England increased, the Continental Congress met in Philadelphia in 1774. The state's delegation only narrowly approved the Declaration of Independence. Much of the will to fight for independence came from the feisty Scotch-Irish frontiersmen. The Quakers opposed bearing arms, and a majority of the Pennsylvania Germans were either loyalists, pacifists, or too isolated on their farms to care about the issues.

Congress left Philadelphia for Lancaster on September 18, 1777, as General Howe approached the city. Washington had failed to halt Howe at the Battle of the Brandywine on September 11, and on September 20 the British killed 300 Americans in a surprise bayonet attack on the camp at Paoli. Two weeks later, Washington's daring attack on the British at Germantown failed, but his audacity and planning helped bring France into the War. In July 1778 a raid by loyalists and Indians tortured and killed settlers defending the town of Forth Fort in the Wyoming Valley, an incident known as the "Wyoming Massacre."

After the Revolution, the state was plagued by border disputes. Connecticut claimed the Wyoming Valley on the Susquehanna River because its settlers had moved there in 1854. The claim was settled in 1782 after some blood was shed. In 1782 a quarrel with Virginia over southwestern Pennsylvania was resolved by both states agreeing to the Mason-Dixon line as a common border. In 1789 New York accepted the forty-second parallel as its boundary.

Pennsylvania's present outline was not set until 1788, when it purchased the Erie Triangle (and acquired a port on Lake Erie) for seventy-five cents an acre.

ALLENTOWN

Liberty Bell Shrine (622 Hamilton at Church St.; 610/435-4232). In the basement of the Zion church is a shrine where the Liberty Bell was hidden in 1777. There is a full-size replica of the original bell, and a mural depicts the journey of the bell. Exhibits. Open Monday through Saturday afternoons.

Trout Hall (414 Walnut St.; 610/435-4664). This restored 1770 Georgian is the oldest house in the city. Period room,

museum, tours. Open Tuesday through Sunday afternoons.

George Taylor House and Park (4 miles north off U.S. 22, at Front and Poplar streets in Catasauqua; 610/435-4664). A signer of the Declaration of Independence lived in this 1768 house, which has period rooms, a museum, and a walled garden. Tours available weekend afternoons, June through October.

Troxell-Steckel House and Farm Museum (6 miles north on PA 145, then 1 mile west on PA 329 at 4229 Reliance St. in Egypt; 610/435-4664). A 1756 stone house of German medieval architecture. Period rooms, museum, Swiss-style bank barn. Tours available weekend afternoons, June through October.

The public reading of the Declaration at Independence Hall in Philadelphia. Courtesy Library of Congress, Prints and Photographs Division.

ALTOONA

Baker Mansion Museum (3500 Oak Lane; 814/942-3916). A circa-1844 Greek Revival home of an early ironmaster, featuring hand-carved Belgian furniture and a gun collection. Open daily except Mondays, mid-April through Memorial Day; Saturdays and Sundays, Labor Day through October.

Fort Roberdeau (8 miles northeast via U.S. 220; 814/946-0048). A reconstructed Revolutionary War log fort contains a smelter, a blacksmith shop, a lead miner's hut, barracks, a storehouse, officers' quarters, and an ammunition magazine. Costumed guides, reenactments, picnicking, visitor center. Open daily except Mondays, mid-May through Labor Day.

AMBRIDGE

Old Economy Village (14th and Church streets; 412-266-4500). A six-acre restoration has seventeen original Harmony Society buildings filled with furnishings of the commune. On the site are the leader's thirty-two-room Great House, Feast Hall, Grotto in the Gardens. Cobblestone streets. Open daily except Mondays.

BEDFORD

Fort Bedford Park and Museum (Fort Bedford Dr., north end of Juliana St.; 814/623-8891). A large-scale replica of the original fort, with antiques, Indian artifacts. Open daily, May through late October.

Old Bedford Village (1 mile north on U.S. Business 220N; 814/623-1156). More than forty 1750–1851 log and frame structures, and an operating pioneer farm. Crafts demonstrations. Open daily, May through October and the first two weekends in December.

Bedford County Courthouse (South Juliana St.; 814/623-4807). A unique spiral staircase in an 1828 Federal-style building. Open weekdays.

BELLEFONTE

Curtin Village (2 miles north on PA 150 at I-80 exit 23; 814/355-1982). A restored 1831 mansion built by industrialist Roland Curtin. Iron furnace, worker's cabin, garden. Open Wednesday through Sunday, Memorial Day through Labor Day, weekends Labor Day to mid-October.

BETHLEHEM

Moravian Museum (Gemeinhaus) (66 West Church St.; 610/867-0173). This 1741 five-story log building has exhibits on the history and culture of the city and the Moravians. Costumed docents conduct walking tours of the city. Open Tuesday through Saturday except January and holidays. Some sites can be visited only on the tour. The *Old Chapel* was once called the "Indian chapel" because so many natives attended the services; this 1751 stone church is still in use. The *Central Moravian Church* is considered the foremost Moravian church in the country. *God's Acre* (Market St.) is an old Moravian cemetery following the tradition that all gravestones are laid flat, indicating that all souls are equal in the sight of God.

Brethren's House (Church and Main streets; 610/861-3916). Residence and shop area for single men of the Moravian community. Built in 1748 and used as a hospital in the Revolution, now part of Moravian College. Open daily.

Historic Bethlehem Inc.'s 18th-century Industrial Quarter (Ohio Rd. and Main St.; 610/691-5300). Tours are given Tuesday through Sunday afternoons. Stops include a

These are the times that try men's souls. The summer soldier and the sunshine patriot will shrink from the service of his country. . . . Tyranny, like Hell, is not easily conquered.

—THOMAS PAINE,
THE CRISIS, 1781

springhouse (1764), a waterworks (1762), a tannery (1761), the Luckenbach Mill (1869), and the Goudie House (1810).

Accommodations: *Wydnor Hall* (3612 Old Philadelphia Pike; 610/867-6851). This 1810 Georgian fieldstone mansion is convenient to the historic district and offers five guest rooms. Meticulously restored, the house has English decor, full breakfast, afternoon tea. Moderate.

BIRD-IN-HAND

Amish Village (1 mile west on PA 340, then 3 miles south on PA 896; 717/687-8511). Original and reconstructed buildings include a blacksmith shop, a schoolhouse, and an operating smokehouse. Tours are given of an Amish farmhouse. Open daily, mid-March through December.

Folk Craft Center and Museum (1½ miles west on PA 340, then north on Mt. Sidney Rd. in Witmer; 717/397-3609). An early-18th-century building displays tools, stoneware pottery, Stiegel glass, toys, quilts, coverlets, and early Pennsylvania Dutch memorabilia. Log cabin loom house, gardens, woodworking and print shops, audiovisual presentation. Open daily, April through November.

BRADFORD

Crook Farm (on Seaward Ave. extension near the Tuna Crossroads; 814/362-3906). The original 1848 home of Erastus and Betsy Crook. On the grounds are an old barn, a one-room schoolhouse, and a carpenter shop. Open Tuesday through Friday afternoons, May through September.

BRISTOL

Pennsbury Manor (5 miles northeast on Pennsbury Memorial Rd. off Bordentown Rd.; 215/946-0400). A reconstruction of William Penn's 17th-century country manor, with formal and kitchen gardens, craft demonstrations. Open daily except Mondays.

Historic Fallsington (4 Yardley Ave., Fallsington, 5 miles north of PA Tpke., off PA 13; 215/295-6567). Restored 17th-to-19th-century buildings include a log house, a schoolmaster's house, the Burges-Lippincott house, a tavern, and a museum store. Self-guided tour. Open daily, May through October.

CARLISLE

Carlisle Barracks (1 mile north on U.S. 11; 717/245-3611). The complex includes the Hessian Powder Magazine, built in 1777 by prisoners captured at the Battle of Trenton. Museum open weekends, May through September. Grounds open daily.

Grave of "Molly Pitcher" (Old Graveyard, East South St.). Soldiers in the Battle of Monmouth gave Mary Ludwig Hays McCauley her nickname because she showed devotion to her husband and other soldiers, and to the Revolutionary cause, by bringing them pitchers of water. When her husband was wounded, Molly allegedly took his place at a cannon and continued fighting for him.

CHESTER

Penn Memorial Landing Stone (Front and Penn streets). This memorial marks the spot where William Penn landed on October 28, 1682.

Caleb Pussy Home, Landingford Plantation (2 miles west at 15 Race St. in Upland; 610/874-5665). Built in 1683 for the manager and agent of Penn's mill, this is the only house remaining in the state visited by

The Bethlehem Gemeinhaus, a National Historic Landmark.

Penn. Period furniture. Also on the twenty-seven acres of the original plantation are a 1790 log house, an 1849 stone schoolhouse-museum, and an herb garden. Open weekend afternoons, May through September.

CORNWALL

Cornwall Iron Furnace (Rexmont Rd. at Boyd St.; 717/272-9711). The furnace was in operation from 1742 to 1883. This site includes an open-pit mine and a miners' village. The furnace building houses a "great wheel" and a 19th-century steam engine. Exhibits, bookstore. Open daily except Mondays.

Historic Schaefferstown (6 miles southeast of Lebanon at jct. of PA 419, 501, and 897; 717/949-3235). Swiss-German settlers established this farm in the 1700s. The village square has log-and-stone and half-timber buildings. It is the site of the first waterworks in the country (1758), still in operation. The museum has a Swiss bank house and barn. Colonial farm garden. Open by appointment, June through September.

DANVILLE

Joseph Priestley House (southwest via U.S. 11, at 472 Priestley St. in Northumberland; 717/473-9474). The 1794 house of the 18th-century English chemist and Unitarian theologian who, in 1774, was the first to isolate the element oxygen. Phone for schedule.

EBENSBURG

Allegheny Portage Railroad National Historic Site (12 miles east on U.S. 22; 814/886-6150). The vestiges of a railroad built in 1831–34 to link the eastern and western divisions of the Pennsylvania Mainline Canal. Cars were pulled up ten inclined planes by ropes powered by steam engines. Horses or locomotives then pulled the cars over the level stretches of the thirty-six-mile route across the Alleghenies. The *Skew Arch Bridge,* an engine house exhibit, and the *Lemon House,* a historic tavern, tell the story of the railroad. The visitor center shows a film. Rangers' programs daily in the summer. Open daily.

EPHRATA

Ephrata Cloister (632 West Main St.; 717/733-6600). In 1732, Conrad Beissel, a German Seventh-Day Baptist, began to lead a hermit's life here. Within a few years he established a religious community of recluses, with a Brotherhood, a Sisterhood, and a group of married "householders." They dressed in concealing white habits, and the buildings (1735–49) were simple and unadorned. Their religious zeal and charity proved to be their undoing. After the Battle of Brandywine, the cloistered community nursed the sick and wounded American soldiers, but its members contracted

typhus, which decimated them. The society was not formally dissolved, however, until 1934. Surviving and restored buildings include the Sisters House, Chapel, Almony, and eight others. Craft demonstrations in summer. Open daily.

Accommodations: *Smithton Inn* (900 West Main St.; 717/733-6094). Opened in 1763 as an inn and tavern on a hill overlooking the Ephrata Cloister, today it has sixteen rooms, eight of which have private bath, canopy or four-poster beds, fireplaces, and a nightshirt provided for each guest. Feather bed on request. Full breakfast. Inexpensive to moderate.

ERIE

On the shore of Presque Isle Bay, Commodore Oliver Hazard Perry built his fleet, floated the ships across the sandbars, and fought the British in the 1813 Battle of Lake Erie.

Wayne Memorial Blockhouse (560 East 3rd St.; 814/871-4531). A replica of the blockhouse in which General "Mad Anthony" Wayne died on December 15, 1796, after becoming ill on a voyage from Detroit. Open daily, Memorial Day through Labor Day.

FORT WASHINGTON

Hope Lodge (1 mile south on Old Bethlehem Pike; 215/646-1595). A 1745 Georgian mansion, headquarters of General John Cochran after the Battle of Germantown. Paintings, period furnishings. Open daily except Mondays.

The Highlands (7001 Sheaf Lane; 215/641-2687). A 1776 Georgian mansion on forty-three acres, built by Anthony Morris, active in government. Formal garden, tours by appointment. Open Monday through Friday.

GREENSBURG

Bushy Run Battlefield (northwest on PA 993; 412/527-5584). Colonel Henry Bouquet defeated united Indian forces here during Pontiac's War on August 5–6, 1763. The battle lifted the siege of Fort Pitt and was the turning point of the war. Picnicking, visitor center. Open daily except Mondays.

Historic Hanna's Town (3 miles northeast via U.S. 119; 412/836-1800). Costumed guides tell the story of the first courthouse west of the Alleghenies. Reconstructed courthouse, tavern, jail, and stockaded fort. Picnicking. Open daily except Mondays, June through August; weekends, May, September, and October.

HARMONY

Harmony Museum (218 Mercer St.; 412/452-7341). In an 1809 building, exhibits depict early life under Harmonists and Mennonites. The Harmony Society was one of the country's most successful experiments in communal living. Tours available. Open Tuesday through Sunday afternoons, June through September. Monday, Wednesday, Friday, and Sunday afternoons, the rest of the year.

HARRISBURG

Fort Hunter Park (6 miles north on North Front St.). On thirty-seven acres is the site of a fort built by the English in 1754, prior to the French and Indian War. The Pennsylvania Canal runs through the park. Some old buildings are open, others are being restored. In the park is the *Fort Hunter Mansion*

(717/599-5751), a Federal stone dwelling built in sections between 1786 and 1814. Period furnishings, toys, clothing, artifacts. Tours available. Open daily except Mondays, May through December.

John Harris Mansion (219 South Front St.; 717/233-3462). The stone home of the city's founder has 19th-century furnishings and artifacts. Tours available. Open weekdays and the second Sunday of each month.

Accommodations: *Kenaga House* (9 miles west on Rte. 11/Carlisle Pike in New Kingstown; 717/697-2714). Built in 1775, this three-story German-style stone house was the home of Joseph Junkin, whose son commanded the American forces in the Battle of the Brandywine. Six guest rooms, five with private bath. Inexpensive.

HAZLETON

Eckley Miners' Village (10 miles northeast on PA 940, near Freeland; 717/636-2070). At the Pennsylvania Anthracite Museum Complex, a coal-patch town of the 1850s portrays life in the mines. Tours available. Open daily except Mondays, Memorial Day through Labor Day.

Hopewell Furnace National Historic Site (15 miles southeast via U.S. 422, PA 82

SHADES OF BLUE

Wealthy colonists imported their clothes from Europe, but the rest either made their own or bought the local product. Flax, from which linen is produced, grew well in America, and American sheep produced good wool. Linen and wool, usually dyed with indigo in various shades of blue, were the most popular materials for clothing, and weaving became an important cottage industry. By 1770, one town, Lancaster, Pennsylvania, was weaving 70,000 yards of cloth a year. A woman working full-time was expected to produce about six yards a day.

to Birdsboro, then southeast on PA 345, 10 miles northeast of PA Tpk., Morgantown Interchange; 610/582-8773). Hopewell grew up around a cold-blast furnace that made pig iron from 1771 to 1883. Nearby mines and forests supplied ore and charcoal for the furnace. Park Service guides interpret the community's role in the country's industrial history. The visitor center has a museum and an audiovisual program. A self-guided tour includes a charcoal house, an anthracite furnace ruin, waterwheel and blast machinery, a casting house, a furnace, a blacksmith shop, tenant houses, and an ironmaster's house. Open daily.

KENNETT SQUARE

Brandywine Battlefield (2 miles west of jct. of U.S. 1 and 202, near Chadds Ford; 610-459-3342). The site of the 1777 battle includes Washington's headquarters and Lafayette's quarters. Visitor center, tours, museum shop, picnicking. Open daily except Mondays.

John Chadds House (7 miles northeast via U.S. 1, then $\frac{1}{4}$ mile north on PA 100, in Chadds Ford; 610/388-7376). An excellent example of early-18th-century Pennsylvania architecture. House museum, costumed guides, baking demonstration in beehive oven. Open weekends, May through September.

Barns-Brinton House ($5\frac{1}{2}$ miles northeast on U.S. 1 in Chadds Ford; 610/388-7376). A restored 1714 tavern, furnished in the style of the period. Tours by costumed guides. Domestic arts demonstrations. Open weekends, June through August.

KING OF PRUSSIA

Mill Grove (5 miles northwest via U.S. 422 and Audubon Rd., north of Valley Forge

NHP; 610/666-5593). A 175-acre wildlife sanctuary, developed around the 1762 house that was the first American home of John James Audubon. A museum has Audubon prints, including a complete "Elephant Folio." Open Tuesday through Saturday, and Sunday afternoons.

Harriton House (6 miles southeast via Old Gulf Rd. to Harriton Rd.; 610/525-0201). The 1704 estate of Charles Thomson, Secretary of the Continental Congresses. Restored in the style of the period. Nature park on $16\frac{1}{2}$ acres. Open Wednesday through Saturday.

LANCASTER

When Congress, fleeing Philadelphia, paused here on September 27, 1777, the city was the national capital for a day.

Fulton Opera House (12 North Prince St.; 717/397-7425). Built in 1852, this is one of the oldest American theaters. Ghosts are believed to haunt the Victorian interior, which houses a professional regional theater. Concerts.

Wheatland (1120 Marietta Ave., $1\frac{1}{2}$ miles west on PA 23; 717/392-8721). This 1828 Federal mansion was the home of President James Buchanan from 1848 to 1868. Period rooms, tours by costumed guides. Open daily, April through November.

Landis Valley Museum (2451 Kissel Hill Rd., $1\frac{1}{2}$ miles west on PA 272; 717/569-0401). A large collection of Pennsylvania German (Dutch) objects. Craft and living-history demonstrations. Exhibit buildings include a farmstead, a tavern, and a country store. Open daily except Mondays.

Hans Herr House (1849 Hans Herr Dr.; 717/464-4438). A 1719 example of medieval German architecture, which served as an early Mennonite meetinghouse and the Colonial home of the Herr family. Exhibits, blacksmith shop, tours. Open daily except Mondays.

Heritage Center of Lancaster County (Penn Sq.; 717/299-6440). A 1795 building houses examples of early Lancaster arts and crafts. Furniture, tall clocks, quilts, needlework, fraktur, silver, pewter, and rifles. Open Tuesday through Saturday, May to mid-November; Friday through Sunday, mid-November to mid-December.

Historic Rock Ford (3 miles south on Rock Ford Rd., south of Duke St. at Lancaster County Park; 717/392-7223). The preserved 1794 home of General Edward Hand, Revolutionary War commander and member of the Continental Congress, includes the *Kauffman Museum,* which has a collection of antiques, folk arts, and crafts. Open daily except Mondays, April through October.

Mill Bridge Village (South Ronks Rd., 4 miles east of jct. of U.S. 30E, PA 462 in Strasburg; 717/687-6521). A historic Colonial mill village restored with an operating water-powered 1738 gristmill, a covered bridge, country crafts, and an Amish kitchen exhibit. Village open daily, early April through October; weekends, November and December.

Watch and Clock Museum (12 miles west via U.S. 30, at 514 Poplar St. in Columbia; 717-687-8976). More than 8,000 timepieces dating from the late 1600s. Open Tuesday through Saturday, and Sunday afternoons, May through September.

Robert Fulton Birthplace (14 miles south via PA 222; 717/684-8261). The man who built the first steamboat, in 1807, was born in this little stone house. Open weekends, Memorial Day through Labor Day.

Historic Lancaster Walking Tour (100 South Queen St.; 717/392-1776). Costumed guides lead a nine-block tour of fifty sites of architectural or historic interest, April through October. Phone for schedule.

Accommodations: *Witmer's Tavern* (2014 Old Philadelphia Pike; 717/299-5305). This 1725 inn is the sole survivor of sixty-two inns that once lined the old Lancaster-to-Philadelphia turnpike. President John Adams once stayed here. The inn has been restored to its original, simple pioneer style. The seven guest rooms (five with shared bath) feature antiques, old quilts, and fresh flowers. Breakfast. Inexpensive.

LEBANON

Stoy Museum (924 Cumberland St.; 717/272-1473). A 1773 building, once the county's first courthouse, contains the local historical museum and thirty room and shop displays on three floors. Tours available. Open daily except Saturdays.

Fort Zeller (11 miles east on U.S. 422, then south on PA 419, in Newmanstown; 610/589-4301). One of the state's oldest existing forts, rebuilt of stone in 1745. The house has a twelve-foot Queen Anne fireplace. Open by appointment.

LEWISBURG

Fort Augusta (9 miles southeast on PA 147, in Sunbury, at 1150 North Front St.; 717/286-4053). A museum collection of county memorabilia and artifacts housed in a 1757 fort. Open Mondays, Wednesdays, and Saturdays.

Packwood House Museum (15 North Water St.; 717/524-0323). A twenty-seven-room late-18th-century log and frame building, once used as a hostelry, has a collection of period furnishings, decorative arts, and Americana. Museum shop, tours. Open daily except Mondays.

LIGONIER

Fort Ligonier (South Market St. on U.S. 30;

Washington crossing the Delaware. Courtesy Library of Congress, Prints and Photographs Division.

412/238-9701). Built in 1758 by the British, this was the scene of a decisive battle in the French and Indian Wars. The reconstructed fort has period furnishings and an orientation film. Open daily, May through October.

Compass Inn Museum (3 miles east on U.S. 30, in Laughlintown; 412/238-4983). A restored 1799 stagecoach stop, of log and stone construction. Cookhouse, blacksmith shop with working forge. Open daily, May through October.

MEADVILLE

Baldwin-Reynolds House Museum (639 Terrace St.; 814/724-6080). The restored 1841 mansion of Henry Baldwin, congressman and U.S. Supreme Court justice. Period furnishings. The third-floor museum has medical, dental, Indian, and military artifacts.

Open Wednesdays and weekends, Memorial Day through Labor Day.

MEDIA

Colonial Pennsylvania Plantation (South on U.S. 1, then north on PA 352 in Ridley Creek State Park; 610/566-1725). A late-18th-century farm is a living-history museum. Period methods and tools are used to perform chores. Open weekends, mid-April through November.

MERCER

Magoffin House Museum (119 South Pitt St.; 412/662-3490). An 1821 house museum with period furniture, tools, toys, clothing, military items, memorabilia, and a restored print shop. Open Tuesday through Saturday.

NEW HOPE

Washington Crossing Historical Park (two sections: Bowman's Hill, 2 miles south on PA 32; and Washington Crossing, 7 miles south on PA 32; 215/493-4076). In a blinding snowstorm on Christmas night, 1776, Washington and 2,400 soldiers crossed the Delaware River and marched to Trenton, surprising the celebrating Hessian mercenaries and capturing the city. The feat was a turning point in the war. At Bowman's Hill, the *Memorial Flagstaff* marks the grave of unknown Continentals. At Washington Crossing, a granite shaft supporting a statue of Washington marks the *Area of Embarkation.* The troops were assembled for the crossing in *Concentration Valley.* Near the *Point of Embarkation,* the *Memorial Building* houses a copy of Emanuel Leutze's painting, *Washington Crossing the Delaware.* The *McConkey Ferry Inn* (1752) has been restored. Both areas are open daily.

Parry Mansion Museum (South Main and Ferry streets; 215/862-5652). A restored 1784 stone house, built by Benjamin Parry, merchant and mill owner. Eleven rooms on view, restored with period furnishings. Open Friday through Sunday, May through October.

Quarry Valley Farm (west on U.S. 202 to Lahaska, at 2302 Street Rd.; 215/794-5882). A farmhouse built in the late 1700s, with a museum of vintage farm equipment, a petting zoo, and pony rides. Open daily.

Accommodations: *Hollyhedge* (6987 Upper York Rd.; 215/862-3136). A 1730 stone manor, furnished with antiques, on twenty acres with a stream and pond. Some of the rooms have private entrances and fireplaces. The innkeepers are former restaurateurs, and the breakfast is notable. Inexpensive to expensive.

NORRISTOWN

Peter Wentz Farmstead (10 miles northwest via U.S. 202, west via PA 73 on Shearer Rd. in Worcester; 610/584-5104). A restored 18th-century country mansion, twice used by Washington during the Pennsylvania campaign. More than seventy acres with demonstration crops of the period. Costumed interpreters, a reconstruction of a 1744 barn with animals. Open daily except Mondays and the second week in September.

ORBISONIA

East Broad Top Railroad (on U.S. 522; 814/447-3011). The oldest surviving narrow-gauge railroad east of the Rocky Mountains. Rides, old equipment and buildings, picnicking. Open weekends, June through October.

Rockhill Trolley Museum (½ mile west off U.S. 522, on PA 994, in Rockhill Furnace; 814/447-9576). Vintage trolleys, car barn, and restoration shop. A two-mile ride on the Shade Gap Electric Railway. Gift shop, tours. Open weekends, Memorial Day through October.

PHILADELPHIA

The first Quakers, who came here in 1681, lived in caves dug into the banks of the Delaware River. By the second year, William Penn's "greene countrie towne" was a city of 600 buildings. The Quakers prospered, and Philadelphia became the leading port in the colonies. Like Boston, the city resented the excesses of the British. In May 1774, 8,000 people rallied to frighten off a British tea ship. The first and second Continental Congresses met here, and Philadelphia became the headquarters of the Revolution. After the

SOCIETY CARPENTERS

Colonists stressed the dignity of labor, and "mechanicks," as people who made things with their hands were called, were essential and enjoyed a higher standing in the colonies than in Europe. In America, craftsmen could be found at every level of society, from the wealthy to the slaves. In Philadelphia, craftsmen (particularly Quakers) often had a high social rank. Members of the Carpenters' Company included some of the leading figures in the city's society. Many early craftsmen, after succeeding as builders, silversmiths, or makers of furniture, became merchants and entered society.

Declaration of Independence was accepted by Congress, the city gave its men, factories, and shipyards to the cause. General Sir William Howe, with 18,000 soldiers, came here on September 26, 1777, and spent a comfortable winter while Washington's troops endured the cold at Valley Forge. When the British evacuated the city, Congress returned. Philadelphia was the seat of government until 1800, except for a brief period when New York City had that honor. The Constitution was written here, and President George Washington governed here.

Independence National Historical Park (Visitor Center, 3rd and Chestnut streets; 215/597-8974). This is "America's most historic square mile." The visitor center has a tour map, a thirty-minute film titled "Independence," and exhibits with interactive computers. The emphasis is on the meaning of the Constitution, how it endured, and its relevance to modern America. Unless noted, all buildings are open daily.

Declaration House (701 Market St.) is a reconstructed house on the site of the writing of the Declaration of Independence by Thomas Jefferson. There is a film about Jefferson and his philosophy on the common man, and on the history of the house.

Liberty Bell Pavilion (Independence Mall) displays the Liberty Bell, created to commemorate the fiftieth anniversary of the

Charter of Privileges, granted by William Penn to his colony in 1701. The bell bears the inscription, "Proclaim liberty throughout all the land unto all the inhabitants thereof." It was rung on the first reading of the Declaration of Independence on July 8, 1776, and was last rung on Washington's Birthday in 1846.

Independence Hall (Chestnut St. between 5th and 6th streets). The site of the adoption of the Declaration of Independence. First used as the Pennsylvania State House, it housed the Second Continental Congress in 1775–83, and the Constitutional Convention in 1787 when the Constitution was written. Admission by tour only. *Congress Hall* (beside Independence Hall) was used by Congress during the 1890s. House of Representatives and Senate chambers are restored. On the other side of Independence Hall is *Old City Hall.* Built in 1789, this was the first home of the U.S. Supreme Court (1791–1800).

Philosophical Hall (5th St. side of Independence Sq.). Benjamin Franklin founded the American Philosophical Society in 1743, the oldest learned society in America. Not open to the public.

Library Hall (5th and Library streets). A reconstruction of the Library Company of Philadelphia (1789–80) building, now occupied by the library of the American

Independence Hall in Philadelphia.

Philosophical Society. Open to scholars only.

The Second Bank of the United States (420 Chestnut St). This 1824 building also was used as the U.S. Custom House, 1824–41. It now contains the park's Portrait Gallery.

Franklin Court (between Market and Chestnut, 3rd and 4th streets.). The site of Franklin's house has been developed as a tribute to him. It includes a working printing office and bindery, and underground museum with multimedia exhibits, archaeological exhibits, and the B. Free Franklin Post Office.

Carpenters' Hall (320 Chestnut St.). Built in 1770, this was the meeting site of the first Continental Congress in 1774. It has been a historical museum since 1857. Original chairs, exhibits of early tools. Open daily except Mondays year-round.

New Hall (4th and Chestnut streets). A reconstruction housing the U.S. Marine Corps Memorial Museum. Also in Carpenters' Court is *Pemberton House,* a reconstruction of a Quaker's house, housing the Army-Navy Museum.

The First Bank of the United States (3rd St. between Walnut and Chestnut streets). The oldest bank building in the country (1797–1811), it housed a bank organized by Alexander Hamilton. Closed to the public.

Bishop White House (309 Walnut St.). Built in 1786, this was the home of the first Episcopal bishop of Pennsylvania. Restored and furnished in the style of the period. *Todd House* (4th and Walnut streets). The 1775 house of Dolley Payne Todd, who married James Madison and became First Lady. Tickets for an hour-long tour of the two houses are available at the visitor center. The tour is given daily, year-round.

The Merchants Exchange (3rd and Walnut streets). One of the finest examples of Greek Revival architecture in the country. Closed to the public.

City Tavern (2nd and Walnut streets). John Adams called this the "most genteel tavern in America." Now rebuilt as an operating Colonial tavern. Reservations: 215/923-6059.

Thaddeus Kosciuszko National Memorial (3rd and Pine streets). The Polish patriot lived here during his second visit to the United States, 1797–98. Kosciuszko was one of the greatest champions of American and Polish freedom and one of the first volunteers to come to the aid of the Revolutionary Army. Exterior and second-floor bedroom restored.

Edgar Allan Poe National Historic Site (532 North 7th St.; 215/597-8780). Poe lived here before his move to New York in 1844. Exhibits and slide show, tours. Open daily.

Betsy Ross House (239 Arch St.; 215/627-5343). The famous seamstress reputedly made the first American flag here. Open daily except Mondays.

Elfreth's Alley (off 2nd St. between Arch and Race streets; 215/627-5343). The oldest continuously residential street in America, with thirty houses dating from 1728 to 1836. Open daily except Mondays.

Society Hill Area (bounded by Front, Walnut, 7th, and Lombard streets). This historic area, named after the Free Society of Traders, was created by William Penn as the city's original land company. *"A Man Full of Trouble" Tavern Museum* (127–129 Spruce St.; 215/922-1759). This 1757 tavern now houses a private collection of 17th- and 18th-century furnishings, silver and porcelain, and English delftware. Costumed guides. Open the second Sunday afternoon every month. *Powel House* (244 South 3rd St.; 215/627-0364). This 1765 Georgian was the town house of Samuel Powel, the last Colonial mayor and the first mayor under the new Republic. Period furnishings, silver, and porcelain. Garden. *Physick House* (321

South 4th St.; 215/925-7866). The restored 1786 Federal mansion of Dr. Philip Syng Physick, "father of American surgery," from 1815 to 1837. Period furnishings, garden. Open daily except holidays. *Athenaeum of Philadelphia* (219 South 6th St.; 215/925-2688). A landmark example of Italian Renaissance architecture, built circa 1845. Neoclassical decorative arts, paintings, sculpture. Furniture and art from the collection of Joseph Bonaparte, king of Spain and brother of Napoleon. Open weekdays.

Washington Square (Walnut and 6th streets). Hundreds of Revolutionary War soldiers and victims of the yellow fever epidemic of 1793 are buried in unmarked graves here. A life-size statue of Washington stands at the tomb of the Revolution's Unknown Soldier.

Walnut Street Theatre (9th and Walnut streets; 215/574-3550). The country's oldest theater, built in 1809, is still in use.

Pennsylvania Hospital (8th and Spruce streets; 215/829-3000). America's first hospital, founded by Benjamin Franklin in 1751.

Germantown. *Deshler-Morris House* (5442 Germantown Ave.; 215/596-1748). George Washington lived in this 1772 house in the summers of 1793–94. Period furnishings, garden. Open daily except Mondays, April through November. *Stenton House* (18th St. between Courtland and Windrim; 215/329-7312). A mansion built by James Logan, secretary to William Penn. Washington spent August 13, 1777, here. General Howe headquartered here for the Battle of Germantown. Barn, gardens. Open Tuesday through Saturday afternoons, April through December. *Clivedon* (6401 Germantown Ave.; 215/848-1777). A stone 1767 Georgian of individual design, built as the summer home of Benjamin Chew, chief justice of Colonial Pennsylvania. British soldiers used the house as a fortress on October 4, 1777, to repulse Washington's

COLONIAL CITIES

The few cities in Colonial America were located along the coast, and all had deep-water harbors, which were essential for trade with Europe. By 1740, Boston, with 17,000 people, was the largest, but its location, on a narrow spit of land, limited its growth and by 1760 New York had 18,000 people and Philadelphia had 24,000. Colonial cities had problems. Fresh water was scarce, there was no organized garbage removal, sanitation was primitive, and fire was a constant threat to life and property.

attempt to recapture Philadelphia. A National Trust property. Open daily, April through December.

Fort Mifflin (Island Ave. from the airport toward the river, follow brown-and-white signs; 215/492-3395). The site of a seven-week siege during the Revolution, the fort served as a military installation until 1959. Tours available. Open Wednesday through Sunday, April through November.

Historic Bartram's Gardens (54th St. and Lindbergh Blvd.; 215/729-5281). Home of John Bartram, naturalist and plant explorer, the royal botanist to the colonies under George II, this is an 18th-century stone farmhouse, stable, and cider mill. Museum shop. Open Wednesday through Sunday afternoons, May through October; Wednesday through Friday afternoons the rest of the year.

Colonial Mansions in Fairmount Park (guided tours from Park Houses: 215/787-5449). Eighteenth-century houses in various architectural styles, authentically preserved and furnished, include the 1761 *Mount Pleasant* (open daily except Mondays), the 1756 *Cedar Grove* (open daily except Mondays), 1797 *Strawberry Mansion* (open daily except Mondays), the 1797 *Sweetbrier*

Cliveden in Germantown.

(open daily except Tuesdays), *Lemon Hill* (Wednesday through Sunday), the 1756 *Woodford* (open daily except Mondays), and the 1760 *Laurel Hill* (open Wednesday through Sunday).

Gloria Dei Church ("Old Swedes") **National Historic Site** (Columbus Blvd. and Christian St.; 215/389-1513). Built in 1700, this is the oldest house in the state, a memorial to John Hanson, President of the United States under the Articles of Confederation. Open daily.

St. George's United Methodist Church (235 North 4th St.; 215/925-7788). The oldest (1789) Methodist church in continuous service in the country. Its collection of Methodist memorabilia includes the only Bishop Asbury Bible and John Wesley Chalice Cup in America.

Burial Ground of the Congregation **Mikveh Israel** (Spruce and 8th streets). Graves of Haym Salomon, Revolutionary financier, and Rebecca Gatz, probable model for "Rebecca" in Sir Walter Scott's *Ivanhoe*.

Old Pine Street Presbyterian Church (412 Pine St.; 215/925-8051). A 1768 church and graveyard, renovated in the 1850s in Greek Revival style.

St. Peter's Church (3rd and Pine streets; 215/925-5968). Many historic figures are buried in the churchyard of this 1761 Greek Revival Episcopal church.

Old St. Mary's Church (252 South 4th St.; 215/923-7930). Commodore John Barry, "father of the U.S. Navy," is buried in the graveyard behind the city's first Catholic cathedral.

Christ Church (2nd St. between Market and Arch streets; 215/922-1695). Benjamin Franklin, George Washington, and Betsy Ross all worshiped here. *Christ Church Burial Ground* (5th and Arch streets) has the grave of Franklin and his wife Deborah, and four signers of the Declaration of Independence.

Arch Street Friends Meetinghouse (4th and Arch streets; 215/627-2667). This 1804 structure may be the largest Friends meetinghouse in the world. Exhibits. Tours daily except Sundays.

Atwater Kent Museum—The History Museum of Philadelphia (15 South 7th St.; 215/922-3031). Artifacts, toys, miniatures, maps, prints, paintings, and photographs of the city's history. Open daily except Mondays.

Historical Society of Pennsylvania (1300 Locust St.; 215/732-6201). On exhibit, among 500 artifacts and manuscripts, is a first draft of the Constitution. Open Tuesday through Saturday.

Philadelphia Museum of Art (26th St. and Benjamin Franklin Pkwy.; 215/763-8100). The American wing includes rural Pennsylvania Dutch crafts, Shaker furniture, and paintings of early American artists, including Gilbert Stuart and Thomas Eakins. Tours available. Open Tuesday through Sunday, and Wednesday evenings.

Pennsylvania Academy of the Fine Arts (118 North Broad St.; 215/972-7600). The oldest art museum and art school in the country, with an outstanding collection of three centuries of American art. Tours available. Open daily except Mondays.

Philadelphia Carriage Company (500 North 13th St.; 215/922-6840). Tours in a horse-drawn carriage cover Society Hill and other historic areas. Daily tours begin and end in front of Independence Hall and the Liberty Bell Pavilion.

Centipede Tours (1315 Walnut St.; 215/735-3123). Candlelight strolls through historic areas, led by guides in 18th-century dress. Tours begin and end at City Tavern. Reservations preferred. Mid-May through mid-October.

Accommodations: *Thomas Bond House* (129 South 2nd St.; 215/923-8523 or 800/845-2663). This handsome 1769 Federal dwelling in Independence National Historic Park recently had a finely executed interior renovation. Twelve guest rooms. Chippendale reproductions, four-poster beds, drop-front desks, working fireplaces, full breakfast and afternoon tea. Moderate.

PITTSBURGH

Fort Pitt Museum (101 Commonwealth Pl.; 412/281-9284). Built on part of the original fort, the museum has exhibits on the fort and on early struggles between France and Britain for western Pennsylvania and the old Northwest Territory. Here also is the *Block House of Fort Pitt,* the last building of the original 1764 fort.

Historical Society of Western Pennsylvania (4338 Bigelow Blvd.; 412/681-5533). Local history exhibits, collection of decorative arts, gift shop. Open Tuesday through Saturday.

The snow lies thick on Valley Forge, The ice on Delaware But the poor dead soldiers of King George They neither know nor care.

—RUDYARD KIPLING, *"THE AMERICAN REBELLION"*

*Pottsgrove Manor in
Pottstown. Photo by
Bob Study.*

POTTSTOWN

Pottsgrove Manor (West King St. and PA 100; 610/326-4014). The restored 1752 Georgian house of John Potts, ironmaster and town founder. Includes recently discovered slave quarters and Potts's office. Period furnishings, audiovisual presentation, museum shop. Open daily except Mondays.

READING

Daniel Boone Homestead (7 miles east on U.S. 422 to Baumstown, then north on Boone Rd.; 610/582-4900). The birthplace of Boone in 1734, some 570 acres include the Boone House, barn, blacksmith shop,

and sawmill. Picnicking. Open daily except Mondays.

Conrad Weiser Homestead (14 miles west via U.S. 422; 610/589-2934). The restored 1729 home of the Colonial "ambassador" to the Iroquois. Picnicking in a twenty-six-acre park. Open Wednesday through Sunday.

SCRANTON

Steamtown National Historic Site (150 South Washington Ave.; 717/961-2033). A large collection of locomotives and other memorabilia of the age of steam. Train rides through the yard (daily, Memorial

Day through October), and twenty-five-mile train excursions (weekends, July through October).

STATE COLLEGE

Columbus Chapel-Boal Mansion Museum (4 miles east on U.S. 322, in Boalsburg; 814/466-6210). The mansion home of the Boal family since 1789. Original furnishings, china, tools, and weapons. The 16th-century chapel belonging to the family of Christopher Columbus was bought in Spain and brought here in 1909 by Boal relatives. The museum has an admiral's desk and explorer's cross that belonged to Columbus. Open daily except Tuesdays.

Accommodations: *The Vincent Douglas House* (490 Meckley Rd.; 814/237-4490). This 1834 brick farmhouse has four guest rooms. A stream on the property is often visited by deer and wild ducks. Full breakfast. Moderate.

TOWANDA

In 1793 the Asylum Company purchased a million acres here as a refuge for Marie Antoinette, should she escape to America. "La Grande Maison," a queenly house, was built, noblemen settled in the area, and a community was planned. Marie Antoinette was executed, the community failed, and most of the founders returned to France.

French Azilium (10 miles southeast via U.S. 6, PA 187; 717/265-3376). The site of a

The American Troops at Valley Forge. Courtesy Library of Congress, Prints and Photographs Division.

colony for refugees of the French Revolution. Five cabins with exhibits, log-cabin museum. The Laporte House, built in 1836 by the son of one of the colony's founders, reflects elegant French influence. Tours available. Open Wednesday through Sunday, September and October; weekends in May.

UNIONTOWN

Fort Necessity National Battlefield (11 miles southeast on U.S. 40; 412/329-5512). The site, in 1754, of Washington's first major battle and the opening battle of the French and Indian Wars. A portion of this land, known as the Great Meadows, was later purchased by Washington, who owned it all his life. A replica of the original fort was built on the site. *Mount Washington Tavern* has been restored as a historic stagecoach inn. A granite monument marks *Braddock's Grave,* where British general Edward Braddock, mortally wounded in battle with the French and Indians on July 9, 1755, is buried. Visitor center. Open daily.

VALLEY FORGE

Some of the darkest days of the Revolution were from December 19, 1777, to June 19, 1778, when the poorly supplied troops of Washington's army were encamped here. More than 2,000 of the 16,000 to 18,000 men died from illness and disease brought on by the freezing weather, lack of supplies, and poor sanitation.

Valley Forge National Historical Park (3 miles north of PA Tpk., interchange 24; 610/783-1077). The park is a 3,600-acre memorial to the trials and success of the brave soldiers who wintered here. A tour route takes the visitor to the primary encampment facilities. Other roads offer a beautiful drive and other historical features.

Bus and auto tours both start at the visitor center (jct. PA 23 and North Gulf Rd., just inside the park). Audiovisual program, exhibits. The sites include *Soldier Life Program Muhlenberg Brigade.* Interpreters present programs detailing camp life (daily in summer; weekends rest of year). *National Memorial Arch* was built in 1917 to commemorate Washington's army. Inscribed in the arch: "Naked and starving as they are, we cannot enough admire the incomparable patience and fidelity of the soldiery." At *Washington's Headquarters,* the general lived and made his headquarters for six months. *General Varnum's Quarters* was the farmhouse of David and Elizabeth Stephens, which quartered General James Varnum of Rhode Island. Period furnishings. The *Washington Memorial Chapel* (on PA 23; 610/783-0120) is on private property within the park. It has stained-glass windows that depict the story of the New World. Hand-carved oak choir stalls, Pews of the Patriots, and Roof of the Republic bearing the seals of all the states. Washington Memorial National Carillon. The *Museum of the Valley Forge Historical Society* (610/783-0535), next door, has exhibits of relics of the winter encampment at Valley Forge. Open daily.

WASHINGTON

LeMoyne House (49 East Maiden St.; 412/225-6740). This abolitionist's home, built in 1812 by the LeMoyne family, was a stop on the Underground Railroad. Paintings, period furnishings, garden, museum shop. Open Wednesday through Friday, and Sunday afternoons, February through December.

David Bradford House (175 South Main St.; 412/222-3604). Restored 1788 frontier home of a leader of the Whiskey

Rebellion. Open Wednesday through Sunday, May through late October.

Meadowcroft Village (19 miles northwest via PA 18, 50 in Avella; 412/587-3412). Many wooden buildings dating from the 18th and 19th centuries, relocated and reconstructed, including general store, barn, log houses, schoolhouse, and blacksmith shop, all with exhibits. Open Wednesday through Sunday, May through October.

WEST CHESTER

Brinton 1704 House (5 miles south, just off U.S. 202, on Oakland Road in Dilworthtown; 302/478-2853). A stone house built by Quaker farmer William Brinton, restored and furnished in the style of the period. Open weekends, May through October.

WRIGHTSVILLE

Donegal Mills Plantation and Inn (5 miles north via U.S. 30, PA 441, 772 in Mount Joy; 717/653-2168). A historic village dating from 1736, with a mansion, bakehouse, and garden. Restaurant and lodging. Plantation tours weekend afternoons, March through December.

YORK

York has a claim to being the first capital of the United States. The Continental Congress met here in 1777 and adopted the Articles of Confederation, which used the phrase "United States of America" for the first time.

Historical Society of York County (250 East Market St.; 717/848-1587). The society maintains historic sites, including the 1750 *Gates House* (157 West Market St.), where Lafayette toasted Washington, marking the end of a movement to replace him as commander of the Continental Army. Two other houses are here, the *Golden Plough Tavern,* circa 1740, which reflects the Germanic background of many of the early settlers, and the circa-1810 *Bobb Log House.* All open daily.

10

DELAWARE

elaware started inauspiciously. Henry Hudson approached Delaware Bay on the *Half Moon* in August 1609, but did not enter because of dangerous shoals. The next year an English explorer, Samuel Argall, took refuge in the bay during a storm and named it in honor of the governor of Virginia, Baron De La Warre.

The first colonists, twenty-eight men sponsored by Dutch investors, landed in 1631 near what is now Lewes, and all but one of them were killed by Indians. In 1639 a group of Swedes established the first permanent settlement, Fort Christina, at a location now in the city of Wilmington. In 1651 the Dutch moved to claim the area by building Fort Casimir, at present-day New Castle. The Swedes drove out the Dutch, the Dutch returned and drove out the Swedes, and then the English took possession of the colony by capturing Fort Casimir.

Charles II, in 1664, granted his brother James, Duke of York, all the territory between the Delaware and Connecticut rivers. This did not include the Dutch holdings on the west bank of the Delaware but James took them anyway. The situation became even more confused in 1681, when King Charles granted the colony of Pennsylvania to William Penn, then ceded Delaware to Penn, as well. The Calverts, the proprietors of Maryland,

also claimed part of Delaware. Mason and Dixon surveyed the boundary in the 1760s, but the Maryland border was not set until 1776.

Except for a minor engagement near Newark, the Revolution passed Delaware by. However, the Delaware regiment in the Continental Army, called the "Blue Hens," distinguished itself. According to General Greene, they would "fight all day and dance all night." Delaware statesman John Dickinson, "penman of the Revolution," was instrumental in the decision to write a new document rather than simply patch up the Articles of Confederation.

Delaware's beginnings as a state date from 1704, when Pennsylvania allowed its three colonies to have their own legislature, but it did not actually become a separate political entity until it adopted a state constitution in 1776. Delaware became the "First State" when, on December 6, 1787, it was the first to adopt the Constitution.

DELAWARE CITY

Fort Delaware State Park (Pea Patch Island, across from the city; 302/834-7941. This grim fort was built for coastal defense in 1859, and used as a prisoner-of-war depot during the Civil War, housing up to 12,500 Con-

The State House in Dover. Photo by Lazlo Bodo, Delaware State Museums, Dover.

I rejoice that America has resisted. Three millions of people, so dead to all feelings of liberty, as voluntarily to submit to be slaves, would have been fit instruments to make slaves of the rest.

—LORD CHATHAM *(William Pitt the Elder), speech in the House of Commons, 1776*

federate prisoners at a time. A museum has Civil War relics, scale models of the fort. Picnicking. A boat trip to the island leaves from Delaware City Wednesday through Sunday, mid-June through August; weekends, late April through mid-June and in September.

DOVER

State House (Federal St. at The Green; 302/739-4266). Built in 1792 and restored in 1976, this is the second-oldest capital in continuous use in the country. Contains legislative chambers, governor's office, county office, courtroom. Open daily except Mondays.

Delaware State Museum (316 South Governors Ave.; 302/739-4266). A complex of three buildings: the 1790 Meetinghouse Gallery, with an archaeology exhibit; the 1880 Gallery, with a vintage drugstore, blacksmith shop, general store, post office, shoemaker's shop and printer's shop; and the Johnson Memorial, a tribute to Eldridge Reeves Johnson, founder of the Victor Talking Machine Company, which has a collection of Victrolas and early recordings. Open Tuesday through Saturday.

John Dickinson Plantation (6 miles southeast, near junction of U.S. 113 and DE 9 on Kitts Hummock Rd.; 302/739-3277). The restored 1740 boyhood residence of Dickinson, the "penman of the Revolution." Reconstructed farm complex open daily except Mondays, March through December; Tuesday through Saturday the rest of the year.

Dover Heritage Trail (302/678-2040). A guided walking tour of historic areas leaves from the State Visitor Center (The Green). By appointment.

LEWES

Zwaanendael Museum (Savannah Rd. and Kings Hwy.; 302/645-9418). A replica of the Hoorn (Holland) Town Hall was built in 1931 as a memorial to the Dutch who founded Lewes (***Loo***-is) in 1631. The museum highlights the town's maritime heritage with Indian, Dutch, and Colonial exhibits. Open daily except Mondays.

Restored buildings. The Lewes Historical Society maintains Cannon Ball House and the U.S. Lifesaving Station, both with marine exhibits, and the lightship *Overfalls*. Other buildings open are the Thompson country store, the Plank house, the Rabbit's Ferry house, the Burton-Ingram house, the Ellegood house, the Hiram R. Burton house, and the old doctor's office. Guided walking tours Tuesdays, Thursdays and Fridays, July to mid-September. Phone 302/645-7670 for details.

Accommodations: *New Devon Inn* (142 Second St.; 302/645-6466 or 800/824-8754). In the heart of the historic district, a half-mile from the shore, this inn has twenty-four individually decorated rooms with antique beds, full breakfast, afternoon tea, and evening snacks. Inexpensive to moderate.

NEW CASTLE

One of the first settlements, the meeting place of the colonial assemblies, the first capital of Delaware, New Castle was a busy port until it was overtaken by Wilmington and Philadelphia. Three signers of the Declaration of Independence lived here: George Read, Thomas McKean, and George Ross Jr.

The Green (3rd and Delaware streets). The public square of this old town was laid out by Peter Stuyvesant.

Old New Castle Court House (2nd and Delaware streets; 302/323-4453). The original Colonial capitol, and the state's oldest surviving courthouse. The cupola is the center of a twelve-mile arc that delineates the Delaware-Pennsylvania border. Open daily except Mondays.

Amstel House Museum (2 East 4th St. at Delaware St.; 302/322-2794). The restored

The George Read II House in New Castle.

SHORT OF CASH

Colonial America always needed money. Literally. English law forbade the export of money, and the colonies were not allowed to mint it. Tobacco, corn, cattle, and wheat all served as "legal tender." Spanish coins were used, but were called by the names of denominations of English currency—pounds, shillings, and pence. And, despite the law, individual colonies did coin their own money and print bills. Massachusetts was the first to issue paper money, in 1690. The soundest Colonial currency was Pennsylvania's, organized by Benjamin Franklin.

The tree of liberty must be refreshed, from time to time, with the blood of patriots and tyrants. It is natural manure.

—THOMAS JEFFERSON, 1787

1730 brick mansion of the seventh governor of Delaware houses period arts and furnishings. Open daily except Mondays, March through December; weekends the rest of the year.

Old Dutch House (32 East 3rd St.; 302/322-2794). Believed to be the state's oldest dwelling in original form, with Dutch colonial furnishings and decorative arts. Open daily, March through December, daily except Mondays the rest of the year.

George Read II House (42 The Strand; 302/322-8411). An 1804 Federal mansion with elegant interiors that feature gilded fanlights, silver door hardware, carved woodwork, relief plasterwork, and period furnishings. Garden. Open daily except Mondays, March through December, weekends in January and February.

Old Library Museum (40 East 3rd St.; 302/322-2794). An unusual semi-octagonal Victorian building houses exhibits relating to the area. Open Thursday through Sunday.

Accommodations: *The Jefferson Home* (5 The Strand, at the Wharf; 302/325-1025). On the lawn of this 1826 house, a sign reads "William Penn landed here." At various times, this was the office of a shipping company, a hotel, and a rooming house. Private access to the river. Four guest rooms with refrigerators. Breakfast, spa. Moderate.

ODESSA

Historic Houses of Odessa (three houses on Main St.; 302-378-4069). *Corbit-Sharp House.* A 1774 Georgian built by William Corbit, the town's leading citizen, and lived in by his family for 150 years, now restored and furnished with family pieces. Garden and library. Maintained by the Winterthur Museum. *Wilson-Warner House.* A handsome red-brick Georgian house, with an L-shaped plan typical of early Delaware architecture, furnished to portray life in the early 19th century. Also maintained by the Winterthur Museum. *Brick Hotel Gallery and Manney Collection of Belter Furniture.* The 19th-century Federal building was a hotel and tavern for nearly a century. It houses the largest collection in existence of high-style Belter Victorian furniture, famous for its carving and workmanship. All open daily except Mondays and in January and February.

WILMINGTON

Swedes seeking their fortunes founded the colony of New Sweden. In 1655 the colony was taken over without bloodshed by soldiers under Peter Stuyvesant, governor of New Amsterdam. Nine years later the English took over and the town grew under the influence of wealthy Quakers.

Holy Trinity (Old Swedes) Church and Hendrickson House (606 Church St.; 302/652-5629). Founded in 1698, the church stands as originally built and still has regular services. The Swedish farmhouse, built in 1690, is now a museum. Open Monday, Wednesday, Friday and Saturday afternoons.

Fort Christina Monument (foot of East 7th St.). A black granite plinth surmounted by a model of the pioneers' ship, *Calmer Nickel,* marks where Swedes settled in 1638.

Wilmington Square (500 block Market Mall). A historic square surrounded by four 18th-century houses that have been moved to this location; one contains the museum gift shop for the Historical Society of Delaware.

Old Town Hall Museum (512 Market St.; 302/665-7161). This Georgian town hall served as the city's meeting chambers, offices, jail, and library in the late 18th and early 19th centuries. Now a museum with artifacts of state history, and restored jail cells. Open Tuesday through Saturday.

Delaware Art Museum (2301 Kentmere Pkwy.; 302/571-9590). The Howard Pyle Collection of American Illustration has works by Pyle, N. C. Wyeth, and Maxfield Parrish. The American painting collection features West, Homer, Church, Glackens, and Hopper, and the Phelps collection of Andrew Wyeth works. Open daily except Mondays.

Winterthur Museum, Garden and Library (6 miles northwest on DE 52; 302/888-4600). A decorative arts collection from 1640 to 1860 includes more than 89,000 objects in two buildings, including an exhibition of 200 years of American antiques, and period rooms in Henry Francis du Pont's nine-story country house. The Galleries at Winterthur have self-guided tours. Open daily except Mondays.

Hagley Museum (3 miles northwest off DE 141; 302/658-2400). The 240-acre historic site of E. I. du Pont's original black-powder mills along the Brandywine River. Working models, an operating water wheel, a stationary steam engine, and an operable 1875 machine shop. There are tours of the 1803 "Eleutherian Mills," residence of five generations of du Ponts. Gardens, museum store. Open daily, mid-March through December, weekends the rest of the year.

I heard the bullets whistle, and, believe me, there is something charming in the sound.

—GEORGE WASHINGTON, *describing his first battle, 1754*

11

MARYLAND

In March 1634, two ships, the *Ark* and the *Dove,* arrived at St. Clements Island at the mouth of the Potomac, carrying 140 settlers. Their leader, Leonard Calvert, knelt, thanked God, and named their new settlement Maryland, in honor of Henrietta Marie, wife of Charles I of England. It would become the fourth permanent English settlement in America.

Calvert's brother, Lord Baltimore, had received a royal charter to some 7 million acres, and he planned to establish a system under which gentlemen who brought a certain number of farmers to Maryland would be given 2,000-acre manors. The lords of the manors would collect rent from the farmers and give part of it to Lord Baltimore. Slaves and indentured servants would do the actual work.

Most of the settlers arrived as indentured servants. They worked off their indentures to pay for their passage, then established their own farms. Most raised tobacco, and by the 1660s, millions of pounds of Maryland tobacco were being shipped to England annually.

The Calverts were Roman Catholics, and proclaimed religious freedom to all who recognized the Trinity. During England's "Glorious Revolution," Maryland Protestants staged a religious revolution of their own, ousting Lord Baltimore's governor and denying Catholics the right to vote. The colony was taken away from Lord Baltimore and placed under a royal governor, who in 1694 moved the capital from St. Mary's to Annapolis, a Protestant stronghold.

Marylanders were active in the early wars fought on American soil. In 1775, British general Edward Braddock, assisted by George Washington, trained his army at Cumberland for the campaign against the French and Indians. In the Revolution, General Howe invaded Maryland on his way to capture Philadelphia. In the Battle of Long Island, Maryland troops made a heroic bayonet coverage of the retreat. The courageous action of the "Old Line" gave the state one of its nicknames.

ACCOKEEK

National Colonial Farm (from Washington, I-95 exit 3A, then 10 miles south on MD 210, right on Bryan Point Rd.; 301/283-2113). A mid-18th-century living-history farm on 150 acres in Piscataway National Park. Replicated farm buildings. Crops, herb garden, livestock. Open daily except Mondays.

ANNAPOLIS

Planned and laid out as the colonial capital in 1695, Annapolis was the first peacetime capital of the United States when Congress met here from November 26,

1783, to August 13, 1784. The U.S. Naval Academy was established here in 1845.

State House (State Circle; 410/974-3400). This building, constructed in 1772–79, is the oldest state house in continuous legislative use. Here, in 1784, Congress ratified the Treaty of Paris, officially ending the Revolution. Visitor center, tours. Open daily.

Old Treasury (south of State House; 410/267-7619). This circa-1735 building is the oldest public building in the state. Open weekdays.

St. John's College (College Ave.; 410/263-2371, ext. 239). The thirty-six-acre campus, which dates from 1784, is a National Historic Landmark. The college succeeded King William's School, founded in 1696.

George Washington's two nephews and a step-grandson studied here. Francis Scott Key was an alumnus. *McDowell Hall,* 1742–89, now the main classroom building, was originally built as the Governor's Palace. *Charles Carroll, Barrister House,* moved to the campus and restored, was the birthplace of the author of the Maryland Bill of Rights. (Open on request.) During the Revolution, the Sons of Liberty met under the *Liberty Tree,* a tulip poplar thought to be more than 400 years old.

Hammond-Harwood House (19 Maryland Ave. at King George St., just west of the U.S. Naval Academy; 410/269-1714). A 1774 Georgian house designed by William Buckland. Matthias Hammond, a Revolution-

City Spring was an amenity of Baltimore, Maryland, in the 1840s. Courtesy Library of Congress, Prints and Photographs Division.

ary War patriot, was the first owner. Period
furnishings, garden. Open daily.

U.S. Naval Academy (enter Gate 1 for
visitor center in Ricketts Hall; 410/263-
6933). A world-renowned school for naval
officers. The remains of John Paul Jones are
in a crypt below the chapel. A museum
exhibits 300 years of American naval his-

tory. A replica of the figurehead of the USS
Delaware (a ship later renamed *Tecumseh*) is
in front of Bancroft Hall. Tours. Parades
three times a year. Open daily.

William Paca House and Garden (186
Prince George St.; 410/263-5553). A five-
part Georgian mansion built circa 1765 for
William Paca, a signer of the Declaration of

Independence and governor of Maryland during the Revolution. The landscaped garden has been faithfully reconstructed, with waterways and formal parterres. Open daily except Tuesdays.

London Town Publick House and Gardens (8 miles southeast via MD 2S, 253 in Edgewater, at the end of Londontown Rd.; 410/222-1919). A circa-1760 Georgian inn on the bank of the South River. Woodland gardens, a log-built 1720 tobacco barn. Exhibits, tours. Open daily except Mondays, March through December.

Accommodations: *Governor Calvert House* (58 State Circle; 410/263-2641 or 800/847-8882). Governor Calvert built this four-story Georgian mansion for his wife, Rebecca, in the 1720s, and more than a century later Victorian touches were added. Tastefully restored, the inn offers fifty-five guest rooms, including several garden mini-suites. Atrium, period gardens. Breakfast extra. Valet parking. Expensive.

BALTIMORE

During the Revolution, when the British threatened Philadelphia, the Continental Congress fled to Baltimore, which served as the nation's capital for two months. In October 1814, a British fleet attacked the city. The defenders of Fort McHenry withstood the naval bombardment for twenty-five hours until the British gave up. Francis Scott Key saw the huge American flag still flying above the fort, and was inspired by it to write "The Star-Spangled Banner."

Washington Monument (Charles and Monument streets). The first major monument to honor George Washington.

Museum and Library of Maryland History (201 West Monument St., between Park Ave. and Howard St.; 410/685-3750). The museum has the original manuscript of the "Star-Spangled Banner," and exhibits of Maryland silver, furniture, and painting. There is also a maritime museum. Open daily except Mondays, October through April; Tuesday through Saturday the rest of the year.

Asbury House (10 East Mt. Vernon Pl.; 410/685-5290). A circa-1850 brownstone with balcony and grillework extending the entire width of the house, a spiral stairway suspended from three floors. Library, drawing room. Open weekdays.

First Unitarian Church (Charles and Franklin streets; 410/685-2330). In this 1817 Greek Revival church, William Ellery Channing preached a sermon that hastened the establishment of the Unitarian denomination.

Basilica of the Assumption of the Blessed Virgin Mary (Cathedral and Mulberry streets; 410/727-3565). The first Catholic cathedral in the country. Bishop John Carroll, head of the diocese of Baltimore from its establishment in 1789, blessed the cornerstone in 1806. The church, designed by Benjamin Latrobe, was dedicated in 1821. Tours are given on the second and fourth Sundays of each month. Open daily.

Peale Museum (225 Holliday St.; 410/396-3523). Built in 1814 as Rembrandt Peale's "Baltimore Museum," this is the nation's oldest museum building. It houses a collection of paintings, including many by members of the Peale family. Walled garden. Open daily except Mondays.

Carroll Mansion (800 East Lombard at Front; 410/396-3523). Residence, circa 1810, of Charles Carroll. When he died here, in 1832, he was the last surviving signer of the Declaration of Independence. Period furnishings. Open daily except Mondays.

Shot Tower (Fayette and Front streets; 410/396-5891). A tapering 234-foot-tall

brick tower where molten lead was dropped to form round shot that hardened when it hit water at the base. Film. Exhibits. Open daily.

Star-Spangled Banner Flag House and 1812 Museum (844 East Pratt St. at Albemarle St.; 410/837-1793). The thirty-by-forty-two-foot banner with fifteen stars and fifteen stripes that Key saw was hand-sewn here by Mary Young Pickersgill. The 1793 house is restored and furnished in the Federal period. The 1812 Museum contains relics, documents, weapons, and memorabilia. Audiovisual program. Garden with unusual stone map of the United States Open daily except Sundays.

Edgar Allan Poe House (203 North Amity St.; 410/396-7932). Poe's home from 1832 to 1835. Open Wednesday through Saturday afternoons, April through July and October to mid-December; Saturday afternoons, August and September. Poe is buried in Westminister Burying Ground (Fayette and Greene streets).

Mother Seton House (600 North Paca St.; 410/523-3443). The home of Saint Elizabeth Ann Bayley Seton from 1808 to 1809. Here she established the forerunner of the parochial school system, and an order of nuns that became the Daughters and Sisters of Charity. Open weekend afternoons.

U.S. Frigate *Constellation* (Pier 1, Pratt St., Inner Harbor; 410/539-1797). The first ship of the U.S. Navy in 1797, and the oldest warship in the world still afloat, now a National Naval Historic Shrine. Early navy relics, self-guided tours. Open daily.

Old Otterbein United Methodist Church (Conway and Sharp streets; 410/685-4703). This fine 1785 Georgian structure is the mother church of the United Brethren. Tours on Saturdays, April through August.

Mount Clare Museum House (in Carroll Park at Monroe St. and Washington Blvd.; 410/837-3262). This 1760 mansion, the oldest in the city, was the home of Charles Carroll, a lawyer. Period furnishings, tours. Open daily except Mondays.

Fort McHenry National Monument and Historic Shrine (east end of Fort Ave.; 410/962-4299). The flag flying over this five-pointed, star-shaped brick fort inspired Francis Scott Key to write "The Star-Spangled Banner." The fort was named for James McHenry, Secretary of War from 1796 to 1800. Replica flagpole. Restored powder magazine, guardroom, officers' quarters, and barracks, all with exhibits. The Fort McHenry Guard, in period uniform, reenacts life at the garrison (weekends, mid-June through August). The visitor center has a film, exhibits, a gift shop. Open daily. *Narrated cruises* (410/745-9216) depart from Inner Harbor Finger Pier to the fort from Memorial Day through Labor Day.

Accommodations: *Union Square House* (23 South Stricker St.; 410/233-9064). A restored Italianate townhouse on "Millionaires' Row," in the Union Square Historic District, offers three guest rooms with original plaster moldings, handsome woodwork, and period furnishings. Inner Harbor and other city attractions are a few blocks away. Full breakfast. Other meals available. Moderate.

BOWIE

Marietta Manor (3 miles west in Glenn Dale, at 5628 Bell Station Rd.; 301/464-5291). A modest Federal plantation house built by Gabriel Duvall, an associate justice of the U.S. Supreme Court from 1811 to 1835. Tours available. Open Sunday afternoons, March through December.

THE REVOLUTIONARY WAR

The roots of the American Revolution were in the French and Indian War. Victory had removed the French threat in North America, but the conflict had doubled the British national debt. Both Britain and the colonies thought the other party should pay for the war. The colonies petitioned Parliament to be reimbursed for the war costs they had incurred. Parliament, however, thought it was high time the colonies paid their own way.

To accomplish this, British officials in America were ordered to enforce all tax laws strictly. The colonies were prohibited from printing their own money, and were required to pay the cost of maintaining British troops in America.

Many colonists saw these measures as taxation without representation. Merchants agreed to boycott British goods until the Stamp Act was repealed. A new organization, the Sons of Liberty, began terrorizing royal tax collectors. Parliament reacted in 1766 by repealing the Stamp Act, but replaced it with the Declaratory Act, which included the right of Parliament to legislate for the colonies in all matters. The next year Parliament passed the Townshend Acts, which put duties on tea, paper, paint, glass, and lead.

The colonists' protests were ignored, and violence flared. In 1770, Redcoats fired on hecklers, killing five in what became known as the Boston Massacre. Parliament repealed the new measures, except for the one on tea. For a while tensions eased.

Then the British Cabinet, now under Lord North, gave the colonists a ready-made issue in the Tea Act of 1772, a scheme to tempt colonists to pay the duty on tea. The act was opposed everywhere, particularly in Boston, where men dressed as Indians threw a shipload of tea into the harbor. American radicals cheered, conservatives were shocked, and Parliament was furious.

Parliament retaliated by passing the so-called Intolerable Acts, which closed the port of Boston until compensation for the tea was paid, and replaced the Massachusetts government with a royal governor. Britain had gone too far. The Virginia Burgesses called for a Continental Congress to convene to discuss their grievances.

When the First Continental Congress met in Philadelphia in 1774, it divided into three factions: radicals, who expected that force eventually would be necessary; moderates, who wanted to seek a peaceful solution; and conservatives, who favored a softening of tax policy, but opposed a break with Britain.

In Congress the colonies made a united protest based on denial of the right of Parliament to legislate for them, although they continued to recognize the Crown. Congress set a date to reconvene to consider any British reply. No reply came.

Massachusetts had had enough. Its dissolved government met outside of British-occupied Boston. General Thomas Gage resolved to seize the leaders—John Hancock and Samuel

To the Public.

THE long expected TEA SHIP arrived laſt night at Sandy-Hook, but the pilot would not bring up the Captain till the ſenſe of the city was known. The committee were immediately informed of her arrival, and that the Captain ſolicits for liberty to come up to provide neceſſaries for his return. The ſhip to remain at Sandy-Hook. The committee conceiving it to be the ſenſe of the city that he ſhould have ſuch liberty, ſignified it to the Gentleman who is to ſupply him with proviſions, and other neceſſaries. Advice of this was immediately diſpatched to the Captain ; and whenever he comes up, care will be taken that he does not enter at the cuſtomhouſe, and that no time be loſt in diſpatching him.

New-York, April 19, 1774.

Adams—and the ammunition that was at Concord. On April 18, 1775, Redcoats set out to raid Concord via Lexington. Alerted by Paul Revere and William Dawes, the "minutemen" met the British and drove them off. The war was on.

The response in America was electric. The Second Continental Congress adopted the poorly organized army assembling outside Boston, and appointed George Washington its commanding general. But it stopped short of declaring independence, and again petitioned King George III.

Before Washington assumed command, the Colonials were pushed off Bunker Hill, near Boston, at a terrible cost to the British, who left Boston nine months later. During the siege of Boston, many Americans reluctantly concluded that the only guarantee of their freedom lay in independence. Their mood was captured by Thomas Paine, whose *Common Sense* sold more than 100,000 copies and helped mobilize Americans to the patriot cause.

On July 4, 1776, the Continental Congress declared independence, based on the natural law of human equality, the right of revolution, and the transgressions of the king. This committed the patriots to resistance, and the loyalists to opposition or emigration. Loyalist regiments fought alongside British troops, and from 40,000 to 100,000 loyalists emigrated, mostly to Canada, and especially to Nova Scotia and New Brunswick.

The patriots raised the Continental Army, a small but dependable regular force composed of state regiments. When they could, they augmented the army with state militia. The soldiers were never adequately supplied or equipped, and most of what they had came from European nations. Their numbers fluctuated from about 4,000 to 90,000. Later the government used a form of draft and opened the ranks to blacks. Near the end of the war, the Continental Army was joined by thousands of French troops.

The British, unable to recruit sufficient men at home, hired German troops and used Indians and loyalists; neither of the latter two groups were particularly dependable. British forces were additionally hampered by governmental financial difficulties, by the difficulties of being supplied from the Atlantic, and by the unfamiliar American climate and terrain.

Before they evacuated Boston, the British attempted to occupy the Carolinas, but were repulsed at Charleston. William Howe, who had succeeded Gage, seized New York City and most of New Jersey. He was repelled at Trenton and Princeton by Washington, but later in 1777 occupied Philadelphia.

General Burgoyne attempted to go to join forces with Howe at New York, but his army was cut off and captured at Saratoga in October 1777, in a pivotal American victory. Washington's army suffered at Valley Forge that winter.

The French, ancient foes of the British, gave secret help to the Americans from the beginning. To prevent a reconciliation of Britain and America, the French openly allied themselves to the American states early in 1778. Spain, long an ally of France, helped in the South and West. The Netherlands also came down on the side of the Americans. Instead of a rebellion in the colonies, Britain now had to fight a world war. Britain, which had once ruled the waves, found herself outnumbered at sea by the combined forces of her enemies. Privateers harassed British merchant shipping and exasperated the navy.

After an indecisive clash at Monmouth in 1778, no large-scale battles were fought in the North, but disaster was narrowly averted when Benedict Arnold tried to sell West Point to the British. Civil war erupted in western New York and Pennsylvania as loyalists and their Indian allies attacked their erstwhile neighbors. The Americans retaliated with devastating expeditions that burned villages and food supplies. George Rogers Clark defeated small British forces in defense of the infant settlements of Kentucky.

Late in the war, most of the fighting was in the South, where the British won victories but lost the war; they could not hold conquered areas or protect their loyalist allies. Exhausted by Nathaniel Greene's dogged defense, Cornwallis settled at Yorktown, Virginia. There he was besieged by Washington and Rochambeau. His escape blocked by a French

fleet, Cornwallis surrendered, ending the war.

Peace negotiations began in earnest after Yorktown. The American negotiators—Benjamin Franklin, John Adams, and John Jay—were supposed to collaborate with the French, but feared they would try to compensate Spain at American expense. In separate negotiations with the British, the Americans fashioned a diplomatic triumph in the 1783 Treaty of Paris. They achieved recognition of the independence of the United States and clearly defined its boundaries. After an eight-year struggle, America had humbled the greatest empire on earth.

CAMBRIDGE

Old Trinity Church, Dorchester Parish (8 miles southwest on MD 16 in Church Creek; 410/228-2940). One of the oldest (circa 1675) churches in the country still holding regular services. Interior restored. Open daily except Tuesdays.

Chesapeake and Ohio Canal National Historical Park. In 1785, George Washington's Potowmack Canal Company cleared obstructions and built skirting canals along the Potomac River to facilitate the transportation of goods between settlements beyond the Allegheny Mountains and the lower Potomac River towns. The system proved inadequate, and in 1828 the Chesapeake & Ohio Canal Company was formed. Its purpose was to connect Georgetown with the Ohio River by river and canal. On July 4, 1828, President John Quincy Adams led the

groundbreaking ceremony. By 1850 the canal was completed as far as Cumberland, Maryland (185 miles from Georgetown), and was used to transport coal, flour, grain, and lumber. But financial and legal difficulties, the coming of the railroad, and improved roads all cut deeply into the commerce on the waterway and it gradually faded into obsolescence.

Today the area along the canal is little changed, and many points of interest can be seen along the way. Exhibits may be seen at Cumberland and Hancock and at a museum near the Great Falls of the Potomac. At Great Falls there are interpretive programs, including a mule-drawn canal boat, a working canal lock, trails, and picnic grounds. At Lock 3 in Georgetown (in Washington, D.C.) there is also a mule-drawn canal boat (next to the Foundry Mall, 30th and Thomas Jefferson streets; 202/472-4376). Visitor center open daily. For information about the canal in Maryland call 301/739-4200.

CUMBERLAND

Washington's Headquarters (in Riverside Park, downtown). Washington was here during the French and Indian Wars, and used this building as his first military headquarters.

   Accommodations: *The Inn at Walnut Bottom* (120 Green St.; 301/777-1629). Two historic houses have been joined to form the inn: the 1815 Cowden House and the 1890 Dent house. There are two parlors, country antiques, and antique reproductions in the twelve guest rooms (four with shared bath). Full breakfast. Arthur's Restaurant provides other meals. Inexpensive.

EASTON

Third Haven Friends Meeting House (405 South Washington St.; 410/822-0293). This circa-1682 building is one of the oldest frame-construction houses of worship in the country. Open daily.

FREDERICK

Roger Brooke Taney Home (123 South Bentz St.; 301/663-8687). This 1799 house was the home of a Chief Justice of the Supreme Court from 1835 to 1864. Taney swore in seven presidents, and issued the famous Dred Scott Decision.

   Trinity Chapel (West Church St., near North Market St.; 301/662-2762). Francis Scott Key was baptized in this graceful 1763 church. The town clock in the steeple has ten-bell chimes. Open daily.

   Schifferstadt (Rosemont Ave. and West 2nd St.; 301/663-3885). An excellent example of German-colonial farmhouse architec-

ture. Tours of the architectural museum are available. Gift shop. Open daily except Mondays, April to mid-December.

   Historical Society of Frederick County Museum (24 East Church St.; 301/663-1188). An early 1800s house, showing both Georgian and Federal details. Doric columns inside. Boxwood gardens, portraits, museum tour. Open Tuesday through Saturday and Sunday afternoons.

HAGERSTOWN

Jonathan Hager House and Museum (19 Key St. in City Park; 301/739-5727). A 1739 house in a park setting. Authentic furnishings. Open daily except Mondays, April through December.

   Miller House (135 West Washington St.; 301/797-8782). A circa-1820 Federal town house with an unusual spiral staircase and collections of clocks, dolls, and Bell pottery. Garden. Headquarters of the Washington County Historical Society. Open Wednesday through Sunday, April through December.

   Fort Frederick State Park (19 miles south and west via I-81 and I-70 to Big Pool, then 1 mile southeast via MD 56 and unnumbered road; 301/842-2155). This partially restored 1756 stone fort overlooks the Chesapeake and Ohio Canal National Historical Park. Military reenactments throughout the year. A museum on the grounds shows a film. Picnicking. Open daily. Phone for hours.

HAVRE DE GRACE

Steppingstone Museum (461 Quaker Bottom Rd. in Susquehanna State Park; 410/939-2299). A self-guided tour of the museum grounds includes a nonworking farm, a farmhouse furnished as a country home, and a barn and shops with exhibits.

No person or persons whatsoever . . . professing to believe in Jesus Christ, shall from henceforth bee any waies troubled, Molested or discountenanced for or in respect of his or her religion . . .

   —*MARYLAND TOLERATION ACT*

The Montpelier Mansion in Laurel. Photo by Mary Jurkiewicz.

Open weekends, May through October.

Concord Point Lighthouse (foot of Lafayette St.). Built in 1827 of granite, this is considered the oldest continually used lighthouse on the East Coast.

LA PLATA

Port Tobacco (3 miles southwest on MD 6; 301/934-4313). Infrared aerial photography and excavations revealed the site here of one of the oldest continuously inhabited English settlements. Appearing as an Indian village on Captain Smith's 1608 map, the area was colonized as early as 1638. The town was chartered in 1727, and the first courthouse erected in 1729. Remaining buildings include Chimney House (1765) and Stagg Hall (1732), an original Colonial home still a private residence, Burch (Catslide) House (1700), the reconstructed Quenzel Store, and a Federal period courthouse. Museum dis-

plays include a film. Open Wednesday through Sunday afternoons, June through August; weekend afternoons in April and May and September through December. Phone ahead for hours.

LAUREL

Montpelier Mansion (3 miles southeast on MD 197; 301/953-1376). A Georgian mansion built around 1780 and owned for generations by the Snowden family. George Washington and Abigail Adams were among the early visitors. Boxwood gardens, summer house, gift shop. Open Sunday afternoons, March through December.

LEONARDTOWN

Sotterley (9 miles east on MD 245; 301/373-2280). A circa-1715 working plantation overlooking the Patuxent River. Chinese

Chippendale staircase. Farming exhibit. Open daily except Mondays, June through October.

ROCKVILLE

Beall-Dawson House (103 West Montgomery Ave.; 301/762-1492). An 1815 Federal dwelling with period furnishings and a vintage doctor's office. Library, museum shop, docent tours. Open Tuesday through Saturday and first Sunday of the month.

ST. MARY'S CITY

Historic St. Mary's City (MD 5 and Rosecroft Rd.; 301/862-0990). An outdoor museum at the site of Maryland's first capital, established in 1634, includes the reconstructed 1676 State House and other exhibits including the *Maryland Dove,* a replica of a 17th-century doctor's office, and a reconstructed inn. Outdoor café, visitor center. Open Wednesday through Sunday. Museum open Wednesday through Sunday, April through November.

ST. MICHAELS

St. Mary's Square. James Braddock laid out this public square in 1770, and several buildings date from the early 1800s, including the Cannonball House and Dr. Miller's Farmhouse. Also in the square is the *St. Mary's Square Museum* (410-745-9535), a mid-19th-century house of half-timber construction. Exhibits of area artifacts. Walking-tour brochures available. Open weekends, May through October.

Chesapeake Bay Maritime Museum (Mill St.; 410/745-2916). A waterside museum with twelve buildings, including a historic lighthouse, a boatbuilding shop with a working exhibit, and workboats. Open daily, mid-March through December, weekends the rest of the year.

Accommodations: *Kemp House Inn* (412 Talbot St.; 410/745-2243). Colonel Joseph Kemp, a shipwright and one of the town founders, built this handsome Georgian dwelling in 1807. The eight guest rooms (two with shared bath) have four-poster rope beds, patchwork quilts, and nightshirts. Robert E. Lee is said to have been a guest here. Breakfast. Inexpensive.

SALISBURY

Poplar Hill Mansion (117 Elizabeth St.; 410/749-1776). A circa-1805 house mixing Georgian and Federal architecture, with a palladium, and bull's-eye windows. Period furnishings. Country garden. Open Sunday afternoons. Phone in advance of your visit.

The Nassawango Iron Furnace (16 miles south via MD 12 to Old Furnace Rd.; 410/632-2032). One of the earliest hot-blast mechanisms still intact, the furnace's stack was restored in 1966. Archaeological excavations found a canal, a dike, and part of the old waterwheel. The area is under restoration. Surrounding the iron furnace is *Furnace Town,* an 1840s industrial village that includes six historical structures and a museum. Both areas open daily, April through October.

TOWSON

Hampton National Historic Site (535 Hampton Lane, ½ mile off Dulaney Valley Rd., I-695 exit 27B; 410/962-0688). An ornate 1790 Georgian mansion, formal gardens, and plantation outbuildings. Tea room, gift shop. Open daily except mid-January through early March.

12

NEW JERSEY

wedish and Dutch traders arrived here, at what
was once the home of the peaceful Lenni-
Lenape Indians, in the early 17th century, and
soon all was confusion over land grants, conflicting claims, shifting allegiances, and resistance to
authority. The Dutch drove out the Swedes, then the
English drove out the Dutch. In 1664 the Duke of York
named it "Nova Caesarea" or New Jersey, after the isle
of Jersey in the English Channel.

In 1676 the colony was divided into East and West
Jersey; the boundary was a line from just north of the
Delaware Water Gap to Little Egg Harbor, north of
Atlantic City. This came about because William Penn
had established his first Quaker settlement in the western
part of the colony. The separation lasted only to 1682,
when Penn purchased East Jersey, but differences
between the two sections persist even into modern times.

West Jersey was settled largely by Quakers, and its
territory included the southern end of the Delaware River
and the flat coastal plain. The long Jersey coastline never
had a major port, and South Jersey has traditionally been
agricultural.

By contrast, East Jersey was settled by New England
Puritans. The Kittatinny Mountains contained the iron
that gave the colony its first industry. At the north, New
Jersey shares a common border with New York, but oth-
erwise it is an island, cut off by the Hudson and
Delaware rivers. East Jersey has gravitated to New York
City, West Jersey to Philadelphia. Shortly after the
Revolution, the influence of both cities was so strong
that New Jersey was described as "a keg tapped at both
ends."

In the Revolution, New Jersey's unique geography
turned it into a battleground. More than a hundred battles
were fought in the state. The prize was the control of the
Hudson and Delaware valleys. George Washington spent
a quarter of this time shuttling back and forth across the
state, and the victories he won at Trenton, Princeton, and
Monmouth were critical. The Continental Army spent
two winters at Morristown in conditions worse than
those they had experienced at Valley Forge.

ALLAIRE STATE PARK

Historic Allaire Village (on county road 524 between
Farmingdale and Lakewood; 908/938-2253). James
Allaire bought this land in 1822 as a source of bog ore for
his ironworks. Some 500 workers turned out cauldrons,
pots, kettles, and pipes for New York City's waterworks.
Today visitors explore the enameling furnace, a bakery, a
carriage house, a general store, a blacksmith shop and
other buildings, much as they appeared in 1853. Rides
are available on a narrow-gauge steam train (daily, mid-
June through Labor Day; weekends May through Labor
Day, weekends, April to mid-June and Labor Day
through November). Grounds open daily; buildings
weekends, May through Labor Day and Labor Day
through November.

ATLANTIC CITY

Historic Town of Smithville (7 miles west on U.S. 30 to Absecon, then 6 miles north on U.S. 9, at Moss Mill Rd.). A restored early-1800s village with carriage rides, train rides, and paddle boats. Shops and restaurants. Village open daily. Rides, April through October.

Historic Gardner's Basin (800 New Hampshire Ave. at north end of city; 609/348-2880). An eight-acre marine park with the state's oldest tugboat, a U.S. Coast Guard Lightship, and Guy Lombardo's speedboat. Picnicking. Open daily.

BORDENTOWN

Clara Barton Schoolhouse (142 Crosswicks St.; 609/298-1740). In 1851, Clara Barton, founder of the American Red Cross, established one of the first free public schools in the country in this building. Open by appointment.

BRANCHVILLE

Peters Valley (8 miles northwest on U.S. 206, county 560, then south on county 615; 201/948-5200). Summer craftspeople live and work in historic buildings in the Delaware Water Gap National Recreational Area. Workshops are offered in blacksmithing, ceramics, fine metals, photography, fibers, and woodworking. Crafts store. Workshops open Friday through Sunday, June through August. Store is open all year.

BRIDGETON

Old Broad Street Church (West Broad St. and West Ave.). This 1792 Georgian church, with Palladian windows, has a wineglass-shaped pulpit, brick-paved aisles, and brass lamps that once burned whale oil. Open daily.

Nanticoke Lenni-Lenape Village (City Park, West Commerce St. and Mayor Aitken Dr., off NJ 49; 609/455-6910). The

*Barclay Farmstead in
Cherry Hill.*

tribe has re-created an ancestral village on this site, with huts, a long house, a ceremonial circle, and an herb garden. A powwow is held in June. Tours are given Wednesday through Sunday, mid-June through Labor Day. Also in City Park is the *New Sweden Farmstead-Museum* (609/455-9785), a reconstruction of the first permanent European settlement in the Delaware Valley, with seven log buildings and a house with period furnishings. Tours are led by costumed guides. Open daily, Memorial Day through Labor Day; Friday through Sunday, mid-April through Memorial Day and Labor Day through October.

Gibson House (7 miles southwest in Greenwich, on Ye Greate St.; 609/455-4055). This 1730 house was the site of New Jersey's only tea-burning party. Tours weekdays. Open daily except Sundays, early April through late November.

BURLINGTON

Historic house tours. Tours are given by the Burlington County Historical Society (457 High St.; 609/386-3993) of the circa-1780 *James Fenimore Cooper House,* birthplace of the author; the *Bard-How House;* and the *Captain James Lawrence House,* birthplace of the commander of the *Chesapeake* during the War of 1812. Tours, Sunday through Thursday.

CALDWELL

Grover Cleveland Birthplace State Historic Site (207 Bloomfield Ave.; 201/226-1810). This 1832 house was the parsonage of the First Presbyterian Church, and the birthplace of Grover Cleveland, who lived here from 1837 to 1841. Open Wednesday through Sunday.

CAMDEN

Walt Whitman House State Historic Site (330 Mickie St.; 609/964-5383). The last residence of the poet, and the only house he ever owned. Whitman lived here until his death in 1892. Original furnishings, books, and mementos. Open Wednesday through Sunday. Whitman is buried in *Harleigh Cemetery* (Haddon Ave. and Vesper Blvd.) in a vault he designed himself. Cemetery open daily.

Camden County Historical Society–Pomona Hall (Park Blvd. at Euclid Ave.; 609/964-3333). A brick Georgian that belonged to descendants of William Cooper, an early Camden settler. Period furnishings, museum. Open Saturday through Thursday.

CAPE MAY

This, the nation's oldest resort, has played host to Presidents Lincoln, Grant, Pierce, Buchanan, and Harrison. The entire town is a National Historic Landmark, with some 600 Victorian homes and buildings. *The Mid-Atlantic Center for the Arts* (609/884-5404) offers a number of interesting tours— Mansions by Gaslight, Cape May INNteriors and Tea, Walking Tours of the Historic District, Ocean Walk Tours, and a Stained Glass Walk tour.

Accommodations: *The Abbey* (34 Gurney St. at Columbia Ave.; 609/884-4506). This inn offers fourteen rooms in two buildings: a Gothic Revival villa with a tower, and a small Second Empire house with a mansard roof. Furnishings in the main house include gas chandeliers, elaborate beds, and floor-to-ceiling mirrors. Full breakfast. Moderate to expensive.

My dear Heart: It is from far away that I am writing, added to this cruel distance is the still worse uncertainty as to when I shall have news of you. . . . How will you have taken my going? Have you forgiven me? . . . As a defender of Liberty which I adore . . . coming to offer my services to this interesting republic, I am bringing nothing but my genuine good will.

—MARQUIS DE LAFAYETTE, *IN A LETTER TO HIS WIFE AFTER LEAVING FRANCE SECRETLY FOR AMERICA*

CAPE MAY
COURT HOUSE

Cape May County Historical Museum (Shore Rd., 1 mile north on U.S. 9; 609/465-3535). Collection includes early-19th-century dining room, 18th-century kitchen, military room with the flag from the Civil War, ironclad *Merrimac,* whaling implements, Indian artifacts, pioneer tools, lens from Cape May Point Lighthouse. Open daily except Sundays, mid-June through Labor Day; Tuesday through Saturday, Labor Day through November and April to mid-June.

CHERRY HILL

Barclay Farmstead (209 Barclay Lane; 609/795-6225). One of the earliest houses (circa 1684) built in the area. Restored Federal farmhouse on thirty-two acres, operating forge barn, springhouse. Grounds open daily. Tours Tuesday through Friday.

CLINTON

Clinton Historical Museum (56 Main St., off I-78; 908/735-4101). A ten-acre park with education center, quarry and lime kilns, general store, blacksmith shop, one-room schoolhouse, log cabin, garden, gift shop. Open daily except Mondays, April through October.

ELIZABETH

First Presbyterian Church and Graveyard (Broad St. and Caldwell Pl.). The first General Assembly convened in an earlier church on this site in 1668. The burned-out church was rebuilt in 1785–87, and again in 1949. Alexander Hamilton and Aaron Burr attended an academy where the parish house now stands. Open daily.

Boxwood Hall State Historic Site (1073 East Jersey St, ½ block west of U.S. 1; 201-648-4540). Late-18th-century home of Elias Boudinot, lawyer, diplomat, president in 1783 of the Continental Congress, and director of the U.S. Mint. He entertained Washington here on April 23, 1789. Open Wednesday through Sunday.

FREEHOLD

Washington defeated General Clinton's Redcoats at the Battle of Monmouth near here on June 28, 1778. Molly Hays carried water to the artillerymen, earning the sobriquet "Molly Pitcher."

Covenhoven House (150 West Main St.; 906/462-1466). Clinton occupied this house prior to the Battle of Monmouth in 1778. Period furnishings. Open Tuesdays, Thursdays, and weekends.

GIBBSTOWN

Hunter-Lawrence-Jessup House (7 miles northwest via NJ 45, county rte. 534 in Woodbury, at 58 North Broad St.; 609/845-7881). This 1765 house contains sixteen rooms of furnishings and memorabilia. Open Wednesday and Friday afternoons, first and third Mondays of the month.

Nothnagle House (406 Swedesboro Rd.; 609/423-0916). Built in 1638–43, this is the oldest surviving log house in the country. Open by appointment.

HACKENSACK

The Church on the Green (42 Court St., northeast corner of the Green; 201/845-0957). Organized in 1686, the original church was built in 1696 and rebuilt in 1791 in Stone Dutch style. Enoch Poor, a Revolutionary general, is buried in the cemetery. Museum. Tours weekdays on request.

Steuben House State Historic Site (¼ mile north of NJ 4, at 1209 Main St. in River Edge; 201/487-1739). This 1713 house was confiscated during the Revolution because the occupants were Loyalists, and given to Baron von Steuben by the state to reward his military services. He later sold it back to the original owners. Period furniture, glassware, china. Open Wednesday through Sunday.

HADDONFIELD

Elizabeth Haddon was a twenty-year-old Quaker whose father sent her from England in 1701 to develop 400 acres of land. She built a house, started a colony, and proposed to a Quaker missionary, who promptly married her. "The Theologian's Tale" in Longfellow's *Tales of a Wayside Inn* celebrates her courtship.

Greenfield Hall (343 King's Hwy. East; 609/429-7375). Built in 1747 and later expanded, the house contains personal items of Elizabeth Haddon. Boxwood garden, library on local history. On the grounds is a house, circa 1735, once owned by Ms. Haddon. Open Monday through Friday mornings.

HOHOKUS

The Hermitage (335 North Franklin Tpke.; 201/445-8311). Stone Gothic Revival superimposed on original 18th-century house. Owned by the Rosencrantz family for more than 150 years. Tours led by costumed docents from mid-April through September and December, also first and third Sundays of the month.

LAMBERTVILLE

Marshall House (62 Bridge St.; 609/397-0770). John Marshall, who discovered gold at Sutter's Mill in California in 1848, lived in this 1816 house until 1834. Period furnishings and memorabilia, museum. Open Sundays, May through mid-October.

John Holcomb House (260 North Main St.). Washington stayed here just before crossing the Delaware. Privately owned.

MILLVILLE

Wheaton Village (2 miles northeast via county rte. 552; 609/825-6800). A tranquil 19th-century town whose livelihood was based on its glassmaking industry. Museum of American glass, working factory with demonstrations of glassmaking, general store, train depot, one-room schoolhouse. Self-guided tours. Restaurant. Hotel. Open daily, April through December.

MONTCLAIR

Israel Crane House (110 Orange Rd.; 201/744-1796). A 1796 Federal mansion with period rooms. Its country store and post office display authentic items. Craft demonstrations. Open Wednesday and Sunday afternoons, September through June.

MORRISTOWN

Morristown National Historical Park (3 miles south on U.S. 202; 201/539-2085). *Ford Mansion,* one of the earliest houses in the area, was built in 1772–74 by Colonel Jacob Ford Jr., who produced gunpowder for American troops during the Revolution. His widow rented the house to the army for General and Mrs. Washington when his army spent the winter of 1779–80 here. Directly to the rear of the house is the *Historical Museum,* with Washington memorabilia, period weapons and 18th-century

Rockingham State Historic Site in Princeton. Photo by Margaret Carlsen.

artifacts. Audiovisual program. *Fort Nonsense* (Ann St.) was given its name after residents here had long forgotten the real reason for the earthworks constructed here in 1777. Overlook marks where fortifications were built to defend military supplies in the village. *Jockey Hollow* (4 miles southwest of town) is the site of the Continental Army's winter quarters in 1779–80 and during the 1781 mutiny of the Pennsylvania Line. Typical log huts and an officer's hut. Signs indicate brigade locations. Summer demonstrations of military and colonial farm life. *Wick House* (Jockey Hollow) *Visitor Center* has exhibits and an audiovisual presentation. Headquarters and museum open daily. Jockey Hollow buildings, daily in the summer.

Macculloch Hall Historical Museum (45 Macculloch Ave.; 201/538-2404). This 1810 house was the home of George P. Macculloch, initiator of the Morris Canal, and his descendants for more than 140 years. Garden, collection of Thomas Nast drawings. Open Thursday and Sunday afternoons, April through November.

Schuyler-Hamilton House (5 Olyphant Pl.; 201/267-4039). The 1760 house of Dr. Jabez Campfield. Alexander Hamilton courted Betsy Schuyler here. Period furniture, colonial garden. Open Tuesday and Sunday afternoons.

Historic Speedwell (333 Speedwell Ave.; 201/540-0211). Home and factory of Stephen Vail, ironmaster who in 1818 manufactured the engine for the SS *Savannah,* the first steamship to cross the Atlantic. In 1838 his son, Alfred Vail, and Samuel F. B. Morse perfected the telegraph and first demonstrated here in the factory. A factory houses exhibits on the history of the telegraph. Water wheel, carriage house, granary, gift shop. Open Thursday through Sunday, May through October.

Acorn Hall (66 Morris Ave.; 201/267-3465). An 1853 Italianate house with original furnishings and a restored garden. Open Thursdays and Sundays, March through December.

MOUNT HOLLY

Mansion at Smithville (on NJ 537, ½ mile west of U.S. 206; 609/265-5068). An 1840 mansion and village of inventor-entrepreneur Hezekiah B. Smith. Home of the "Star" high-wheeled bicycle. Tours available. Open Wednesdays and Sundays, May through October.

Burlington County Prison-Museum (128 High St.; 609/265-5068). Robert Mills, architect of the Washington Monument, designed this 1810 jail, said to be the first fireproof building in the country. Phone for tour information.

Mount Holly Library (307 High St.; 609/267-7111). Chartered in 1765 by King George III, the library is now housed in an 1830 Georgian mansion. The historic Lyceum contains original crystal chandeliers and has boxwood gardens. Its archives date from 1765. Open Monday through Thursday and Saturdays.

NEW BRUNSWICK

Buccleuch Mansion (George St. and Easton Ave., in Buccleuch Park; 908/297-2438).

AARON BURR

Aaron Burr, intelligent, ambitious and cynical, sought fame but found notoriety. He was a revolutionary, a soldier, an adventurer, and came within a hair's breadth of being President. His quick temper cost him his fortune.

He got off to a fast start. The son of one president of Princeton and the grandson of another, he studied at Princeton, became a lawyer in 1782, attorney general in 1789, and U.S. senator in 1791, and in 1800 he and Thomas Jefferson received an equal number of electoral votes for President. After thirty-six ballots in the House of Representatives, Jefferson was elected President, and Burr became Vice-President.

Alexander Hamilton had supported Jefferson over Burr, a fellow New Yorker, and Burr was resentful. Upon leaving the vice-presidency, Burr sought the governorship of New York, but Hamilton blocked him. Enraged, Burr challenged Hamilton to a duel. Hamilton fired his pistol into the air; Burr then shot him dead. He fled to Virginia and went into hiding.

Burr decided he would win fame and power in the West. He and others plotted to create a new country by detaching Mexico from Spain, and the land west of the Appalachian Mountains from the United States. The plans were exposed in 1806. Burr was arrested and charged with treason.

Chief Justice John Marshall presided at the trial, which was notable for its constitutional significance. Jefferson was subpoenaed but refused to appear, asserting the independence of the presidency from the courts. Marshall also set a precedent with his narrow construction of the constitutional law of treason. Burr was acquitted.

He then went to Europe, where he continued his schemes, but nothing came of them. He returned home in 1812 and practiced law in New York.

Built in 1739 by Anthony White, son-in-law of Lewis Morris, a Colonial governor of New Jersey, the mansion has period rooms. Open Sunday afternoons, June through October.

PATERSON

Great Falls Historic District (McBride Ave. Ext. and Spruce St.; 201/279-9587). Renovated 19th-century buildings, raceway system, high falls, park, and picnic area. Phone for tour information.

American Labor Museum–Botto House National Monument (north on NJ 504, at 83 Norway St. in Haledon; 201/595-7953). The history of the working class is presented through period rooms and exhibits. Ethnic

Waterloo Village Restoration near Stanhope. Photo by Pat Conklin.

gardens. Tours available. Open Wednesday through Sunday.

PRINCETON

In 1776 the first legislature of New Jersey met in Princeton University's Nassau Hall. In the 1777 Battle of Princeton, Washington surprised and defeated a superior British force. When Princeton was the nation's capital, Washington stayed at Rockingham in nearby Rocky Hill, where he wrote and delivered his famous "Farewell Orders to the Armies."

Nassau Hall (Princeton University; 609/258-3603). New Jersey's first legislature met here in 1776, and the Continental Congress in 1783, when Princeton was the

Old Barracks Museum in Trenton.

capital. During the Revolution it served as a barracks and hospital for Continental and British troops. Phone for information on campus tours.

Princeton Battle Monument (on Monument Dr., off Stockton St., near Morven). The work of Frederick West MacMonnies, this fifty-foot-tall block of limestone commemorates the 1777 battle at which Washington defeated the British.

Morven (55 Stockton St.). The 1755 house was the home of Richard Stockton, a signer of the Declaration of Independence. It was used as a Continental Army headquarters, and frequently visited by Washington. View exterior only; not open to the public.

Bainbridge House (158 Nassau St.; 609/921-6748). This circa-1776 house was the birthplace of the commander of the USS *Constitution* during the War of 1812. Period rooms, exhibits on Princeton history. Phone for schedule and information on Sunday walking tours of historic district.

Rockingham State Historic Site (4 miles north on U.S. 206, then 2 miles east on county rte. 518 in Rocky Hill; 609/921-8835). On a five-acre site are three buildings: main house, kitchen, and wash house. This was Washington's headquarters, from August 23 to November 10, 1783. Period furnishings in ten rooms. Open Wednesday through Sunday.

Accommodations: *Peacock Inn* (20 Bayard Lane; 609/924-1707). This 1775 Georgian mansion was relocated from Nassau Street to this location. The seventeen guest rooms (nine with private bath) are individually decorated. One block from Princeton campus. Antiques. Breakfast. Moderate.

RED BANK

Holmes-Hendrickson House (west on NJ 520 to Longstreet Rd. in Holmdel; 908/462-1466). A fourteen-room circa-1750 Dutch Colonial farmhouse with period furnishings. Open Tuesday, Thursday, Saturday, and Sunday afternoons, May through October.

Marlpit Hall (137 Kings Hwy. in Middletown, on NJ 35; 908/462-1466). An enlarged 1685 Dutch cottage done in 1740 English style, with period furnishings. The schedule is the same as Holmes-Hendrickson House (see above).

Allen House (2 miles south on NJ 35, at jct. with Sycamore Ave. in Shrewsbury; 906/462-1466). The lower floor of this circa-1750 house was restored as a tavern of the revolutionary period. Two upstairs galleries have historic exhibits. The schedule is the same as Holmes-Hendrickson House (see above).

Spy House Museum Complex (4 miles northwest on NJ 35 to Middletown, then 3 miles north to Port Monmouth, at shore end of Wilson Ave.; 908/787-1807). The Whitlock-Seabrook-Wilson House cabin was built in 1683, and later named "Spy House" because it was used as the meeting place for both British and American spies. Shoal Harbor Marine Museum. Penelope Stout Museum of the Crafts of Man. Open afternoons daily.

SOMERVILLE

Wallace House State Historic Site (38 Washington Pl.; 908/725-1015). General and Mrs. Washington made their home here immediately after the house was built in 1778, while his army was at Camp Middle-

brook. Period furnishings. Open Wednesday through Sunday.

Old Dutch Parsonage State Historic Site (65 Washington Pl.; 908/725-1015). Moved from its original location, this 1751 brick building was the home of the Rev. Jacob Hardenbergh from 1758 to 1781. He founded Queens College, now Rutgers University, while living here. Some original furnishings and memorabilia. Open Wednesday through Sunday.

STANHOPE

Waterloo Village Restoration (I-80 exit 25, follow signs; 201/347-0900). Known as the Andover Forge during the Revolution, this was once a busy town on the Morris Canal. The 18th-century buildings include the Stagecoach Inn, houses and craft barns, a gristmill, an apothecary shop, and a general store. There is a summer music festival. Open daily except Mondays, mid-April through December.

Accommodations: *Whistling Swan Inn* (100 Main St.; 201/347-6339). A Queen Anne with a steep-roofed turret, filled with polished woodwork and family antiques, offers ten guest rooms and a full breakfast. Moderate.

TRENTON

The Old Barracks Museum (Barrack St., opposite West Front St.; 609/396-1176). One of the finest examples of a Colonial barracks in the country. Built in 1758–59, it housed British, Hessian, and Continental troops during the Revolution. A museum contains restored soldiers' squad room, period furniture, firearms. Guides in period costumes. Open daily except Mondays.

William Trent House (15 Market St.;

609/989-3027). Trenton's oldest house (1719), an example of Queen Anne architecture, was the home of Chief Justice William Trent, for whom the city was named. Period furnishings, Colonial garden. Open daily.

Washington Crossing State Park (8 miles northwest on NJ 29; 609/737-0623). This 841-acre park commemorates the crossing on Christmas night, 1776, by George Washington and his army. Continental Lane, at the park, is the road over which Washington's army began its march to Trenton. In the park is the *Ferry House State Historic Site,* a building that sheltered Washington and some of his men after they crossed the Delaware from the Pennsylvania side, now restored as a living-history Colonial farmhouse. Picnicking, open-air summer theater, visitor center. Open Wednesday through Sunday.

WAYNE

Van Riper-Hopper (Wayne) Museum (533 Berdan Ave.; 201/694-7192). A circa-1786 Dutch Colonial farmhouse with period furnishings and an herb garden. Also here is the *Mead Van Duyne House,* a restored Dutch farmhouse. Open Friday through Tuesday.

Day Mansion (199 Totowa Rd.; 201/696-1776). A restoration of a 1740 house that served as Washington's headquarters in 1780. Period furnishings, tours, picnicking. Open Wednesday through Friday. Phone for exact schedule.

13

W A S H I N G T O N ,   D . C .

The youngest of the great cities in the East, Washington, D.C., was created in 1790 in a swamp at the confluence of the Potomac and Anacostia rivers. The site was part of a deal between the new federal government and Virginia and Maryland. In return for taking over the Revolutionary War debts of those states, the states ceded their sovereignty over one hundred square miles. (Originally the District was a ten-mile square crossing the Potomac into Virginia, but the Virginia portion was returned to the state in 1846.) In this area were the small river ports of Georgetown and, downriver, Alexandria.

George Washington appointed Major Pierre Charles L'Enfant, a French officer of engineers, to plan the capital city, and his plan was both radical and aesthetically pleasing. It combined a grid pattern for streets and grand avenues sweeping through the city, which would allow vistas to circles or squares to be occupied by statues and fountains. L'Enfant sited the Capitol on Jenkins Hill, from which an avenue would run northwest to the President's house. At the suggestion of Thomas Jefferson, he included a mall at the foot of the hill.

The government was scheduled, by law, to occupy the city by 1800, and work began in the early 1790s on the Capitol and the President's house. Growth was slow; no commercial enterprises attracted residents or investors. A visitor wrote in 1808 that "all around are premature symptoms of decay . . . so many houses built, not inhabited, but tumbling into ruins." During the War of 1812, British troops burned the city. A bill in Congress to abandon the city was defeated by only nine votes.

The Capitol (between Constitution and Independence avenues, at Pennsylvania Ave.; 202/225-6827). George Washington laid the cornerstone in 1793, and part of the building opened in 1800. The Capitol was rebuilt after the British burned it in 1814, and construction continued on and off over a number of years. The original building, crowned with a low copper-covered dome, was completed in 1826. Expansion in the 1850s and 1860s included the Senate and House wings and the present cast-iron dome, which was completed during the Civil War. The Old Senate Chamber has been restored to its 1850s appearance. There is a public dining room in the Senate wing. Tours available. Open weekdays.

Library of Congress (10 lst St., SE; 202/707-6400). The collection includes manuscripts, newspapers, maps, recordings, prints, photographs, and more then 30 million books. Exhibitions. In the Madison Building, a twenty-two-minute audiovisual program, "America's Library," is an introduction to the facility. Open daily.

The National Archives (Pennsylvania Ave. between 7th and 9th streets, NW; 202-501-5000). Original copies of the Declaration of Independence, the Bill of Rights, the Constitution, a 1297 version of the Magna Carta and other historic documents are on display. For tours, 202/501-5205. The Archives is available to the public for research. Open daily except Sundays.

The burning of Washington during the War of 1812.

Sewall-Belmont House (144 Constitution Ave., NE; 202/546-3989). This is a living monument to Alice Paul, the author of the Equal Rights Amendment. From this 1800 house she led the fight for passage. The house contains portraits, sculptures, and memorabilia of women from the beginning of the suffrage movement. Headquarters of the National Women's Party. Open daily except Mondays.

Smithsonian Institution (Information Office, The Castle, 1000 Jefferson Dr., SW, on the Mall; 202/357-2700). The collections are housed in several buildings. All buildings are open daily. *National Museum of American History* (Constitution Ave. between 12th and 14th streets, NW) exhibits include the original flag that flew over Fort McHenry in the War of 1812 (see page 135), political history, gowns of First Ladies, ship models, a Railroad Hall. Cafeteria. *Arts and Industries Building* (900 Jefferson Dr., SW). The exhibit "1876: A Centennial Exhibition" is a re-creation of the Centennial Exhibition in Philadelphia.

Washington Monument (The Mall at 15th St., NW; 202/426-6839). At 555 feet, this obelisk is the tallest masonry structure in the world. An elevator takes visitors to the observation room at the 500-foot level. Open daily.

The White House (1600 Pennsylvania Ave., NW; 202/456-7041). Constructed under the supervision of George Washington, the house has been lived in by every President since John Adams. It was burned by the British during the War of 1812, and reconstructed under the guidance of James Monroe. Tours, Tuesday through Saturday mornings, mid-March through October.

Decatur House Museum (Lafayette Sq., 748 Jackson Pl., NW; 202/842-0920). This 1818 Federal town house, operated by the National Trust, was built for naval hero

My movements to the chair of Government will be accompanied by feelings not unlike those of a culprit who is going to the place of his execution.

—GEORGE WASHINGTON, *ON HIS INAUGURATION AS PRESIDENT, 1789*

A PANIC OR TWO

Business cycles, the ebb and flow of economic activity, were a legacy of the Industrial Revolution. Economic downturns, now called "recessions," in early times were called "panics" because some sudden and unexpected collapse signaled the arrival of bad times. Two early panics are of note.

The Panic of 1819. The boom that followed the War of 1812 ended in 1818. Two factors triggered the downturn: European agriculture rebounded after the end of the Napoleonic Wars; and credit was contracted by the Second Bank of the United States, which was paying off loans made to finance the Louisiana Purchase. Sales of land on the frontier then slowed to a trickle, and the price of cotton and other crops dropped sharply. Many farmers, unable to pay their debts, lost their farms, and numerous banks failed. Many Westerners blamed the Bank of the United States for the troubles. President Jackson vetoed a bill to extend the charter of the bank in 1832. Ironically, this set in motion a chain of events that led to another panic.

The Panic of 1837. After the Jackson veto, federal moneys were transferred to state banks, which enabled them to make credit available on easy terms. Land sales in the West increased tenfold, and the construction of roads and canals boomed. But in July 1836, Jackson issued the "Specie Circular," which required purchasers of government land to pay for it with gold or silver. As a result, people withdrew specie from the banks. Land sales slowed. With less gold and silver in their reserves, many state banks failed and the others tightened credit requirements. The panic occurred when all the banks in the country suspended the conversion of paper currency into specie on demand. The economy remained depressed until 1843.

Stephen Decatur by Benjamin H. Latrobe, second architect of the Capitol. After Decatur's death in 1820, the house was occupied by a succession of statesmen, and was a center of political and social life in the city. Ground-floor family rooms reflect Decatur's lifestyle. The second-floor rooms are Victorian. Open daily except Mondays.

Octagon House (1799 New York Ave., NW, at 18th and E streets; 202/638-3105). A 1799 Federal town house built for Colonel John Tayloe III, which served as temporary quarters for President and Mrs. James Madison after the burning of the White House in the War of 1812. It was the site of the signing of the Treaty of Ghent. Period furnishings, changing architectural exhibits.

Open daily except Mondays.

St. John's Church (3240 O St., NW; 202/338-1796). Established in 1796, this is the oldest Episcopal congregation in Georgetown. Francis Scott Key was a founding member, and many presidents have worshiped here. Open daily.

Old Stone House (3051 M St., NW; 202/426-6851). Considered the oldest building in the capital, this 1765 house was built on Parcel Number 3 of the original tract of land that was then Georgetown. Period furnishings, beautiful grounds. Open Wednesday through Sunday.

Tudor Place (1644 31st St., NW; 202/965-0400). An 1805 twelve-room Federal mansion designed by William Thornton, one

The Sewell-Belmont House.

Dumbarton Oaks.

of the architects of the capitol, for Martha Custis Peter, granddaughter of Martha Washington. Her descendants lived in the house for 180 years. Original furnishings, five acres of gardens. Docent tours are given Tuesday through Saturday by reservation.

Dumbarton Oaks (1703 32nd St. NW; 202/342-3200). This 1800 mansion has antiques and European art, including El Greco's *The Visitation.* There is a famous collection of pre-Columbian artifacts. The gardens cover sixteen acres. Garden open daily; house and museum, Tuesday through Sunday afternoons.

Anderson House Museum (2118 Massachusetts Ave., NW; 202/785-2040). Museum of the American Revolution and national headquarters of the Society of the Cincinnati. Portraits by Early American artists. Displays of medals, swords, Continental Army artifacts. Open Tuesday through Saturday.

Frederick Douglass National Historic Site, "Cedar Hill" (1411 W St., SE; 202/

426-5961). The twenty-one-room house on nine acres was the home, from 1877 to 1895, of Douglass, a former slave who became minister to Haiti and a leading black spokesman. The visitor center has a film, memorabilia. Open daily.

Marine Barracks (G St. between 8th and 9th streets, NE; 202/433-6060). The oldest continuously occupied public building in the capital. Historic structures, including the Commandant's House. An evening parade is open to the public on Fridays in summer.

Navy Yard (M St. between 1st and 11th streets, SE). Along the Anacostia River, at a location chosen by George Washington, the yard was founded in 1799. Inside are two museums. *Navy Museum* (Bldg. 76; 202/433-2651) tells the story of the navy from the Revolution up to modern times. Dioramas of the accomplishments of early heroes. Some 5,000 objects are on display, including paintings, ship models, flags, and uniforms. A two-acre park has guns and can-non. *Marine Museum* (202/433-3840), in a restored 19th-century building nearby, displays weapons, uniforms, flags, and other artifacts describing the history of the Marine Corps. Both are open daily.

Tourmobile Sightseeing (202/554-7950, or 202/554-7020). Narrated tours to eighteen historic sights on the Mall and in Arlington National Cemetery. Unlimited reboarding. Daily.

Potomac Cruises (202/554-8000). A boat departs for Mount Vernon from Pier 4, two departures daily except Mondays late March to mid-June; one departure daily, September to mid-October.

Accommodations: *Morrison-Clark Inn* (1015 L St., NW; 202/898-1200 or 800/332-7898). Two Italianate mansions that once housed the Soldiers, Sailors and Marines Club now have become an elegant inn. Many of the fifty-four guest rooms have twelve-foot ceilings and period furnishings. Breakfast, lunch, and dinner are available in an intimate dining room. Moderate.

A view of Louisville, Kentucky, from the old blind asylum.
Courtesy Library of Congress, Prints and Photographs Division.

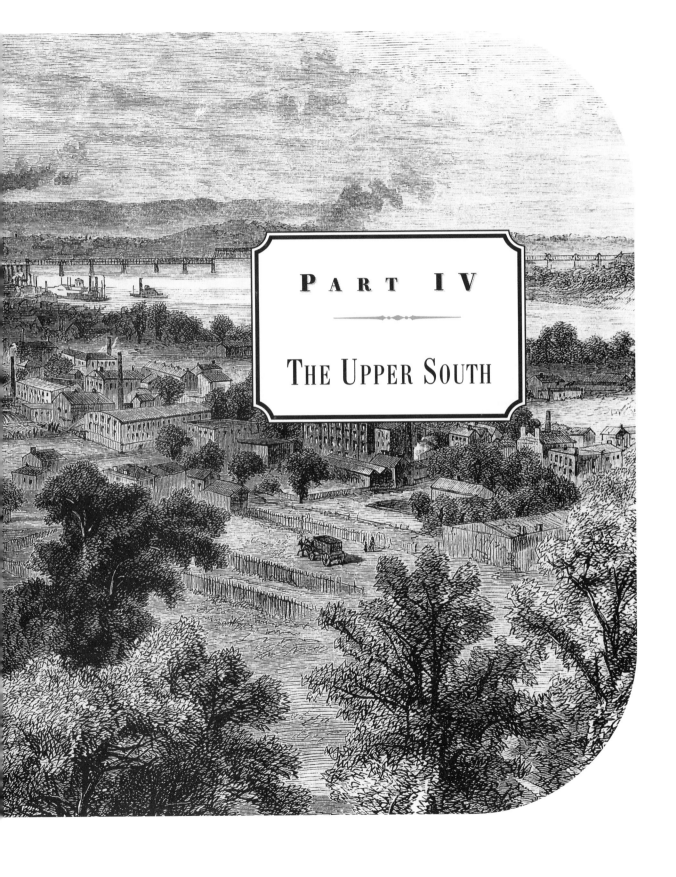

PART IV

THE UPPER SOUTH

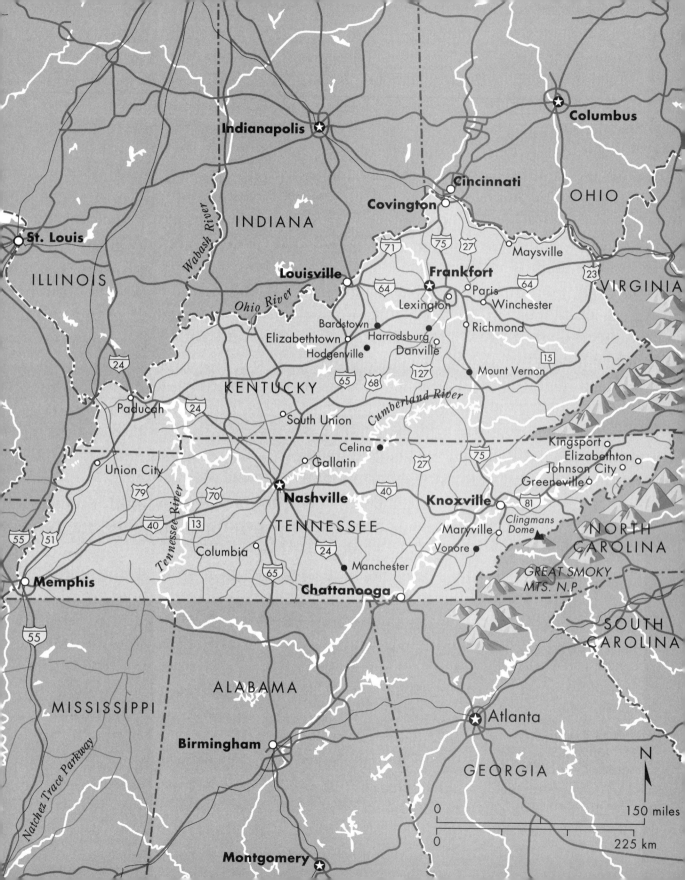

14

KENTUCKY

The Cumberland Gap, a natural passageway through the mountains that seal off the Kentucky wilderness from Virginia, was the gateway of the pioneers. Dr. Thomas Walker, the first recorded explorer to make a thorough land expedition into Kentucky, arrived in 1750. Later, Daniel Boone and a company of axmen hacked the Wilderness Road through the Cumberland Gap and far into the wilds.

The first permanent settlement was at Harrodsburg in 1774, followed by Boonesborough in 1775. Richard Henderson, founder of the Transylvania Company, asked Congress to recognize Transylvania as the fourteenth state, but Virginia claimed Kentucky as one of its counties, and Transylvania passed into history. Kentuckians met in Danville in December 1784, the first of ten conventions, to discuss separation from Virginia. By April 1792 they had agreed on a constitution, and that June Kentucky was admitted to the Union as the fifteenth state, the first on the western frontier.

BARDSTOWN

My Old Kentucky Home State Park (1 mile east on U.S. 150; 502/348-3502). Composer Stephen Foster occasionally visited his cousin, Judge John Rowan, at the stately 1795 house *Federal Hill.* These visits inspired him to write "My Old Kentucky Home." The house is on 290 acres. Period furnishings, costumed guides, picnicking. Open daily, March through December; daily except Mondays the rest of the year.

Lincoln Homestead State Park (20 miles southeast on U.S. 150, to KY 528; 606/336-7461). A replica of the cabin built here by Abraham Lincoln Sr., grandfather of the President. This was the home of Thomas Lincoln, the President's father, until he was twenty-five. It has been furnished in pioneer style. Also here is the *Berry House,* the home of Nancy Hanks during her courtship by Thomas Lincoln. Pioneer relics. A replica of the blacksmith and carpenter shop where Thomas Lincoln worked is also in the compound, which is enclosed by a split-rail fence. Picnicking. Open daily, May through September, and October weekends.

St. Joseph's Cathedral (310 West Stephen Foster, at jct. U.S. 31E and Rte. 62; 502/348-3126). This 1818 church was the first Catholic church west of the Allegheny Mountains. Paintings donated by Pope Leo XII. Open daily.

Wickland (east on U.S. 62; 502/348-5428). This Georgian mansion, built 1813–17, was the residence of two governors. Original furnishings. Open daily.

The Stephen Foster Story (J. Dan Talbott Amphitheater, in My Old Kentucky Home State Park; 502/348-5971). A musical with fifty Foster melodies traces the composer's triumphs and romance. Nightly except Monday and Saturday matinees, early June through early

September. An indoor theater is used in the event of rain.

Accommodations: *The Mansion* (1003 North 3rd St.; 502/348-2586). An 1851 Greek Revival mansion, on the National Register of Historic Places, nine blocks from the court-house, has eight guest rooms furnished with antiques. Three acres of gardens and tall trees. The Confederate flag was raised for the first time in Kentucky on this property. Breakfast. Inexpensive to moderate.

COVINGTON

MainStrasse Village (5 blocks in city's old German area; 606/491-0458). A historic district of residences, shops, and restaurants in more than twenty restored buildings, dating from the mid-1800s.

Riverboat Cruises (BB Riverboats, 606/261-8500, or Queen City Riverboats; 606/292-8867). Sightseeing cruises on the Ohio River in vintage steamboats.

Accommodations: *Sandford House* (1026 Russell St.; 609/291-9133). Built in the Federal style in 1820, this inn was reconstructed in the 1880s to incorporate Victorian features. The inn, once a finishing school for young ladies, now offers guests one bedroom, a suite, and two apartments. The inn is in the Seminary Historic District. Full breakfast. Inexpensive.

DANVILLE

Constitution Square State Shrine (on U.S. 127 in center of town at 105 East Walnut; 606/236-5089). A reproduction of Kentucky's first courthouse stands where the first state constitution was framed and adopted in 1792. An original post office, a restored row house, replicas of jail, courthouse, and meetinghouse. Dr. Goldsmith House and Grayson Tavern. Open daily.

McDowell House and Apothecary Shop (125 South 2nd St.; 606/236-2804). Residence and shop of Dr. Ephraim McDowell, noted surgeon of the early 19th century, restored and refurbished with period pieces. Large apothecary ware collection, gardens. Open daily March through October; daily except Mondays the rest of the year.

Accommodations: *Twin Hollies Retreat* (406 Maple Ave.; 606/236-8954). This 1835 Greek Revival house, listed on the National Register, is furnished in the period and offers three guest rooms, two with shared bath. Formal gardens. Inexpensive.

ELIZABETHTOWN

The Lincolns knew this town well. Thomas Lincoln owned property and worked here, and it was here he brought his bride, Nancy Hanks, immediately after their marriage. Abraham's oldest sister, Sarah, was born here, and after his first wife's death, Thomas returned to marry Sarah Bush Johnston.

Abraham Lincoln Birthplace National Historic Site (3 miles south on U.S. 31E/KY 61; 502/358-3137). Abraham Lincoln was born February 12, 1809, on the Sinking Spring Farm. Less than three years later, in 1811, his father, Thomas Lincoln, moved the family to Knob Creek Farm, located about ten miles northeast. Later moves eventually took the Lincolns to Indiana and Illinois. Today 110 acres of the original Lincoln farm are within this 116-acre park. The Memorial Building was built of granite and marble in 1911 with contributions from more than 100,000 people. Inside is the log cabin believed to be the Lincoln birthplace. It was disassembled, moved, exhibited, and stored many times before becoming reconstructed permanently here. The visitor center has an audiovisual program and exhibits. Thomas

Lincoln's Bible is on display. Open daily.

Lincoln Heritage House (1 mile north on U.S. 31 west in Freeman Lake Park; 502/765-2175). This double log cabin, built 1789–1805, the home of Hardin Thomas, has unusual trimwork done by Thomas Lincoln, as well as pioneer implements, early surveying equipment, period furniture. A one-room schoolhouse is nearby. Open daily except Mondays, June through September.

Brown-Pusey Community House (128 North Main St. at Poplar St.; 502/765-2515). This 1825 stagecoach inn is a fine example of Georgian architecture. George Custer lived here 1871–73. Restored as a community house with a garden. Open daily except Sundays.

FRANKFORT

Old State Capitol Building (Broadway and Lewis streets; 502/564-3016). The state's third capitol building, erected in 1827–29, was used as the capitol from 1829 to 1909 and was the first Greek Revival statehouse west of the Alleghenies. Completely restored and furnished in the style of the period, it has an unusual self-balanced double stairway. In the annex is the *Kentucky History Museum.* Both open daily.

Old Governor's Mansion (420 High St.; 502/564-3449). Georgian residence of thirty-three governors until 1914, now restored to the style of the 1800s. Tours available. Open Tuesday and Thursday afternoons.

Daniel Boone's Grave (Frankfort Cemetery, 215 East Main St.). Boone died in Missouri, but his remains were brought here in 1845. There is a monument to Boone and his wife. Open daily.

Liberty Hall (218 Wilkinson St. at West Main St.; 502/227-2560). A Georgian mansion built circa 1796 by John Brown, the first U.S. senator from Kentucky, it has been restored and furnished with family pieces and has period gardens. Open daily except Mondays, March through December.

Orlando Brown House (202 Wilkinson St.; 502/227-2560). An early Greek Revival house built for Orlando Brown, son of Senator John Brown, it has original furnishings and artifacts. Open daily except Mondays, March through December.

HARRODSBURG

Old Fort Harrod State Park (on U.S. 68/127 in town; 606/734-3314). The fort, originally known as Old Fort Hill, has been reproduced on the site of the original 1774 fort. The stockade shelters the Ann McGinty Block House, the George Rogers Clark Block House, the James Harrod Block House, and the first school in the state, complete with hand-hewn benches. The Mansion Museum includes a Lincoln Room, a Confederate Room, a gun collection, and Indian artifacts. The Lincoln Marriage Temple shelters the log cabin in which Lincoln's parents were married on June 12, 1806. Pioneer cemetery, picnicking, gift shop. A living-history program is offered in summer. Open daily, mid-March through November.

Morgan Row (220-222 South Chiles St.; 606/734-5985). Probably the oldest standing row houses, built 1807–45, west of the Alleghenies. Once a stagecoach stop and tavern, the building now houses the Harrodsburg Historical Society Museum. Open weekdays.

Old Mud Meeting House (4 miles south off U.S. 68; 606/734-5985). Built in 1800, this was the first Dutch Reformed Church west of the Alleghenies. Original mud-thatch walls have been restored. Open by appointment.

Shaker Village of Pleasant Hill (7 miles

All [Washington's] features were indicative of the most ungovernable passions, and had he been born in the forests . . . he would have been the fiercest man among the savage tribes.

—GILBERT STUART, *AFTER PAINTING WASHINGTON'S PORTRAIT FOR THE FIRST TIME, 1795*

Old Fort Harrod at Harrodsburg.

northeast on U.S. 68; 606/734-5411). Thirty structures, built 1805–59, include frame, brick and stone houses, furnished with Shaker reproductions. Center Family House has exhibits; Trustees' House a restaurant and twin spiral staircases. Craft shops have reproductions of Shaker furniture. Craft demonstrations. There is lodging in fifteen restored buildings. A stern-wheeler offers one-hour excursions on the Kentucky River, late April through October. Open daily.

Accommodations: *Canaan Land Farm* (4355 Lexington Rd.; 609/734-3984). This 1795 farmhouse, listed on the National Register, is one of the oldest brick houses in the state. The inn offers four rooms appointed with antiques, quilts, and feather beds. Sheep and other farm animals graze in the pasture of the 189-acre farm. Inexpensive.

HODGENVILLE

Lincoln's Boyhood Home (7 miles northeast on U.S. 31E, on Knob Creek Farm; 502/549-3741). A replica of the log cabin where Lincoln lived for five years during his childhood, from 1811 to 1816. Historic items and antiques. Open daily, April through October.

LEXINGTON

Ashland (East Main St. at Sycamore Rd.; 606/266-8581). The 1806 home of Henry Clay, statesman, orator, senator, and would-be President, and occupied by his family for four generations is furnished with family possessions. A number of outbuildings still stand. Open daily except Mondays and in January.

Hunt-Morgan House (201 North Mill St.

The Center family dwelling at Shaker Village of Pleasant Hill.

at West 2nd St.; 606/253-0362). A circa-1812 Federal mansion with a cantilevered elliptical staircase and fanlight doorway. Built for John Wesley Hunt, Kentucky's first millionaire. Later occupied by his grandson, General John Hunt Morgan, known as the "Thunderbolt of the Confederacy." Nobel Prize–winning geneticist Thomas Hunt Morgan was born here. Family furniture, portraits, and porcelain. Walled courtyard garden, gift shop. Open daily except Mondays and late December through February.

Mary Todd Lincoln House (578 West Main St.; 606/233-9999). The childhood home of the President's wife is authentically restored, furnished in the style of the period. Personal items are on display. Open Tuesday through Saturday, April to mid-December.

Waveland State Historic Site (225 Higbee Mill Rd.; 606/272-3611). A Greek Revival mansion built in 1847, with three original outbuildings. Exhibits depict plantation life of the 1840s. Gift shop. Open daily, March through December.

LOUISVILLE

Zachary Taylor National Cemetery (4701 Brownsboro Road, 7 miles east on U.S. 42; 502/893-3852). The twelfth President is buried here, near where he lived from infancy to adulthood. The Taylor family plot is surrounded by a national cemetery. Open daily.

Jefferson County Courthouse (Jefferson St. between 5th and 6th streets; 502/925-5000). A Greek Revival building designed by Gideon Shryock and built 1835–60, the courthouse has a splendid cast-iron monumental stair and balustrade in a sixty-eight-foot rotunda. Tours by appointment. Open weekdays.

Farmington (3033 Bardstown Rd. North, at jct. Watterson Expwy., 6 miles southeast on U.S. 31E; 502/452-9920). A Federal house built in 1810 from plans drawn by Thomas Jefferson. Lincoln visited here in 1841. Furnished with pre-1820 antiques, the house has an enclosed stairway, octagonal rooms, and a museum room. There is a blacksmith

Locust Grove in Louisville.

*Old Mulkey Meeting
House near
Monticello. Courtesy
Kentucky Department
of Parks.*

shop, a stone barn, and a 19th-century garden. Open daily.

Locust Grove (6 miles northeast on River Road, then 1 mile southwest, at 561 Blankenbaker Lane; 502/897-9845). The circa-1790 home of George Rogers Clark from 1809 to 1818, this is a handsome Georgian mansion on fifty-five acres, with original paneling, authentic furnishings, a garden, eight restored outbuildings. The visitor center presents an audiovisual program. Open daily.

Thomas Edison House (731 East Washington; 502/585-5287). A restored 1850 cottage where Edison lived while working for Western Union after the Civil War. The bedroom has been furnished in the style of the period. Four display rooms display Edison memorabilia and some of his inventions. Open Tuesday through Thursday and Saturdays.

Accommodations: *The Inn at the Park* (1332 South 4th St.; 502/637-6930 or 800/700-7275). A handsome Richardson Romanesque inn, located in the historic district, offers six guest rooms, two with a shared bath. Fourteen-foot ceilings, stone balconies, elaborate fireplaces. Full breakfast, afternoon tea. Inexpensive to moderate.

MAYSVILLE

Blue Licks Battlefield State Park (26 miles southwest on U.S. 68; 606/289-5507). The site of one of the bloodiest battles of the frontier, and the last Kentucky battle of the Revolutionary War, on August 19, 1782, one year after Cornwallis's surrender. Museum exhibits depict the history of the area. Picnicking. Open daily, April through October.

MONTICELLO

Mill Springs Park (10 miles northeast on Rte. 1275, off Rte. 90; 502/487-8481). Built in 1804 and used as a church until 1885, the *Old Mulkey Meetinghouse* is the oldest log meeting house in the state. Daniel Boone's sister Hannah and fifteen Revolutionary War soldiers are buried in the cemetery. Picnicking. Open daily.

MOUNT VERNON

William Whitley House Historic Site (15 miles northwest on U.S. 150; 606/355-2881). Built in 1785–92, this was the first brick house west of the Alleghenies. It was used as a fort against Indian attacks, and as a haven for travelers on the Wilderness Road. Called Sportsman's Hill because of the circular racetrack built nearby, which was the first track in the country and ran counterclockwise, unlike those in England. Panels over the parlor mantel symbolize each of the thirteen original states. Restored and furnished in the style of the period. Open daily, June through August.

Old Washington (4 miles south on U.S. 68; 606/759-7411). Founded in 1786 and once the second-largest settlement in Kentucky, with 119 buildings, this was the original seat of Mason County. Restored buildings include the Paxton Inn (1810), the Albert Sidney Johnston House (1797), the Old Church Museum, Mefford Fort, the Simon Kenton trading store, and the Cane Brake, thought to be one of the original cabins. Tours available. Open daily, mid-March through December.

PADUCAH

Whitehaven (I-24 exit 7; 502/554-2077). An antebellum mansion remodeled in neoclassical style in 1903. Elaborate plasterwork, stained glass, 1860s furnishings. Tours available. Open daily.

PARIS

Duncan Tavern Historic Shrine (323 High St.; 606/987-1788). The 1788 Duncan Tavern, made of local limestone, and the adjoining 1800 Anne Duncan House, of log construction, have been restored and furnished in the style of the period. Open Tuesday through Saturday.

DANIEL BOONE

A frontiersman and pioneer, Daniel Boone wrote history while others wrote about him. He was the model for James Fenimore Cooper's Leatherstocking, and his adventures inspired incidents in hundreds of works of fiction. Even Lord Byron mentiotied him in *Don Juan.*

Born near Reading, Pennsylvania, in 1734, the son of Quaker parents, Daniel was a scrappy lad who loved hunting, the wilderness, and independence. The Boone famlly moved to northwestern North Carolina in 1750. He served as a wagoner for General Braddock's ill-fated expedition to Fort Duquesne in 1755. He married, bought some land from his father, but loved to roam too much to be a serious farmer.

Boone found fame in Kentucky. In 1767 he was first into eastern Kentucky. Returning in 1769 with a small party, he followed an Indian trail known as the Warrior's Path deep into unexplored territory, remaining behind for two years after his party returned home. He had fallen in love with the "dark and bloody ground" known as "Kentuck." He tried to return in 1773 with forty settlers, but the Indians drove them back.

Two years latter he hacked out the Wilderness Road, and as soon as he reached his destination, he began building Boonesboro. For the next four years he was a militia captain, busily defending the Kentucky settlements. To a great extent, the early history of Kentucky was written by Daniel Boone.

Although highly respected, Boone was not a good businessman, and lost his Kentucky lands. In 1799 he set out for Missouri to join one of his sons. He settled there and continued to hunt and roam until his death. A quarter of a century later his remains were returned to Kentucky for burial.

Old Cane Ridge Meeting House (8 miles east on KY 537; 606/987-5350). This 1791 log meetinghouse, the birthplace of the Christian Church (Disciples of Christ), has been restored within an outer building of stone. In the early 1800s, revival meetings here attracted 20,000 to 30,000 people at a time. Tours by appointment.

Accommodations: *Rosedale* (1917 Cypress St.; 606/987-1845). This 1862 Italianate house once was the home of Civil War general John Croxton. The four guest rooms are filled with antiques, paintings, and fresh flowers, and have down comforters and ceiling fans. Duncan Tavern Historic Shrine is close by. Full breakfast. Inexpensive.

RICHMOND

Courthouse (Main St. between North 1st and North 2nd streets). This 1849 Greek Revival courthouse in the historic district was used as a hospital by Union and Confederate forces during the Civil War. The Squire Boone Rock, one of the Wilderness Road markers, is in the lobby. Open weekdays.

White Hall State Shrine (9 miles north, at I-75 exit 95; 606; 623-9178). The restored 44-room home of Cassius M. Clay, abolitionist, diplomat, and publisher of *The True American,* an antislavery newspaper. The 1799 Georgian house incorporates an Italianate addition from the 1860s, and has period furnishings, some original, as well as personal mementos. Picnicking. Open daily, April through Labor Day; Wednesday through Sunday, Labor Day through October.

SOUTH UNION

Shaker Museum (on U.S. 68; 502/542-4167). The Shakers settled this town as a religious community, but by 1922 there were only nine members left, and they sold their property and dispersed. The museum, in an original 1824 building, houses Shaker furniture, crafts, textiles, and tools. Nearby are many historic buildings. Open daily, mid-March to mid-November.

WINCHESTER

Fort Boonesborough State Park (9 miles southwest via KY 627; 606/527-3131). On the Kentucky River, this is the site of the settlement where Daniel Boone defended his fort against Indian sieges. The fort now houses craft shops where costumed interpreters produce wares. A museum has Boone memorabilia and an audiovisual program. Exhibits recreate life at the fort. Picnicking. Open daily, April through Labor Day; Wednesday through Sunday, Labor Day through October.

Old Stone Church (6 miles south, off KY 627). Built in the late 1700s, this landmark church is the oldest active church west of the Allegheny Mountains. Daniel Boone and his family worshiped here.

15

TENNESSEE

In 1541, Hernando de Soto planted the flag of Spain on the banks of the Mississippi, near what is now Memphis. Although French traders explored the Tennessee Valley, it was traders and hunters from the English colonies to the east who came over the mountain ranges, settling among the Cherokee and laying claim to the area. One recorded his presence in the winderness by carving on a tree: "D. Boone killed a bar on tree in the year 1760."

Settlers, who were called "overmountain men," were coming into East Tennessee by 1770, despite a proclamation declaring the lands west of the Appalachians Indian territory. Outside the protection of the law, they banded together, and made and administered their own laws. Dissatisfied and insecure, they formed the independent state of Franklin in 1784. But formal recognition of the independent state never came, and after four chaotic years the federal government took over and in 1790 established "the Territory of the United States South of the River Ohio."

BRISTOL

Rockey Mount Historic Site (11 miles southwest on U.S. 11E; 615/538-7396). A 1770 log house that served under William Blount as the capital of the Territory of the United States South of the River Ohio. Restored slave cabin, barn, blacksmith shop, smokehouse. Open daily.

COLUMBIA

Ancestral Home of James K. Polk (301 West 7th St., U.S. 412; 615/388-2354). The father of the President, Samuel Polk, built this Federal-style house in 1816. It is furnished with family possessions, including furniture and portraits used in the White House. Gardens link the house to an adjacent 1818 building once owned by the President's sisters. There is a visitor center. Open daily.

ELIZABETHTON

Sycamore Shoals State Historic Area (1½ miles southeast via U.S. 19E, then 3 miles east on TN 67; 615/543-5808). The first settlement west of the Blue Ridge Mountains has a reconstructed fort consisting of five buildings and palisade walls. The visitor center has a theater and museum. Picnicking. Open daily.

GALLATIN

Cragfont (5 miles east on TN 25, in Castalian Springs; 615/452-7070). This 1798 Georgian-style house was built for General James Winchester, a hero of the Revolution. It has a galleried ballroom, a weaving room, a wine cellar, Federal furnishings, and restored gardens. Open daily except Mondays, mid-April through early November.

Wynnewood (7 miles east on TN 25, in Castalian

Springs; 615/452-5463). This 1828 log inn, the oldest and largest log structure in the state, was a stagecoach inn and resort. Andrew Jackson was a frequent guest. Open daily except Mondays, mid-April through early November.

Trousdale Place (183 West Main St.; 615/452-5648). A two-story brick house built in the early 1800s, the residence of Governor William Trousdale. Period furniture, a military-history library. Open daily except Mondays.

GREENVILLE

Andrew Johnson National Historic Site (Monument Ave., College and Depot streets; 615/638-3551). The tailor shop, two houses, and the burial place of the seventeenth Presi-

dent are preserved here. Apprenticed to a tailor as a youth, Johnson came to Greenville in 1826. After years of service in local, state, and federal government, Senator Johnson remained loyal to the Union when Tennessee seceded. After serving as military governor of Tennessee, Johnson was elected Vice-President in 1864, and became President following the assassination of Lincoln. Continued opposition to the radical program of Reconstruction led to his impeachment in 1868. Acquitted by the Senate, he continued to serve as President until 1869. In 1875, Johnson became the only former President to be elected to the U.S. Senate.

The visitor center houses the Johnson tailor shop, preserved with some original furnishings and tools of the craft, as well as a museum. Opposite is the *Johnson Homestead,*

Lookout Mountain towers 2,100 feet above Chattanooga, Tennessee.

◆–❉–◆

By the Eternal, they shall not sleep on our soil!

—ANDREW JACKSON, *ON LEARNING OF BRITISH LANDINGS, 1814*

Andrew Johnson Homestead in Greenville. Courtesy National Park Service.

occupied by the family from 1851 to 1875, except during war and presidential years. *The Grave* (Monument Ave.) has an eagle-capped marker. Open daily.

Davy Crockett Birthplace State Park (3 miles east off U.S. 11E; 615/257-2167). This sixty-six-acre site overlooking the Nolichucky River is a memorial to Crockett—humorist, bear hunter, congressman, and hero of the Alamo. A small monument marks his birthplace. Nearby is a replica of the log cabin in which he was born in 1786. Visitor center and museum, picnicking. Park open daily, museum and visitor center weekdays.

Accommodations: *Hilltop House* (6 Sanford Circle; 615/639-8282). On a bluff overlooking the Nolichucky River valley, this inn offers guests three rooms, including one with a sitting area and a verandah with a river and sunset view. Innkeeper Denise Ashworth is a horticulturist and landscape architect. Full breakfast. Inexpensive.

JOHNSON CITY

Rocky Mount Historic Site (4 miles northeast on U.S. 11E; 615/538-7396). The 1770 log house that was the territorial capitol in 1790-92, under Governor William Blount, is restored to its original simplicity and furnished in the period. Slave cabin, barn, blacksmith shop, smokehouse, costumed interpreters. Tours include the Cobb Massengill House and the adjacent *Museum of Overmountain History.* Open daily, May through December, weekdays the rest of the year.

Tipton-Haynes Historic Site (1 mile off I-181 exit 31, at south edge of town; 616/926-3631). The site of the 1788 "Battle of the Lost State of Franklin." Six original buildings and four reconstructions span the period from Colonial days to the Civil War. Gift shop, visitor center. Open daily, April through October, weekdays the rest of the year.

KINGSPORT

Located at a natural gateway, this area was on the Great Indian Warrior and Trader Path, and, in 1761, the Island Road, which was the first road built in Tennessee. The trail later became the Great State Road and was used for 150 years, marking the beginning of Daniel Boone's Wilderness Road.

Netherland Inn (on the bank of the Holston River; 615/247-3211). A large 1818 stone-and-frame structure on the site of King's Boat Yard was a celebrated stop on the Great Stage Road, and was operated for more than 150 years as an inn. It is now a museum with 18th- and 19th-century furnishings, a circa-1770 log cabin, well house, and garden. Costumed interpreters. Open daily except Mondays, May through September.

KNOXVILLE

The first capital of Tennessee, Knoxville was a frontier outpost on the edge of the Cherokee Nation, the last stop on the way west. Founded by a Revolutionary War veteran and named after Secretary of War Henry Knox, it was famous as a provisioning place for westward-bound wagons and infamous for whiskey and wild times.

General James White's Fort (205 East Hill Ave.; 615/525-6514). An original 1786 pioneer house built by the founder and first settler of Knoxville. Smokehouse and blacksmith shop, museum. Open daily except Sundays, March to mid-December.

Governor William Blount Mansion (200 West Hill Ave.; 615/525-2375). The 1792 house of the governor of the Southwest Territory and a signer of the U.S. Constitution, this was the center of political and social activity in the territory. Restored with period furnishings and garden, and Blount

memorabilia. Tennessee's first constitution was drafted in the governor's office behind the mansion. The 1818 *Craighead-Jackson House* on the grounds serves as the visitor center, and has an audiovisual presentation and exhibits. Open daily, March through October; daily except Mondays the rest of the year.

Ramsey House (Swan Pond) (6 miles northeast on Thorngrove Pike; 615/546-0745). The first stone house in the county was built in 1797 for Colonel Francis A. Ramsey and became a political, religious, and social center. The restored gabled house, with attached kitchen, features ornamental cornices, keystone arches, and period furnishings. Open daily except Mondays.

Crescent Bend (Armstrong-Lockett House) and W. Perry Toms Memorial Gardens (2728 Kingston Pike; 615/637-3163). The 1834 house has collections of American and English furniture and English silver, as well as extensive terraced gardens.

Marble Springs (6 miles south via U.S. 441, TN 33, then west on TN 168; 615/573-5508). The restored farmhouse of John Seiver, state's first governor. The original cabin and other buildings stand on thirty-six acres. Open Tuesday through Sunday.

MANCHESTER

Old Stone Fort State Archaeological Park (1½ miles west off I-24; 615/723-5073). In a 600-acre park are the earthen remains of a 200-year-old walled structure built along the bluffs of the Duck River. Picnicking, museum. Open daily.

MARYVILLE

Sam Houston Schoolhouse (5 miles northeast, off U.S. 411, follow signs; 616/983-1550). The restored 1794 log building where

The Hermitage, Andrew Jackson's home in Nashville.

Houston taught in 1812. He moved to this area from Virginia with his widowed mother and eight brothers in 1807. Picnicking. The visitor center has a museum of Houston memorabilia. Open daily.

MEMPHIS

Victorian Village (600 block of Adams Ave.). Eighteen landmark buildings, either preserved or restored, range in style from neoclassical to Gothic Revival. Three houses are open to the public. *Magevney House* (198 Adams Ave.; 901/526-4464). The restored 1836 house of pioneer schoolmaster Eugene Magevney is the oldest middle-class dwelling in the city. Period antiques. Open Tuesday through Saturday. *Woodruff-Fontaine House* (680 Adams Ave.; 901/526-1469). A restored and furnished 1870 Second Empire/ Victorian mansion with a collection of antique costumes. Open daily. *Mallory- Neely House* (652 Adams Ave.; 901/523- 1484). A preserved 1852 Italianate twenty- five-room mansion with original furnishings. Open daily except Mondays.

Chucalissa Archaeological Museum (1987 Indian Village Dr., in T. O. Fuller State Park; 901/785-3160). The site of an Indian village founded around A.D. 900 and abandoned in about 1500. The 354-acre park is where de Soto is believed to have crossed

ANDREW JACKSON

America's first six presidents were aristocrats, to the manor born. Then came Andrew Jackson, a parvenu if there ever was one. All the contradictory qualities of young America were mirrored in this forceful, sometimes violent man.

Jackson was born in the South Carolina backwoods to an immigrant Irish farmer. All but one of his immediate family had died in connection with the Revolution. Jackson himself was captured and imprisoned by the British. An intensely ambitious teenager, alone and adrift, he decided to study law and head west.

His rise was mercurial. A prosecuting attorney, he served as a delegate to the Tennessee constitutional convention, and was the state's first elected congressman, then senator. He returned to Nashville in 1798, and won a seat on the state supreme court. He bought a modest estate, the Hermitage, which he would build into a major cotton plantation.

Jackson won national fame as a soldier. He crushed the Creek Indians in the Mississippi Territory, then led the American forces to victory at New Orleans, emerging as the great hero of the War of 1812. Later, fighting the Seminole Indians in Florida, he provoked controversy by executing two British subjects suspected of aiding the Indians. This delighted his supporters, who dubbed him "Old Hickory" for his physical and mental toughness.

Now immensely popular, Jackson turned to politics. Reclaiming his Senate seat, he ran for President in 1824. In a four-man race he won a plurality, but not sufficient electoral votes to win. When the House of Representatives chose John Quincy Adams, Jackson claimed that he was the victim of a "corrupt bargain" between Adams and Henry Clay. He defeated Adams four years later, which proved, he claimed, that "the majority is to govern."

Thomas Jefferson took a dim view of a Jackson presidency. "I feel much alarmed at the prospect of seeing General Jackson President," he wrote. "He is one of the most unfit men I know of for such a place. He has very little respect for laws and constitutions, and is, in fact, an able military chief. His passions are terrible."

It soon became clear that Jackson was a new kind of President. He made wide use of the spoils system, replacing competent government workers with his loyal supporters. He halted an internal improvement program, saying it was a dangerous expansion of federal power. Ignoring his critics, he opened up land for settlers by relocating eastern Indian tribes west of the Mississippi River. As antislavery agitation mounted, he condemned the abolitionists and curtailed their activities. Yet he defeated southern nationalists who defied federal authority in the name of states' rights.

Jackson's war on the Second Bank of the United States consolidated his popularity. An advocate of "hard money" and suspicious of personal debt, he believed the bank gave a few unelected private bankers power over the people's money. He proceeded to veto the bank's charter, a move that helped him gain reelection.

By the end of his second term, Jackson had created a new political party, fashioned in his own image. After his protégé, Martin Van Buren, was elected as his successor, he returned to the Hermitage, where he spent his final years as a country gentleman and elder statesman.

the Mississippi. Indian houses and temple have been reconstructed. Archaeological exhibits, museum. Open daily.

NASHVILLE

State Capitol (6th and Charlotte avenues; 615/741-1621). A Greek Revival structure built in 1845–59 with an eighty-foot tower. Architect William Strickland died before the building was completed, and is buried within its walls. Grand stairway, library, murals in the gubernatorial suite. Open weekdays.

Fort Nashborough (170 1st Ave. North, at Church St., in north end of Riverfront Park; 615/259-4747). Patterned after the

*The Belle Meade
Plantation in
Nashville.*

*The Belle Meade
Plantation in
Nashville.*

pioneer fort established nearby in 1779, this stockade-walled replica is smaller and has fewer cabins. There are exhibits of pioneer implements. Open daily.

The Hermitage (12 miles east, off I-40 exit 221A, follow sign; 615/889-2941). The Greek Revival mansion of President Andrew Jackson, built in 1819 and rebuilt after a fire in 1834, is furnished with family pieces associated with his military and White House years. On the 660-acre estate is a garden with graves of Jackson and his wife, Rachel; there are also two log cabins and a church. Nearby is *Tulip Grove,* the 1836 Greek Revival house of Andrew Jackson Donelson, Mrs. Jackson's nephew and her husband's private secretary. The visitor center has an audiovisual presentation and a museum. Open daily.

Belle Meade (7 miles southwest at Harding Rd. and Leake Ave.; 615/356-0501). Mansion and outbuildings were once part of a 5,300-acre working plantation. At the turn of the century, this was considered the greatest thoroughbred breeding farm in the country. The fourteen-room 1853 Greek Revival mansion contains Empire and Victorian furnishings. On the grounds are the 1793 Dunham Station log cabin, and a circa-1890 carriage house containing the South's largest collection of carriages. Open daily.

Traveller's Rest Historic House (I-65 exit 78, south on U.S. 31, then follow signs; 615/832-2962). The restored 1799 Federal house of Judge John Overton is maintained as a museum with period furniture, records, and letters. The eleven-acre grounds have gardens, a kitchen, and a smokehouse. Gift shop. Open daily except Mondays.

Accommodations: *The Drake Farm on Lumsley Creek* (5508 Brick Church Pike; 615/859-2425 or 800/586-7539). This 1850 Greek Revival inn, a fifteen-minute drive from downtown Nashville, has pastures and woodlands. The two guest rooms share a bath but have their own fireplaces. Breakfast. Inexpensive.

UNION CITY

Davy Crockett Cabin (20 miles south on U.S. 45W, in Rutherford; 901/643-6428). The frontiersman's cabin is now a museum with period artifacts. The grave of Crockett's mother is on the grounds. Open daily except Mondays, late May through September.

VONORE

Fort Loudoun (follow signs from U.S. 411, north of town; 615/884-6217). The southwestern outpost of England during the French and Indian Wars, this 1758–60 fort was the first permanent structure erected by the English west of the Appalachians. Besieged by Cherokees in 1760, the starved garrison was forced to surrender. Although promised safe conduct, soldiers and their families were attacked fifteen miles away from the fort, and twenty-three persons were slain. The restored site, enclosed within high palisades, includes rebuilt barracks, powder magazine, and blacksmith shop. Also here is the *Tellico Blockhouse,* an American outpost constructed in 1794–97, during Tennessee's territorial period. The fort was later converted to a federal trading post. In 1798 and 1805, two treaties with the Cherokees were negotiated here. Museum, self-guided tours. Open daily.

Sequoyah Birthplace Museum (follow signs from U.S. 411, north of town, on Citico Rd.; 615/884-6246). Displays include archaeological artifacts, Cherokee crafts, and the Cherokee syllabary developed by Sequoyah. Gift shop. Open daily.

16

NORTH CAROLINA

In 1584 two English explorers described what is now North Carolina in glowing terms, and Sir Walter Raleigh founded a colony there the next year, on Roanoke Island, the first English settlement in America. It lasted less than a year. Raleigh's next colony, in 1587, produced one of America's great mysteries—the "Lost Colony." In 1591 a supply ship found that the colony had vanished without a trace.

In the 1660s, Charles II granted eight lords proprietors the right to govern the territory between Virginia and Spanish Florida, from the Atlantic to the "South Seas." Proprietary rule didn't sit well with the settlers here, though, and they deposed six royal governors between 1663 and 1730. The region was settled slowly. The first town, Bath, was incorporated in 1705, and Wilmington, which became the major port, in 1730.

The lords proprietors sold the territory to George II in 1729, and it became the royal colony of Carolina. The next year it was divided into its north and south provinces. The first settlers were mostly English who came down from Virginia. In the eighteenth century, German and Scotch-Irish settlers came from Pennsylvania and Maryland to settle the backcountry, now called the Piedmont.

The British lost control of North Carolina early in the Revolution. At the Battle of Moores Creek Bridge, in February 1776, a patriot force defeated loyalist Scots on their way to join the royal governor. Fighting did not

come again until 1781, when Cornwallis invaded from South Carolina. He assumed that large numbers of loyalists would rally to him, but found himself "in a damned rebellious country." He pursued Nathanael Greene's army through the woods without success, then won a costly victory at Guilford Courthouse. "Another such victory would destroy the British Army," said an official in London. Cornwallis, his army seriously weakened, left North Carolina for Virginia, where he would lose the war.

Some "mountain people," isolated and independent, singing songs dating back to Elizabethan England, still live here. Individual and democratic from the beginning, North Carolina refused to ratify the Constitution until the adoption of the Bill of Rights.

ALBEMARLE

Town Creek Indian Mound State Historic Site (11 miles south on U.S. 52, then 12 miles east on NC 731 to state road, follow signs; 919/439-6802). A reconstructed 16th-century Indian ceremonial center with stockade, temples, and mortuary. Visitor center, exhibits, audiovisual presentation. Open daily, April through October; daily except Mondays the rest of the year.

Albemarle-Stanly County Historic Preservation Commission (112 North 3rd St.; 704/983-8116). An 1850s log cabin has been expanded to house a museum of period artifacts. Adjacent is Mark's House, built in the 1850s, the town's oldest building. Both open Monday through Thursday.

ASHEVILLE

Zebulon B. Vance Birthplace State Historic Site (9 miles north on U.S. 19/23, exit New-Stock Rd., then 6 miles north on Reems Creek Rd. in Weaverville; 704/645-6706). A reconstructed log house and outbuildings on the site where the Civil War governor of North Carolina grew up. Visitor center, exhibits, picnicking. Open daily, April through October; daily except Mondays rest of the year.

BEAUFORT

Beaufort Historic Site (Old Burying Ground). A restored 1829 jail, restored houses (1767–1830), and a 1796 courthouse. Information, self-guided walking tour map from Beaufort Historical Assn., 138 Turner St.; 919/728-5225. Open daily except Sundays.

Accommodations: *Pecan Tree Inn* (116 Queen St.; 919/728-6733). Built in 1866 as a Masonic lodge, over the years the inn has acquired Victorian porches, turrets, and gingerbread trim. Located in the heart of the town's historic district. Flower and herb gardens, seven guest rooms, breakfast. Inexpensive to moderate.

A bird's-eye view of New Bern, North Carolina. Courtesy Library of Congress, Prints and Photographs Division.

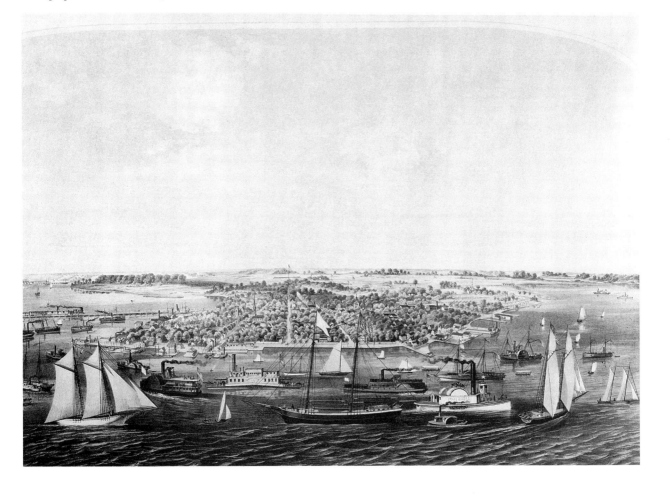

*James K. Polk
Memorial in Pineville.*

BURLINGTON

Alamance Battleground State Historic Site (6 miles southwest on NC 62; 910/227-4785). In a two-hour battle fought here on May 16, 1771, colonial militia under Royal Governor William Tryon defeated some 2,000 rebellious "Regulators." A restored log house is on the site. The visitor center has exhibits and an audiovisual presentation. Picnicking. Open daily, April through October; daily except Mondays the rest of the year.

CHARLOTTE

James K. Polk Memorial State Historic Site (12 miles south on U.S. 521, in Pineville; 704/889-7145). A replica of a log cabin and outbuildings at the birthsite of the eleventh President. The visitor center has a film and exhibits. Open daily, April through October; Sundays the rest of year.

CHEROKEE

This is the capital of the Eastern Band of the Cherokee, who live on the Qualla Reservation at the edge of the Great Smoky Mountains National Park. It is the largest reservation east of the Mississippi, and is populated by the descendants of tribe members who avoided being driven to Oklahoma over the "Trail of Tears."

Oconaluftee Indian Village ($\frac{1}{2}$ mile north on U.S. 441; 704/497-2111). A replica of an Indian village of 250 years ago includes a seven-sided council house. Lectures, craft demonstrations, tours. Open daily, mid-May through late October.

Museum of the Cherokee Indian (on U.S. 441 at Drama Rd., on Cherokee Reservation; 704/497-3481). Arts and crafts, audiovisual programs, artifacts. Open daily.

Cherokee Heritage Museum and Gallery (on U.S. 441 and Big Cove Rd., in Saunooke's Village; 704-497-3211). This

... 'tis a thorough aversion to labor that makes new people file off to North Carolina, where plenty and a warm sun confirm them in their disposition to laziness ...

—WILLIAM BYRD
OF VIRGINIA

Duke Homestead in Durham. Photo by Marian K. O'Keefe.

facility interprets Cherokee history and culture. Gift shop. Open daily except three weeks from late December through early January.

Unto These Hills (Mountainside Theater, U.S. 441, ½ mile from jct. U.S. 19; 704/497-2111). Kermit Hunter's drama re-creating the history of the Cherokee Nation from 1540 to 1848 is presented in a natural amphitheater. Nightly except Sunday, mid-June through late August.

CONCORD

Reed Gold Mine State Historic Site (10 miles southeast on U.S. 601 and NC 200 to Georgeville, then 2 miles south on NC 1100; 704/786-8337). The first documented discovery of gold in the United States occurred here in 1799. Panning area, demonstrations, underground tour. The visitor center has exhibits

and shows a film. Picnicking. Open daily, April through October; daily except Mondays the rest of the year.

DURHAM

Duke Homestead State Historic Site (2828 Duke Homestead Rd., ½ mile north of jct. I-85 and Guess Rd.; 919/477-5498). The ancestral home of the Duke family includes a tobacco factory, curing barn, and outbuildings. The Tobacco Museum has exhibits and shows a film. Tours available. Open daily, April through October; daily except Mondays the rest of the year.

Stagville Preservation Center (7 miles northeast via Roxboro Rd. and Old Oxford Hwy.; 919/620-0120). Once part of the Bennehan-Cameron plantation, the seventy-seven-acre property now has several 18th-

and 19th-century plantation buildings. Open weekdays.

West Point on the Eno (I-85, Duke St. exit, then 3½ miles north; 919/471-1623). A 371-acre park on the scenic Eno River has a restored 1850 farmhouse, a working gristmill, a blacksmith shop, and a museum of photography. Picnicking. Park open daily; farmhouse and museum open weekends, March through December.

EDENTON

One of the oldest communities in North Carolina, Edenton was the capital of the colony for more than twenty-two years. The women of the town staged their own "tea party" on October 25, 1774, signing a resolution protesting British injustice. A bronze teapot on the Courthouse Green commemorates the event.

Historic Edenton. Tours of historic properties start at the Visitor Center (108 North Broad St.; 919/482-2637) daily, April through December, daily except Mondays the rest of the year. Stops include the 1767 Georgian *Chowan County Courthouse,* in continuous use since it was built; *St. Paul's Episcopal Church* (1736); the *John Iredell House* (1773); the home of a George Washington appointee to the Supreme Court; and the *Cupola House* (1758), considered an outstanding example of Jacobean architecture.

Nerwbold-White House (15 miles north on U.S. 17 Bypass to Hereford, then southeast on county rte. 1336; 919/426-7567). The oldest house in the state, this 1680 brick structure was a meeting place for the proprietary government of North Carolina. Open daily except Sundays, March through December.

Somerset Place State Historic Site (18

INDENTURED SERVITUDE

The Virginia Company devised the system of indentured servitude in the 1610s to help finance the recruitment and transport of workers from England to the colony. Those who couldn't afford the Atlantic passage could "borrow" the funds. In return they signed contracts of "indentures" to work for their masters for a fixed number of years. It was a popular system, and during the Colonial era, some 200,000 to 300,000 people, from one half to two thirds of all European emigrants, used it to come to America.

The system was inspired by "service in husbandry," a major source of agricultural labor in England. Typically, farm servants were children from poor families who left home in their early teens to work for more-prosperous farmers until they married. They lived in their masters' households, agreeing to an annual contract for wages, food, and lodgings.

Indentured servitude was harsher than service in husbandry, but it was not a form of slavery. Servants entered into their contracts voluntarily, and they retained some legal rights. They could own property, bring suit, testify, and appeal to the courts for protection against abusive masters. Terms varied considerably, however, from four years for skilled adults to a decade or more for unskilled minors. Servants could not marry without their masters' permission, they had little control over the terms or conditions of their labor and living standards, and they could be sold without their consent.

They put up with a lot, because they expected a lot in America. A few joined the ranks of the Colonial Elite, but more died in poverty, often while still servants. Cheap land and the rapid growth of the Colonial economy lured successive migrants to take a chance on America. As the years went by, African slaves proved a less expensive form of labor, and indentured servitude was not a factor in the American economy after 1800.

Cades Cove in the Great Smoky Mountains National Park. Courtesy National Park Service.

miles southeast via NC 32, U.S. 64 to Crewsell, then 7 miles south on Lake Phelps in Pettigrew State Park; 919/797-4560). One of the largest plantations in the state, encompassing more than 100,000 acres. Mansion and outbuildings date from about 1830. Open daily, April through October; daily except Mondays the rest of the year.

Accommodations: *The Lords Proprietors' Inn* (33 North Broad St.; 919/482-3641, or 800/348-8933). The inn, dating from 1801, consists of three houses in the historic district, offering a total of twenty guest rooms. Full breakfast, dinner available.

Meals served in a separate dining room on the patio. Expensive.

GREAT SMOKY MOUNTAINS NATIONAL PARK

Half in North Carolina, half in Tennessee, this is a hiker's dream. Nearby are the cabins, barns, and mills of the mountain people whose ancestors came from England and Scotland. It also is a place to see the descendants of the once-mighty Cherokee Nation, whose ancestors hid in the mountains from the soldiers in the winter of 1838–39 to avoid being driven over the "Trail of Tears" to Oklahoma. This is the tribe of Sequoyah, the brilliant chief who invented a written language for the Cherokee people.

Cades Cove (8 miles southwest of Townsend, TN; 615/436-1200). An outdoor museum reflecting the life of the original mountain people, with log cabins and barns. Park naturalists conduct campfire programs and hikes during spring and summer. Self-guided nature trails. Open daily, mid-March through November.

GREENSBORO

Guilford Courthouse National Military Park (6 miles northwest and ¼ mile east off U.S. 220 on New Garden Rd.; 910/288-1776). On March 15, 1781, Cornwallis won a costly victory here, a step toward his surrender at Yorktown in October of the same year. After destroying a quarter of the British force, General Nathanael Greene made a successful retreat and then severely hampered the British plan of subduing the Southern colonies. Self-guided auto tours of the 220-acre park are available; there are also walking trails. The visitor center has a museum housing a collection of Revolutionary War weapons and other relics, and shows a film. Open daily.

MANTEO

Fort Raleigh National Historical Site (3 miles north, off U.S. 64; 919/473-5772). The first English colony in the New World was attempted here on Roanoke Island in 1585. Virginia Dare, born here August 18, 1587,

Fort Raleigh National Historic Site at Manteo.

Compelling the colonies to pay money without their consent would be rather like raising contributions in an enemy's country than taxing Englishmen for their own benefit.

—BENJAMIN FRANKLIN, *1764*

was the first child of English parents born in America. A few days after her birth, Governor John White left the island for England, intending to return with supplies. He was detained by the war with Spain and did not get back until August 1590. The colony had disappeared, leaving only the mysterious word "CROATOAN" cut into a tree. What happened to the colonists is unknown. Some believe the present-day Lumbee Indians descend from them. Fort Raleigh has been excavated and the fort built by the colonists reconstructed. The visitor center has an audiovisual program, exhibits, and relics. Open daily.

***Elizabeth II* State Historic Site** (town waterfront; 919/473-1144). A replica of a 16th-century ship similar to those that brought the first colonists here more than 400 years ago. A living-history interpretation is presented in summer. The visitor center has exhibits and an audiovisual program. Open daily, April through October; daily except Mondays the rest of the year.

The Lost Colony (Waterside Theater, 3 miles northwest of Manteo on U.S. 64/264; 919/473-3414). This outdoor drama by Pulitzer Prize winner Paul Green is about the colony and its curious disappearance. Nightly except Sundays, mid-June through late August. Reservations advised.

NEW BERN

Tryon Palace Sites and Gardens (610 Pollock St., south end of George St., 1 block south of U.S. 17, 70 Business, NC 55; 919/638-1560). Built in 1767–70 by the royal governor, William Tryon, this "most beautiful building in the colonial Americas" burned by accident in 1798 and lay in ruins until rebuilt between 1952 and 1959. It served as the Colonial and first state capitol. Reconstruction, furnishings and 18th-century gar-

den are beautiful and authentic. Dramas are performed on the grounds daily during summer. On the site are two other historic houses: the *Dixon-Stevenson House* (1830), an early Federal structure that reflects the marine history of the area in its interior woodwork and widow's walk; and the Georgian *John Wright Stanly House* (circa 1780), furnished in the period. Formal gardens are typical of the period. Tours available. Open daily.

New Bern Academy (4 blocks from Tryon Palace in the historic district; 919/638-1560). This circa-1790 structure is the major surviving landmark of an educational institution founded in the 1760s, now restored as a museum of local history. Open daily.

Attmore-Oliver House (510 Pollock St.; 919/638-8558). This circa-1790 house, the headquarters of the New Bern Historical Society, exhibits 18th- and 19th-century furnishings and objects. Open Tuesday through Saturday, early April to mid-December.

Accommodations: *King's Arms Inn* (212 Pollock St.; 919/638-4409 or 800/872-9306). In the heart of the historic district, four blocks from Tryon Palace, this 1848 house has a mansard roof and touches of Victorian architecture. The ten guest rooms (two with a shared bath) are decorated with antiques, and have canopy or four-poster beds and fireplaces. Breakfast. Inexpensive.

RALEIGH

State Capitol (Capitol Square; 919/733-4994). A stately 1840 Greek Revival building. The old legislative chambers, in use until 1963, have been restored to their original appearance, as have the old state library room and the state geologist's office. Tours may be scheduled for this and other state buildings at the *Capital Area Visitor Center* (301 North Blount St.; 919/733-3456). Open daily.

Mordecai Historic Park (Mimosa St. and Wake Forest Rd.; 919/834-4844). The park includes a preserved 1785 plantation home with many original furnishings, noted for its neoclassical architecture; an early Raleigh office building; St. Mark's chapel; the Basdger-Iredell Law Office; the house in which Andrew Johnson, seventeenth President, was born; and an 1830s herb garden. Tours available. Open daily.

ROANOKE RAPIDS

Historic Halifax State Historic Site (9 miles southeast off U.S. 301, or south on I-95 to exit 168; 919/583-7191). The Halifax Resolves, the first formal sanction of American independence, were adopted here on April 12, 1776. Buildings include the Owens House (1760), the Burgess Law Office, the Eagle Tavern (1790), the Sally-Billy House, the clerk's office, the jail, and the Montfort Archaeology Exhibit Center. There are also a garden and an old churchyard. The visitor center has audiovisual programs, exhibits. Historical dramas are presented during the summer. Open daily, April through October; daily except Mondays the rest of the year.

SALISBURY

Daniel Boone spent his youth and Andrew Jackson studied law here. Salisbury's wide, shady streets were twice taken over by the military: first by Lord Cornwallis during the Revolution, then by General Stoneman during the Civil War.

Dr. Josephus Hall House (226 South Jackson; 704/636-0103). A large 1820 house with original Federal and Victorian furnishings, set amid giant oaks and century-old boxwood. The house was used as a Union commander's headquarters after the Civil War. Open Thursday through Sunday afternoons.

Rowan Museum (116 South Jackson St.; 704/633-5946). In the 1819 Maxwell Chambers house, the museum has period rooms, regional furniture, and a 19th-century garden. Open Thursday through Sunday.

Old Stone House (4 miles southeast off U.S. 52 in Granite Quarry; 704/633-5946). Built in 1766 of hand-laid granite, with walls two feet thick, the house was restored in 1966 and authentically furnished. It includes a family burial ground. Open Saturday and Sunday afternoons, April through November.

SANFORD

House in the Horseshoe State Historic Site (12 miles west on NC 42 to Carbonton, then 5 miles south on state road 1644; 919/947-2051). This circa-1770 house was the home of Governor Benjamin Williams and the site of a Revolutionary War skirmish. Open daily, April through October; daily except Mondays the rest of the year.

SOUTHERN PINES

Shaw House (Southwest Broad St. and Morganton Rd.; 910/692-2051). This antebellum house of simple style has unusual mantels of carved cypress. Also on the premises are the Britt Sanders Cabin and the Garner House. Tours Wednesday through Sunday afternoons, mid-January through June and September to mid-December.

SOUTHPORT

Brunswick Town–Fort Anderson State Historic Site (14 miles north on NC 133, then 5 miles south on Plantation Rd.; 910/371-6613). Brunswick, founded in 1726, thrived as a major port. Fearing a British attack, its citizens fled when the Revolution began. In 1776 the town was burned by British sailors. Built

The times that tried men's souls are over and the greatest and completest revolution the world ever knew gloriously and happily accomplished.

—THOMAS PAINE, *1783*

Poplar Grove Plantation in Wilmington.

across the town are the Civil War earthworks of Fort Anderson, which held out for thirty days after the fall of Fort Fisher in 1865. The visitor center has an audiovisual program and exhibits. Nature trail, picnicking. Open daily, April through October; daily except Mondays the rest of the year.

WASHINGTON

Bath State Historic Site (14 miles east on U.S. 264 and NC 92; 919/923-3971). The oldest incorporated town in the state (1705), its buildings include the Bonner House (circa 1820), the Van Der Veer House (circa 1790), the Palmer-Marsh House (circa 1745), and the St. Thomas Episcopal Church (circa 1735). Open daily, April through October; daily except Mondays the rest of the year.

WILLIAMSTON

Hope Plantation (U.S. 13 to Windsor, then 4 miles west on NC 308; 919/794-3140). A circa-1800 Georgian plantation house built by Governor David Stone, with period furnishings, outbuildings, and gardens. The tour includes the 1763 King-Bazemore House, a unique Colonial with gambrel roof, dormer windows, and brick ends. This house also has period furnishings, outbuildings, and gardens. Open daily, March through December.

WILMINGTON

In 1765, eight years before the Boston Tea Party, the citizens of Wilmington prevented the British from unloading their stamps for the Stamp Act. Cornwallis held the town for almost a year in 1781 as his main base of operations. After the battle of Guilford Courthouse, the Lord General came back to Wilmington before heading for Yorktown and defeat.

Burgwin-Wright House (224 Market St. at 3rd St.; 910/762-0570). A restored 1770 town house built on the foundation of the abandoned town jail. Cornwallis had his headquarters here during April 1781. Period furnishings, garden. Tours available. Open Tuesday through Saturday.

Moores Creek National Battlefield (17 miles north on U.S. 421, then 3 miles west on NC 210; 910/283-5591). In 1776, the colonists took sides—patriots opposing loyalists. Colonels Moore, Lillington, and Caswell, with the blessing of the Continental Congress, broke up the loyalist forces, captured their leaders, and seized gold and weapons. This ended British hopes of an early invasion through the South and encouraged North Carolina to instruct its delegates to vote in Philadelphia for independence. Visitor center, picnicking. Open daily.

Orton Plantation Gardens (18 miles south on NC 133; 910/371-6851). This former rice plantation now has beautiful gardens with ancient oaks, magnolias, ornamental plants, lawn and water scenes, and a waterfowl refuge in the former ricefields. Orton House (circa 1730) can be seen but is not open to the public. Gardens open daily, March through November.

Poplar Grove Plantation (9 miles northeast on U.S. 17; 910/686-9989). A restored circa-1850 Greek Revival plantation manor house with smokehouse, tenant house, blacksmith and weaver workshops, restaurant, country store, tours. Open daily except late December through early January.

Henrietta II Paddlewheel Riverboat Cruises (downtown at riverfront; 910/343-1611). Narrated sightseeing cruises down the Cape Fear River to North Carolina State Port. Two cruises daily except Mondays, June through August; one cruise daily except Mondays April–May and September–October.

Accommodations: *Historic Stemmerman's 1855 Inn* (130 South Front St.; 910/763-7776). Overlooking the Cape Fear River, this Federal-style inn has seven guest rooms with period furnishings and equipped kitchenettes. A restaurant is on the premises. Breakfast. Inexpensive to expensive.

WINSTON-SALEM

Historic Bethabara Park (2147 Bethabara Rd.; 910/924-8191). The site of a 1753 Moravian settlement. Restored buildings include Gemeinhaus (1788), Potter's House (1782), Buttner House (1803), and a reconstructed palisade fort (1756–63). God's Acre graveyard, reconstructed community gardens, picnicking. The visitor center has a slide program. Open daily, April through November.

Historic Old Salem (south of business district on Old Salem Rd.; 910/721-7300). A restoration of a planned Moravian community, which was the 18th-century trade and cultural center of North Carolina's Piedmont. Many of the structures have been restored and furnished with original or period pieces. Nine houses plus outbuildings are open to the public. Craft demonstrations. Nearby are the *Salem Academy and College* (Church St. on Salem Sq.; 910/721-2702), founded by the Moravians in 1772; and the *Museum of Early Southern Decorative Arts* (924 South Main St.; 910/721-7360). Tours start at the visitor center on Old Salem Road. Open daily.

Accommodations: *Augustus T. Zevely Inn* (803 South Main St.; 910/748-9299, or 800/929-9299). Each of the thirteen guest rooms in this 1844 Georgian inn is individually decorated in Moravian style. Breakfast is served on a covered porch shaded by a magnolia tree. Moderate to expensive.

17

VIRGINIA

In 1607, thirteen years before the Pilgrims set foot on Plymouth Rock, three ships—the *Susan Constant,* the *Godspeed,* and the *Discovery*—landed a hundred or so men and boys on the coast of Virginia at a place they would name Jamestown, after their king, James I. It proved to be an unhealthy and dangerous choice, and the settlement would not have survived were it not for the able leadership of Captain John Smith and the strict discipline maintained by the first governors.

During the first decade, the Virginia Company of London, the settlement's sponsor, saw little progress or profit beyond survival and the development of tobacco as an export product. It tried various schemes to attract new settlers, but an Indian attack in 1622 that killed 347 settlers was the last straw. The king revoked the charter and made Virginia a crown colony in 1624, and it thrived. By 1650 it had 16,000 settlers, and it grew to 40,000 by 1660.

The original boundaries of Virginia were enormous, stretching to the Mississippi. The Carolinas were made separate from Virginia in 1626, and Maryland in 1632. After the Revolution, land severed from Virginia would be made into the states of Kentucky, Ohio, Indiana, Illinois, Michigan, and Wisconsin—the old Northwest Territory.

An economic pattern was developing, in which the best land was accumulated in large holdings by a small group of planters. This brought pressure from have-nots and newcomers for additional land in the backcountry to the west, and this led in turn to hostilities with Indians on the frontier, and frequently the forced removal of the Indians.

Because tobacco cultivation required large amounts of land, the plantations were spread out and became virtually self-sufficient economic units. As a result, few towns of any size developed. Williamsburg, the seat of the Colonial government, was almost deserted most of the year. Planters came to town for a few weeks when the House of Burgesses was in session, then went home.

Under Governor Sir William Berkeley, who dominated the politics of Virginia for thirty years, the House of Burgesses, which was sanctioned in 1639, became an exclusive club of the large landowners, heavily weighted in favor of the easternmost counties. When Berkeley failed to put down an Indian uprising on the frontier in 1676, settlers there took matters into their own hands. Led by Nathaniel Bacon, they took control of the colony for a brief time, and even burned Jamestown. Although "Bacon's Rebellion" fizzled after Bacon died of natural causes, it was the most serious challenge to royal authority in the colonies until the outbreak of the Revolution.

Virginia provided much of the political and military leadership to the cause of independence—Washington, Jefferson, Patrick Henry, George Mason, and the five Lee brothers. Washington was named commander-in-chief of the Continental Army, and Daniel Morgan and "Light-Horse" Harry Lee were both brilliant field commanders.

At the outbreak of the Revolution, the Virginia militia chased Governor Dunmore from the colony. Norfolk was burned to the ground by fires set by British shells. Thereafter the fighting took place in the northern states and the Carolinas, until Cornwallis invaded Virginia from the Carolinas in 1781. That October he was trapped at Yorktown, between a French fleet and a Franco-American army, and his surrender signaled the end of the war.

ALEXANDRIA

Walking tour of historic sites. Start at the Visitor Bureau in the circa-1725 *Ramsay House* (221 King St. at Fairfax St.; 703/838-4200), the oldest house in town. Guided walking tours are led by costumed guides daily from spring through fall, weather permitting. Free parking tickets. Open daily.

Carlyle House (121 North Fairfax St.; 703/549-2997). This 1792 Palladian stone mansion was the site of a 1755 meeting between General Edward Braddock and five Colonial governors to plan the French and Indian Wars. Open daily.

Stabler-Leadbeater Apothecary Museum (105 South Fairfax St.; 703/836-3373). A museum of early pharmacy with a collection of more than 1,000 apothecary bottles. Washington, Robert E. Lee, and John Calhoun were regular customers. Open daily except Sundays.

Patrick Henry gave the coming Revolution a battle cry when he declared, "give me liberty, or give me death!" in St. John's Church in Richmond.

Arlington House, the Robert E. Lee Memorial. Courtesy Library of Congress.

─┼─

Kings are the servants, not the proprietors of the people.

—THOMAS JEFFERSON, *A SUMMARY VIEW OF THE RIGHTS OF BRITISH AMERICA, 1774*

Christ Church (118 North Washington St.; 703/549-6670). Washington and Robert E. Lee were pewholders in this 1773 church, which has a Palladian window and a crystal chandelier brought from England. Gift shop. Open Mondays and weekend afternoons.

Lee-Fendall House (614 Oronoco St.; 703/548-1789). Built in 1785 by Phillip Richard Fendall, and lived in by the Lee family for 118 years. Furnished with Lee family belongings. Open daily except Mondays.

Boyhood Home of Robert E. Lee (607 Oronoco St.; 703/548-8454). Federal architecture, antique furnishings and paintings. Open daily, February through mid-December.

Gadsby's Tavern Museum (134 North Royal St.; 703/838-4242). This famous 1770 hostelry, now a restaurant, combines two 18th-century buildings. Open daily.

George Washington Masonic National Memorial (101 Callahan Dr., west end of King St.; 703/683-2007). This 333-foot-high structure houses a collection of Washington belongings compiled by the Masonic lodge, where he served as its first master. Tours of a replica of the lodge's first hall, library, museum, and observation deck. Open daily.

Alexandria Black History Resource Center (638 North Alfred St.; 703/838-4399). Exhibits, documents and artifacts tell the story of African-Americans in Alexandria. Open Tuesday through Saturday.

Gunston Hall (18 miles south on U.S. 1, then 4 miles east on VA 242 in Lorton, at 10709 Gunston Rd.; 703/550-9220). The 550-acre, circa-1750 estate of George Mason, framer of the Constitution and father of the Bill of Rights. Restored mansion, outbuildings, museum, boxwood gardens, gift shop. Open daily.

Pohick Episcopal Church (9301 Richmond Hwy., 18 miles south on U.S. 1, in Lorton; 703/550-9449). The 1774 parish church of Mount Vernon and Gunston Hall,

THOMAS JEFFERSON

Although he served as governor of Virginia, minister to France, secretary of state, Vice-President, and President, Thomas Jefferson is remembered less for the offices he held than for what he stood for—the belief in the natural rights of man, as he expressed them in the Declaration of Independence, and his faith in the people's ability to govern themselves. Few people have ever made a greater impact on their times.

As a young member of the Virginia House of Burgesses, Jefferson questioned British colonial policies and was an early advocate of American rights. In 1774 his pamphlet *A Summary View of the Rights of British America* brought him recognition and a place on the committee of the Continental Congress charged with drafting the Declaration of Independence. As its principal author, he gave eloquent expression to the principles of the natural rights of man.

Jefferson's intellect led some to dismiss him as a visionary, but he was remarkably successful in politics. He led the opposition to the Federalist policies of Alexander Hamilton and John Adams, and ran against Adams in the election of 1796 to succeed Washington as President. He lost, but four years later defeated Adams and presided over the first transfer of political power in the history of the young republic.

In his inaugural address, Jefferson called for faith in majority rule, simplicity and frugality in government, limited central authority, and the protection of civil liberties and minority rights.

Jefferson had boundless intellectual curiosity, and his interests included science and natural history, the classics, music, and the arts. He translated his interests into action. His study of natural law and political thought reinforced his commitment to republican government. His devotion to science inspired numerous agricultural pursuits. His interest in architecture and the arts was evident in the design of his home at Monticello. His concern about education led to the founding of the University of Virginia, for which he was champion, architect, and academic planner.

His sense of priorities was revealed when he instructed that his tombstone be inscribed only with the words that he was the author of the Declaration of Independence and the Statute of Virginia for Religious Freedom, and the father of the University of Virginia.

Alexis de Tocqueville, visiting America five years after Jefferson's death, declared him to be "the greatest democrat whom the democracy of America has as yet produced."

Red Hill, the Patrick Henry National Memorial, in Brookneal.

built under the supervision of George Mason and George Washington. The interior has been fully restored. Open daily.

ARLINGTON

Arlington House, Robert E. Lee Memorial (Arlington National Cemetery; 703/557-0613). Built in 1802–18 by George Washington Parke Custis, Martha Washington's grandson and foster son of George Washington. In 1831, Custis's daughter, Mary Anna Randolph Custis, married Lieutenant Robert E. Lee here, and six of their seven children were born here. As executor of the estate, Lee took extended leave from the army and devoted his time to managing and improving the property. It was the Lee homestead for thirty years before the Civil War. The Lees lost the house during the war, and much of what was to become the Arlington National Cemetery was built on what had been their property. The Greek Revival house has been restored and furnished in the style of the period. Open daily.

ASHLAND

Patrick Henry Home "Scotchtown" (1 mile northwest via VA 54, 671, county rte. 685; 804/227-3500, or 804/883-6917). This graceful 1830 mansion was also the girlhood home of Dolley Madison. Open daily except Mondays, April through October.

BLACKSBURG

Smithfield Plantation (¼ mile west off U.S. 460 Bypass, at VA Tech exit; 703/951-2060). The restored 1773 home of Colonel

William Preston and three governors represents an architectural link between Tidewater and Piedmont plantations and those of the Mississippi Valley. Open April through November, Thursday through Sunday afternoons.

BROOKNEAL

Patrick Henry National Memorial, "Red Hill" (3 miles east on VA 40, 2 miles south on VA 600 and 619; 804/376-2044). The last home and burial place of Henry, the site includes a restoration of the family cottage, cook's cabin, smokehouse, stable, and kitchen, as well as Henry's law office, a museum, and a gift shop. Open daily.

CHARLOTTESVILLE

Monticello (2 miles southeast on VA 53; 804/295-8181). One of the most beautiful estates in Virginia, and a classic of American architecture. Thomas Jefferson designed Monticello and built it on a mountaintop over the course of forty years, moving into the first completed outbuilding in 1771, though construction continued until 1809. Most interior furnishings are original, and the estate includes a restored orchard, a vineyard, and a vegetable garden. Jefferson died here, and is buried in the family cemetery. The visitor center (on VA 20S, at I-64; 804/295-8181) displays Jefferson family memorabilia, architectural models, and a film. Both open daily.

Ash Lawn-Highland (4½ miles southeast on county rte. 795; 804/293-9539). Jefferson personally selected this site for the 535-acre estate home, built in 1799, of President James Monroe. Furnished with family possessions. Craft demonstrations. Boxwood gardens, peacocks, picnicking, special events. Open daily.

Monticello, home of Thomas Jefferson. From The American Revolution, Dover Publications, Inc., New York.

JAMES MADISON

Short, soft-spoken, scholarly, James Madison was one of the less colorful but more important of the Founding Fathers. In a career of more than forty years, he was involved in every major phase of the Revolution and the early republic. Although he served in a number of high offices, including the presidency, he is best remembered as a political theorist and for his role in launching the Constitution.

At the Constitutional Convention of 1787, Madison was the best prepared and the most influential. He led the search for, as he put it, "a republican remedy for the diseases most incident in republican government." He hoped that a new government that rested directly on the people would prevent factional disorder without endangering liberty.

Madison worked tirelessly for ratification. He co-authored the brilliant collection of essays explaining the Constitution, *The Federalist*, still considered a masterpiece of political theory.

A member of the first Congress, he drafted laws and established precedents that gave shape and force to the new Constitution. He guided the process that produced the first ten amendments, known as the Bill of Rights.

Madison served eight years as Jefferson's secretary of state, and succeeded him as President for two terms. Most historians consider him a weak chief executive, citing his inept leadership during the War of 1812, although the new nation emerged from the "Second War of Independence" with new unity and self-confidence. In retirement he was revered for his role both in founding and in securing the first great modern republic.

Historic Michie Tavern (1 mile south on VA 20; 804/977-1234). Built circa 1780 on land granted to Patrick Henry's father and later bought by James Michie. One of the oldest homesteads remaining in the state. A lunch buffet is served in a converted 200-year-old log house. Open daily.

University of Virginia (2 miles southeast on VA 53; 804/924-1019). Founded by Thomas Jefferson and built according to his design. Red brick buildings with white trim, striking vistas, rolling lawns, and ancient trees mark this "academic village." Serpentine walls, one brick thick, are famous. Room 13, West Range, occupied by Edgar Allan Poe when he was a student, is open to the public. Walking tours start at the rotunda. Open daily.

Accommodations: *Silver Thatch Inn* (3001 Hollymead Dr.; 804/978-4686). This white clapboard inn was built in 1780 for British officers by Hessian mercenaries. Later it was a boys' school and the manor house on a tobacco plantation. The original house, now called the Hessian Room, was enlarged several times. The public spaces and the seven guest rooms are filled with antiques. Breakfast. Dinner (at extra cost) is served in three intimate dining rooms. Moderate.

CLARKSVILLE

Prestwould (2 miles north on U.S. 15; 804/374-8672). This manor house was built in 1795 by Sir Peyton Skipwith. It has rare French scenic wallpaper, original and period furnishings. Interpretive programs are offered. Open daily.

FAIRFAX

Sully (10 miles west on U.S. 50, then north on VA 28 near Chantilly; 703/437-1794). The restored 1794 house of Richard Bland Lee, brother of Light-Horse Harry Lee, has some original furnishings. On the grounds are a log store, a smokehouse, and a kitchen-washhouse. Tours available. Open daily except Tuesdays.

FALLS CHURCH

The Falls Church (115 East Fairfax St. at Washington on U.S. 29; 703/532-7600). This 1769 building replaced the original 1732 wooden church. It served as a recruiting station during the Revolution, was then abandoned until 1830, and used during the Civil War as a hospital and later as a stable for cavalry horses. Restored in 1959. Open daily except Saturdays.

FREDERICKSBURG

Captain John Smith visited this area in 1608, and thought it was a good place for a settlement. In 1727 the General Assembly directed that fifty acres of "lease-land" be laid out, and that the town be called Fredericksburg after the Prince of Wales. Here is where George Washington went to school, and where his sister Betty and his mother, Mary Ball Washington, lived. Guns for the Revolution were manufactured here, and four of the most savage battles of the Civil War were fought here.

Hugh Mercer Apothecary Shop (1020 Caroline St.; 703/373-3362). The 18th-century pharmacy and medical office of Dr. Hugh Mercer, who left his practice to serve as a general in the Revolution. Period medical instruments are displayed. Open daily.

Rising Sun Tavern (1308 Caroline St.; 703/371-1494). Built in 1760 by George Washington's youngest brother, Charles, this tavern, a stagecoach stop and social and political center, has been restored and furnished in the style of the period. It has a pewter collection. Open daily.

Fredericksburg Area Museum (Town Hall) (907 Princess Anne St.; 703/371-3037). The museum interprets history of the area from the first settlers to the 20th century. Open daily.

St. George's Episcopal Church and Churchyard (Princess Anne and George streets; 703/373-4133). Patrick Henry's uncle and namesake was the first rector here. Many illustrious Virginians are buried in the churchyard. Open daily.

Fredericksburg Masonic Lodge Number Four (Princess Anne and Hanover streets; 703/373-5885). Washington became a member in 1752, and the building, which dates from 1812, contains relics of his initiation and membership, and a Gilbert Stuart portrait. Open daily.

James Monroe Museum (908 Charles St.; 703/899-4559). Monroe lived and worked in town as a young man, from 1786 to 1789. This museum has the largest collection of his memorabilia in the country, including original documents, a desk bought in France in 1794 while he was ambassador, attire worn at the court of Napoleon, and books from his library. The museum has a garden, and is a National Historic Landmark. Open daily.

Old Slave Block (William and Charles).

Kenmore Plantation in Fredericksburg. Photo by Robb Gassie.

A circular sandstone block about three feet high, from which slaves were once auctioned.

Mary Washington House (1200 Charles St.; 703/373-1569). George Washington bought this house for his mother in 1772, and she lived here until her death in 1789. Some original furnishings, boxwood garden. Open daily.

Accommodations: Kenmore (1201 Washington Ave.; 703/373-3381 or 800/437-7622). The home of Colonel Fielding Lewis, commissioner of Fredericksburg gunnery, who married George Washington's only sister, Betty. A magnificent 1752 home, one of the finest restorations in Virginia is now an inn with thirteen guest rooms, some with fireplaces and canopy beds. Breakfast, other meals available in dining room. Moderate.

Chatham Manor (Fredericksburg and Spotsylvania National Military Park; 703/373-4461). This 18th-century Georgian mansion, the home of William Fitzhugh, one of the wealthiest landowners in Virginia, became the headquarters of various Union generals during the Civil War. Robert E. Lee is believed to have met Mary Custis, his future bride, at a house party here. Open daily.

George Washington Birthplace National Monument (38 miles east on VA 3, then 2 miles east on VA 204; 804/224-1732). George, first child of Augustine and Mary Ball Washington, was born February 11, 1732 (February 22, according to the Gregorian calendar adopted in 1752), at his father's estate on Popes Creek on the shore of the Potomac. The family moved in 1735 to Little Hunting Creek Plantation (later called Mount Vernon), then in 1738 to Ferry Farm, near Fredericksburg. The original house burned in 1779 and was never rebuilt. Memorial House is not a replica, but represents a composite of typical 18th-century Virginia plantation houses, with period furnishings and a period garden, a spinning and weaving room, and household slave quarters. There is also a farm with livestock. Picnicking, visitor center. Open daily.

HAMPTON

Hampton, settled in 1610, is one of the oldest continuously English-speaking communities in the country. The settlement began at a place then called Kecoughtan, with the building of Fort Algernourne as protection against the Spanish. Later the area was harassed by pirates. In 1718 the notorious Edward Teach, known as Blackbeard, was killed by Lieutenant Robert Maynard, and this brought an end to organized piracy. The town was shelled in the Revolution, sacked by the British in the War of 1812, and burned in the Civil War by retreating Confederates.

St. John's Church and Parish Museum (West Queen's Way and High Court Lane; 804/722-2567). This is the fourth church of the Episcopal parish, which was established in 1610. The museum has a Bible dating from 1599, communion silver from 1618, and a Colonial vestry book. Open daily.

Fort Monroe (3 miles southeast via Mercury Blvd., Ingalls Rd.; 804/727-3391). Fort Algernourne was built here in 1609, then Fort George, which was destroyed by a hurricane in 1749. The present fort was completed about 1834. Jefferson Davis, president of the Confederacy, was confined in a cell

here on false charges of plotting against the life of Lincoln. Casement Museum has relics of the fort and Davis's imprisonment. Open daily.

HOPEWELL

Merchants Hope Church (6 miles east on VA 10, then $\frac{1}{2}$ mile south on VA 641; 804/858-6197). Named for a plantation that was in turn named for a barque that sailed between Virginia and England, this 1657 church is the oldest operating Protestant church in the country. Experts consider it the most beautiful Colonial brickwork in America. Open daily.

Flowerdew Hundred (10 miles southeast on VA 10; 804/541-8897). An outdoor museum on the site of an early English settlement on the south bank of the James River. Originally inhabited by Indians, it was settled by Governor George Yeardley in 1618. Thousands of archaeological artifacts are on display in the museum. A replica of a 19th-century detached kitchen and an 18th-century windmill are open to visitors. Exhibits, interpretive tours, picnicking. Open daily except Mondays, April through November.

IRVINGTON

Historic Christ Church ($4\frac{1}{2}$ miles west, off VA 3; 804/438-6855). Built in 1735 by Robert Carter, forefather of eight governors of Virginia, two presidents, three signers of the Declaration of Independence, a chief justice, and many others who served their country with distinction. The church has been restored, with original furnishings, three-decker pulpit, and family tombs. The nearby Carter Reception Center has artifacts from Corotoman, home of Robert Carter, and a narrated slide show. Open daily.

JOHN SMITH

Jamestown probably would not have become the first permanent English colony in the New World if John Smith had been less of a man. He was primarily responsible for the colony's survival. His bold leadership, military experience, and determination brought discipline to the dissolute colonists, and his negotiations with the Indians kept them from starving. However, his greatest contribution to creating England's American empire was achieved not as a man of action but as a writer.

His early career had prepared Smith for the challenges of the New World. As a teenager he fought in the Low Countries, then joined a Christian army fighting the Turks, during which campaign he was captured and enslaved. Smith killed his master, then wandered through Eastern Europe and North Africa before returning to England. He later wrote, "The Warres in Europe, Asia, and Africa taught me how to subdue the wilde Savages in . . . America."

The promoters of the Virginia colony appreciated Smith's worth to an outpost likely to be attacked by French or Spanish forces and certain to be on uneasy terms with the Indians.

As the colony's president, Smith ruled fairly but firmly. Everyone, regardless of rank, worked or suffered his wrath, which earned him the enmity of the local gentry. He dealt with the Indians more brazenly, using threats and sometimes force to get corn, which annoyed Chief Powhatan. He wrote a detailed account of the colony's first year, including the story of his capture by Indians. However, he neglected to mention his timely rescue by the chief's daughter, Pocahontas—a tale that became part of American folklore.

Under pressure from his enemies at Jamestown and wounded by a gunpowder explosion, Smith relinquished the presidency and returned to England. His literary achievements during the next two decades were probably more important to England's imperial aspirations than were his actions in Virginia.

From 1608 until the eve of his death, Smith was British America's most insistent and prolific champion. After a voyage along the northern coast in 1614, he insisted that the area he named "New England" had great potential in fish, furs, and other resources, and that England's imperial future lay in people committed to hard work and realistic goals. He published nearly a dozen tracts, including a comprehensive *Generall Historie of Virginia, New England, and the Summer Isles.*

JAMESTOWN
(COLONIAL NATIONAL
HISTORICAL PARK)

The first permanent English settlement in the New World was founded here on May 13, 1607. The settlers came here after a landing at Cape Henry. This is where the English succeeded in settling in America, twenty years after the tragic failure to establish a colony at Roanoke Island and thirteen years before the Pilgrims landed at Plymouth, Massachusetts. The landing was not promising. Captain John Smith, the ablest man in the company, was in chains, and most of the others had no aptitude to adapt to a hostile wilderness. Smith soon emerged as the acknowledged leader.

For years the little band did not have an easy day. Crops failed, and rats ate the corn. The Indians were unfriendly until John Rolfe married Pocahontas, daughter of Chief Powhatan. Disease plagued the settlers. The winter of 1609–10 was called "the starving time." The 500-person colony was reduced to about sixty emaciated, defeated survivors who decided to give up and return to England. The June 1610 arrival of reinforcements and supplies dissuaded them.

Hope returned and the colony began to build. They made glass in 1608, began commercial tobacco cultivation in 1612, and pro-

duced the country's first representative legislative body in 1619. They made clapboard, brick, fishing nets, pottery, a variety of tools, and other items needed in the colony. When Jamestown became a Royal Colony in 1824, feeling against the government began to mount, and by 1676 there was open revolt, led by Nathaniel Bacon the younger. Bacon's forces burned the town, calling it a "stronghold of oppression." It was partially rebuilt, but never regained its prominence. The statehouse burned in 1698, and in 1699 the government moved to Middle Plantation and renamed it Williamsburg. But by the time of the Revolution, Jamestown was no longer an active community. At about this time the James River washed away the sandy isthmus, and the site became an island.

Nothing of the original settlement remains today except the Old Church Tower. Since 1934, though, archaeological exploration has made the outline of the town clear. Foundations have been explored, streets restored, and ditches, hedgerows, and fences replaced. Today markers, recorded messages, paintings, and monuments are everywhere. Open daily.

Colonial National Historical Park (I-64 to Rte. 199 W exit 57A, then west to Colonial Pkwy., follow signs to Jamestown Island; 804/898-3400). The *Visitor Center* has film and exhibits. Walk from here to *New Towne,* the area where Jamestown expanded around 1620. It contains "Back Streete" and other original sites. Reconstructed foundations indicate the sites of Country House and Governor's House, as well as the homes of Richard Kemp, builder of one of the first brick houses in America; Henry Hartwell, a founder of the College of William and Mary; and Dr. John Pott and William Pierce, who led the "thrusting out" of Governor John Harvey in 1635.

First Landing Site is a point in the river,

A re-creation of the original settlement at Jamestown.

The men bestow their times in fishing, hunting, warres, and such man-like exercises, which is the cause that the women be very painefull, and the men often idle. The women and children doe the rest of the worke.

—JOHN SMITH, *DESCRIBING THE INDIANS OF VIRGINIA, 1607*

Why will you take by force what you may have quietly by love? Why will you destroy us who supply you with food? What can you get by war? . . . In these wars, my men must sit up watching, and if a twig breaks, they all cry out, "Here comes Captain Smith!" So I must end my miserable life. Take away your guns and swords, the cause of all our jealousy, or you may all die in the same manners.

—POWHATAN *TO* JOHN SMITH, 1607

near the seawall, upriver from the Old Church Tower. The first fort may have been in this area. *Old Church Tower* is the only standing ruin of the 17th-century town, believed to be part of the first brick church, built in 1639. *Memorial Church* was built in 1907 by the Colonial Dames of America, over the foundations of the original church. Within are two foundations believed to be of earlier churches, including one from 1617 that housed the first assembly. *First Statehouse* is the foundation of a brick building discovered near the river, which may have been the first seat of government. *Tercentenary Monument* was erected in 1907 to commemorate the 300th anniversary of Jamestown. Other monuments include the Captain John Smith statue, the Pocahontas Monument, and the House of Burgesses Monument. Craft demonstrations. Five-mile auto trail with audio tape. Open daily.

Jamestown Settlement (adjacent to historic Jamestown; 804/229-1607). This living-history museum re-creates the first permanent English settlement in the New World, with full-scale reproductions of the three ships that arrived in 1607, and the triangular James Fort. The Powhatan Indian village depicts Indian culture encountered by English colonists. The museum has an orientation film, a gallery, and exhibit areas. Cafeteria, gift shop. Open daily.

WOMEN WANTED

Plymouth was settled by families, but the original settlers at Jamestown were all men. By 1608 there were only two women in the colony, and it was not until 1619 that a large number of women arrived. The Virginia Company in England recruited unmarried women to go to Jamestown to improve morale and, it was hoped, increase the colony's population.

LEESBURG

Waterford (3 miles northwest on VA 7, ¼ mile on VA 9, then 3 miles north on VA 662; 703/882-3018). An 18th-century Quaker village, now a National Historic Landmark, has been restored as a residential community. Open daily.

Oatlands (6 miles south on U.S. 15; 703/777-3174). A Greek Revival mansion, built by George Carter in 1803 on 261 acres, was once the center of a 5,000-acre plantation. English and French furnishings reflect the period between 1897 and 1965, when the house was owned by William Corcoran Eustis, a prominent Washingtonian. The formal garden has some of the finest boxwood in the country. Open daily early April to mid-December.

Accommodations: *The Norris House Inn* (108 Loudoun St. SW; 703/777-1806 or 800/644-1806). The Norris brothers, Northern Virginia's foremost architects and builders, purchased this 1806 mansion and made extensive renovations, remodeling the exterior to an Eastlake style. The inn has six guest rooms, all with shared bath. Full breakfast, afternoon tea. Moderate.

LEXINGTON

Stonewall Jackson House (8 East Washington St.; 703/463-2552). The Confederate general lived in this simple brick townhouse in 1859–61 while he was a teacher at Virginia Military Institute. Many of the furnishings were owned by the Jackson family. Restored gardens. Guided tours daily. Jackson is buried in the *Stonewall Jackson Memorial Cemetery* on the east side of South Main Street.

Washington and Lee University (West Washington St.; 707/463-8400). Founded as Augusta Academy in 1749, the school became Liberty Hall in 1776, changed its name to Washington Academy in 1798 after receiving 200 shares of James River Canal stock from George Washington, and then became Washington College. Many of the colonnaded buildings date from the late 18th century. Robert E. Lee served as president from 1865 to 1870, and soon after his death Washington College became Washington and Lee University. Lee is entombed in the Lee Chapel on the grounds. Displayed in the chapel is a portion of the art collection of the Washington and Lee families. Chapel open daily.

Virginia Military Institute (on U.S. 11; 707/464-7000). Stonewall Jackson taught physics and artillery tactics at this school, founded in 1839. A fellow professor was Matthew Fontaine Maury, the famed naval explorer and inventor. A dress parade takes place on the grounds Friday afternoons, September through May, weather permitting. A museum displays a collection of military items. Open daily.

LYNCHBURG

Point of Honor (112 Cabell St.; 804/847-1459). This restored 1815 mansion on Daniel's Hill, above the James River, was built by Dr. George Cabell Sr., Patrick Henry's physician. It is a Federal-style building with an octagon-bay façade, finely crafted interior woodwork, and period furnishings. Gardens and grounds are being restored. Open daily.

Old Court House Museum (901 Court St.; 804/847-1459). In a restored 1815 Greek Revival building are three galleries with exhibits on area history, including an early Quaker settlement. Open daily.

Pest House Medical Museum (Old City Cemetery, 4th and Taylor streets; 804/847-1811). The white frame medical office, circa

1850, of Quaker physician Dr. John J. Terrell has been joined with the Pest House quarantine hospital to represent medicine as it was practiced during the late 1800s. On display are original medical instruments. Open daily.

South River Meeting House (5810 Fort Ave.; 804/239-2548). This stone building, completed in 1798, was the site of Quaker worship and activity until the 1840s. Open daily.

MARTINSVILLE

Blue Ridge Farm Museum (VA 40 in Ferrum; 703/365-4415). Reconstructed farmsteads and "folklife" galleries present the heritage of this mountain region. Authentic buildings from 1800 includes a German-heritage farm, log house, kitchen, blacksmith shop, and barn. Costumed interpreters. Open weekends, May through August.

MCLEAN

Claude Moore Colonial Farm at Turkey Run (2 miles east on VA 193; 703/442-7557). An example of a 1770s low-income working farm. Costumed interpreters work with crops and animals using period techniques. Open Wednesday through Sunday, April to mid-December.

MONTROSS

Stratford Hall Plantation (6 miles north on VA 3 to Lerty, then east on VA 214; 804/493-8038). The boyhood home of Richard Henry Lee and Francis Lightfoot Lee, and the birthplace of Robert E. Lee. The center of a restored, working plantation is a monumental Georgian house, circa 1735, famous for its grouped chimney stacks. Interiors span a 100-year period and feature a Federal-era parlor and neoclassical panel-

Stratford Hall Plantation in Montross, the birthplace of Robert E. Lee.

ing in the Great Hall. Flanking dependencies include a kitchen, a plantation office, and a gardener's house, also a boxwood garden and a working mill. The visitor center has a museum with slide presentations. Gift shops, restaurant. Open daily.

Montross (Courthouse Square; 804/493-9097, or 800/321-0979). A 1683 residence offering six guest rooms furnished with four-poster beds, antiques, and original art. Dining room. Inexpensive.

MOUNT VERNON

Mount Vernon (16 miles south of Washington, D.C., on Mount Vernon Memorial Hwy.; 703/780-2000). Washington brought his bride here in 1759, and set about becoming the leading scientific farmer in America. He kept detailed notes, conferred with other farmers, tried crop rotation and other new experiments, added to the house, which became a stately Georgian Colonial mansion, and planned for the family that nature denied him. He and his wife, Martha, brought up her two children by a previous marriage and raised two of her grandchildren.

But when duty called in 1775 to lead the armies of his country, he did not hesitate. He returned after the war, determined to live as he wished. But four years later he was called to preside at the Constitutional Convention, and in 1789 he became the new nation's first President. From March 1797 until his death on December 14, 1799, he lived here. He and Martha are buried here.

The nucleus of the existing house was built circa 1735 by Augustine Washington, George's father. George acquired it in 1754,

GEORGE WASHINGTON

The greatness of George Washington, commander of the Continental Army and first President of the United States, is beyond question. Unfortunately, so is his austerity. Despite the quaint fiction about cutting down a cherry tree, he remains the coldest, least approachable personage in American history.

The facts are well known. He was born in 1732 to a Virginia planter of modest means, and when his father died, in 1743, he went to live with an older brother at Mount Vernon, a property he later inherited. As a young man, he worked as a surveyor and served in the militia. In 1753 he was sent to warn the French against encroaching in the Ohio Valley. Although the French ignored the warning, his superiors noted his tenacity in making a hazardous winter trek of a thousand miles.

A lieutenant colonel at twenty-two, Washington returned to Ohio to protect the Ohio Company. His surprise attack (the first engagement in the French and Indian Wars) on a French detachment didn't succeed, and he was forced to surrender. When Braddock's army arrived in Virginia, he was appointed the British general's aide-de-camp. After Braddock was slain at Fort Duquesne, Washington was appointed commander-in-chief of all the Virginia forces.

He resigned his commission in 1755, at twenty-six years of age, returned to Mount Vernon, and married Martha Dandridge Custis, a widow, the next year. The union brought him considerable wealth and two stepchildren, the offspring of Martha and her first husband, Daniel Parke Custis. He and Martha had no children of their own. He proved a resourceful landowner, became prominent in local politics, and served in the House of Burgesses for seven years. In 1774 he represented Virginia in the first Continental Congress. Returning to the second Congress in 1775, he was made commander-in-chief of the combined colonial military forces.

His greatest wartime achievement was holding his ragtag army together, rallying them at Valley Forge during the bitter winter of 1777–78. Dogged by defeats, desertions, sickness, and starvation, his troops reached the lowest ebb of their campaign morale. Their subsequent recovery and notable victories prompted French involvement in the war, ensuring ultimate victory.

When the war was over, Washington returned to Mount Vernon, and continued to work for a strong constitutional government. He was president of the Constitutional Convention in 1787, and his force of character was instrumental in the adoption of the Constitution. In 1789 he was unanimously elected first President of the United States, and reluctantly returned to public life.

In his first term he formed a cabinet of the foremost men in the country, evenly balanced between the two political parties. It included Thomas Jefferson and Alexander Hamilton. By his second term, however, the differences between Jefferson's Democratic-Republicans and Hamilton's Federalists became increasingly acrimonious. Washington leaned toward the Federalists, but was dismayed that his cabinet could not put aside party differences.

Faced with increasingly virulent personal attacks, he retired from the presidency in 1797, and returned to Mount Vernon. He died in 1799, following exposure from riding around the estate in wintry conditions. On learning of his death, his former enemy paid him a touching tribute: the British fleet fired a twenty-gun salute.

JAMES MONROE

James Monroe rode to the presidency on the coattails of his predecessors, but he became his own man when he got there. Jefferson was his mentor, Madison his close friend, and for years he was overshadowed by their more brilliant minds, broader interests, and greater impact on their times.

Politics was a consuming interest for Monroe, and he was a pragmatic man, keenly sensitive to political currents. He was a junior officer under Washington and was wounded at the Battle of Trenton. He served in the Continental Congress, and later was elected senator. He joined with Representative Madison and Secretary of State Jefferson to oppose Alexander Hamilton. When Jefferson became President, he sent Monroe to purchase Louisiana and later made him minister to Great Britain.

Monroe ran unsuccessfully against his friend Madison for the presidency after Jefferson retired. Despite the differences between the two, Jefferson kept the circle of friendship unbroken, and in 1811 President Madison brought Monroe into his cabinet as secretary of state.

The Federalist Party barely survived the War of 1812, and Monroe was elected President in 1816 with barely any opposition. He sought to end party divisions and created what was called "the era of good feelings." His presidency is best remembered for the Monroe Doctrine. Addressing Congress in 1823, he declared that the United States would not tolerate intervention in the Americas by European nations.

after the death of his half brother Lawrence. Today Mount Vernon has been accurately restored to its appearance in the last year of Washington's life. Since 1858 the estate has been maintained by the Mount Vernon Ladies' Association, and was, in effect, the nation's first tourist attraction of historic interest. Gift shop, nearby restaurant. Open daily.

Spirit of Washington (202/554-8000). Potomac River cruises from Washington, D.C. to Mount Vernon. The stop at Mount Vernon is sufficient for a complete tour. Two trips daily, mid-March through October.

Woodlawn Plantation (3 miles west of George Washington Pkwy., on U.S. 1; 703/780-4000). In 1789, George Washington gave 2,000 acres of land as a wedding present to Eleanor Parke Custis, his foster daughter, who married his nephew, Major Lawrence Lewis. Dr. William Thornton, first architect of the U.S. Capitol, designed the mansion, which has been restored with many original furnishings and formal gardens. A National Trust for Historic Preservation property. Open daily, February through December.

NORFOLK

In 1682 the General Assembly bought from Nicholas Wise, a pioneer settler, fifty acres on the Elizabeth River for "ten thousand pounds of tobacco and caske." By 1736 the town that developed here was the largest in Virginia. During the Revolution, Norfolk was shelled by the British and later burned by the colonists to prevent a British takeover.

St. Paul's Episcopal Church (201 St. Paul's Blvd.; 804/627-4353). This 1739 church was the only building to survive the burning of Norfolk in 1776. Open Tuesday through Friday.

Moses Myers House (323 East Freemason St.; 804/622-1211, ext. 283). An excellent example of Georgian architecture, with many original furnishings, including silver and china. Open daily except Mondays, April through December; Tuesday through Saturday the rest of the year.

Willoughby-Baylor House (601 East Freemason St.; 804/622-1211, ext. 283). A restored 1794 town house with period furnishings, herb and flower gardens. Open by appointment; inquire at Moses Myers House.

American Rover (Waterside Marina, Waterside Dr. exit off I-264; 804/627-SAIL). This 135-foot, three-masted topsail schooner makes two- and three-hour cruises around the Hampton Roads historical harbor past historic forts, merchant and navy ships. Sails daily, May through mid-October.

ORANGE

Montpelier (4 miles southwest on VA 20; 703/672-0006). The residence of James Madison, fourth President of the United States. He was the third generation to live on this plantation. He inherited Montpelier and enlarged it twice. After his presidency, he and Dolley Madison retired to the estate, which Dolley sold after his death to pay her son's gambling debts. In 1901 the estate was bought by William du Pont, who enlarged the house and added many outbuildings, including a private railroad station and gardens. Now a property of the National Trust for Historic Preservation. Tours available. Open daily, mid-March through December, weekends the rest of the year.

Accommodations: *The Holladay House* (155 West Main St.; 703/672-4893, or 800/358-4422). Each of the six guest rooms

in this Federal-style inn is furnished with family pieces and has a sitting area and fresh flowers. Breakfast is served to guests in their rooms. Moderate to expensive.

PETERSBURG

Trapezium House (Market and High streets; 804/733-2402). An eccentric Irish bachelor, Charles O'Hara, built this house in 1817 in the form of a trapezium, with no right angles and no parallel sides. O'Hara is said to have believed in the superstitions of his West Indian servant, who thought that ghosts and evil spirits inhabited right angles. Tours depart from *Siege Museum* (15 West Bank St.; 804/733-2404). Open daily, April through October.

Centre Hill Mansion (Center Hill Ct.; 804/733-2401). A Federal-style mansion visited by Presidents Tyler, Lincoln, and Taft. Chandeliers, fine detail carvings, period furnishings. Open daily.

PORTSMOUTH

In Gosport, long a part of Portsmouth, Andrew Sprowie, a Scot, built a marine yard in 1767, which became in turn a British naval repair station and, after the Revolution, a federal navy yard. Now called the Norfolk Naval Shipyard, it is the largest naval shipyard in the world.

Hill House (221 North St.; 804/393-0241). Built in the early 1830s, this four-story English-basement-style house contains original furnishings collected by generations of the Hill family. Garden. Open Wednesdays and weekends, April through December.

Trinity Church (500 Court St.; 804/393-0431). This 1762 Episcopal church is the oldest in Portsmouth. Legend says that the church bell cracked while ringing the news of Conwallis's surrender. Open on request,

Monday through Friday. Inquire at office in parish hall.

Monumental United Church (Queen and Dinwiddie streets; 804/397-1297). This 1772 church is the oldest Methodist church in the South. Guided tours by appointment on weekdays.

Historic houses. Portsmouth has many excellent examples of Colonial, Federal, and antebellum houses. They are private, and may be viewed only from outside. Obtain an Olde Towne Portsmouth walking-tour brochure, with a map and descriptions of the houses, from the Portside Visitor Information Center (804/393-5111).

RICHMOND

Settlers and Indians once fought where this city now stands. In 1775, Patrick Henry made his "liberty or death" speech in St. John's Church, and in 1780 the city was named capital of Virginia. At that time Virginia extended all the way to the Mississippi. British soldiers plundered it brutally in the Revolution. It was the capital of the Confederacy. In 1865, Richmond was evacuated. Retreating Confederate soldiers burned the government warehouse, and a portion of the rest of the city went up in flames.

State Capitol (9th and Grace streets; 804/786-2220). Designed by Thomas Jefferson, the Capitol, built from 1785–88, was modeled after La Maison Carrée, an ancient Roman temple at Nîmes, France. In the building, where America's oldest continuous English-speaking legislative bodies still meet, is the famous Houdon statue of Washington. The old Hall of the House of Delegates features the first interior dome in the country. Here Aaron Burr was tried for treason, Virginia ratified the Articles of Secession, and Robert E. Lee accepted command of the Confederate forces of Virginia. The Confederate Congress also met here. Open daily.

Governor's Mansion (east of the Capitol; 804/786-2220). This two-story, Federal-style house was built in 1813 after the capital was moved from Williamsburg. It is the oldest governor's mansion in the United States still in use. Tours by appointment.

Equestrian Statue of Washington (Capitol Square). The statue was created by Thomas Crawford and cast in Munich over an eighteen-year period. Its base features allegorical representations of six famous Revolutionary War figures from Virginia.

St. Paul's Church (9th and Grace streets; 804/643-3589). Established in 1843, this church was where Jefferson Davis received the news of Lee's retreat from Petersburg to Appomattox. It has eight Tiffany stained-glass windows, and a Tiffany mosaic of da Vinci's *Last Supper* surmounts the altar. Open daily.

Monumental Church (1226 East Broad St). This octagonal domed building, designed by Robert Mills, the architect of the Washington Monument, was built in 1812 on the site where many prominent people, including the governor, perished in a theater fire in 1811. Interior not open to the public.

John Marshall House (9th and Marshall streets; 804/648-7998). The restored house of the famous Supreme Court justice features original woodwork and paneling, family furnishings, and mementos. Open daily except Mondays.

Valentine Museum (1015 East Clay St.; 804/649-0711). Exhibits of decorative arts, costumes, and textiles relating to the industrial and social history of Richmond. Tours of the restored 1812 Wickham House. Lunch served in a walled garden. Open daily, April through October.

White House of the Confederacy (12th and East Clay streets; 804/649-1861). An 1818 Greek Revival house used by Jefferson Davis as his official residence, restored to its pre-wartime appearance, with original furnishings. Next door is the *Museum of the Confederacy* (804/649-1861), which contains the largest collection of Confederate artifacts in the country. Both open daily.

Kanawha Canal Locks (12th and Byrd streets; 804/281-2000). These impressive stone locks were part of the nation's first canal system, planned by George Washington. A film explains the workings of the locks and the canal. Picnicking. Open daily.

St. John's Episcopal Church (25th and Broad streets; 804/786-2050). Patrick Henry delivered his stirring "liberty or death" speech here. Tours available. Open daily.

Edgar Allan Poe Museum (1914 East Main St.; 804/648-5523). The Old Stone House portion of this building, built in 1743, is believed to be the oldest structure in the city. Four additional buildings house Poe mementos, including James Carling illustrations of "The Raven," a scale model of Richmond in Poe's time, and a slide presentation of Poe's life here. Tours available. Open daily.

Accommodations: *Linden Row* (entrance at 101 North 1st St.; 804/783-7000 or 800/348-7424). This inn was built in 1847 around a courtyard where Edgar Allan Poe played as a boy. Part of a downtown block of Greek Revival row houses, the inn has sixty-nine guest rooms and seven suites. Breakfast. Restaurant on the premises. Concierge. Moderate.

STRASBURG

Belle Grove (4 miles north on U.S. 11; 703/869-2028). Thomas Jefferson influenced the design of this limestone mansion, which has unusual interior woodwork and an herb garden. It was used as Union headquarters during the Battle of Cedar Grove, October 19, 1864. A National Trust for Historic Preservation property. Open daily, April through October.

WILLIAMSBURG

A palisade was constructed across the peninsula between the James and York rivers after the Indian massacre of 1622. The settlement that grew up around it was called Middle Plantation, now Colonial Williamsburg. It figured prominently in Bacon's Rebellion against Governor Berkeley. In 1693 it was chosen as the site of the College of William and Mary, and in 1699 the seat of Virginia government was settled here. Renamed in honor of William of England, the new capital gradually became a town of about 200 houses and 1,500 residents. For eighty-one years Williamsburg was the political, social, and cultural capital of Virginia.

The first Continental Congress was called from here in 1774 by the dissolved House of Burgesses. Two years later the Second Continental Congress was led by delegates from Virginia to declare independence. George Mason's Declaration of Rights, which became the basis for the first ten amendments to the Constitution, was adopted here. Williamsburg's exciting period came to an end in 1780, when the capital was moved to Richmond for greater safety and convenience.

Williamsburg slumbered until 1917, when a munitions factory was built nearby, and housing for its 15,000 workers was hastily erected. In 1926, though, John D. Rockefeller Jr. and Dr. W. A. R. Goodwin, rector of Bruton Parish Church, shared the vision that inspired the restoration of Williamsburg. For more than thirty years,

Is life so dear or peace so sweet as to be purchased at the price of chains and slavery? . . . I know not what course others may take, but as for me, give me liberty or give me death!

—PATRICK HENRY, *SPEECH TO THE HOUSE OF BURGESSES, 1755*

George Washington's plantation at Mount Vernon. From The American Revolution, Dover Publications, Inc., New York.

Rockefeller gave his personal attention to the project and contributed funds to the non-profit undertaking.

Today the Historic Area, approximately a mile long and a half-mile wide, encompasses most of the 18th-century capital. Eighty-eight of the original buildings have been restored, and fifty major buildings, including houses and shops, and many outbuildings, have been reconstructed on their original sites. Forty-five buildings contain more than 200 exhibition rooms, furnished either with original pieces or accurate reproductions. Visitors stroll Duke of Gloucester Street, mingling with people in 18th-century attire. Craftsmen at about twenty different sites ply such trades as wigmaking and black-smithing, using tools, techniques, and materials of Colonial days.

Colonial Williamsburg (Colonial Pkwy. and VA 132; 804/220-7645 or 800-HISTORY). The *Visitor Center* has sightseeing information and an orientation film, and provides lodging and dining assistance. Bookstore, gift shop, transportation. Open daily.

The Capitol (east end of Duke of Gloucester St.). The meeting place of the House of Burgesses, 1704–79, and the scene of Patrick Henry's speech against the Stamp Act. North of the Capitol, across Nicholson Street, is the *Public Gaol,* where criminals, debtors, and pirates (including Blackbeard's crew) were imprisoned. A few steps west is the *Raleigh Tavern,* a frequent meeting place for Jefferson, Henry, and other patriots, and a social center for the colony. Opposite is *Wetherburn's Tavern,* which was one of the most popular inns of the period.

Governor's Palace and Gardens (north end of Palace Green). The residence of the Royal Governor, set in a ten-acre restored garden, was one of the most elegant mansions in Colonial America. Nearby is the *Brush-Everard House,* the home of an early mayor, with a carved staircase and a box-wood garden. To the southeast is the *Peyton Randolph House,* the 1716 home of the president of the First Continental Congress. Rochambeau made the house his headquarters prior to the Yorktown campaign. To the southwest is the *James Geddy House,* once the home of a silversmith, with a working brass, bronze, silver, and pewter foundry. Across Palace Green, at the corner of Prince George St., is the *Wythe House,* the home of George Wythe, America's first law profes-

sor, the teacher of Jefferson, Clay, and Marshall. Washington made his headquarters here before the siege of Yorktown.

The Magazine (Duke of Gloucester St., 1 block east of Palace Green). The arsenal and military storehouse of the Virginia Colony. Exhibits of vintage arms. Also nearby is the *Courthouse,* where county and city business was conducted from 1770 until 1932. The interior has been restored to its original appearance. Nearby is the *Public Hospital,* a reconstruction of the first public institution in the English colonies devoted exclusively to the treatment of mental illness. Adjoining the hospital is the *DeWitt Wallace Decorative Arts Gallery,* a modern museum with displays, films, and lectures on British and American decorative arts.

Abby Aldrich Rockefeller Folk Art Center (York St., ½ block southeast of the Capitol). An outstanding collection of American folk-art items: paintings, sculpture, needlework, ceramics, toys, and other media.

Bruton Parish Church (Duke of Gloucester St., just west of Palace Green; 804/229-2891). One of the oldest Episcopal churches in America, it has been in continuous use since 1715. Open daily.

Tours. Orientation tours are available for first-time visitors; special tours are devoted to African-American life, gardens, religion, and women of Williamsburg (reservations at the Lumber House, next to Greenhow Store, south end of Palace Green). *Lantern Tour:* A costumed interpreter conducts an evening walking tour of selected shops that are lit by candlelight (tickets at Lumber House). *Children's Tours:* Special programs, tours, and experiences for children are offered in

The Moore House in Yorktown, where terms for surrender were negotiated. Courtesy National Park Service.

the summer. *Carriage and wagon rides:* A drive through the Historic Area in a carriage or wagon driven by a costumed coachman (tickets at Lumber House). All tours are given daily, weather permitting.

College of William and Mary (west end of Duke of Gloucester St.; 804/221-4000). The second oldest college in America, William and Mary initiated the honor system and schools of law and modern languages. The Phi Beta Kappa society was founded here in 1776. The restored *Wren Building* (1695–99), designed by the English architect Sir Christopher Wren, is the oldest academic building in the country. Tours daily.

Accommodations: *Piney Grove at Southall's Plantation* (Old Main Rd.; 804/829-2480). The inn consists of two historic homes: Piney Grove, a rare Tidewater log building, listed on the National Register of Historic Places; and the 1857 Ladysmith House. Both are furnished with artifacts that help illustrate the history of the area. Four guest rooms, full breakfast, dinner available. Expensive.

WINCHESTER

Washington's Office-Museum (Cork and Braddock streets; 703/662-4412). This building, used by Washington in 1755–56 during the erection of Fort Loudoun, has displays of French and Indian, Revolutionary, and Civil War artifacts. Open daily, April through October.

Stonewall Jackson's Headquarters (415 North Braddock St.; 703/667-3242). Jackson lived here from November 1861 to March 1862 while waging his campaign in the Shenandoah Valley. Museum displays Jackson memorabilia and Confederate relics. Open daily, April through October, and weekdays in November, December, and March.

Abram's Delight and Log Cabin (1340 South Pleasant Valley Rd.; 703/662-6519). This 1754 house, the oldest in the city, has been restored and furnished in 18th-century style. Log cabin, boxwood garden. Open daily, April through October.

Old Stone Presbyterian Church (306 East Piccadilly St.; 703/662-3824). This 1788 structure, restored in 1941, has been used as a church, a stable by Union troops in the Civil War, a public school, and an armory. Open daily.

WOODSTOCK

Shenandoah County Court House (Main St.). Built in 1792, this is the oldest courthouse still in use west of the Blue Ridge Mountains. The interior has been restored to its original design. Open weekdays.

WYTHEVILLE

Shot Tower Historical Park (at Jackson's Ferry, 6 miles east on I-81, then 7 miles south on U.S. 52; 703/699-6778). One of three shot towers still standing in the country, its fortress-like stone shaft has two-and-a-half-foot-thick walls that rise seventy-five feet above ground and descend seventy-five feet below ground to a water tank. Molten lead was poured through sheet-iron colanders from the tower's top. During the 150-foot descent it became globular before hitting the water, which instantly cooled it, hardening it into lead balls. Picnicking, visitor center. Open daily, Memorial Day through Labor Day.

YORKTOWN

In 1630, settlement here began when free land was offered to those adventurous enough "to seate and inhabit" the fifty-foot bluffs on the south side of the York River "formerly known by the Indyan name of Chiskiacke."

When the Assembly authorized a port, built here in 1691, the town quickly expanded and in the following years became a busy shipping center, with prosperity reaching a peak about 1750. It declined from then on, along with the Tidewater Virginia tobacco trade.

Yorktown's great moment came in 1781, when General Cornwallis was sent here to establish a port in which British ships-of-the-line would winter. The Comte de Grasse's French fleet then effectively blockaded the British by controlling the mouth of the Chesapeake Bay. At the Battle of the Capes, on September 5, 1781, a British fleet sent to relieve Cornwallis was defeated by the French. Cornwallis found himself bottled up in Yorktown by combined American and French forces under Washington. Shelling began on October 9, and the siege of Yorktown ended October 17 with Cornwallis requesting terms of capitulation. On October 19, Cornwallis's troops marched out with flags and arms cased, their band playing "The World Turned Upside Down." Then they laid down their arms, bringing the American Revolution to an end.

Yorktown Battlefield (surrounds and includes part of town; 804/898-3400). The remains of 1781 British fortifications, modified and strengthened by Confederate forces in the Civil War. Reconstructed American and French lines lie beyond. Roads lead to headquarters and encampment areas of Americans and French. The visitor center (east side of town, at end of Colonial Parkway) has special exhibits and Washington's field tents. A self-guided battlefield tour includes headquarters sites of Lafayette, von Steuben, Rochambeau, Washington, American Battery No. 2, and the Grand French Battery. Battlefield and visitor center open daily.

Moore House (Nelson and Main streets). A restored mansion built by "Scotch Tom" Nelson in the early 1700s, later the home of his grandson, Thomas Nelson Jr., a signer of the Declaration of Independence. An impressive example of Georgian architecture. Open daily, mid-June through mid-August.

York County Courthouse (Main St.). Reconstructed in 1955 to resemble the 1733 courthouse. Open weekdays.

Grace Episcopal Church (Church St.; 804/898-3261). Built in 1697, walls damaged in 1781, gutted by fire in 1814. The 1649 communion service is still in use. Open daily.

Yorktown Victory Center (½ mile west on VA 238; 804/887-1776). The American Revolution is chronicled here with exhibits, a living-history military camp, and a Colonial farm site. There is also a docudrama on the final days of the Revolution. Open daily.

18

WEST(ERN) VIRGINIA

Pioneers who ventured here in the eighteenth century found forests, curative springs, and beautiful rivers, but in those days it was considered "the wild West." Originally the western part of Virginia, this mountainous area was largely ignored by the Commonwealth. Before 1860, only one governor was elected from this area. When the western counties formed their own state during the Civil War, it was the result of many years of strained relations with the parent state. The move had been debated for years, and the war provided the opportunity the counties needed to break away from Virginia. West Virginia became the thirty-fifth state when it entered the Union on June 20, 1863. Although many in the new state remained loyal to the South, West Virginia stayed in the Union.

CHARLES TOWN

Jefferson County Courthouse (North George and East Washington streets; 304/725-9761). This red brick Georgian Colonial building, constructed in 1836, was the scene of the trial of John Brown after his capture at Harpers Ferry. The original courtroom is open to the public. Open weekdays.

Zion Episcopal Church (East Congress St. between South Mildred and South Church streets; 304/725-5312). Buried in the cemetery of this 1852 church are about seventy-five members of the Washington family,

as well as many Revolutionary and Confederate soldiers. Interior viewed by appointment only.

Accommodations: *Gilbert House* (9 miles west on U.S. 11 in Middleway; 304/725-0637). When this 1760 stone Georgian was being restored, graffiti found on a bedroom wall included a drawing of President James Polk. On the original pioneer's trail, the village has an outstanding collection of log houses. Inn appointments include oriental rugs, art, and antique furnishings. Four guest rooms, fireplaces, full breakfast. Moderate.

CLARKSBURG

Stealy-Goff-Vance House (123 West Main St.; 304/842-3073). This 1807 house has been restored by the Harrison County Historical Society as a museum with period rooms, local artifacts. Open Fridays, May through September.

Fort New Salem (12 miles west on campus of Salem-Teikyo University; 304/782-5245). A collection of twenty log houses relocated from throughout the state. Crafts and folklore. Open Wednesday through Sunday, Memorial Day through October.

FAIRMONT

Pricketts Fort State Park (I-79 exit 139, then 2 miles west; 304/367-2731). A reconstructed 18th-century log

fort. Costumed interpreters, museum, picnicking, visitor center. Fort and museum open daily mid-April through October.

GAULEY BRIDGE

Contentment Museum Complex (7miles east on U.S. 60, 1 mile west of Ansted; 304/465-0165). The circa-1830 former residence of Confederate colonel George W. Imboden contains period furniture and a toy collection. The adjacent *Fayette County Historical Society Museum* features Indian relics and Civil War items. Also on the premises is a restored one-room schoolhouse. Open daily, June through September; Sundays the rest of the year.

HARPERS FERRY

Harpers Ferry, at the junction of the Shenandoah and Potomac rivers, where West Virginia, Virginia, and Maryland meet, was the scene of abolitionist John Brown's raid in October 1859. A U.S. armory and rifle factory made this an important town in early Virginia. Brown and sixteen of his followers seized the armory and arsenal, then took refuge in the engine house when attacked by local militia. The engine house was stormed, and Brown was captured by marines under the command of Colonel Robert E. Lee. Taken to nearby Charles Town, Brown was tried and hanged. Harpers Ferry was strategic in

A heroic frontiersman nonchalantly makes his escape from an Indian war party in Western Virginia by leaping on horseback from a cliff to the river far below. Courtesy Library of Congress, Prints and Photographs Division.

the Civil War, and changed hands several times.

Harpers Ferry National Historic Park (on U.S. 340; 304/535-6298). The old town has been restored to its 19th-century appearance. Tours, exhibits and interpretive presentations explore the town and its history. From the *Visitor Center* (off U.S. 340) a bus takes visitors to the Lower Town. Visitor center and park are open daily. A walking tour includes the following sites:

Master Armorer's House Museum (Shenandoah St., near High St.). A restored 1859 Federal house containing a museum with exhibits on gunmaking. Farther down Shenandoah Street and right under the trestle is *The Point,* where three states and two rivers meet at the Blue Ridge Mountains. Back under the trestle is *John Brown's Fort,* on Arsenal Square, where Brown made his last stand. The structure was rebuilt and moved here from its original site. Across the street is the *John Brown Museum,* which has a slide presentation. Nearby are two Civil War museums and two African-American history museums. *Harper House,* up stone steps from High Street, is a three-story stone structure built between 1775 and 1782 by the founder of the town, restored and furnished in the style of the period. Both Washington and Jefferson stayed here. Behind the house is *Marion Row,* four restored private houses, circa 1832–50. Up the hill are the *Ruins of St. John's Episcopal Church,* and 100 yards farther on is *Jefferson's Rock,* from which Thomas Jefferson, in 1783, pronounced the view "one of the most stupendous scenes in nature." *Lockwood House,* above the cemetery, is an 1848 Greek Revival dwelling used as a headquarters during the Civil War

and later as a classroom for nearby Storer College. All houses and museums open daily.

MARTINSBURG

General Adam Stephen House (309 East John St.; 304/267-4434). The restored 1789 residence of Revolutionary War soldier and surgeon Adam Stephen, founder of Martinsburg. Period furnishings. Restored log cabin and smoke house. Open weekends, May through October.

Accommodations: *Aspen Hall Inn* (405 Boyd Ave.; 304/263-4385). This 1745 Georgian manor, listed in the National Register, overlooks acres of lawns, gardens, and a stream. During the French and Indian Wars, Washington sent troops to protect the house, and later attended a wedding here. It features double parlors, a library, and an elegant dining room. Five guest rooms are furnished with antiques and canopy beds. Full breakfast and afternoon tea. Moderate.

POINT PLEASANT

Point Pleasant Battle Monument State Park (1 Main St.; 304/675-0869). An eighty-four-foot granite shaft was erected in 1909, after the U.S. Senate agreed to a claim that the first battle of the Revolution was fought here. A nearby marker notes where Joseph Celeron de Bienville buried a lead plate in 1749, claiming the land for France, and the graves of Chief Cornstalk and "Mad Anne" Baily, a noted pioneer scout. In the park is *Mansion House* (304/675-0869), the oldest log building in Kanawha Valley. The 1796 structure has been restored as a museum. Open daily, May through October.

THE NATIONAL ROAD

A demand arose in the early 1800s for surfaced roads to facilitate travel to the West. The government responded with the National Road, which later was called the Cumberland Road. In 1800, Congress approved the route for the first section, largely along an Indian trail that ran from the end of the Baltimore Turnpike in Cumberland, Maryland, to Wheeling, in western Virginia, where travelers could board ships on the Ohio River. Planning began immediately, but contracts were not granted until 1811, and the War of 1812 put construction off until 1815. The road finally reached Wheeling in 1818.

The road became a political football. Easterners had no particular interest in facilitating travel to and from the West. Southern states wanted state rather than federal programs. But westerners pressed for improvements no one state could finance. Henry Clay of Kentucky became their champion in 1824 by proposing the American System—a combination of protective tariffs and internal improvements designed to build domestic Industry and trade.

Was federal involvement in such a project constitutional? President Monroe thought not, and vetoed an 1822 bill to establish tolls and use them for road repair. President Jackson got around the problem by turning the completed sections of the road over to the states, permitting them to finance repairs through tolls.

In 1850 the National Road reached Vandalia, Illinois, but before it could be extended to St. Louis, railroad construction had become the national priority. In the years that followed, the road lost importance, until automobile travel brought it back into use as part of U.S. Route 40.

PART V

THE DEEP SOUTH

19

F L O R I D A

When Ponce de León explored Florida in 1513, he didn't find the fountain of youth, nor establish a colony, but he did map its long coast. Hernando de Soto traversed the land, beginning his march in 1539 from what now is the Tampa Bay area to discover the Mississippi River and stake Spain's claim to the Southwest.

Spanish settlements were made at St. Augustine and Pensacola in the seventeenth century. Florida was taken as a British province in the eighteenth century, but Spanish rule resumed after the British defeat in the Revolution. In 1912, a group of Americans took over the peninsula and declared it an independent republic. Finally, in 1819, the United States took formal possession of Florida through a treaty of purchase.

APALACHICOLA

Fort Gadsden State Historic Site (east on U.S. 98/319, then 17 miles north on FL 65, just north of Bucks Siding; 904/670-8616). The British built a fort here in 1814 as a base for recruitment during the War of 1812. The fort was later destroyed by U.S. forces, but Andrew Jackson ordered another built as a supply base. Some earthworks remain visible. A kiosk has a miniature replica of Fort Gadsden. Exhibits, picnicking. Open Friday through Monday and Wednesdays.

BRADENTON

Gamble Plantation State Historic Site (1 mile north, then 2 miles east on U.S. 301, in Ellenton; 813/723-4536). The only antebellum house still standing in south Florida. Major Robert Gamble ran a 3,500-acre sugar plantation here with 190 slaves. In May 1865, Judah P. Benjamin, Secretary of State of the Confederacy, fled to the plantation to hide from Union forces. He then escaped to the Bahamas and England. The restored mansion is furnished with period pieces. Picnicking, tours, visitor center. Open Thursday through Monday.

De Soto National Monument (2 miles north off FL 64, at the end of 75th St. NW, on Tampa Bay; 813/792-0458). De Soto landed somewhere near here on May 30, 1539, with 600 conquistadors, to begin the first European expedition into the interior of what now is the southeastern United States. In a 4,000-mile, four-year wilderness odyssey, he and his army explored beyond the Mississippi, staking out claims to a vast empire for Spain. The visitor center has armor and weapons of the era, and a film depicting the expedition. Living-history program. Open daily, December to mid-April.

DADE CITY

Pioneer Florida Museum (½ mile north via U.S. 301N,

at 15602 Pioneer Museum Rd.; 904/567-0262). A twenty-five-acre complex contains the restored two-story, circa-1864 Overstreet House with period furnishings, a one-room schoolhouse, a church, an old train depot and engine, and relics and photographs from pioneer times. Open Tuesday through Saturday afternoons.

Dade Battlefield State Historic District (22 miles north on U.S. 301, off FL 476W in Bushnell; 904/793-4781). A memorial to Major Francis L. Dade and the more than 100 soldiers who were ambushed and massacred here by Seminoles in 1835. Picnicking. Museum. Open daily.

DRY TORTUGAS

Dry Tortugas National Park (68 miles west of Key West, reached by boat or seaplane; 305/242-7700). This national park includes the remains of what was once the largest of the 19th-century American coastal forts and

the cluster of seven islands known as the Dry Tortugas. The coral keys were named *las tortugas* ("the turtles") by Ponce de León in 1513 because so many turtles inhabited the bits of land. The epithet "dry" came from the absence of fresh water. Spanish pirates used the Tortugas as a base until 1821, when they were driven away. In 1846 the United States began construction of a fort. For more than thirty years, laborers worked on the fort, a rampart one-half mile in perimeter with fifty-foot-high walls and three tiers designed for 450 guns. Called "the Gibraltar of the Gulf," it needed a garrison of 1,500 men. Only partially completed, Fort Jefferson never saw battle.

Resting on an unstable foundation, the walls began to crack and shift, making it unsuitable for military defense. In 1863 it became a military prison, confining some 2,400 men. Among them was Dr. Samuel Mudd, who set the broken leg of John Wilkes Booth, Lincoln's assassin. After two yellow-

Tallahassee, the capital of Florida, in the 1840s. Courtesy Library of Congress, Prints and Photographs Division.

Gamble Plantation in Bradenton.

fever epidemics and a hurricane, the fort was abandoned.

The fort and islands are accessible by boat or by seaplane from Key West. Tours, visitor Center. Open daily. (For transportation information, contact the Greater Key West Chamber of Commerce; 305/294-2587.)

HOMOSASSA SPRINGS

Yulee Sugar Mill Ruins State Historic Site (on FL 490, west of U.S. 19; 904/628-2311). On a six-acre site are the remnants of an antebellum sugar mill, including its boiler casing, chimney, engine, and connecting gears. Picnicking. Open daily.

JACKSONVILLE

Kingsley Plantation (north on FL A1A, on Fort George Island at 11678 Palmetto Ave.,

reached by ferry from Mayport or via FL 105; 904/251-3537). An antebellum plantation house, kitchen house, barn, and tabby (a kind of cement made with oyster shells) slave quarters reflect 19th-century life on a Sea Island cotton plantation. Ranger programs. Open daily.

Fort Caroline National Memorial (13 miles east of Jacksonville on FL 10, then north on Monument Rd., then east on Fort Caroline Rd.; 904/641-7155). Fort Caroline, a triangular wood-and-earth fortress, once stood here. René de Laudonniere established a short-lived foothold for France in the battle for supremacy in the New World, but the 300 colonists, mostly Huguenots, spent more time searching for treasure than growing food. Driven by famine, the colonists were about to abandon the outpost in August 1565 when reinforcements arrived from France. At about this time, however, King

The mass of mankind has not been born with saddles on their backs, nor a favored few booted and spurred, ready to ride them legitimately, by the grace of God.

—THOMAS JEFFERSON, *1826*

Philip II ordered Captain-General Pedro Menéndez de Avilés to clear Florida for colonization.

Foiled in his initial efforts to destroy Fort Caroline, Menéndez sailed thirty miles south and established a settlement known today as St. Augustine. The French tried to attack, but their fleet was destroyed in a storm. Menéndez then took a force overland to Fort Caroline, where he killed about 140 of the French and took some seventy women and children prisoner. In 1568 a French expedition attacked and burned the fort, now held by the Spanish, and killed most of its occupants. But Florida was to remain under Spanish control for the next 250 years.

A scale model of the fort is on the riverfront. A visitor center overlooks the St. Johns River near the former site of the fort. Open daily.

KEY WEST

Audubon House and Gardens (205 Whitehead St. at Greene St.; 305/294-2116). The gracious antebellum house of sea captain and wrecker (salvage operator) John Geiger has a collection of 18th- and 19th-century furnishings, and re-creates the ambiance of Key West when Audubon visited the island. Many Audubon engravings are on display. Open daily.

Wreckers Museum (322 Duval St.; 305/294-9502). Built circa 1830, the oldest house in Key West has a unique "conch" construction. Once the home of sea captain and wrecker (salvage operator) Francis B. Wattington, it is now a museum with displays of the wrecking industry, historic documents, ship models, and other memorabilia. Open daily.

The John Overstreet House at the Pioneer Florida Museum in Dade City. Photo by Eric Herrmann.

NEW SMYRNA BEACH

New Smyrna Sugar Mill Ruins State Historic Site (2 miles west of U.S. 1, south off FL 44; 904/423-3300). The remains of a large sugar mill destroyed during the Seminole War. Construction of the building began in 1830. All that remains are a walking beam from a steam engine and cooking pots. Open daily.

ORMOND BEACH

Bulow Plantation Ruins State Historic Site (8 miles north off FL A1A, on FL 5, south of Flagler Beach; 904/439-2219). The plantation, which flourished in the early 1800s, was destroyed by Seminole Indians in 1836. Only the ruins of its sugar mill remain on this 109-acre park. Picnicking, interpretive center. Open daily.

PENSACOLA

In 1559, the Spanish established a settlement here, which lasted only two years. However, in 1698 they reestablished the site and built a fort. After three battles in 1719, the French took over, but Spain returned in 1723. The British came in 1763, but Spain returned again in 1781. Andrew Jackson led invasions of the city in 1814 and 1818, and returned in 1821 to accept Florida as a U.S. territory.

Fort Barrancas (on the Naval Air Station; 904/455-5167). On the site of the 18th-century Spanish fortifications, this fort and its attached Water Battery, a 19th-century American fort, have been authentically restored from old drawings and documents. Now part of Gulf Islands National Seashore, the area comprises sixty-five acres of the naval base. Tours, visitor center. Open daily.

Historic Pensacola Village (Seville

Kingsley Plantation on Fort George Island near Jacksonville. Courtesy National Park Service.

Castillo de San Marcos in St. Augustine. Photo by Richard Frear for the National Park Service.

Square, East Government and South Alcaniz streets; 904/444-8905). The park contains several historic buildings. *Pensacola Historic Museum* (405 South Adams St. at Zaragoza St.; 904/433-1559) is in the 1832 *Old Christ Church,* which was used by Union soldiers as a barracks and hospital. Open daily except Sundays. The 1805 *Charles LaValle House* (205 East Church St.) is one of the oldest in the city. Its apron roof and plastered interior are typical of French Creole architecture. *Dorr House* (311 South Adams St. at Church St.) is a Classical Revival dwelling, restored and furnished with mid-Victorian pieces. The 1825-60 *Quina House* (204 South Alcaniz St.) is furnished in the style of the period.

Gulf Islands National Seashore (south on U.S. 98 and FL 399 to Pensacola Beach, then west on Fort Pickens Rd. to Fort Pickens Area; 904/934-2600). Old Fort Pickens, built circa 1834, was one of the largest masonry forts in the United States with concrete batteries. Geronimo and his Apache followers were imprisoned here. Tours available. Open daily.

ST. AUGUSTINE

St. Augustine was under a Spanish flag longer than it has been under the Stars and Stripes. On September 8, 1565, Pedro Menéndez de Avilés dropped anchor and rowed ashore here to found the oldest permanent settlement in the United States. To protect this strategic outpost, the Spanish built Castillo de San Marcos, a massive gray fortress that still dominates the town. Through the centuries, St. Augustine has been repeatedly attacked, counterattacked, pillaged, and burned. The Spanish, British, Confederate, and U.S. flags all have flown over the town.

Castillo de San Marcos National Monument (overlooking Matanzas Bay at jct. of Castillo Dr. and Avenida Menendez; 904/829-6506). The symbol of Spain's ubiquitous presence here and throughout Florida, this massive masonry structure, constructed in 1672–95, was intended to permanently replace a succession of nine previous wooden fortifications. Hispanic artisans and convicts, Indian laborers, black slaves, and English prisoners erected walls twenty-five feet high, fourteen feet thick at the base, nine feet thick at the top, and four feet thick at the parapet. Castillo de San Marcos was never completed. It withstood a fifty-day siege when St. Augustine was captured by South Carolinians in 1702, and another siege of thirty-eight days in 1740. During the American Revolution, the British imprisoned rebels here. The United States later used the fort as a battery in the coastal defense system, as a military prison, and as a magazine. Open daily.

Mission of Nombre de Dios (San Marco Ave.; 904/824-2809). A 208-foot stainless-steel cross marks the site of the founding of St. Augustine, September 8, 1565. Also here is the 1603 Shrine of Our Lady of La Leche. Open daily.

Gonzalez-Alvarez House (14 St. Francis St.; 905/824-2872). The house, built in the early 1600s, is the oldest in town, and its furnishings and neighborhood reflect the Spanish period. Other buildings here include the Manucy Museum of St. Augustine History and the Tover House, which contains the Museum of Florida's Army. All open daily.

Spanish Quarter (904/825-6830). A restoration by the Historic St. Augustine Preservation Board of the 18th-century Spanish colonial village. Six buildings are open daily. *Gallegos House* (21 St. George St.) is a reconstruction of a two-room tabby (an oyster-shell cement) house occupied in the 1750s by a Spanish soldier and his family. Depictions of the lifestyle of the period include demonstrations of period outdoor cooking. *Gomez House* (23 St. George St.) is a reconstructed one-room wooden dwelling occupied by a Spanish infantryman in 1763. *Paso de Burgo and Pellicer Houses,* circa 1780, are two reconstructed frame houses sharing a common center wall. Inside is the Spanish Quarter Museum Store. *De Mesa-Sanchez House* (43 St. George St.) is one of thirty-three surviving original houses. Demonstrations of spinning, weaving and textile arts. *Blacksmith Shop,* built of tabby, now provides hardware for the museum village.

Old Wooden Schoolhouse (14 St. George St.; 904/824-0192). This circa-1760 structure served as a private residence and schoolhouse. Open daily.

Pena-Peck House (143 St. George St.; 904/829-5064). The circa-1700 home of the Spanish Royal Treasurer, and from 1837 to 1930 the residence of the Peck family. Tours available. Open daily.

Ximenez-Fatio House (20 Aviles St.; 904/829-3575). Built in 1798 of coquina, it

Asking one of the States to surrender part of her sovereignty is like asking a lady to surrender part of her chastity.

—JOHN RANDOLPH, *CIRCA 1805*

was a house and general store, then used as an inn during the 1800s. The kitchen in the rear is the only original such structure remaining in town. The museum houses the Society of Colonial Dames of America. Open Thursday through Monday, February through August.

Fort Matanzas National Monument (on Anastasia Island, 14 miles south on FL A1A; 904/471-0116). To protect St. Augustine, the Spanish erected the first of several watchtowers in 1569. The importance of this inlet was demonstrated during a British siege in 1740, when Spanish relief ships ran the blockade. Around 1740 the Spanish built Fort Matanzas to control the inlet. A few years later British attempts to destroy the fort failed. After the transfer of Florida to the United States in 1821, the unmanned fort fell into ruin. The structure was stabilized in the early part of the 20th century and the fort designated a national monument. It is considered a fine representative of a vanished style of military architecture. The fort is visible from the visitor center on Anastasia Island, and a ferry boat there takes visitors to the national monument. Open daily.

Tours. A sightseeing train (904/829-6545) makes regular seven-mile, one-hour trips with stop-off privileges at eight stations. *Colee's Horse-drawn Carriage Tours* (904/829-2818) give one-hour narrated tours of the historic area.

TALLAHASSEE

The Columns (100 North Duval St.; 904/244-8116). An 1830 three-story brick mansion, moved here from its original site, once served as a bank, boardinghouse, doctor's office, and restaurant. Restored and furnished in the style of the period, it now serves as the office of the Chamber of Commerce. Open weekdays.

San Marcos de Apalache State Historic Site (24 miles south via FL 363, on Canal St. in St. Marks; 904/922-6007). This site was visited by Pánfilo de Narváez in 1527 and Hernando de Soto in 1539. There are ruins of a 1739 fort. A museum is on the site of an old federal hospital. Open Thursday through Monday.

ZEPHYRHILLS

Fort Foster Historic Site (6 miles southwest on U.S. 301, adjoining Hillsborough River State Park; 813/987-6771). A reconstruction of a circa-1835 fort built during the Second Seminole War. Living-history program. Tours depart from Hillsborough River State Park. Open weekends.

20

GEORGIA

James Oglethorpe sold King George II (for whom Georgia is named) on granting his group a charter to a vast tract of land between the Carolinas and Florida, stretching westward to the Mississipi. Intending it as a place where debtors, dissentors, and the working poor would have a second chance, he landed his first group at Yamacraw Bluff on February 12, 1733, and set about building what would become the city of Savannah.

The colony also had a military purpose: It would serve as a buffer between the British Carolinas and Spanish Florida. Oglethorpe failed to capture St. Augustine from the Spanish, but in 1742 he repulsed Spanish assaults on St. Simons Island.

Georgia did not live up to Oglethorpe's hopes. Despite efforts to recruit settlers, only a few of the deserving poor migrated to the colony. Land restrictions were eased and the ban on slavery lifted in 1751, but the discouraged trustees returned the colony to the Crown the next year. Georgia then began to grow as settlers from South Carolina came to establish plantations to cultivate rice and other staple crops.

ATHENS

Taylor-Grady House (634 Prince Ave.; 706/549-8688). A restored 1839 Greek Revival mansion surrounded by thirteen columns said to symbolize the thir-

teen original states. Period furniture. Open weekdays.

Church-Waddell-Brumby House (280 East Dougherty St.; 706/353-1820). This circa-1820 Federal structure thought to be the oldest house in the state. It houses the *Athens Welcome Center,* which has information on self-guided tours of other historic homes and buildings. Schedule varies, phone in advance.

Founders Memorial Gardens and House (325 South Lumpkin St., on Univ. of Georgia campus; 706/542-3631). Built in 1857 as a residence for professors, the house has been restored and furnished with period pieces as a museum and headquarters of the Garden Club of Georgia. The surrounding gardens are a memorial to the founders of the Ladies' Garden Club of Athens, the first garden club in the country. Gardens open daily, house weekdays.

Other historic houses. Circa-1820 *University President's House* (570 Prince Ave.), 1842 *Ross Crane House* (247 Pulaski St.), 1858 *Lucy Cobb Institute* (200 Milledge Ave.), 1841 *Joseph Henry Lumpkin House* (248 Prince Ave.), 1845 *Old Franklin Hotel* (480 East Broad St.), 1842 *Governor Wilson Lumpkin House* (South Campus, Univ. of Georgia).

ATLANTA

Tullie Smith Farm (Atlanta History Center, 130 West Paces Ferry Rd.; 404/814-4000). An 1840 plantation-

style farmhouse. Garden, log cabin and outbuilding, craft demonstrations. Open daily.

Wren's Nest (1050 Ralph D. Abernathy Blvd. SW; 404/753-8535). The eccentric Victorian home of Joel Chandler Harris, journalist and transcriber of the "Uncle Remus" stories. Family furnishings, books, photographs. Open daily except Mondays.

Stone Mountain Park (19 miles east on U.S. 78; 404/498-5600). The major attraction is the world's largest granite monolith, rising 825 feet, on which has been carved the three major figures of the Confederacy: Robert E. Lee, Stonewall Jackson, and Jefferson Davis. In the park an antebellum plantation features nineteen buildings, moved here and restored and furnished with 18th- and 19th-century antiques. Cookhouse, slave quarters, country store, and other outbuildings, formal and kitchen gardens, museum, boat and train rides, three restaurants. Open daily.

Accommodations: *Ansley Inn* (253 15th St. NE; 404/872-9000 or 800/446-5416). This Tudor-style inn, in the historic Ansley Park section of midtown Atlanta, once was a chaperoned boardinghouse for young women. The fifteen guest rooms now have wet bars and Jacuzzis, and some have fireplaces and four-poster beds. Breakfast. Moderate.

AUGUSTA

The second town marked off for settlement was Augusta, which became a military outpost and upriver trading town. During the Revolution, the town changed hands several times, but Fort Augusta, renamed Fort Cornwallis by its British captors, was finally surrendered to "Light-Horse" Harry Lee on June 5, 1781.

Harris House (1822 Broad St.; 706/724-0436). The circa-1795 house of tobacco merchant Ezekiel Harris. Period furnishings. Tours available. Open Monday through Friday afternoons and Saturday mornings.

Meadow Garden (1320 Independence Dr.; 706/724-4174). The 1791–1804 house of George Walton, a signer of the Declaration. Open Monday through Friday.

St. Paul's Episcopal Church (605 Reynolds St.). A granite Celtic cross in the yard of this 1750 church marks the site of the fort, and the spot where Augusta began, established in 1736 in honor of Princess Augusta. Open daily.

BLAKELY

Kolomoki Mounds State Park (6 miles north off U.S. 27; 912/723-5296). Indian mounds, temple mound, and excavations indicate that a settlement was here between A.D. 800 and 1200. The museum interprets the civilization of Kolomoki, Weeden Island, and Swift Creek cultures. Picnicking. Park open daily, museum daily except Mondays.

BRUNSWICK

Laid out in 1771 by the Colonial Council of the Royal Province of Georgia, this town was named to honor George III of the House of Brunswick (Hanover). It later became the seat of Glynn County, named in honor of John Glynn, member of Parliament and a sympathizer with the colonists' struggle for independence.

Fort Frederica National Monument (12 miles northeast via St. Simons/Sea Island Causeway; 912/638-3639). One of the largest forts ever built by the British in America, Fort Frederica was carefully planned by the Trustees in London in 1736, and included the town of Frederica. Forty-four men and seventy-two women landed at St. Simons Island on March 16, 1736.

In 1738, a regiment of 650 British soldiers arrived. The town was enclosed with earth and timber works from ten to thirteen feet high, which included towers and a moat. The fort was Oglethorpe's command post for his invasion of Florida. In July 1742, Spaniards launched an attach on the fort, but it was repulsed with an ambush at Bloody Marsh, ending Spanish attempts to gain control of Georgia. Frederica flourished as a military town until after the peace of 1748, but did not survive for long after the British troops left.

Today, archaeological excavations have exposed some of the old foundations.

Outdoor exhibits make it easy to visualize the town as it was. The visitor center has a film and exhibits. Self-guided tour. Open daily.

The Tullie Smith Farm at the Atlanta History Center.

CALHOUN

New Echota State Historic Site ($\frac{1}{2}$ mile east of I-75 on GA 225; 706/629-8151). After establishing a government in 1817, the legislature of the Cherokee Nation in 1825 established a capital surrounding the site of their Council House. The written form of the Cherokee language had been created by Sequoyah in 1821, and the print shop was built in 1827. The first issue of the newspaper, the *Cherokee Phoenix,* was printed here in 1828. In 1827, Samuel A. Worcester, a missionary, arrived from Boston and built a house, the only original building still standing here. At the height of Cherokee prosperity, gold was found in the Indians' territory. In 1835, after a long legal battle, the Cherokee were forced to agree to sell their territory and move to Oklahoma. Today the restoration of the final capital here includes

THE TRAIL OF TEARS

In 1838, some 15,000 Cherokee were driven out of their homeland in Georgia and forced to march to Indian Territory, which today is Oklahoma. One out of four, an estimated 4,000, died along the way. The route they followed is called the Trail of Tears. Now a National Monument, it is a symbol of the wrongs suffered by Indians at the hands of the U.S. government.

A 1791 treaty had recognized Cherokee territory in Georgia as independent, and the Cherokee had created a thriving republic with a written constitution. For decades the state of Georgia sought to enforce its authority over the Cherokee Nation, but was unsuccessful until the election of President Andrew Jackson, a supporter of Indian removal. Although the Supreme Court declared Congress's 1830 Indian Removal Bill unconstitutional, the harassment continued, culminating in the rounding up of the Cherokee by troops in 1838.

The Cherokee were forced to abandon their property, livestock, and tribal burial grounds and move to camps in Tennessee. From there, in severe winter weather, they were marched another 800 miles to Indian Territory.

the 1828 Worcester House, the Council House, the print shop, the 1805 Vann Tavern, an 1830s log store, the courthouse, and a museum and orientation center. Open daily except Mondays.

CARTERSVILLE

Etowah Indian Mounds Historic Site (3 miles south, off GA 113, 61; 404/387-3747). This village, occupied from A.D. 1000 to 1500, now is the most impressive of more than 100 settlements in the Etowah Valley. It was home to several thousand people of a relatively advanced culture. Six earthen pyramids grouped around two public squares, the largest of which occupied several acres, served as funeral mounds, bases for temples,

and the residences of the chiefs. A museum displays artifacts and a painted white marble mortuary. Open daily except Mondays.

CHATSWORTH

Vann House State Historic Site (3 miles west on Alt GA 52 at jct. GA 225 in Spring Place; 706/695-2598). This 1804 modified-Georgian brick house was the showplace of the Cherokee Nation. James Vann, half Scottish, half Cherokee, helped establish the nearby Moravian Mission for the education of the young Cherokee. The three-story house is partly furnished. Open daily except Mondays.

Fort Mountain State Park (7 miles east via GA 52; 706/695-2651). In the park are the ruins of a prehistoric wall. Open daily.

DAHLONEGA

Scottish Highlanders were recruited in 1736 by Oglethorpe to protect Georgia's frontier on the Altamaha River. They guarded Savannah from Spanish and Indian attack, and carved out plantations from the south Georgia wilderness.

Dahlonega Courthouse Gold Museum State Historic Site (on the Square; 706/864-2257). In the 1836 Lumpkin County Courthouse, a film and exhibits tell of the country's first major gold rush. Open daily. Visitors pan for gold in an authentic mining setting at *Gold Miners' Camp* (2½ miles south via GA 60; 706/864-2257). Open daily, May through October.

Accommodations: *Worley Homestead Inn* (410 West Main St.; 706/864-7002). An 1845 Colonial Revival inn, four blocks from the town square, offers seven guest rooms with fireplaces and antique beds, full breakfast. Inexpensive.

DARIEN

Fort King George State Historic Site (1½ miles east of U.S. 17 on Fort King George Dr.; 912/437-4770). South Carolina scouts built this fort in 1721 near an abandoned Indian village, to block Spanish and French expansion into Georgia. The fort and its blockhouse have been entirely reconstructed. There is a museum. Open daily except Mondays.

Hofwyl-Broadfield Plantation State Historic Site (6 miles south on U.S. 17; 912/264-9263). The evolution of a rice plantation is depicted through tours of the 1851 plantation, museum, and trails. Open daily except Mondays.

EATONTON

Bronson House (114 North Madison Ave.; 706/485-6442). An 1822 Greek Revival mansion, now the headquarters of the Eaton-Putnam Historical Society, has restored rooms, local memorabilia. Open by appointment.

Uncle Remus Museum (3 blocks south of courthouse on U.S. 441, in Turner Park; 706/485-6856). A log cabin, made from two original slave cabins, has a fireplace, shadow boxes with illustrations of Uncle Remus sto-

The John Jarrell House at Jarrell Plantation near Forsyth.

ries. First editions, relics, and mementos. Open daily, June through August, daily except Tuesdays the rest of the year.

FORSYTH

Jarrell Plantation State Historic Site (18 miles east of I-75 exit 60 on GA 18E; 912/986-5172). A plantation with twenty buildings dating from 1847, including sawmill, gristmill, and blacksmith shop. Farm animals, seasonal demonstrations. Open daily except Mondays.

JEKYLL ISLAND

Horton House (northwest side of island; 912/635-3636). The ruins of the 1742 house of William Horton, sent from St. Simons as captain by Oglethorpe. Here he established an outpost and plantation. Horton became major of all British forces at Fort Frederica after Oglethorpe's return to England. The house later was occupied by the du Bigon family as part of their plantation. Open daily.

LA GRANGE

Bellevue (Ben Hill St.; 706/884-1832). A Greek Revival house, built 1852-53, for U.S. senator Benjamin Harvey Hill. Period furnishings. Open Tuesday through Saturday.

LUMPKIN

Westville (1 mile south of town; 912/838-6310). A living-history village of restored circa-1850 buildings. Craft workers demonstrate quilting, weaving, candlemaking, potterymaking, blacksmithing, and basket weaving. Open daily except Mondays.

MACON

City Hall (700 Poplar St.; 912/751-7170).

The main entrance of this 1836 Classical Revival building is flanked by panels depicting area history. It was the state capitol during the last session of the Georgian General Assembly under the Confederacy. Tours available. Open weekdays.

Sidney Lanier Cottage (935 High St.; 912/743-3851). This 1840 Gothic Revival house was the birthplace of the poet. It has period furnishings, and is the headquarters of the Middle Georgia Historical Society. Open daily except Sundays.

Old Cannonball House (856 Mulberry St.; 912/745-5982). This 1853 Greek Revival house was struck by a Union cannonball, which went through one of the house's columns, entered the parlor, and landed, unexploded, in the hall. The house contains the Macon-Confederate Museum. Open daily.

Hay House (934 Georgia Ave.; 912/742-8155). An Italian Renaissance Revival villa built in 1855–59 with twenty-four rooms, elaborate ornamental plaster, woodwork, and stained glass. Ornate period furnishings and objets d'art. Open daily.

Ocmulgee National Monument (2 miles east on U.S. 80, Alt 129; 912/752-8257). This major Indian archaeological site shows evidence of 12,000 years of settlement, including six successive occupations from at least 10,000 B.C. to A.D. 1825. The major remains consist of nine ceremonial mounds, a funeral mound, and a restored ceremonial earth lodge of the early Mississippian Period (A.D. 900–1100). Exhibits and dioramas in the museum show Indian culture from its earliest origins. The Great Temple Mound is more than forty feet high. An audio program is presented in the restored earth lodge. Open daily.

Historic District comprises nearly all of old Macon; forty-eight buildings and houses have been cited for architectural excellence and listed on the National Register of

Historic Places. Tour maps are available at the *Convention and Visitors Bureau* (in Macon Coliseum, 200 Coliseum Dr.; 912/743-3401; open daily).

Tours. *Heart of Georgia Tours,* operated by the Middle Georgia Historical Society (935 High St.; 912/743-3851), offer bus tours and guides for private tours of the city. *Sidney's Old South Tours* (200 Cherry St.; 912/743-3401), operated by the Convention and Visitors Bureau, has daily city tours.

Accommodations: *1842 Inn* (353 College St.; 912/741-1842). A restored 1842 Greek Revival structure is now a handsome inn with twenty-one guest rooms that are individually decorated and named. Fireplaces, antiques, breakfast. Victorian cottage nearby. Moderate.

SAVANNAH

This charming city is a legacy of its founder, James Oglethorpe, who landed at Yamacraw Bluff with 120 settlers on February 12, 1733. His plan was to make the "inner city" spacious, beautiful, and all that a city should be. Bull Street, named for Colonel William Bull, one of his aides, stretches south from the high bluffs overlooking the Savannah River and is punctuated by five handsome squares and Forsyth Park.

By the time of the Revolution, wharves served ocean trade. The town had its liberty pole and a patriots' battalion when news of Lexington came. The Declaration of Independence led to Savannah's designation as capital of the new state. By December, however, the British had retaken the town. An attempt to recapture Savannah failed, and more than 1,000 Americans and 700 Frenchmen were killed. General "Mad Anthony" Wayne's forces finally drove out the British in 1782.

U.S. Customs House (Bull and East Bay streets). Built in 1850 on the site of the colony's public building, the carved capitals on the granite columns were modeled on tobacco leaves. A tablet on Bay Street marks the site of Oglethorpe's headquarters.

Factors Walk (between Bull and East Broad streets). Named by cotton factors of the 19th century, this row of business houses "on the Bay" is accessible by a network of iron bridgeways over cobblestone ramps.

Pirates' House (20 East Broad St.; 912/233-1881). In the Trustee's Garden Site, this 1734 former inn for visiting seamen has been restored and is a restaurant. Robert Louis Stevenson referred to the inn in *Treasure Island.* Open daily.

Telfair Mansion (121 Barnard St.; 912/232-1177). On the site of the Royal Governor's Residence is an 1818 Regency mansion, one of three surviving buildings in Savannah designed by the English architect William Jay. Period rooms with family furnishings. The mansion houses an art museum with a collection of American and European paintings, sculpture, and decorative arts. Open daily except Mondays.

Owens-Thompson House (124 Abercorn St.; 912/233-9743). An authentically furnished circa-1816 Regency house designed by William Jay. Lafayette was a guest in 1825. Walled garden. Open daily.

Davenport House (324 East State St.; 912/236-8097). Built in 1815–20 by master builder Isaiah Davenport, this is a splendid example of Federal architecture, restored and furnished in the style of the period. Gardens. Open daily.

Juliette Gordon Low Birthplace (142 Bull St.; 912/236-4501). This restored 1818–21 Regency town house was, in 1860, the birthplace of the founder of the Girl Scouts of America. Many Gordon family pieces.

Andrew Low House (329 Abercorn St.; 912/233-6854). An 1848 house built for Andrew Low, this later was the residence of

Let us compare every constitution we have seen with those of the United States of America, and we shall have reason to blush for our country. On the contrary, we shall feel the strongest motives to fall upon our knees, in gratitude to heaven for having been graciously pleased to give us birth and education in that country, and for having destined us to live under her laws!

—JOHN ADAMS, *A DEFENSE OF THE CONSTITUTIONS OF GOVERNMENT OF THE UNITED STATES OF AMERICA, 1787–88*

Juliette Gordon Low. Period furnishings. Open daily except Thursdays.

Green-Meldrim House (14 West Macon St.; 912/233-3845). This antebellum house, used by General Sherman during the occupation of the city, now is the parish house of St. John Church. Tours Tuesday and Thursday through Staurday; closed the two weeks before Easter.

Christ Episcopal Church (Johnson Sq.; 912/232-4131). Built in 1838 for a congregation dating from 1733, this is the mother church of Georgia. Among its early rectors were John Wesley and George Whitfield. Open Tuesdays and Fridays.

Congregation Mickve Israel (20 East Gordon St., east side of Monterey Sq.; 912/233-1547). The only Gothic-style synagogue in the country contains a Torah brought here in 1733 by the Portuguese and German Jews who founded the congregation. A museum has portraits, religious objects, and letters from Washington, Jefferson, and Madison. Tours available. Open weekdays.

Tours. *Helen Salter's Savannah Tours* (1113 Winston Ave.; 912/355-4296) and *Old Savannah Tours* (516 Lee Blvd.; 912/354-7913) both offer daily bus tours of the historic sites of the city.

Accommodations: *East Bay Inn* (225 East Bat St.; 912/238-1225, or 800/500-1225). Once a cotton warehouse, this three-story inn on the historic Savannah River waterfront now offers twenty-eight guest rooms. Antiques, breakfast, restaurant on premises. Moderate.

THOMASVILLE

Pebble Hill Plantation (5 miles southwest via U.S. 319; 912/226-2344). A circa-1820s plantation with an elaborate Greek Revival mansion furnished with art, antiques, porcelains, crystal, and silver belonging to the Hanna family, who rebuilt the house and outbuildings

after a fire in the 1930s. Gardens, wagon rides, tours. Open daily except Mondays.

TOCCOA

Traveler's Rest State Historic Site (6 miles northeast off U.S. 123; 706/886-2256). A plantation house built in about 1840 on land granted in 1785 to Jesse Walton, a Revolutionary War soldier and political leader. The two-story structure covers 6,000 square feet. Later owned and enlarged by Devereaux Jarrett, it served as a stagecoach inn and post office. Today it houses a museum. Open daily except Mondays.

WASHINGTON

Robert Toombs House State Historic Site (216 East Robert Toombs Ave.; 706/678-2226). The restored 1797 residence of a Confederate statesman and soldier, this is a frame Federal house with a Greek Revival portico. Period furnishings, exhibits. Open daily except Mondays.

Callaway Plantation (5 miles west on U.S. 78; 706/678-2013). A working plantation complex includes a red brick 1869 Greek Revival mansion and frame Federal "plain style" 1785 house with period furnishings. Open daily except Mondays.

Elijah Clark State Park (23 miles northeast on U.S. 378, on Clark Hill Lake; 706/359-3458). The park includes a log-cabin museum with Colonial-life demonstrations. Nature trails, cottages, picnicking. Open daily.

Alexander H. Stephens State Park (19 miles southwest on GA 47 to Crawfordville, then ½ mile north; 706/456-2602). In this 1,190-acre park is the circa-1830 Liberty Hall, the restored home of A. H. Stephens, Vice-President of the Confederacy. Museum, picnicking. Open Wednesday through Sunday.

21

SOUTH CAROLINA

oth the Spanish and the French attempted to settle here, but the first permanent settlement in what now is South Carolina was English, in 1670, on the Ashley River. It was named Charles Towne (or Charleston, as it was officially renamed in 1783) for Charles II, who granted the Carolina province to eight lords proprietors. The province originally included both of the Carolinas as well as Georgia and northern Florida. The settlement had moved, by 1680, to the present site of Charleston.

Proprietary rule proved unpopular and was overthrown in 1719, although two years later the legislature voted to accept the king's appointed governor, Sir Francis Nicholson. There were other things to worry about. Coastal settlers were plagued by pirates; upcountry settlers by Indians. Planters were importing slaves from Africa, and there was constant fear of insurrection.

The Carolina province was divided into North and South Carolina in 1729, although the boundary was not settled until 1815. Another division was between Low Country planters and upcountry farmers, who resented Charleston's reluctance to acknowledge their rights. Undeveloped upcountry land was taxed at the same rate as that of the rich planters.

South Carolina sent delegates to the Continental Congress in 1774, and ousted its royal governor. When the British attacked Charleston in 1776, General William Moultrie successfully defended the city. In the Revo-

lution, South Carolina was the scene of 137 military engagements, ranging from skirmishes to major battles. Although local militia triumphed at Kings Mountain and Cowpens, but lost at Camden, bitter and brutal guerrilla warfare set the tone of the war here. In one of the final actions of the war, the British were driven out of Charleston, which they had occupied since 1780.

AIKEN

Redcliffe (15 miles east, off U.S. 278 near Beach Island; 803/827-1473). A circa-1850 Greek Revival mansion built on 350 acres by James Henry Hammond, now furnished with family and period pieces. Art collection, historic documents, picnicking. Open Thursday through Monday.

ANDERSON

"The Old Reformer" (Main and Whitner streets, in front of courthouse). The cannon bearing this nickname was used by both British and Americans during the Revolution, and was fired again in 1860 when the Ordinance of Secession was signed.

Pendleton Historic District (7 miles northwest of I-85, off U.S. 76; 803/646-3782 for tour information). Guided and self-guided tours of the area, which contains forty-five historic homes and buildings, leave from the

239

Pendleton District Historical and Recreational Commission, 125 East Queen St. Visitor center. Arts and crafts in the circa-1850 Hunter's Store. Tours weekdays.

Accommodations: *River Inn* (612 East River St.; 803/226-1431). This Georgian plantation house, bordering the town's historic district, has ten-foot beamed ceilings and working, coal-burning fireplaces. Each of the three guest rooms has its own fireplace and bath. On the inn's five acres are azaleas, camellia sasanqua trees, roses, and crape myrtles. Full breakfast, dinner available. Inexpensive.

BEAUFORT

Spanish explorers first noted the harbor here in 1514–15. In 1526, colonists from Spain made an unsuccessful attempt to settle the area. In 1562 a group of Frenchmen established the first colony, which also failed. English and Scottish attempts followed, and

success finally came when the present city was laid out for the Duke of Beaufort. The town was almost completely destroyed in 1715, captured by the British in the Revolution, and menaced by British cannon in 1812. Nearly all the population left when the town was captured by Union troops in the Civil War. The second-oldest town in the state, Beaufort's name is pronounced *Bewfert*.

John Mark Verdier House Museum (801 Bay St.; 803/524-6334). Built about 1790, this Federal house once was known as the Lafayette Building; the marquis reputedly spoke from the piazza here in 1825. Open Monday through Friday and Saturday mornings.

George P. Elliott House Museum (Bay and Charles streets; 803/524-8450). This 1844 Greek Revival house was used as a hospital during the Civil War. Period furniture. Open weekdays.

St. Helena's Episcopal Church (507 Newcastle St. at North St.; 803/522-1712).

The watermelon market in Charleston, South Carolina.

The John Mark Verdier House in Beaufort.

Built in 1712 and still in use, this church was used as a hospital in the Civil War, and tombstones from the burial ground became operating tables. Open daily except Sundays.

Accommodations: *Old Point Inn* (212 New St.; 803/524-3177). Built by William Waterhouse as a wedding present for his wife, this Queen Anne has wraparound verandahs in the "Beaufort Style" that overlook the Intercoastal Waterway. Four pillared fireplaces, pocket door, and eyelash windows. Four guest rooms, breakfast. Moderate.

CAMDEN

Historic Camden (South Broad St.; 803/432-9841). The archaeological site of the state's oldest inland town. The visitor area includes two early-19th-century log cabins and a restored 18th-century town house. Trails lead to the reconstructed foundation of a pre-Revolutionary powder maga-

zine, the Kershaw-Cornwallis House, and two reconstructed British fortifications. The visitor center presents an audiovisual program. Natural trail, picnicking, self-guided tour. Open daily except Mondays.

Bethesda Presbyterian Church (on U.S. 1; 502 DeKalb St.). Designed by Robert Mills, architect of the Washington Monument, this 1820 church is considered a masterpiece, and is called the House of Five Porches. The steeple is at the rear of the building. Open daily except Sundays.

CHARLESTON

The first permanent settlement in the Carolinas, Charles Towne, as it was first called, was established as a small colony at the Ashley River, by Anthony Ashley Cooper, Earl of Shaftesbury. He also established the only American nobility in history, with barons, landgraves (dukes), and caciques (earls), all of whom owned great

[Visitors saw only] opulent and lordly planters, poor and spiritless white and vile slaves.

—HENRY LAURENS *describing Charleston, 1750*

*The American com-
mander General
Johann Kalb was mor-
tally wounded in the
Battle of Camden dur-
ing the Revolution.
Despite repeated tries,
the Americans failed to
recapture the town.
Most of the battles in
the latter part of the
war were fought in the
South. Courtesy
Library of Congress,
Prints and
Photographs Division.*

plantations. This nobility lasted less than fifty years, but it was the foundation for an aristocratic tradition that still exists, even though the rice and indigo that made the nobility rich are gone.

Colonists from England, Ireland, and Barbados came to enlarge the settlement in 1670, and by 1680 the colony moved across the river to become a city-state. Many of the colonists went to the Carolina Low Country and established large plantation. Every year on the traditional date of May 10, the planters and their families moved back to Charleston to escape the mosquitoes and malarial heat. From spring to frost, these planters created a season of dancing, socials, theater, and musicales. The city founded the first playhouse, the first museum, and the first public school in the colony, the first municipal college in America, and the first fire-insurance company on the continent. Charleston became famous throughout the world as "a flourishing capital of wealth and ease."

The First Provincial Congress of South Carolina met in Charleston in 1775 and prepared the city to repulse a British attack. But the city was captured in 1780 and for two and a half years was occupied by the enemy. With peace came great prosperity, but rivalry between the small farmers of the interior and the merchants and plantation owners of the Low Country resulted in removal of the capital to Columbia. The convention that authored the Ordinance of Secession came to Charleston to pass that declaration. South Carolina was the first state to leave the Union, and the Civil War began with the bombardment of Union-occupied Fort Sumter in Charleston Harbor.

Today the aristocratic old city lives up to its reputation for cultivated manners. Its homes, historic shrines, old churches, lovely gardens, winding streets, and intricate iron lace gateways exude charm and dignity.

Edmondston-Alston House (21 East Battery; 803/722-7171). Built in about 1825 by a wealthy merchant and wharf owner, remodeled in Greek Revival style by the next owner, a rice planter, the house has an uninterrupted view across the harbor. It contains portraits and documents, elaborate woodwork, and original furnishings. Tours available. Open daily.

Heyward-Washington House (87 Church St.; 803/722-0354). Once owned by Thomas Heyward Jr., a signer of the Declaration of Independence, this 1772 Georgian house has exquisite period furnishings, a colonial garden, and a carriage house. Open daily.

Thomas Elfe House (54 Queen St.; 803/722-2142). The restored circa-1760 home of a furniture maker, with original cypress paneling. Tours on weekday mornings.

Nathaniel Russell House (51 Meeting St.; 803/724-8483). The 1808 Adam-style home of a wealthy merchant, the house has a free-flying staircase, oval drawing rooms, and period furnishings. Open daily.

Joseph Manigault House (350 Meeting St.; 723-2926). This 1803 house is an outstanding example of Adam architecture, and is furnished with antiques and has a curving staircase. Open daily.

Aiken-Rhett House (48 Elizabeth St.; 803/723-1159). Built in 1817 and enlarged in 1833 in Greek Revival style, subsequent additions have created some of the finest rooms in the city, including a Rococo Revival art gallery. Many original furnishings. Open daily.

Old Exchange and Provost Dungeon (122 East Bay St.; 803/727-2165). Built in 1771, this was the last building constructed by the British here prior to the war. It served as an exchange and customs house, then as a prison during the Revolutionary War, and has been the site of many important events. Extensively restored. Open daily.

The Powder Magazine (79 Cumberland St.; 803/722-3767). Built in about 1710 as part of the city's original fortifications, this is now the oldest public building in Charleston.

The Edmondston-Alston House in Charleston.

SONS OF LIBERTY

As Americans rallied in 1765 to resist the Stamp Act, a loose affiliation of patriot groups became known as the Sons of Liberty. The movement began when a New York City group initiated correspondence with Sons of Liberty groups in New England and later in the South. Originally middle- and upper-class secret societies, the groups worked to build a broad base of political support. British officials accused them of plotting to overthrow the government, although the aims of the Sons of Liberty were narrower: while organizing resistance to the Stamp Act, they maintained their loyalty to the king.

The movement broke up after the repeal of the Stamp Act in 1766, but was revived in 1768 in response to the Townshend Acts. From then until the Revolution, Sons of Liberty groups took the lead in organizing and enforcing resistance movements in the colonies.

Colonial museum. Open weekdays.

City Hall Art Gallery (80 Broad St.; 803/724-3799). On the site of the Colonial marketplace, this 1801 building first housed the Bank of the United States, then became the city hall in 1818. Its superb picture gallery has John Trumbull's portrait of Washington in his late years, and Samuel F. B. Morse's painting of President Monroe. Tours. Open weekdays.

Huguenot Church (110 Church St.; 803/722-4385). Built in 1845 on the site of an earlier structure that burned in 1796, it was the only church in the United States to use the Calvinist Huguenot liturgy; services were in French until 1928. Open daily.

St. Philip's Church (142 Church St.). The lofty steeple of this 1838 Georgian church became a target for Union guns in the Civil War. John C. Calhoun and other notables are buried in the graveyard. Open daily.

St. Michael's Church (Meeting and Broad streets; 803/723-0623). The steeple of this 1752 church rises 186 feet, and its tower has a four-faced clock that has been in operation since 1764. The steeple bells were captured by the British, returned after the Revolution, sent to Columbia, South Carolina, during the Civil War, and partly destroyed by fire there. Later they were sent back to England to have them melted down and recast in the original molds, and were returned to St. Michael's in 1867. Open weekdays.

St. Mary's Church (93 Hassell St.; 803/722-7696). The mother church of the Catholic dioceses of the Carolinas and Georgia. The congregation was established in 1789; the church was built in 1836. Open daily.

Kahal Kadosh Beth Elohim (90 Hassell St.; 803/723-1090). Founded in 1749, this was the first (1624) Reform Jewish congregation in America. The 1840 synagogue has a museum and gift ship. Open weekday mornings.

Unitarian Church (4 Archdale St.; 803/723-4617). This 1772 church has a fan tracery ceiling and an interior modeled after the Henry VII Chapel in Westminster Abbey. Open daily.

St. John's Lutheran Church (Archdale and Clifford streets; 803/723-4617). The congregation was established in 1742, and this church was built in 1817. Pastor John Bachman (1815–74), who co-authored *Quadrupeds of America* with John James

Audubon, is buried beneath the altar in the church nave. Open weekdays.

Charles Towne Landing (1500 Old Town Rd., on SC 171; 803/556-4450). An unusual sixty-six-acre park on the site of the state's first permanent settlement, it has reconstructed fortifications, a replica of *Adventure* (a 17th-century trading vessel), formal gardens, and a 1670 experimental crop garden. Colonial village, tram tour, restaurant, picnicking. The visitor center shows a movie, *Carolina*. Open daily.

Fort Sumter National Monument (on island in harbor; tour boat leaves from Municipal Yacht Basin, Lockwood Blvd.; 803/883-3123). The national monument also includes *Fort Moultrie* (U.S. 17 to SC 703; turn right and follow signs), which was originally built in 1776 of sand and palmetto logs. Colonel William Moultrie's forces drove British ships from Charleston Harbor at Fort Moultrie in June 1776. The present fort was completed in 1809 and garrisoned by Union forces in late 1860. South Carolina seceded in December 1860, and the surrender of Fort Sumter was demanded in April 1861. When the demand was refused, an intense bombardment ensued, and the fort surrendered after thirty-four hours. The fall of Fort Sumter caused President Lincoln to call for 75,000 volunteers to put down the rebellion, and the Civil War began. The fort's ruins have been partially excavated, and there is a museum on the site. Fort Moultrie has been restored. The visitor center has an audiovisual program depicting the development of the seacoast defense. Both forts are open daily.

Boone Hall Plantation (8 miles north off U.S. 17 on Long Point Rd. in Mount Pleasant; 803/884-4371). A 738-acre estate with nine original slave houses and a circa-1750 ginhouse. Several rooms in the 1681 house are open to the public. "Avenue of Oaks." Open daily.

Drayton Hall (9 miles northwest via SC 61; 803/766-0188). Built in 1738, this is one of the oldest surviving plantation houses in the area. The Georgian Palladian house is surrounded by live oaks and is on the Ashley River. Held in the Drayton family for seven generations, the mansion is in virtually its original condition. A National Trust for Historic Preservation property. Tours available. Open daily.

Magnolia Plantation and Gardens (10 miles northwest on SC 61; 803/571-1266). Internationally famous circa-1680 gardens are America's oldest. They cover fifty acres with camellias, azaleas, magnolias, and hundreds of other species. Audubon Swamp Garden. Plantation home and local art gallery. Open daily.

Middleton Place Gardens, House, and Stableyards (14 miles northwest on SC 61; 803/556-6020). Once the home of Arthur Middleton, a signer of the Declaration of Independence, it encompasses the Gardens, the Plantation Stableyards, and the restored House Museum. The Gardens, laid out in 1741, highlight ornamental butterfly lakes, sweeping terraces, and a wide variety of flora and fauna. The Stableyards feature craftspeople demonstrating skills necessary for a self-sufficient 18th-century plantation. Tours available. Open daily.

Old Dorchester State Park (19 miles northwest on SC 642; 803/873-1740). Here, at the head of the Ashley River, Congregationalists from Massachusetts established a village in 1696. It was a trading center until 1752, when there was an exodus to Georgia in a search for plentiful land and a better climate. By 1780 the town was occupied by the British, and had only forty houses and a church. The next year, Colonel Wade Hampton advanced against Dorchester, but the British destroyed the town and retreated to Charleston. Remains of the church tower

Carolina is in the spring a paradise, in the summer a hell, and in the autumn a hospital.

—DR. JOHANN DAVID SCHOEPH

and Fort Dorchester remain. The ninety-seven-acre area has been partially excavated. Picnicking. The visitor center has drawings and artifacts. Open Thursday through Monday.

Tours. *Charleston Carriage Co.* (96 North Market St.; 803/577-0042) and *Palmetto Carriage Tours* (40 North Market St.; 803/723-8145) offer narrated, horse-drawn carriage tours of Old Charleston. Both have shuttle service from downtown hotels. *Carolina Lowcountry Tours* (803/ 797-1045) offers a variety of tours of the city and the neighboring plantations. All operate daily.

Accommodations: *The Battery Carriage House Inn* (20 South Battery; 800/775-5575). The inn was built in 1843; renovations have preserved its antebellum charm. It was used in the filming of the miniseries *North and South.* Modern amenities include Jacuzzis, cable television, and computer hookups. Garden. Eleven guest rooms, breakfast. Expensive.

CHERAW

Historic District (803/537-7681). The 214 downtown acres contain more than fifty antebellum homes and public buildings. The circa-1765 Town Green is the site of the 1820 Lyceum Museum. Other buildings of note include the circa-1855 Town Hall, the circa-1835 Market Place, and the Inglis-McIver Law Office. Chamber of Commerce on the Green has self-guided tour booklets.

Old St. David's Episcopal Church (Front and Church streets; 803/537-8425). Built in 1768 and restored to the 1820s period, this church was used as a hospital by the British during the Revolution, and by Union forces in the Civil War. Many British soldiers are buried in the graveyard. Tours by appointment.

CLEMSON

Clemson University (11 miles northwest of I-85, at jct. of U.S. 76 and SC 93; 803/656-3311). The university was founded in 1889 and named for Thomas G. Clemson, son-in-law of John C. Calhoun, who bequeathed the bulk of his estate, Fort Hill, for the establishment of a scientific college. On the 1,400-acre campus are two historic houses: *Fort Hill* (803/656-2475), an 1803 mansion acquired by Calhoun during his first term as Vice-President; and *Hanover House* (803/ 656-2241), a 1716 French Huguenot house moved here from its original site. Fort Hill is open daily, Hanover House on weekends.

CLINTON

Rose Hill (15 miles east on SC 72, 2 miles north on SC 176, then west on Sardis Rd.; 803/427-5966). This circa-1865 restored mansion was the home of William H. Gist, the state's secession governor. It is a Federal-style house with 1860 furnishings. Museum. Open weekends.

COLUMBIA

The General Assembly met here in the State House for the first time in January 1790. Washington was a guest here during his Southern tour the next year. On December 17, 1860, a convention met in the First Baptist Church here and drew up the Ordinance of Secession. At war's end, the capital city was occupied by General Sherman, whose troops reduced it to ashes, burning an area of eighty-four blocks and 1,386 buildings.

State House (Main and Gervais streets; 803/734-2430). Built in the late 1850s, this is considered one of the most beautiful state capitols. On the porticoes are giant columns made of blue granite. The building was

The Robert Scruggs House at Cowpens National Battlefield in Gaffney. Courtesy National Park Service.

under construction when Sherman shelled the city, and metal stars mark where Union shells struck. The dome differs from the architect's plans, which were destroyed in the burning of Columbia. Open weekdays.

Governor's Mansion (800 Richland St.; 803/737-1710). Built in 1855 as officers' quarters for the Arsenal Academy. Tours Tuesday through Thursday by appointment.

Hampton-Preston Mansion (1615 Blanding St.; 803/252-1770). This 1818 mansion was purchased by Wade Hampton I, and later occupied by the family of his daughter, Mrs. John Preston. In 1865 it was the headquarters of Union general J. A. Logan. The mansion contains many Hampton family furnishings and decorative arts. Open daily except Mondays.

Robert Mills Historic House and Park (1616 Blanding St.; 803/252-1770). This 1823 house was designed by Robert Mills, the architect of the Washington Monument. Regency furnishings. Open daily except Mondays.

Trinity Cathedral (1100 Sumter St., opposite State House; 803/771-7300). An 1846 reproduction of the cathedral of Yorkminster, England, this is the oldest church building in Columbia, and home of one of the largest Episcopal congregations in the country. It has a baptismal font sculpted by Hiram Powers, as well as box pews and English stained glass. Many prominent South Carolinians are buried in the church-yard. Open Monday through Friday, spring and fall.

First Presbyterian Church (1306 Hampton St.; 803/799-9062). Woodrow Wilson's parents are buried in the churchyard of this 1853 church. Open daily.

First Baptist Church (1324 Marion St. at Lady St.; 803/256-4251). The first Secession Convention met here on December 17, 1860. Open daily except Saturdays.

Accommodations: *Chesnut Cottage* (1718 Hampton St.; 803/256-1718, or 800/898-8555). Built in 1850, this originally was the home of Confederate general James

Chesnut and his wife, Mary Chesnut, who wrote *A Diary from Dixie*. The white frame, one-and-a-half-story house has a central dormer and an arched window above the entrance. Four guest rooms, full breakfast, afternoon tea. Moderate to expensive.

FLORENCE

Timrod Park (Timrod Park Dr. and South Coit St.; 803/665-3253). Here is the one-room schoolhouse in which Henry Timrod, Poet Laureate of the Confederacy, once taught. Picnicking. Nature trails. Open daily.

GAFFNEY

Cowpens National Battlefield (11 miles northwest on SC 11, ½ mile from jct. with SC 110; 803/461-2828). General Daniel Morgan's army defeated a superior British force here on January 17, 1781. The British suffered heavy casualties; American losses were minimal. Victory was followed by the Battle of Guilford Courthouse, and then the forces moved on to Yorktown, where Cornwallis was forced to surrender. An 843-acre tract with a self-guided tour road, a walking trail, and the restored circa-1830 Robert Scruggs House. Picnicking. The visitor center has exhibits and a slide program. Open daily.

Kings Mountain National Military Park (20 miles northeast off I-85, near Grover, NC; 803/936-7921). In October 1780, frontiersmen broke up Britain's southern campaign in a battle here. The mountain men were faced with the invasion of their homes by advancing Tories. After traveling more than 200 miles, the Americans surrounded and attacked Cornwallis's left wing, which was encamped atop a spur of Kings Mountain, under the command of Major Patrick Ferguson. Although untrained in for-

mal warfare, the Americans killed, wounded, or captured Ferguson's entire force of 1,104 Tories. The battle led to renewed resistance and to the American victory at Yorktown. Near the center of the park is the battlefield ridge, with several monuments. Self-guided tours. The visitor center has a film and exhibits. Open daily.

GEORGETOWN

The shore of Winyah Bay, where Georgetown is situated, was the site of the first European settlement on the North American mainland, outside of Mexico. In 1526 a groups of Spaniards settled here, only to be driven out within a year by disease and Indian attacks. Georgetown, founded in 1729, was occupied for a while by British troops during the Revolution.

Tower Clock Building (Front and Screven streets; 803/546-7423). Rebuilt in 1842, the building houses the *Rice Museum,* which traces the development of the crop that once was the basis for the local economy. Open daily except Sundays.

Prince George, Winyah Church (Broad and Highmarket streets; 803/546-4358). This 1750 church has been in continuous use except during the Revolution and the Civil War. Tours weekdays.

Harold Kaminski House (1003 Front St.; 803/546-7706). A circa-1760 house furnished in the style of the period. Tours available. Open weekdays.

Hopsewee Plantation (12 miles south on U.S. 17; 803/546-7891). A preserved circa-1740 rice plantation house on the North Santee River, the birthplace of Thomas Lynch Jr., a signer of the Declaration of Independence. Open Tuesday through Friday, March through October.

Hampton Plantation State Park (20 miles south off U.S. 17, at 1950 Rutledge

Rd., McClellanville; 803/546-9361). The restored 18th-century mansion was the centerpiece of a large rice plantation, the ancestral home of the Rutledge family. Tours available. Open Thursday through Monday.

Accommodations: *1790 House* (630 Highmarket St.; 803/546-4821). This restored West Indies Colonial, in the heart of the historic district, has eleven-foot ceilings and seven fireplaces, three in the seven guest rooms. Some accommodations are in the renovated slave quarters. Full breakfast. Moderate.

GREENWOOD

Ninety Six National Historic Site (9 miles east on SC 34 to the town of Ninety Six, then 2 miles south on SC 248; 803/543-4068). The site of old Ninety Six, an early village in the backcountry, so named because it was ninety-six miles from the Cherokee village of Keowee. The South's first land battle of the Revolutionary War was fought here in 1775, and the twenty-eight-day siege of Ninety Six took place in 1781. The earthworks of the British-built star fort remain, along with reconstructed siegeworks and other fortifications. The visitor center has a video presentation and a museum. Also on the site are the remains of two village complexes, a trading post/plantation complex, and a network of early roads. Open daily.

SANTEE

Eutaw Springs Battlefield Site (12 miles southeast, off SC 6). Colonials fought the British here on September 8, 1781, and both sides claimed victory in what is considered the last major engagement in South Carolina. Three acres are maintained by the state. No facilities. Open daily.

Fort Watson Battle Site and Indian Mound (4 miles north, 1 mile off U.S. 15/301). A forty-eight-foot-high mound, the site of the Revolutionary War battle (April 15–23, 1781) during which General Francis Marion, the "Swamp Fox," attacked and captured the British fortification with its garrison, supplies, and ammunition. Three acres are maintained by the state. No facilities. Open daily.

TENNESSEE

13

40

55   51

24

65

Tennessee River

Memphis

40

Corinth

Florence

72

Huntsville

Chattanooga

78

45

Decatur

79

61

65

6

MISSISSIPPI

Mississippi River

ALABAMA

75

65

Greenwood

82

55

Columbus

78

59

Birmingham

20

Greenville

Natchez Trace Parkway

61

Tuscaloosa

21

82

65

280

Alexander Ci

20

Vicksburg

Meridian

20 59

Demopolis

Selma

Montgomery

Jackson

Port Gibson

20

Pearl River

49

59

Alabama River

82

Eufaula

17

84

Natchez

61

43

65

Woodville

55

FLORIDA

Mobile

85

10

Baton Rouge

12

Biloxi

10

Gulf Shores

20

231

10

Pascagoula

Dauphin Island

90

New Orleans

Gulf Islands
Nat'l. Seashore

N

Gulf of Mexico

0   150 miles

0   225 km

Mississippi
Delta

22

ALABAMA

Cliff-dwelling Indians lived in the Alabama region 8,000 years ago. Later residents included the Cherokee, Creek, Choctaw, and Chickasaw. Settlers called them the Civilized Tribes because they adopted European customs. Several Spanish explorers came in the early sixteenth century, but Hernando de Soto, who came in 1540, was the first to explore the interior. The first permanent settlement was French. In 1699, Pierre Le Moyne, Sieur d'Iberville, and his brother Jean-Baptiste founded Fort Louis near Mobile Bay, and it became the capital of the colony known as Louisiana. The settlement later moved to Mobile and was renamed Fort Conde.

In 1763 the French gave most of Louisiana to the British in the Treaty of Paris. Spain declared war on Britain in 1779, and won back the Mobile region. In the late 1700s, all of present-day Alabama except the Mobile area became part of the Mississippi Territory. During the War of 1812, the United States seized the Mobile area from Spain. On April 15, 1813, the Stars and Stripes flew over the entire Alabama region for the first time. After Andrew Jackson subdued the Creek Indians in the Battle of Horseshoe Bend, the Alabama Territory was organized, and in 1819 Alabama became a state.

ALEXANDER CITY

Horseshoe Bend National Military Park (13 miles northeast on AL 22 to New Site, the south on AL 49;

205/234-7111). After the Revolution, a horde of settlers moved south and west of the Appalachians. Despite territorial guarantees in the Treaty of 1790, the United States repeatedly forced land concessions from the Creeks. In Georgia, the Lower Creeks adjusted to life with the settlers, but the Upper Creeks in Alabama did not, and vowed to defend their land. When a few Upper Creeks, called Red Sticks, killed settlers near the Tennessee border, the Indian Agency ordered the Lower Creeks to execute them. As a result, civil war broke out within the Creek Nation.

By the summer of 1813, settlers became involved, attacking an Upper Creek munitions convoy at Burnt Corn Creek. The Upper Creeks then attacked Fort Mims and killed an estimated 250 people. The militia of Georgia, Tennessee, and the Mississippi Territory were brought in to combat the uprising of the "Red Sticks." Georgia troops defeated the Creeks at Autosee and Calabee Creek. The most effective fighting force, though, was Andrew Jackson's Tennessee Militia, which triumphed at Talladega, Emuckfaw, and Enitachopoco.

In March 1814, they struck and routed the Creeks at the Horseshoe Bend of the Tallapoosa River, the bloodiest battle in the Creek War. This would cost the Creeks more than 20 million acres, opening a vast domain to settlement, and eventually leading to the statehood of Alabama in 1819. In the 1830s, during Jackson's presidency, the Creeks were forced to leave Alabama and

Slaves work the land near the thriving city of Montgomery, Alabama. Courtesy Library of Congress, Prints and Photographs Division.

move to Indian Territory (present-day Oklahoma).

A three-mile-loop road tour traverses the battle area in the 2,040-acre park. Picnicking. The visitor center has a museum depicting the battle. Open daily.

BIRMINGHAM

Indians who painted their faces and weapons red were known by early settlers as "Red Sticks." Even when the red paint was found to be hematite iron ore, it was considered worthless, and many years passed before Red Mountain ore became the foundation of Birmingham's steel industry.

Arlington (331 Cotton Ave. SW; 205-780-5656). The city's last remaining antebellum Greek Revival house, built in 1850, has a diverse collection of 19th-century decorative arts, Indian art, and the largest collection of Wedgwood outside of England.

DAUPHIN ISLAND

Spaniards visited here and mapped the island in the sixteenth century. Pierre Le Moyne, Sieur d'Iberville, used the island as a base in 1699. Indians left the "Shell Mound," an ancient monument.

Fort Gaines (east end of island; 334/861-6992). A five-sided fort begun in 1821 and completed in the 1850s, it was manned by Confederates until its capture by Union land troops on August 23, 1864. Museum. Open daily.

DECATUR

Mooreville (6 miles east on AL 20; 205/350-2431). The oldest incorporated town in the state is preserved as a living record of 19th-century life. It includes the house of Andrew Johnson, who was a tailor's apprentice here; a circa-1840 brick church; an 1825 stagecoach tavern; and the frame 1854 Church of Christ, in which James Garfield is said to have preached during the Civil War. Open daily except Sundays.

DEMOPOLIS

Settled by a group of French exiles who were habitués of the French court and officers of Napoleon's army. They were granted four townships by Congress in July 1817 as the "French Emigrants for the Cultivation of the Vine and the Olive." The colonists, however, failed to cope with the wilderness and were gone by the mid-1820s.

Gainswood (805 South Cedar St.; 334/289-4846). A restored 1860 20-room Greek Revival mansion furnished with many original pieces. Open daily.

Bluff Hall (405 North Commissioners St.; 334/289-1666). A restored 1832 mansion built by the slaves of Allen Glover, a planter and merchant, as a wedding gift for his daughter. Its interior has Corinthian columns in the drawing room, period furniture, many marble mantels. Clothing museum and craft shop. Open daily.

EUFAULA

Hart House (211 North Eufaula Ave.; 334-687-9755). A one-story, circa-1850 Greek Revival frame house with fluted Doric columns on the porch is headquarters for the Historic Chattahoochee Trace of Alabama and Georgia. Open weekdays.

Seth Lore and Irwinton Historic District (information and driving tour brochure at Eufaula Heritage Association, 340 North Eufaula Ave.; 334/687-3793). Some 582 registered landmarks includes a mixture of Greek Revival, Italianate, and Victorian churches and commercial structures built from 1834. Bus tour.

The planters are full of money . . .

—HENRY LAURENS, *1750*

Bluff Hall in Demopolis.

FLORENCE

Pope's Tavern (203 Hermitage Dr.; 205/760-6439). Andrew Jackson stayed in this 1830 stage stop, which served as a hospital for both sides during the Civil War. Open Tuesday through Saturday.

Indian Mound and Museum (South Court St.; 205/760-6247). The largest ceremonial mound in the Tennessee Valley. Its museum has a collection of Indian artifacts. Open Tuesday through Saturday.

GULF SHORES

Fort Morgan Park (22 miles west on AL 180; 334/540-7125). This area on the western tip of Mobile Point was explored by the Spanish in 1519. Between then and 1813, Spain, France, England, and, finally, the United States held this strategic point. This was the site of two engagements during the War of 1812. In the park is *Fort Morgan,* a star-shaped brick fort. Built in 1819, it replaced a sand-and-log fort that figured in the War of 1812 battles. Its most famous moment occurred during the Battle of Mobile Bay in August 1864. The use of mines, then called torpedoes, was the source of Admiral Farragut's legendary command, "Damn the torpedoes, full speed ahead!" Following the battle, the fort withstood a two-week siege before surrendering to Union forces. Open daily.

HUNTSVILLE

Alabama's Constitution Village (404 Madison St.; 205/535-6565). A complex of re-created buildings commemorating the state's entry into the Union at the 1819 Constitutional Convention. Costumed guides, craft demonstrations. Open daily except Sundays.

Twickenham Historic District (south and east of Courthouse Sq.; Visitors Bureau,

Pope's Tavern in Florence.

700 Monroe St.; 204/551-2230). This living museum of period architecture contains the state's largest concentration of antebellum homes. Self-guided tours daily.

MOBILE

Oakleigh (350 Oakleigh Pl.; 334/432-1281). This circa-1830s house stands on the highest point of Simon Favre's old Spanish land grant. Bricks for the first story were made on the site; the upper portion is of hand-hewn timber. The Historic Mobile Preservation Society has furnished the house in the period. The Cox-Deasy Creole cottage is included in the tour. Open daily.

Bragg-Mitchell Mansion (1906 Springhill Ave.; 334/471-6364). A twenty-room, 1855 Greek Revival mansion set on twelve acres of landscaped grounds. Its restored interior includes extensive faux-grained woodwork and stenciled moldings. Period furnishings. Open daily except Saturdays.

Richards-DAR House (256 North Joachim St.; 334/434-7320). A circa-1860 restored Italianate town house with elaborate ironwork, curved suspended staircase, and period furniture. Open daily except Mondays.

Carlen House Museum (54 Carlen St. at Willcox St.; 334/470-7768). An 1842 "Creole cottage" furnished in the period. Open daily.

Fort Conde Mobile Visitor Welcome Center (150 South Royal St. at Church St.; 334/434-7304). A reconstruction of the 1724–35 French fort features working reproductions of 1740s naval cannon, muskets, and other arms. Soldiers in period French uniforms. Open daily.

Conde-Charlotte Museum House (104 Theatre St., next to Fort Conde; 334/432-4722). Built in 1822–24 and once a jail, the museum is furnished with period pieces and artifacts. Spanish garden. Open Tuesday through Saturday.

Cathedral of the Immaculate Conception (Dauphin and Claiborne streets; 334/

434-1565). This 1835 church has a Greek Revival minor basilica with German art-glass windows, a bronze canopy over the altar, and hand-carved stations of the cross. Open daily.

Accommodations: *Malaga Inn* (359 Church St.; 334/438-4701, or 800/235-1586). Brothers built these adjoining town houses in 1862, but shortly after they were completed, Admiral Farragut steamed into Mobile Bay. Today they offer guests forty rooms and an attractive courtyard with a fountain. Many original furnishings. Restaurant. Inexpensive.

MONTGOMERY

State Capitol (Bainbridge between Washington and Monroe avenues; 334/242-4169). The seat of Alabama's government since

1851. Opposite is the *First White House of the Confederacy* (644 Washington Ave.; 334/242-1861), an 1835 two-story, white frame house that was the residence of Jefferson Davis and his family while Montgomery was the Confederate capital. Moved from its original location at Bibb and Lee streets, it is now a museum containing period furnishings, personal belongings, and paintings of the Davis family. Tours available. Open daily.

Teague House (468 South Perry St.; 334/834-6000). An 1848 Greek Revival mansion used as headquarters for Union general James H. Wilson after April 12, 1865. Antiques and period reproductions. Open weekdays.

Murphy House (Bibb and Coosa streets; 334/240-1600). An 1851 Greek Revival mansion with fluted Corinthian columns and wrought-iron balcony, now the headquarters of the city water works. The parlor has period furnishings. Open weekdays.

Old Alabama Town (334/240-4500). The site includes the circa-1850 Ordermann-Shaw House, an Italianate town house with period furnishings and a reconstructed 1840 barn, a carriage house, an 1820s log cabin, a shotgun cottage depicting black urban life, a country doctor's office, a drugstore museum, and a cotton-gin museum, also an exhibition hall. Films, tours, visitor center. Open daily.

St. John's Episcopal Church (113 Madison Ave. and North Perry St.; 334/262-1937). Stained-glass windows, Gothic pipe organ, Jefferson Davis's pew.

Fort Toulouse/Jackson Park National Historic Landmark (12 miles northeast, 2 miles west off U.S. 231, near Wetumpka; 334/567-3002). The fort, at the confluence of the Coosa and Tallapoosa rivers, was opened by Bienville in 1717 to establish trade in

Sturdivant Hall in Selma.

Creek territory. It was abandoned in 1763, but Andrew Jackson built a fort on the same site in 1814 after the Battle of Horseshoe Bend. Fort Toulouse has been reconstructed, and Fort Jackson partly reconstructed. This is also the site of Indian mounds dating from A.D. 1100. Open daily.

Accommodations: *Red Bluff Cottage* (551 Clay St.; 205/264-0056). A raised cottage overlooking the Alabama River in the city's Cottage Hill District. The four guest rooms, furnished with family antiques, are on the first floor, and the living room, dining room, kitchen, and music room with piano and harpsichord are on the second. Full breakfast. Inexpensive.

SELMA

Sturdivant Hall (713 Mabry St.; 334/872-5626). This Greek Revival mansion designed by Thomas Helm Lee, cousin of Robert E. Lee, features massive Corinthian columns, original wrought-iron balconies, and a belvedere on the roof. Restored with period furnishings. Kitchen with slave quarters above. Smokehouse, carriage house, garden. Tours available. Open daily except Mondays.

Joseph T. Smitherman Historic Building (109 Union St.; 334/874-2174). Restored with period pieces and artifacts. Art pavilion. Open weekdays.

Old Town Historic District (Chamber of Commerce, 513 Lauderdale St.; 334/875-7241). The district comprises more than 1,200 structures, including museums, specialty shops, and restaurants. Self-guided cassette tours weekdays, also weekends by appointment.

Cahawba (9 miles west on AL 22, then 4 miles south on county road; 334/875-2529). Alabama's first permanent capital, this was a flourishing town from 1820 to 1860. By 1822, 184 town lots were sold for $120,000. Nearly swept away by floods in 1825, the capital was moved to Tuscaloosa in 1826, and Cahawba was nearly abandoned by 1828, but rose again. By 1830 it was the most important shipping point on the Alabama River. Despite an 1833 flood, the city reached a peak population of 5,000 in 1850, but the Civil War and a third flood finally finished the town. Today only a few structures still stand. The site is under development as a historical park. Welcome center open daily.

Accommodations: *Grace Hall Inn* (506 Lauderdale St.; 205/875-5744). Guest rooms on the first floor of this 1857 mansion open on a New Orleans–style garden, and larger, more opulent rooms are upstairs. All have woodburning fireplaces. The inn is conveniently located in the historic district. Walking tours. Full breakfast. Inexpensive.

TUSCALOOSA

Gorgas House (9th Ave. and Castone Dr., Univ. of Alabama campus; 205/348-6010). A three-story 1829 brick structure named for General Josiah Gorgas, a university president. One of the school's original structures, it now houses a museum with historical exhibits. Open daily.

Battle-Friedman House (1010 Greensboro Ave.; 205/758-6138). This circa-1835 house, built by Alfred Battle, and acquired by the Friedman family in 1875, contains antiques and has large period gardens. Open Tuesday through Saturday.

Old Tavern (University Blvd. and 28th Ave. on Historic Capitol Park; 205/758-8163). This 1827 tavern was frequented by Governor Gayle in the early 1830s, and by members of the Alabama legislature when Tuscaloosa was the state capital. Open daily except Mondays.

Moundville Archaeological Park (16 miles south on AL 69 in Moundville; 205/371-2572). A group of twenty Indian ceremonial mounds, dating from A.D. 1000–1450. A reconstructed village and temple with displays depicting Indian lifestyles and activity. The museum traces the prehistoric record of the Indians of the Southeast. The site is part of the Alabama Museum of Natural History. Picnicking. Open daily.

23

MISSISSIPPI

Seeking gold, Hernando de Soto and his men crossed through what is now Mississippi eighty years before the *Mayflower* landed in Massachusetts. De Soto died on his fruitless search. Pierre Le Moyne, Sieur d'Iberville, established the first permanent settlement in Mississippi near Biloxi in 1699. There was no gold, but the Mississippi River had created something of greater value—an immense valley of rich, productive land on which cotton could be grown. It was cotton that made the great plantations possible. Andrew Jackson became a hero in Mississippi after defeating the Creek Nation. He was honored again during a triumphal return through the state after victory in the Battle of New Orleans in 1815. Mississippians named their capital after "Old Hickory," and they entertained him when he returned as an elder statesman in 1840.

After the Revolution, the United States took possession of the territory north of the thirty-first parallel, while the area south of that line remained part of Spanish West Florida. Mississippi did not attain its present borders until it became a state, in 1817. At that time, Alabama, which had been part of the Mississippi Territory, was split off as a separate territory. The way was open for large numbers of white settlers to come to Mississippi, and before long the Choctaw and Chickasaw were forcibly removed to make room for them.

BILOXI

Tullis-Toledano Manor (360 Beach Blvd.; 601/435-6293). A historic 1856 mansion on oak-shaded grounds. Open weekdays.

COLUMBUS

This was a stopover on the Military Road that Andrew Jackson ordered built between New Orleans and Nashville. It was originally called "Possum Town" because Indians thought the tavernkeeper who served them looked like a wizened old opossum. Columbus welcomed the steamboat *Cotton Plant* in 1822, a year after Mississippi's first public school was established here.

Historic houses. More than 100 antebellum houses, some open for tours. An auto-tour map and a taped narrative describing the houses are available from the Historic Foundation, 601/329-3533. Open daily.

Waverly Plantation (10 miles northwest via U.S. 45, MS 50, near West Point; 601/494-1399). An 1852 mansion with twin, circular self-supporting stairways leading to a sixty-five-foot-high, octagonal observation cupola. Original gold-leaf mirrors. Open daily.

A Mississippi planter's house and plantation along the river. Courtesy Library of Congress, Prints and Photographs Division.

America is an independent empire, and ought to assume a national character. Nothing can be more ridiculous, than a servile imitation of the manners, the language, and the vices of foreigners.

—NOAH WEBSTER,
SKETCHES OF
AMERICAN POLICY,
1785

CORINTH

Curlee House (705 Jackson St.; 601/287-9501). A restored 1857 home that served as headquarters for Generals Bragg, Halleck, and Hood during the Civil War. Hours vary, phone in advance.

Jacinto Courthouse (15 miles southeast, in Jacinto). The first courthouse (1854) for old Tishomingo County, this fine example of Federal architecture was later used as both a school and a church. Open daily.

Accommodations: *Generals' Quarters* (924 Fillmore St.; 601/286-3325). Guests of this Queen Anne Victorian may choose from three bedrooms and a suite. Innkeeper J. L. Aldridge often leads tours of the historic district. Full breakfast. Inexpensive.

FAYETTE

Springfield (off Route 553; 601/786-3802). One of the largest plantation houses in

Mississippi, Springfield, built circa 1789 by Thomas Marston, a Virginia planter, is still a working plantation. It is believed that Andrew Jackson's 1791 marriage to Rachel Robards took place here. Open daily.

GREENVILLE

Winterville Mounds State Park (3 miles north, off MS 1; 601/334-4684). One of the largest groups of Indian mounds in the Mississippi Valley, this was a religious site and economic center for thousands of Indians. The Great Temple mound is surrounded by ten smaller mounds used for a variety of purposes. Picnicking, museum. Open Wednesday through Sunday.

GREENWOOD

Florewood River Plantation (2 miles west on U.S. 82; 601/455-3821). A re-creation of a circa-1850 plantation house and outbuildings. Crops are planted and harvested. There is a cotton museum. Craft demonstrations, tours. Open daily except Mondays.

JACKSON

Governor's Mansion (300 East Capitol St.; 601/359-3175). The mansion has been restored to its original 1842 plan and Greek Revival style, with period furnishings. The grounds occupy an entire block, with gardens and gazebos. Tours available. Open Tuesday through Friday mornings.

Old Capitol (east end of Capitol St. at State St.; 601/359-6920). The capitol from 1839 to 1903, the Greek Revival building now houses the State Historical Museum. Monthly exhibits. Open daily.

The Oaks House Museum (823 North Jefferson St.; 601/353-9339). This 1846 Greek Revival cottage, built of hand-hewn timber by James H. Boyd, mayor of Jackson, was occupied by General Sherman during the siege of 1863. Period furniture, garden. Open Tuesday through Saturday.

Manship House (420 East Fortification St.; 601/961-4724). A circa-1855 restored Gothic Revival cottage, the residence of Charles Henry Manship, mayor of Jackson during the Civil War. Period furnishings. Open Tuesday through Saturday.

Accommodations: *Millsaps Buie House* (628 North State St.; 601/352-0221). A restored Victorian dwelling with vintage furnishings offers eleven guest rooms with refrigerators and balconies or private patios. Full breakfast. Moderate.

NATCHEZ

If there were a museum of the antebellum plantation South, it would look just like this Mississippi River town. A center of cotton wealth, Natchez emerged from the war intact, a treasure trove of Greek Revival

Springfield Plantation near Fayette.

mansions and manicured lawns and gardens. The fall and spring pilgrimages attract thousands from all over the world to tour more than thirty mansions.

The House on Ellicott Hill (Jefferson and Canal streets; 601/442-2011). The site where, in 1797, Andrew Ellicott raised the first American flag in the lower Mississippi Valley. Built in 1798, the house overlooks both the Mississippi and the terminus of the Natchez Trace. Restored and authentically furnished. Open daily.

Rosalle (100 Orleans St.; 601/445-4555). This circa-1820 red-brick Georgian mansion with a Greek Revival portico, on a bluff above the Mississippi, served as headquarters for the Union Army during the occupation of the city. Original furnishings, gardens. Open daily.

Stanton Hall (401 High St.; 601/446-6631). A highly elaborate 1851–57 mansion surrounded by giant oaks. Original chandeliers, Sheffield hardware, French mirrors. Owned and operated by the Pilgrimage Garden Club. Open daily.

Magnolia Hall (South Pearl St. at Washington St.; 601/442-6672). The last great mansion to be built in the city before the outbreak of the Civil War, this 1858 house is an outstanding example of Greek Revival architecture. Period antiques, costume museum. Open daily.

Accommodations: *Dunleith* (84 Homochitto St.; 601/446-8500, or 800/433-2445). A National Historic Landmark circa-1856 Greek Revival mansion surrounded by colonnaded galleries. The estate includes forty acres of pastures and wood bayous. French and English antiques, eleven guest rooms, house tour, full breakfast. Moderate.

Accommodations: *Monmouth* (36 Melrose Ave.; 601/442-5852, or 800/828-4531). A National Historic Landmark, this monumental circa-1818 Greek Revival house and auxiliary buildings were once owned by Mexican War hero John Anthony Quitman. Completely restored and furnished in the style of the period. Gardens, twenty-five guest rooms in slave quarters, house tour, full breakfast. Moderate to expensive.

Longwood (140 Lower Woodville Rd.; 800/647-6742). An enormous, Italianate "octagon house" crowned with an onion dome. Under construction at the start of the Civil War, the interiors were never completed above the first floor. Period furnishings. Owned and operated by the Pilgrimage Garden Club. Open daily.

Historic Jefferson College (6 miles east on U.S. 61, in Washington; 601/442-2901). This campus was the site, in 1817, of the first state Constitutional Convention. Jefferson Davis attended the college. No longer in use, the buildings are being restored as a historic site. Picnicking, museum. Open daily.

Historic Springfield Plantation (20 miles northeast via U.S. 61, Natchez Trace Pkwy., then 12 miles north on MS 553; 601/786-3802). Believed to be the first mansion erected in Mississippi, 1786–90, the structure, built for Thomas Marston Green Jr., a wealthy planter from Virginia, remains nearly intact, with little remodeling over the years. Original hand-carved woodwork. The site of Andrew Jackson's wedding. Displays. Open daily.

Emerald Mound (12 miles northeast on Natchez Trace Pkwy.; 601/680-4025). This eight-acre mound, the second largest in the country, dates roughly from A.D. 1250–1600 Unlike earlier peoples who constructed mounds to cover tombs and burials, the Mississippians (ancestors of the Natchez, Creek, and Choctaw) built mounds to support temples and ceremonial buildings. When de Soto passed through in the 1540s, the flat-topped temple mounds were still in use. Open daily.

NATCHEZ TRACE PARKWAY

The Natchez Trace Parkway stretched from Natchez, Mississippi, to Nashville, Tennessee, and was the most heavily traveled road in the old Southwest from about 1785 to 1820. Boatmen floated their products downriver to Natchez or New Orleans, sold them, and walked or rode home over the Natchez Trace. A "trace" is a trail or road. This trace was shown on French maps as early as 1733.

When completed, the Natchez Trace Parkway, operated by the National Park Service, will be a 445-mile-long road. Some 425 miles are now paved and open, most of them in Mississippi. A continuous stretch of 338 miles is open between Jackson and TN 96 west of Franklin, Tennessee. A seventy-nine-mile stretch is open west of Jackson to near Natchez. The parkway crosses and recrosses the original trace, passing many points of historic interest, including Emerald Mound.

The parkway headquarters and visitor center are five miles north of Tupelo, at the junction of U.S. 45 Business and the parkway. Interpretive facilities include a museum and an audiovisual program (601/680-4025). Open daily.

PASCAGOULA

Old Spanish Fort and Museum (4602 Fort St., 5 blocks north of U.S. 90; 601/769-1505). Built by the French in 1718, later captured by the Spanish, the fort's walls of massive cypress timbers, cemented with oyster shells, mud, and moss, are eighteen inches thick. This is said to be the oldest structure in the Mississippi Valley. The museum has Indian relics and historic artifacts. Open daily.

PORT GIBSON

First Presbyterian Church (Church and Walnuts streets). This 1859 structure has a gold-leafed hand atop the steeple, with a finger pointing to the sky. The interior features an old slave gallery and chandeliers taken from the steamboat *Robert E. Lee*. Open daily.

Oak Square (1207 Church St., 1 mile off Natchez Trace Pkwy.; 601/437-4350). A restored circa-1850 mansion with six fluted Corinthian columns. Period furnishings, extensive grounds with courtyard and gazebo. Guest rooms. Tours daily.

The Ruins of Windsor (Old Rodney Rd.). All that remains of a four-story mansion built in 1860 and consumed by fire in 1890 are twenty-three stately columns. The size of the mansion and its proximity to the river made it a landmar for Mississippi River pilots, including Samuel Clemens.

Accommodations: *Rosswood Mansion* (9 miles south on U.S. 61 to Loman, then 2½ miles east on MS 552; 800/533-5889). This classic 1857 Greek Revival mansion designed by David Shroder, architect of Windsor, features columned galleries, ten fireplaces, fifteen-foot ceilings, a winding stairway, and slave quarters in the basement. The first owner's diary has survived, and offers details of life on a cotton plantation. Furnished with antiques. Four guest rooms, breakfast. Moderate.

VICKSBURG

Old Court House Museum (Court Sq., 1008 Cherry St.; 601/636-0741). Built in 1858 with slave labor, the building offers a view of the Yazoo Canal from its hilltop location. Here General Ulysses S. Grant raised the U.S. flag on July 4, 1863, signifying the end of the forty-seven-day Union siege of the city. The courthouse now has an extensive display of Americana, including a Confederate Room, a Furniture Room, a Pioneer Room, and a Native American Room. Open daily.

Martha Vick House (1300 Grove St.; 601/636-7036). Built in 1830 by the daughter of the founder of Vicksburg, Newit Vick. Greek Revival façade and restored original interior. Furnished in the period. Outstanding art collection. Open daily.

McRaven Home (1445 Harrison St.; 601/636-1663). The most heavily shelled house during the siege now provides an architectural record of local history, from a 1797 frontier cottage to an 1836 Empire dwelling, and finally to an 1849 Greek Revival town house. Many original furnishings. Original brick walks surround the house. Garden, guided tours. Open daily, except the month of January.

The Martha Vick House in Vicksburg.

Accommodations: *Cedar Grove* (2200 Oak St.; 601/636-1605, or 800/862-1300). This elegant 1840 mansion was shelled by Union gunboats, and a cannonball is still lodged in the parlor wall. A roof garden provides views of the Mississippi and Yazoo rivers. Tea room, gift shop, many original furnishings, four acres of formal gardens, courtyards, fountains, gazebos. Twenty-six guest rooms decorated in the style of the period. House tour, breakfast. Moderate.

Accommodations: *Anchuca Inn* (1010 First East St.; 601/636-4931, or 800/262-4822). A restored 1830 Greek Revival house furnished with period pieces and gas-burning chandeliers. It once belonged to the brother of Jefferson Davis. Gardens, brick courtyard, twelve elegant guest rooms, house tour, breakfast. Moderate.

Tourist Information Center (U.S. 80E;

601/636-9421, or 800/221-3536). Information, maps, and brochures on historic houses and other points of interest. Guide service. Open daily.

WOODVILLE

Rosemont Plantation (1 mile east on MS 24; 601/888-6809). The circa-1810 home of Jefferson Davis and his family. His parents moved here and built the house when Davis was two years old. He grew up here, and returned to visit his family throughout his life. Five generations of the Davis family are buried on the property. Many family furnishings. Original working atmosphere on the 300-acre plantation. Open weekdays, March to mid-December.

Rosemont Plantation in Woodville.

Even though it was not settled until 1803, Chicago was a major city by the eve of the Civil War.

PART VI

THE OLD NORTHWEST

24

ILLINOIS

The word *Illinois* is from the confederated tribes who inhabited the valley of the Illinois River and called themselves the Iliniwek ("superior men"). The first white men to come to the land of the Iliniwek were Father Jacques Marquette and Louis Jolliet, who, in 1673, paddled down the Mississippi, returned up the Illinois, and carried their canoes across the portage where Chicago now stands. Five years later, René-Robert Cavelier de La Salle established Fort Crevecoeur, near Peoria Lake. French interest then shifted to the area around Cahokia and Kaskaskia. Fort de Chartres was built in 1720, and trappers and traders soon followed. The area called the French Corridor was designated Illinois, the first official use of the name.

French rule came to an end when the British seized Fort de Chartres in 1765, but the British, distracted by the wars with the Ottawa chief Pontiac and then by the Revolution, never established a presence in the area.

During the Revolution, the only action in Illinois was the 1778 campaign of George Rogers Clark, who seized a vast area between the Mississippi and Ohio rivers for the state of Virginia. Virginia then passed Illinois County, as it was called, to the Continental Congress in 1782. Order was not established, however, until after the Northwest Ordinance of 1787 and the arrival of the first governor, Arthur St. Clair.

Settlement in Illinois was retarded because of Indian attacks and Britain's reluctance to give up its hold on the territory. During the War of 1812 a major American setback was the defeat and massacre of some sixty soldiers by the Potawatomi at Fort Dearborn, at the tiny trading post of Chicago. By 1818, however, the federal government had title to most of Illinois, the territory achieved statehood, and settlement began in earnest.

AURORA

Blackberry Historical Farm Village (west on I-88 to Orchard Rd., south to Galena Blvd., then west to Barnes Rd.; 708/892-1550). A working farm of the 1840s, and a children's animal farm. Craft demonstrations include blacksmithing, weaving, quilting, pottery making. Wagon and pony rides. One-room schoolhouse, gift shop. Open daily, May through Labor Day; Friday through Sunday, Labor Day through October.

BISHOP HILL

Bishop Hill State Historic Site (2 miles north on unnumbered road; 309/927-3345). Settled in 1846 by Swedish immigrants seeking religious freedom, this communal-utopian colony was led by Erik Jansson until his assassination in 1850. Descendants of the settlers still live in the community. The Colony Hotel, the Colony Church, and fifteen of the original twenty-one buildings still stand. Tours available. Open daily.

CAHOKIA

Historic Holy Family Mission Log Church
(at jct. of IL 3 and IL 157; 618/337-4548).
Built in 1799 and restored in 1949, the original walnut logs of the church's walls stand
upright in Canadian fashion. Old cemetery.
Open daily, June through August.

Cahokia Courthouse State Historic Site
(214 West 1st St., off IL 3; 618/332-1782).
The former house of François Saucier, son of
the builder of Fort de Chartres, was built
around 1735, and is believed to be the oldest
house in the state. Sold in 1793, it was used
as a territorial courthouse and jail until 1815.
An on-site museum has interpretive program.
Open afternoons, Tuesday through Saturday.

Cahokia Mounds State Historic Site
(I-255 exit 24, west on Collinsville Rd.;
618/346-5160). This site preserves the central section of the only prehistoric city north
of Mexico. Archaeological finds indicate that
it was first inhabited around A.D. 700, and
eventually a complex community developed.
The city covered six square miles and had a
population of tens of thousands. Sixty-eight
earthen mounds, used primarily for ceremonial purposes, are preserved. Monks Mound
is the largest prehistoric earthen construction
in the New World, covering fourteen acres
and rising to a height of 100 feet. Resident
archaeologist, self-guided tours, museum.
Open daily, March through November;
Wednesday through Sunday the rest of the
year.

CHESTER

Fort Kaskaskia State Historic Site (8 miles
northwest, off IL 3; 618/859-3741). In this
275-acre park are the earthworks of the old
fort, built in 1733, rebuilt in 1736 by the
French, and finally destroyed to prevent
British occupation. During the anarchy that
followed the Revolution here, the ruins of the
fort, while in the hands of John Dodge, a
Connecticut renegade, were the scene of rev-
elry and murders. Nearby is the *Garrison
Hill Cemetery,* which holds the remains of
some 3,000 settlers. The *Pierre Menard
Mansion,* at the base of the bluffs along the
Mississippi, was built in 1802. General
Lafayette was entertained in the mansion,
which has been called "the Mount Vernon of
the West." Tours available. Open daily.

GALENA

Dowling House (220 North Diagonal St.;
815/777-1250). This restored circa-1826
stone house, the oldest in Galena, is furnished as a trading post. Tours available.
Open daily, May through December.

Old Stockade and Refuge (208 Perry St.
at North Main St.; 815/777-1646). Underground space used as a refuge from the
Indians during the Black Hawk War. A
museum has Black Hawk War and pioneer
artifacts. Open daily, May through October,
April weekends.

GLEN ELLYN

Stacy's Tavern (557 Geneva Rd. at Main
St.; 708/858-8696). An 1846 inn, once a pop-
ular stagecoach stop for travelers going from
Chicago to the Fox River Valley, has been
restored with period furnishings. Open
Wednesdays and Sundays, March through
December.

GLENVIEW

The Grove National Historic Landmark
(1421 North Milwaukee Ave., just south of
Lake Ave.; 708/299-6096). An eighty-two-
acre nature preserve with two historic structures: the 1856 Kennicott House, and the

Redfield Center, a house designed by a student of Louis Sullivan, which was the home of author Donald Culross Peattie, who wrote *A Prairie Grove* about his experiences at the Grove. Open daily.

LOCKPORT

Illinois and Michigan Canal Museum (803 South State St.; 815/838-5080). Lockport was the headquarters of the Illinois and Michigan Canal, and in its heyday it boasted five locks, of which four remain today. The museum has documents relating to the construction and operation of the canal. Tours are led by costumed docents. Open daily. The *Pioneer Settlement* has log cabins, a village jail, a blacksmith and a tinsmith, a farmhouse, and a railroad station. Open daily, mid-April through October.

NAPERVILLE

Naper Settlement (Aurora Ave. between Webster St. and Porter Ave.; 708/420-6010). A twelve-acre living-history museum of twenty-five buildings depicts an 1830 northern Illinois town. Costumed guides lead tours of four residences of the period. There are also several public buildings and various shops and businesses. Museum shop. Open daily.

NAUVOO

When the Mormon prophet Joseph Smith was driven out of Missouri, he came here with his Latter-day Saints and established what was virtually an autonomous state. A city of 8,000 houses was created, and in 1841 construction was begun on a great temple. Prejudice and the threat of Mormon political power led to riots and to persecution of the Mormons. Joseph Smith and his brother were arrested and murdered by a mob while in jail. Brigham Young became the Mormon leader, and when armed clashes broke out anew, he led the Mormons westward in 1846 to their final settlement in Utah. Nauvoo became a ghost city, and the nearly completed temple was burned by an arsonist.

In 1856 the Icarians, a band of French communalists, came here from Texas and established their short-lived experiment in communal living. They attempted to rebuild the former Mormon temple, but it was destroyed in a storm. The Icarians did not prosper, and moved on in 1856. The city was gradually resettled by a conventional group of Germans.

Nauvoo Restoration, Inc. (Young and North Main streets; 217/453-2237). A number of homes, shops, and public buildings of the Mormon settlement have been restored or reconstructed. The visitor center has a twenty-minute film on the town's colorful history. Points of interest include the 1803 Joseph Smith Homestead, Smith's Mansion, a Federal-style house that the prophet built in 1843, the Brigham Young Home, the grave of Joseph Smith, and the Old Carthage Jail where Smith was killed.

Accommodations: *Hotel Nauvoo* (1290 Mulholland, center of town on IL 86; 217/453-2211). Eight guest rooms in a restored 1840 Mormon residence. Restaurant. Inexpensive.

PERU

Matthiessen State Park (9 miles southeast via I-80E and IL 178S in Utica; 815/667-4868). In this 1,938-acre park is a replica of a small fort stockade of the type built by the French in the Midwest during the late 16th and early 17th centuries. Hiking, picnicking. Open daily.

Sell [our] country! Why not sell the air, the clouds, and the great sea? Did not the Great Spirit make them all for the use of his children?

—CHIEF TECUMSEH, TO GENERAL WILLIAM HENRY HARRISON, *1810*

O! ye that love mankind! Ye that dare oppose not only tyranny but the tyrant, stand forth!

—THOMAS PAINE,
COMMON SENSE,
1776

PETERSBURG

Lincoln's New Salem State Historic Site (2 miles south on IL 97; 217/632-4000). A complete reconstruction, based on maps and family archives, of New Salem as the village appeared when Lincoln lived there (1831–37). New Salem consisted of twelve timbered houses, a school, and ten shops, including the Denton Offutt store, where Lincoln first worked, the Lincoln-Berry Store, the Rutledge tavern, and the sawmill and gristmill. Most interior furnishings are authentic to the period. The grave of Ann Rutledge, believed to be Lincoln's first love, is in Oakland Cemetery nearby. A variety of programs are offered throughout the year. Interpreters in period costumes, wagon rides. The visitor center shows an 18-minute orientation film. Gift shop.

QUINCY

John Wood Mansion (425 South 12th St.; 217/222-1835). This 1835 Greek Revival mansion, the residence of the founder of Quincy and a former governor of Illinois, was moved to its present location in about 1860. Restored and furnished in the style of the period. Three-story Victorian doll house. Museum. Open weekends, April through October.

ROCK ISLAND

Black Hawk State Historic Site (south edge of town; 309/788-0177 or 309/788-9536). In these steeply rolling hills was fought the westernmost battle of the Revolution. The area was occupied for nearly a century by the villages of the Fox and Sauk Nation. Today the Watch Tower, on a promontory 150 feet above the Rock River, provides a view of the countryside. The Haubert Indian Museum

contains an outstanding collection of artifacts, paintings, and relics, as well as dioramas of Sauk and Fox daily life. Open daily.

Accommodations: *Potter House* (1906 7th Ave.; 309/788-1906 or 800/747-0339). This handsome Greek Revival house, built in 1907 for the publisher of the local newspaper, offers five guest rooms, all with private bath and a full breakfast. The house, listed on the National Register of Historic Places, has six fireplaces and a player piano. Moderate.

SALEM

Halfway Tavern (7 miles east on U.S. 50). The tavern received its name from its location, halfway between St. Louis, Missouri, and Vincennes, Indiana. This is a reconstruction of the 1818 original, which served as a stagecoach stop until 1861, located on the trail used by George Rogers Clark when he crossed Illinois. Interior not open.

Ingram's Log Cabin Village (12 miles north via IL 37 in Kinmundy; 618/547-7123). On seventy-four acres are seventeen authentic log structures dating from 1818. Thirteen are authentically furnished and open to the public. Picnicking. Open daily, mid-April through mid-November.

SPRINGFIELD

Illinois was already a state when Elisha Kelly from North Carolina came by and was impressed by the fertile land and plentiful game. He returned with his father and four brothers, and soon a small community surrounded their small cabin. Springfield became the county seat in 1821. As a result of a campaign led by Abraham Lincoln, this town of 1,500 was named the state capital in 1837. Lincoln practiced law, married, bought a house, and raised his family in Springfield.

The Abraham Lincoln Home in Springfield. Courtesy National Park Service.

On February 11, 1861, he left Springfield for Washington and the presidency. His body was returned in May 1865 to be buried in the city's Oak Ridge Cemetery.

Old State Capitol State Historic Site (City Square; 217/785-7960). Called the most historic structure west of the Alleghenies, this restored Greek Revival sandstone structure was the first statehouse in Springfield (the state's fifth). It was here that Lincoln made his famous "house divided" speech. Open daily, March through November; Wednesday through Staturday, December through February.

Lincoln-Herndon Law Office Building (6th and Adams streets, opposite Old State Capitol; 217/782-7960). A restored building in which Lincoln practiced law. Open daily.

Lincoln Home National Historic Site (426 South 7th St.; 217/492-4150). The site includes four city blocks restored to their 1860 appearance, the last year of Lincoln's seventeen-year residency. The Federal-style house was originally a single-story cottage, which Mary Todd Lincoln remodeled to her own design. The interior has been restored, and has Lincoln family furnishings. Exhibits, orientation film, bookstore. Open daily.

Lincoln Depot (Monroe St. between 9th and 10th streets; 217/544-8695 or 217/788-1356). The restored station where Lincoln delivered his farewell address before departing for Washington on February 11, 1861. Slide show, exhibits. Open daily, April through August.

Edwards Place (700 North 4th St.; 217/523-2631). Built by Benjamin Edwards (brother of Ninian Edwards, the early Illinois governor who married Mary Todd Lincoln's older sister), this 1833 Italianate mansion was the city's social and political center. Lincoln addressed the public from the front gallery. Furnished with original pieces and period antiques. Open Wednesday through Sunday.

25

WISCONSIN

Indians called this land *Ouisconsin* which means "where the waters gather." In 1634, four years after the Pilgrims landed in Massachusetts, Jean Nicolet, a French explorer seeking the Northwest Passage to the Orient, landed near Green Bay and was greeted by Winnebago Indians, whom he thought were Asians. The Winnebago made a treaty of alliance with the French and, for the next 125 years, traded furs with them.

White settlement of Wisconsin started with Father Claude Allouez, who established Green Bay on the banks of the Fox River. Agents of John Jacob Astor, the New York fur trader, built their houses on 10,000-year-old Indian mounds on the Mississippi River at Prairie du Chien. Bayfield, on Chequamegon Bay, was settled as a natural deep-water port with a view of the beautiful Apostle Islands. Sturgeon Bay grew up around the narrow isthmus and portage point on the Door Peninsula. Milwaukee was settled after pioneers figured out how to drain a tamarack swamp.

The British won Wisconsin from the French in 1760, but lost it to the United States after the American Revolution. Both the French and the British lived in relative harmony with the Indians because all they wanted were furs. The Americans, however, wanted land, a concept foreign to Indians. When the U.S. government became intent on removing the Indians from their ancestral land, it resulted in local conflicts throughout Wisconsin. The defeat of Chief Black Hawk in 1832 ended the Indian wars. After the campaign, word spread in the East of Wisconsin's fertile land and beauty, which opened the doors to a flood of settlers. Wisconsin entered the Union as the thirtieth state on May 29, 1848.

APPLETON

Charles A. Grignon Mansion (8 miles east off U.S. 41 in Kaukauna, at 1313 Augustine St.; 414/766-3122). This 1837 Greek Revival house of one of the early French settlers was built on land that was, in 1793, the first deeded property in Wisconsin. Period furnishings, picnic area, tours. Open Tuesday through Sunday, Memorial Day through Labor Day.

BARABOO

Founded by Jean Barbeau as a trading post for the Hudson's Bay Company, this city was the original winter quarters of the Ringling Brothers and Gollmar circuses.

Circus World Museum (426 Water St.; 608/356-0800). Fifty acres and eight buildings of circus lore. Live circus acts under the "Big Top." Daily circus parade, display of circus parade wagons, steam calliope concerts, P. T. Barnum sideshow, wild animal menagerie, merry-go-round. Open daily, mid-May through mid-September. Exhibit hall open year-round.

Sauk County Historical Museum (531 4th Ave.;

608/356-1001). Pioneer household goods, toys, china, textiles, military items, Indian artifacts, circus memorabilia, photos. Open daily except Mondays, mid-May to mid-September.

Mid-Continent Railway Museum (5 miles west via WI 136, then 2 miles south to North Freedom; 608/522-4261). A restored 1894 depot and complete rail environment. Steam locomotives, coaches, snowplows, a steam wrecker, artifacts and historical exhibits, picnicking, gift shop. A one-hour steam train ride runs four times a day when the museum is open. Open daily, mid-May through Labor Day; weekends, Labor Day to mid-October.

BELOIT

Hanchett-Bartlett Homestead (2149 St. Lawrence Ave.; 608/365-7835). A restored 1857 Greek Revival limestone homestead with Italianate details, set on fifteen acres and furnished in the style of the period. The barn has a collection of farm implements. On the premises is a one-room schoolhouse. Picnicking. Open Wednesday through Sunday, June through September.

ELKHART LAKE

Old Wade House Historic Site (2 miles north on county rte. P, then SW via county rtes. P and A in Greenbush; 414/526-3271). The restored 1850 Wade House was an early stagecoach inn. Also on the site are a smokehouse, a blacksmith shop, a mill dam, the Robinson House, and the Jung Carriage Museum, which displays more than a hundred vehicles. Carriage rides, picnicking. Open daily, May through October.

Pioneer Corner Museum (Main St.;

In 1837 trading with the Indians was big business in Fond du Lac, Wisconsin. Courtesy Library of Congress, Prints and Photographs Division.

What then is the American, this new man? . . . I could point to you a man, whose grandfather was an Englishman, whose wife was Dutch, whose son married a French woman, and whose present four sons have now four wives of different nations. *He* is an American . . . . Here individuals of all nations are melted into a new race of men, whose labours and posterity will one day cause great change in the world.

—MICHEL
GUILLAUME DE
CREVECOUR,
*LETTERS FROM AN
AMERICAN FARMER,*
1782

414/898-9006). A collection of early German immigrant furniture, a button collection, a general store, and a post office. Open Sundays, June through September.

Accommodations: *52 Stafford* (12 miles south on WI 67, south of jct. with WI 23; 414/893-0552 or 800/421-4667). An 1892 Victorian dwelling, restored and furnished as an Irish guest house, offers nineteen guest rooms, some with four-poster beds and in-room whirlpools. Breakfast, dinner in restaurant on premises. Moderate.

ELKHORN

Webster House (9 East Rockwell St.; 414/723-4348). The restored 19th-century home of Joseph Philbrick Webster, composer of "Sweet Bye and Bye" and "Lorena." Open Wednesday through Sunday, Memorial Day to mid-October.

FOND DU LAC

Galloway House (336 Old Pioneer Rd.; 414/922-6390). A restored thirty-room Victorian with four fireplaces, carved woodwork, and stenciled ceilings. Nearby is a village of twenty-two buildings, including a one-room schoolhouse, a print shop, a general store, a gristmill, and a museum with a collection of Indian artifacts. Open daily, Memorial Day through Labor Day; weekends the rest of the year.

Octagon House (276 Linden St.; 414/922-1608). A twelve-room octagonal house built in 1856 by Isaac Brown and designed by Orson Fowler has a hidden room, secret passageways, and a tunnel. Period antiques, Indian display, collection of model ships, guided tours. Open Mondays, Wednesdays, and Fridays, Memorial Day through Labor Day.

Silver Wheel Manor (east on WI 23,

then south on county rte. K; 424/922-1608). A thirty-room mansion, once part of a 400-acre farm, has antique furnishings, a collection of more than 1,200 dolls, model trains, and a circus room. A trick-horse show is given. Open daily except Sundays, Memorial Day through Labor Day.

FORT ATKINSON

In 1872, William Dempster Hoard, who later became governor, organized the Wisconsin State Dairyman's Association here. He toured the state, preaching the virtues of the cow, "the foster mother of the human race." More than anyone else, Hoard was responsible for Wisconsin's becoming a leading dairy state.

Hoard Historical Museum (407 Merchants Ave.; 414/563-7769). In a historic home, the museum features period rooms, antique quilts, old costumes and clothing, and antique firearms. Open daily, June through August, daily except Mondays the rest of the year. On the premises is the 1841 *Dwight Forster House* (414/563-7769), the Greek Revival home of the city's founder. Open daily, June through August; daily except Mondays the rest of the year. Also here is the *National Dairy Shrine Museum,* which traces the industry's development over the past century. The museum displays include a memorabilia collection, an old creamery, a replica of an early dairy farm kitchen, old barn and milk-hauling equipment, and a multimedia presentation. Open daily except Mondays June through August; Tuesday through Saturday, the rest of the year.

GREEN BAY

Heritage Hill State Park (2640 South Webster; 414/497-4368). A forty-acre living-history museum with twenty-six historical buildings that illustrate the development of northeastern Wisconsin. The restored structures include the circa-1840 *Beaupre Place,* the restored Greek Revival home of Captain John and Mary Cotton; the 1835 *Baird Law Office;* and the circa-1750 *Roi-Portlier-Tank Cottage,* the home of Otto and Carolina Tank, Norwegian and Dutch immigrants. Open daily, June through August; daily except Mondays in May and September.

National Railroad Museum (2285 South Broadway; 414/435-7245). A collection of seventy-five steam and diesel locomotives and railroad cars, with related exhibits. Theater, gift shop. Open daily, May to mid-October.

HUDSON

Octagon House (1004 3rd St.; 715/386-2654). An 1855 octagonal house lavishly furnished in the style of the Victorian era. A garden-house museum has country store and lumbering and farming implements. A carriage-house museum has a blacksmith shop. Open daily except Mondays, May through October.

JANESVILLE

Lincoln-Tallman Restoration (440 North Jackson St., 4 blocks north on U.S. 14 Business; 608/752-4519). One of the finest examples of American culture at the time of the Civil War. Buildings here include the Tallman House, an 1855 twenty-six-room Italianate mansion; the 1842 Greek Revival Stone House; and the circa-1855 Horse Barn, which serves as a visitor center and museum shop. Tours available. Open daily except Mondays, June through August; weekends, September to mid-October.

Accommodations: *Jackson Street* (210

South Jackson St.; 608/754-7250). A High Victorian with oak paneling, cross-beam ceilings, and elaborate fireplaces offers four guest rooms with private bath, breakfast. Inexpensive.

MENOMONEE FALLS

Old Falls Village (½ mile north on County Line Rd.; 414/255-8346). This complex of historic buildings includes the 1858 Greek Revival Miller-Davidson farmhouse, an 1873 Victorian cottage, an 1851 schoolhouse, an 1890 railroad depot, two restored log cabins, and a barn museum. Open Sundays, May through September.

MENOMONIE

Wilson Place Museum (Wilson Circle; 715/235-2283). The former home of Senator James H. Stout, founder of the University of Wisconsin. Original furnishings, tours. Open daily, Memorial Day to Labor Day.

MINERAL POINT

Pendarvis (114 Shake Rag St.; 608/987-2122). A guided tour of six restored log and limestone homes, circa-1845, of Cornish miners. Nature walk through old mining area. Open daily May through October.

Shake Rag Under the Hill (18 Shake Rag St.; 608/987-2122). A craft community in a restored mining village. Demonstrations, traditional marketplace. Open daily, May through October; weekends, November and December.

Accommodations: *Chesterfield Inn–Ovens of Brittany* (20 Commerce St.; 608/987-3682). An 1834 cut-stone building offers eight rooms, two with private baths. Antiques, garden terrace, continental breakfast, dining room for other meals. Inexpensive.

NEW GLARUS

Swiss Historical Village (612 7th Ave.; 608/527-2317). Replicas of buildings erected by settlers, including shops, a cheese factory, and a schoolhouse, all with original furnishings and tools. Guided tours. Open daily, May through October.

PORTAGE

Old Indian Agency House (1 mile east on WI 33 to Agency House Rd.; 608/742-6362). Restored 1832 home of John Kinzie, U.S. Indian agent to the Winnebago and an important pioneer. His wife, Juliette, wrote *Waubun,* an early history of their voyages to Fort Winnebago. Period furnishings. Open daily, May through October.

Fort Winnebago Surgeons' Quarters (1 mile east on WI 33; 608/742-2739). An original 1828 log house from Old Fort Winnebago, used by medical officers stationed at the fort, restored with many original furnishings. Nearby is the 1850 garrison school. Open daily, mid-May to mid-October.

PRAIRIE DU CHIEN

The site of the second oldest European settlement, this town dates from June 1673. Marquette and Jolliet discovered the Mississippi River just south of here. The site became a gathering place and trading fort. The War of 1812 led to the construction of Forts Shelby and Crawford. Stationed here were Jefferson Davis, later President of the Confederacy, and Zachary Taylor, later President of the United States. In 1828, Hercules Dousman, an agent for John Jacob Astor's American Fur Company, built a personal fortune here and became the state's first millionaire. When Fort Crawford was moved, Dousman bought the site and erected Villa Louis, a palatial mansion.

Villa Louis (521 Villa Louis Rd., off U.S. 18; 608/326-2721). An 1870 mansion restored to its original splendor with original furnishings and a collection of Victorian decorative arts. Tours available. Open daily, May through October.

Fort Crawford Medical Museum (717 South Beaumont Rd.; 326-6960). Artifacts of 19th-century medicine, Indian herbal remedies, a dentist's and physician's office, and a drugstore. Dedicated to Dr. William Beaumont, who did some of his famous digestive-system studies here. Open Wednesday through Sunday, May through October.

Kickapoo Indian Caverns and Native American Museum (6 miles south on U.S. 18, then 9 miles east on WI 60 in Wauzeka, at West 200 Rhein Hollow; 608/875-7723). The largest caverns in the state, used by Indians for centuries for shelter. Sights include a subterranean lake, Cathedral Room, Turquoise Room, Stalactite Chamber, and Chamber of the Lost Waters. Tours available. Open daily, mid-May through October.

REEDSBURG

Historical Society Log Village and Museum (3 miles east via WI 33; 608/524-2807). On fifty-two acres are a log cabin, an 1876 log house, a log church and library, a schoolhouse, a blacksmith shop, an apothecary shop, and Indian and army memorabilia. Open weekends, June through September.

RHINELANDER

Rhinelander Logging Museum (Pioneer Park, on U.S. 8, WI 47; 715/369-5004). "Five Spot," the last narrow-gauge locomotive to work the state's north woods, a restored depot, and a one-room schoolhouse. The museum houses "hodag, the strangest animal known to man," which was created as a hoax and became the symbol of the city. Open daily, Memorial Day through Labor Day.

WATERTOWN

Octagon House and First Kindergarten (919 Charles St.; 414/261-2796). This 1854 fifty-seven-room mansion has a forty-foot spiral cantilever hanging staircase and vintage furnishings. On the premises is the kindergarten founded by Margarethe Meyer

Schruz in 1856, the first in the nation. Barn with early farm implements. Open daily, May through October.

WAUKESHA

Old World Wisconsin (14 miles southwest on WI 67; 414/594-2166). A 576-acre outdoor museum with more than fifty historic structures: church, town hall, schoolhouse, stagecoach inn, blacksmith shop, and ten complete 19th-century farmsteads. All buildings have period furnishings and are staffed by costumed interpreters. Tram system, restaurant. Open daily, May through October.

26

INDIANA

The first white men came to Indiana in 1679, and Miami Indians graciously showed René-Robert Cavelier de La Salle and his party the portage from the Saint Joseph River to the Kankakee River, connecting Lake Michigan and the Gulf of Mexico via the Illinois and Mississippi rivers. Another river system—the Maumee-Wabash—linked Indiana with Lake Erie.

The French used these waterways for trapping fur-bearing animals, and to protect their interests they built three fortified villages along the Wabash: Fort Miami, which would become the city of Fort Wayne; Fort Ouiatenon, near present-day Lafayette; and Fort Vincennes on the lower Wabash. For more than a century these forts were crucial in the struggle among the French, the British, and the Americans for control of the territory.

First, Indiana was part of the French provinces of Canada and Louisiana. Then, after the French and Indian War, in 1763, it came under British control. The British were opposed by an Indian confederation led by Chief Pontiac. In 1779, General George Rogers Clark occupied southern Indiana with French assistance and claimed it for the state of Virginia. Virginia, however, was unable to control the region. It became public domain in 1784, and remained chiefly Indian territory for the next fifteen years.

As America spread westward, the great Shawnee chief, Tecumseh, formed a confederation of Indian nations extending from the Great Lakes to the Gulf of Mexico. In 1811, while Tecumseh was in the South, General William Henry Harrison forced the Battle of Tippecanoe, which dealt a fatal blow to the Indian confederation. The next year, the Indians, their towns and granaries having been burned by federal troops and local militia, made a last, furious attempt to defend their land. But Tecumseh's death, in the Battle of the Thames, in 1813, marked the end of the Indian era. In 1816, Indiana became the nineteenth state.

ANDERSON

Mounds State Park (2 miles east on IN 232; 317/642-6627). In the park are several well-preserved earth formations constructed by the Indian mound builders. On bluffs overlooking the White River, these mounds once were the center of an ancient civilization. The largest is nine feet high and nearly a quarter mile in circumference. Open daily.

BATESVILLE

Whitewater Canal State Historic Site (14 miles north on U.S. 52 in Metamora; 317/647-6512). Part of a restored fourteen-mile section of the Whitewater Canal, which provided transportation between Hagerstown and the Ohio River from 1836 to 1860. There are horse-drawn cruises through the Duck Creek aqueduct in the canal boat *Ben Franklin III,* to the only lock still operat-

Fort Harrison was built in 1812 to protect settlers in Indiana from the Indians. Courtesy Library of Congress, Prints and Photographs Division.

ing. Open Wednesday through Sunday, May through October.

Accommodations: *Sherman House* (35 South Main St.; 812/934-2407). This two-story inn, welcoming guests since 1852, has twenty-five rooms and a restaurant. Inexpensive.

CORYDON

Corydon Capitol State Historic Site (Capitol Ave.; 812/738-4890). This small town was the seat of the Indian Territorial government, 1813–16, when the constitutional convention assembled here. After admission to the Union, this building was the state capitol until 1825. Construction of the blue limestone building began in 1814 and was completed in 1816. Open daily except Mondays.

Governor Hendricks' Home (202 East Walnut St.; 812/738-4890). The executive mansion, 1822–25. Exhibits portray home life in three time periods between 1820 and 1880. Open daily except Mondays.

Squire Boone Caverns and Village (10 miles south on IN 135; 812/732-4381).

Daniel Boone's brother, Squire, discovered these caverns in 1790 while hiding from Indians. The village includes a restored gristmill, craft shops, and nature trails. Hay rides, cavern tours. Open daily, June through August; weekends in spring and fall.

Accommodations: *Kinter House* (101 South Capitol Ave.; 812/738-2020). This brick Victorian, furnished in the style of the period, has fifteen guest rooms, pool, tennis, and golf privileges, full breakfast. Inexpensive.

CRAWFORDSVILLE

Lane Place (212 South Water St.; 317/362-3416). The Greek Revival residence of Henry S. Lane, governor and U.S. senator, houses a collection of Colonial, Federal, and Victorian furnishings, dolls, and china. On the premises is a furnished log cabin. Open Tuesday through Sunday, April through October.

EVANSVILLE

Angel Mounds State Historic Site (7 miles east on IN 662 at 8215 Pollack Ave.; 812/853-3956). The largest and best preserved group of prehistoric Indian mounds in the state. Reconstructed dwellings. An interpretive center has a film, exhibits, and artifacts. Open daily except Mondays, mid-March through December.

GREENFIELD

James Whitcomb Riley House (250 West Main St.; 317/462-8539). This 1850 house was the boyhood home of the poet (1850–69). He wrote "When the Frost Is on the Punkin" and many other verses in Hoosier dialect. Tours, museum. Open daily, April through late December.

The Old Capitol at Corydon.

HUNTINGTON

Forks of the Wabash (2 miles west on U.S. 24; 219/356-5725). This was once the treaty grounds of the Miami Indians. Tours of Miami Chief Richardville Home and Log House. Open daily, June through August.

Accommodations: *Purviance House* (326 South Jefferson; 219/356-4218). This 1859 Greek Revival–Italianate house, listed on the National Register, has interior shutters, ornate ceiling designs, and tile fireplaces. Four guest rooms, all with shared bath, full breakfast. Inexpensive.

JEFFERSONVILLE

Howard Steamboat Museum (1101 East Market St.; 812/283-3728). In the twenty-two-room Victorian mansion are steamboat models, shipyard artifacts, tools, pictures, and other steamboat memorabilia covering the years from 1834 to 1941. Tours available. Open daily except Mondays.

LAFAYETTE

Fort Ouiatenon (4 miles southwest of West Lafayette on South River Rd.; 317/743-3921). A replica blockhouse with an 18th-century French trading post. A museum interprets the history of French, Indian, British, and American struggles to control the Wabash Valley. Open daily except Mondays, June through August; weekends, early April and May and September through late October.

Tippecanoe Battlefield County Park (I-65 at IN 43 exit, in Battle Ground; 317/567-2147). The site of the 1811 battle in which soldiers of the Fourth Regiment and local militia, led by Gen. William Henry Harrison, territorial governor, defeated a

confederation of Indians headed by the Prophet, brother of Tecumseh. The Wabash Heritage Trail begins here. Open daily.

MADISON

Lanier State Historic Site (511 West 1st St.; 812/265-3526). An 1844 Greek Revival mansion built for James F. D. Lanier, a financier who loaned the state more than $1 million when the treasury was in need during the Civil War. Some original furnishings. Open daily except Mondays.

Shrewsbury House (301 West 1st St.; 812/265-4481). A circa-1846 Greek Revival dwelling with a free-standing spiral staircase and period furnishings. Open daily, mid-March through December.

Schofield House (217 West 2nd St.; 812/265-4759). A circa-1809 two-story Federal-style tavern constructed of sun-dried brick. Open daily, April through early December.

MITCHELL

Spring Mill State Park (3 miles east of Mitchell on IN 60; 812/849-4129). An abandoned pioneer village has been restored in a valley among wooded hills. Near the 1816 gristmill are the shop and homes of a trading post. The main street has a tavern, a distillery, a post office, and an apothecary shop. Open daily, April through October.

NEW ALBANY

Scribner House (State and Main streets; 812/944-7330). Built by a city founder in 1814, this is the oldest house in New Albany. Period furnishings, collections of paintings, toys, textiles, and antiques.

NEW HARMONY

The experimental community here was founded by members of the Harmony Society, under the leadership of George Rapp, who had come with his followers from Wurttenberg, Germany, and settled at Harmony, Pennsylvania. In 1814 the society came to Indiana. The deeply religious members believed in equality, mutual protection, and common ownership of property. They practiced celibacy and prepared for the imminent return of Christ. In a decade they transformed 30,000 acres of forest and swampland into farms and a town. In 1825, however, everything was sold to Robert Owen, a Scottish industrialist, social reformer, and communal idealist, after which Rapp and his followers returned to Pennsylvania.

Owen attempted to organize a new social order with equal opportunities for all, and with advanced educational facilities to develop the highest type of human being. Many of the world's most distinguished scientists and educators came to New Harmony, which evolved into one of the country's scientific centers. Owen's absences from the center and rivalry among his followers caused the experiment to fail, but the scientists and educators stayed on. The first U.S. Geological Survey was done here, and the Smithsonian Institution had its origins here. Many of the original buildings and homes can be visited today.

The Athenaeum Visitor Center (North and Arthur streets; 812/682-4488). The orientation area is in a building designed by the architect Richard Meier. Audiovisual presentation, tours. The visitor center and most buildings are open daily. More than twenty buildings are on the tour, ranging from the oldest building, the 1775 Macluria Double-Log Cabin, to the 1959 Roofless Church,

designed by Philip Johnson and containing Jacques Lipchitz's sculpture *Descent of the Holy Spirit,* a tribute to New Harmony's religious heritage.

RICHMOND

Levi Coffin House State Historic Site (113 U.S. 27N; 317/847-2432). An 1839 Federal brick home of the Quaker abolitionist who helped some 2,000 slaves escape to Canada. Period furnishings, tours. Open Tuesday

THE NORTHWEST ORDINANCE

On July 13, 1787, Congress approved the Northwest Ordinance, which spelled out rules for governing the old Northwest, the area north of the Ohio River and east of the Mississippi. Three years earlier, Thomas Jefferson had written the first ordinance for the territory, calling for a division of the region into states. Each state was to have the same political powers as the original thirteen, and was to prohibit slavery after 1800. The ordinance was adopted in 1784, but it hadn't gone into effect because no settlers as yet held legal title to land in the area.

Pressure from land speculators induced Congress to issue a revised Northwest Ordinance in 1787, providing for federal controls while local governments were being developed. The new law called for dividing the area into separate territories, but specified that each would be administered initially by a governor. Whenever a district reached a population of 5,000 free males, it could elect a legislature and send a nonvoting member to Congress. When its population reached 60,000, a district would be eligible for statehood. The ordinance guaranteed freedom of religion, trial by jury, and public support for education, and prohibited slavery.

The Northwest Ordinance was one of the most important acts passed by Congress under the Articles of Confederation. It laid out the process through which a territory could move to statehood, it guaranteed that new states would be on an equal footing with the old, and it protected civil liberties in the new territories. And it was the first national legislation that set limits on the expansion of slavery.

The Lincoln Living Historical Farm near Santa Claus.

through Sunday, June to mid-September; weekends, mid-September through October.

Huddleston Farmhouse Inn Museum (1 mile west on U.S. 40, at edge of town, in Cambridge City; 317/478-3172). A restored circa-1840 farmhouse and inn that once served travelers on the National Road. Open daily except Mondays, May through August; Tuesday through Saturday the rest of the year.

ROCKVILLE

Historic Billie Creek Village (1 mile east on U.S. 36; 317/569-3430). A re-created pioneer village and working farm with more than thirty buildings and three covered bridges. Craft demonstrations. Open daily except late December.

Accommodations: *Suit's Us* (514 North

College; 317/569-5660). A Colonial Revival inn offering four guest rooms. Fireplace and library. Inexpensive to moderate.

SANTA CLAUS

Lincoln Boyhood National Memorial and Lincoln State Park (4 miles west on IN 162; 812/937-4541). Lincoln spent his boyhood years, 1816–30, in this area, clerking in a store, helping his father on the farm, and reading books. When he was twenty-one, his family moved to Illinois, where his political career began. This 200-acre wooded and landscaped park encloses the grave of Nancy Hanks Lincoln, his mother. She was thirty-four years old, Abraham nine, when she died in 1818. Visitor center open daily. Nearby, in the original Thomas Lincoln tract, is the *Lincoln Living Historical Farm,* with a furnished log cabin similar to the one the Lincolns lived in, as well as other log buildings, animals, and crops of a pioneer farm. Costumed interpreters carry out family living and farming activities typical of an early-19th-century farm. Open daily, mid-April through September.

VINCENNES

This is the oldest settlement in Indiana. French fur traders roamed the area as early as 1683 and built Fort Vincennes in 1732. In 1778, Virginia ordered George Rogers Clark (brother of William Clark, who, with Meriwether Lewis, explored the Northwest to the Pacific Ocean) to secure all land northwest of the Ohio River for the state. His victory at Vincennes was a great coup. Exhausted from crossing the icy, flooded Illinois plains in mid-February, Clark's 175 men made the British think they were outnumbered by shooting extra rounds and making a lot of noise, a ruse that worked. The recapture of Vincennes in 1779 opened up the entire Northwest Territory. Virginia was unable to maintain law and order, however, and in 1784 the territory was ceded to the United States and became a public domain. Until 1800 the town was populated by descendants of the French founders. From 1808 to 1811, Vincennes was the capital of the Indiana Territory.

George Rogers Clark National Historic Park (downtown off U.S. 50 and U.S. 41; 812/882-1776). On the site of Fort Sackville, captured from the British by Clark's force in 1779, a memorial building commemorates the George Rogers Clark campaign during the Revolution. The visitor center has a movie and exhibits. In the summer, uniformed interpreters stage military drills and firearms demonstrations. Open daily.

The Old Cathedral Minor Basilica (2nd and Church streets, off U.S. 50; 812/882-1776). Behind this 1826 structure is the Old French Cemetery, in which are buried William Clark, Judge of the Indiana Territory, and local Frenchmen who served in George Rogers Clark's army. Both open daily.

William Henry Harrison Mansion "Grouseland" (2 West Scott St., opposite old capitol; 812/882-2096). The circa-1803 residence of the ninth President of the United States while he was governor of the Indiana Territory. Period furnishings. Open daily.

Indiana Territory Capitol, State Historic Site (Harrison and 1st streets, in Harrison Historical Park; 812/882-7472). From this two-story frame building, an area consisting of the present states of Indiana, Illinois, Michigan, Wisconsin and part of Minnesota was governed. Nearby is the Maurice Thompson Birthplace, the restored 1842 home of the author of *Alice of Old Vincennes*. Tours daily, June through September; weekends only in spring and fall.

Michel Brouillet Old French House (509 1st St.; 812/882-7886). A circa-1806 French Creole house with period furnishings. Open daily, May through September.

Fort Knox II (2 miles north via Fort Knox Rd.). Site of an American military post built during the early 1800s to protect the western frontier. As tensions increased, the fort was enlarged and strengthened by Captain Zachary Taylor in 1810. The outline of the fort is marked for a self-guided tour. Open daily.

Any man's son may become the equal of any other man's son; and the consciousness of this is certainly a sport to that coarse familiarity, untempered by any shadow of respect, which is assumed by the grossest and the lowest in their intercourse with the highest and most refined. . . . Strong, indeed, must be the love of equality in an English breast, if it can survive a tour through the Union.

—FRANCES TROLLOPE, *DOMESTIC MANNERS OF THE AMERICANS, 1832*

27

MICHIGAN

Michigan comes in two parts, the Upper Peninsula and the Lower Peninsula. It is surrounded by four of the five Great Lakes—Superior on the north, Michigan on the west, and Huron and Erie on the east. As a result, Michigan has some 3,000 miles of shoreline.

In the seventeenth century the Upper Peninsula was in the path of French exploration, and later became a hub of its fur-trading empire. In search of a northwest passage, Etienne Brulé, in 1816, and Jean Nicolet, in 1634, made the portage where rapids are formed by Lake Superior's twenty-foot descent into Lake Huron. At the rapids, in 1668, Father Jacques Marquette founded Sault Sainte Marie, the first settlement in Michigan. The priest also founded the second permanent settlement, Mission Saint Ignace, at the Straits of Mackinac.

Antoine de La Mothe Cadillac, the commandant of the fort at Mission Saint Ignace, was concerned with British encroachment in the fur business, and shifted operations to another strategic strait, the river between Lakes Saint Clair and Erie, where he founded Detroit in 1701.

During the French and Indian War, the Revolution, and the War of 1812, the French fortifications changed hands several times, usually without bloodshed except when Indians were involved. Pontiac's War, in 1763, was a fierce attempt by the Ottawa chief to drive back the encroachments of the British. Pontiac captured Forts Michilimackinac and Saint Joseph and laid siege to Detroit for five months before the British were able to turn them back. But the Indians soon aligned themselves with the British against the American settlers.

Lewis Cass, territorial governor from 1813 to 1831, negotiated the 1819 Treaty of Saginaw, whereby the Indians relinquished the eastern half of the Lower Peninsula, and the 1821 Treaty of Chicago, which gave the southwestern part to Michigan. In 1818 the first steamship arrived at Detroit. In 1820, Cass made a three-month tour of inspection, and through his efforts Detroit was linked by road to Saint Joseph on Lake Michigan, and to Chicago. In 1825 the Erie Canal opened. Settlers poured in, and the territory's population tripled between 1820 and 1830, and increased sevenfold in the next decade.

Michigan applied for statehood in 1834, but had to wait until the so-called Toledo War was settled. The dispute involved a strip of land around Lake Erie that included the port of Toledo. The settlement gave Ohio the Toledo Strip, Michigan the Upper Peninsula. Michigan joined the Union in 1837.

DEARBORN

Greenfield Village (20900 Oakwood Blvd., ½ mile south of U.S. 12; 313/271-1620 or 800/343-1929). Henry Ford's collection of more than eighty 17th- and 19th-century buildings, moved here from all over the country,

includes historic homes, shops, schools, mills, stores, and laboratories that figured in the lives of such personages as Lincoln, Webster, Burbank, McGuffey, Carver, the Wright brothers, Edison, Firestone, and Ford himself. Craft demonstrations, tours. Open daily.

MACKINAC ISLAND

Mackinac (pronounced *MAK-i-naw*) was called "great turtle" by the Indians, who believed its towering heights and rock formations were shaped by supernatural forces. Its strategic position made the island the key to the struggle between England and France for control of the fur trade in the great Northwest. Held by the French until 1760, it became English after Wolfe's victory at Quebec, and became American after the Revolution. It was captured by British troops during the War of 1812, but was later returned to the United States. Today 80 percent of the island is a state park (906/847-3328).

Fort Mackinac. On a bluff overlooking the Straits of Mackinac, this military outpost has massive limestone ramparts, cannon, a guardhouse, blockhouses, and barracks. In all, fourteen buildings have been restored. Costumed interpreters, reenactments, craft demonstrations, rifle and cannon firings,

Built by the French in 1715 to protect the fur trading center on Mackinac Island, an elaborate fort looks out over the northern waters of Lake Michigan. Courtesy Library of Congress, Prints and Photographs Division.

SIX NOTABLE INDIANS

Pocahontas. Saving the life of John Smith made her famous, but her contribution was greater as the wife of John Rolfe, the man who introduced the cultivation of tobacco in Virginia. By her marriage and her conversion to Christianity, Pocahontas helped preserve peace between the colonists and the Indians. In 1616, Rolfe took her to England, where people saw in her evidence that the New World could be "civilized" and made a welcoming place for settlers.

Squanto. Kidnapped and taken to Europe in 1615 by an early explorer, Squanto learned to speak English, returned to America as the pilot of a ship, and decided to remain in his native land. He befriended the Pilgrims and proved to be a godsend. According to William Bradford, the Pilgrim leader, "he directed them how to set their corne, wher to take fish . . . and was also their pilott to bring them to unknowne places for their profitt, and never left them till he dyed."

Pontiac. As chief of the Ottawa, Pontiac pestered the British in the Ohio Valley during the French and Indian Wars. After the wars, though, he organized a "conspiracy" in a desperate attempt to drive white settlers back across the Appalachian Mountains. "We must exterminate from our land this nation whose only object is our death," he told his followers. He won some early victories, but eventually he was worn down by sheer numbers, and in 1776 he made peace with the British.

Tecumseh. The organizer of what was probably the most formidable Indian military alliance in American history, Tecumseh was a charismatic leader. His opponent, General William Henry Harrison, called him "one of those uncommon geniuses who spring up occasionally to produce revolutions." He roused nearly all the tribes east of the Mississippi in a campaign to drive back the whites and erase all signs of their civilization from Indian culture. He and his followers were defeated by Harrison at the Battle of Tippecanoe in 1811, and two years later, at the Battle of the Thames, Tecumseh was slain.

Tenskwatawa. An Indian religious leader called "the Prophet," Tenskwatawa was Tecumseh's brother. He had visions, burned rivals as witches, and practiced mystic rites that brought him a wide following. He urged Indians to give up alcohol and European clothes and tools, and to return to their traditional way of life. He was headstrong and a poor soldier. He precipitated the disastrous Battle of Tippecanoe, although Tecumseh, who was absent at the time, had warned him not to engage in battle.

Black Hawk. A Sauk chief, Black Hawk believed, with good reason, that his tribe had been tricked into surrendering its land east of the Mississippi. He joined Tecumseh's confederation and took part in many battles during the War of 1812. He organized a new confederation in 1831 and attempted to invade his old homeland in Illinois. The resulting Black Hawk War ended in his capture in 1832. He was taken to Washington, D.C., imprisoned briefly, then returned to Iowa, where he spent the rest of his life. The Black Hawk War is well known because Abraham Lincoln served in it as a captain of volunteers.

audiovisual presentation. Open daily, mid-June to mid-October.

Indian Dormitory. Built near the fort as a place to house Indians during their annual visits to the Mackinac Island office of the U.S. Indian Agency, the building has interpretive displays and craft demonstrations. Open mid-June through Labor Day.

Accommodations: *Haan's 1830 Inn* (Huron St.; 906/847-6244). This structure is the oldest example of Greek Revival architecture in the Northwest Territory, and the oldest building used as an inn in the state. Haan's once was the home of Colonel William Preston, the first mayor of Mackinac Island City. The seven guest rooms are furnished in the style of the period. Continental breakfast. Moderate.

MONROE

River Basin Battlefield Visitor Center (1402 Elm Ave., off I-75 at Elm Ave. Ext.; 313/243-7136). During the War of 1812, the Battle of River Basin was fought here, in January 1813, when nearly a thousand American soldiers from Kentucky clashed with British, Canadian, and Indian forces. Only thirty-three Americans escaped death or capture. Exhibits of weapons and uniforms, dioramas, audiovisual map program. Open daily, Memorial Day through Labor Day; weekends the rest of the year.

NILES

Fort St. Joseph Museum (508 East Main St.; 616/683-4702). Collections include material from Fort St. Joseph (1691–1781), Potawatomi artifacts, local memorabilia, and one of the finest collections of Sioux art in the country. Open weekdays and Sunday afternoons.

ST. IGNACE

Marquette Mission Park and Museum of Ojibwa Culture (500 North State St.; 906/643-9161). The gravesite of Father Marquette. The museum interprets 17th-century Indian life and the coming of the French. Open daily, Memorial Day through Labor Day; Tuesday through Saturday the rest of September.

TRAVERSE CITY

Con Foster Museum (in Clinch Park, Grandview Pkwy. and Cass St.; 616/922-4905). Exhibits on local history, Indian and pioneer life. Open daily, Memorial Day through Labor Day. Docked in the park marina is the schooner *Madeline,* a full-scale replica of a Great Lakes vessel of the 1850s, which served as the first school in the Grand Traverse region. Tours Wednesday through Sunday afternoons, early May through late September.

28

OHIO

The first part of the Northwest Territory to be settled was Ohio (from the Iroquois for "something great"), the area between Lake Erie and the Ohio River. The river was the highway of settlement, and New Englanders of the Ohio Company bought land and founded Marietta on the river in 1788.

Several thousand years earlier, Indians had built more than 10,000 mounds here, many of them effigy mounds of great beauty. The first European in the area probably was the French explorer La Salle, around 1669. The French and the British had conflicting claims in the area, which led to the French and Indian Wars. France lost, and ceded to Britain most of its territory east of the Mississippi.

With the outbreak of the Revolution, both the British and the Americans urged the Indians to remain neutral, but they were soon involved, once again on the losing side. The new republic had no intention of halting settlement at the Ohio River regardless of Indian unrest, and the Northwest Ordinance of 1787 spelled out how the area would be colonized.

Settlers did attempt for a time to avoid trouble with the Indians by staying north of the Ohio River. Indians remained a problem, however. Between 1783 and 1790, raiding parties along the Ohio killed, wounded, or took prisoner some 1,500 settlers.

In 1790, President Washington directed federal troops to remove the Indians by force, and the Ohio Indian Wars, fought along the present-day Ohio-Indiana boundary, lasted four years. The treaty of Greene Ville, in 1795, gave up all claims to territory in Ohio.

Meanwhile, Governor Arthur St. Clair was able to provide a framework for settlement. The Ordinances of 1785 and 1787 created a body of laws that paved the way for settlement and statehood. Ohio became a state in 1803, and its population grew from 42,000 in 1800 to 230,000 in 1810.

AKRON

Perkins Mansion (550 Copley Rd. at South Portage Path; 216/535-1120). An 1837 Greek Revival home built by Simon Perkins Jr., on ten landscaped acres. The Summit County Historical Society, housed in the Perkins Mansion, also administers the *John Brown Home* (514 Diagonal Rd. at Copley Rd.), the house, now remodeled, where the abolitionist lived from 1844 to 1846. Both open daily except Mondays and the month of January.

Hale Farm and Western Reserve Village (10 miles south of I-80 exit 11, in Cuyahoga Valley National Recreation Area; 216/666-3711). A circa-1825 Western Reserve house and other authentic buildings in a village setting depict rural life in the area in the mid-19th century. Farming, craft demonstrations, costumed interpreters. Open Wednesday through Sunday, May through October.

Cincinnati, Ohio, from the canal at Plum and Twelfth streets, in the late 1850s. Courtesy Library of Congress, Prints and Photographs Division.

Accommodations: *O'Neil House* (1290 West Exchange; 216/867-2650). The 20,000-square-foot Tudor mansion, once the home of the founder of General Tire, now offers four guest rooms. The house is on four acres, separated into seven English gardens. Breakfast is served on the terrace or in a room overlooking the reflecting pool. Moderate to expensive.

CHARDON

Geauga County Historical Society-Century Village (8 miles south on OH 44, then 3 miles east on OH 87, at 14653 East Park St. in Burton; 216/834-4012). A restored Western Reserve village with homes, school, shops, and store. All original, with period furnishings. Open daily, May through October; daily except Mondays, March–April and November–December.

CHILLICOTHE

Knoles Log Home (39 West 5th St.; 616/772-1936). A two-story log home, built in 1800–25, with open-hearth cooking, garden, vintage utensils and tools. Demonstrations. Open Tuesday through Sunday, April through November.

Adams State Memorial (south end of Adena Rd., off Pleasant Valley Rd.; 614/772-1500). The restored 1807 mansion of Governor Thomas Worthington. Period furnishings. Open Wednesday through Saturday, June through September.

Hopewell Culture National Historical Park (west bank of Scioto River, 4 miles north on OH 104; 614/774-1125). The site of twenty-three prehistoric Hopewell Indian burial mounds, dating from 200 B.C. to A.D. 500, in a thirteen-acre area within an earth wall. Self-guided tours, visitor center with museum. Open daily.

The William Howard Taft House in Cincinnati. Courtesy National Park Service, William Howard Taft National Historic Site.

Seip Mound State Memorial (14 miles southwest, on south side of U.S. 50; 614/297-2630). An Indian burial mound 250 feet long and 30 feet high, surrounded by smaller mounds and earthworks. Exhibit pavilion. Open daily.

Fort Hill State Memorial (via U.S. 50, 41; 513/588-3221). The site of a prehistoric Indian hilltop earth-and-stone enclosure. A 2,000-foot trail leads to the ancient earthworks. Open daily.

Accommodations: *Old McDill-Anderson Place* (3656 Polk Hollow Rd.; 614/774-1770). This 1820 brick Italianate house has a screened breakfast porch that looks out on the inn's two acres. Four guest rooms, including a family suite. Feather beds. Inexpensive.

CINCINNATI

By 1790 there were four small settlements here, at an important Ohio River crossroads. Arthur St. Clair, governor of the Northwest Territory, changed the name of Losantville to Cincinnati, in honor of the Revolutionary officers' Society of the Cincinnati. Despite smallpox, floods, and crop failures, 15,000 settlers came in the next five years under the protection of General Anthony Wayne, who broke the resistance of the Indians in Ohio.

William Howard Taft National Historical Site (2038 Auburn Ave.; 513/684-3262). The circa-1840 birthplace and boyhood home of the twenty-seventh President and Chief Justice of the Supreme Court. Four rooms with period furnishings. Exhibits on Taft's life and career. Open daily.

Harriet Beecher Stowe Memorial (2950 Gilbert Ave.; 513/632-5120). The author of *Uncle Tom's Cabin* lived here from 1832 to 1836. Restored with some original furnishings. Open Tuesday through Thursday.

John Hauck House Museum (812 Dayton St.; 513/721-3570). An ornate 19th-century town house in the historic district. Period furnishings, children's toys, memorabilia. Open Thursdays and Sundays.

Sharon Woods Village (north on I-75, east on I-275, exit at U.S. 42 S, then 1 mile south; 513/563-9484). A historic village showing life in the area before 1880. Nine buildings (1804–80) reconstructed and authentically restored and refurnished. Special exhibits, craft demonstrations, tours. Open Wednesday through Sunday, May through October.

Accommodations: *Prospect Hill* (408 Boal St.; 513/421-4408). On a wooded hillside in the Prospect Hill Historic District, this 1867 Italianate town house offers views of downtown Cincinnati. Each of the three guest rooms (two share a bath) is decorated in a particular historic period. Moderate.

CLEVELAND

Dunham Tavern Museum (6709 Euclid Ave.; 216/431-1060). A restoration of an 1824 stagecoach stop on the route between Buffalo and Detroit. Period furnishings, museum. Open Wednesdays and Sundays.

Oldest Stone House Museum (5 miles west, 1 block north of U.S. 5 in Lakewood, at 14710 Lake Ave.; 216/221-7343). An 1838 house, authentically restored and refurnished. Herb garden. Tours led by costumed guides. Open Wednesdays and Sundays, February through November.

COSHOCTON

Roscoe Village (northwest edge of town on OH 16; 800/877-1830). A living museum of an 1830s Erie Canal town with old-time shops, antiques, gardens, exhibits, and crafts. *Johnston-Humrickhouse Museum* (614/622-8710) has four galleries: Native American and Eskimo, Oriental Room, Early American, and Decorative Arts. *Village Exhibit Tour* includes the Township Hall, the Craftsman's House (1825), the Dr. Maro Johnston House (1833), and the Canal Toll House. The visitor center has an audiovisual presentation. Open daily.

GALLIPOLIS

Our House State Memorial (434 1st St.; 614/448-0586). A restored 1819 tavern where Lafayette, Jenny Lind, and other celebrities once stayed. Open Tuesday through Saturday, May through August.

GENEVA-ON-THE-LAKE

Shandy Hall (south on OH 5234, then 2 miles west on OH 84, to 6333 South Ridge West Rd.; 216/466/3680). An 1815 Western Reserve home with original furnishings.

MCGUFFEY'S READER

In 1836 a Cincinnati publishing firm asked William Holmes McGuffey, an Ohio college professor and Presbyterian minister, to compile a series of graded readers adapted to the values, beliefs, and way of life of "Western people." Within the year he produced the *Eclectic First Reader* and *Eclectic Second Reader,* and two more the next year. They contained stories of widely varied subject matter appealing to youngsters. They taught religious, moral, and ethical principles that reflected both McGuffey's personality and the society he lived in.

The original publishing partnership dissolved in 1841, and the books passed through a series of seven owners while their content evolved during almost a hundred years of publication. Although the revised texts of 1857 added McGuffey's name to the title, they moved away from the Calvinist values of a broader American society. The first editions sold 7 million copies. By 1879, more than 60 million had been sold, and twice that number by 1922. In 1980 the books were still in use in some school systems.

The birthplace of General William Tecumseh Sherman in Lancaster.

Tours available. Open Tuesday through Saturday, May through October.

GNADENHUTTEN

Gnadenhutten Historical Park and Museum (1 mile south; 614/254-4756). A monument to the ninety Christian Indians who were massacred here in 1782. Indian burial mound, reconstructed log church, and cooper's cabin. Open daily, June through early September.

LANCASTER

Sherman House Museum (137 East Main St.; 614/687-5891). Birthplace of General William Tecumseh Sherman and Senator John Sherman, sponsor of the Sherman Antitrust Act. Museum. Open Tuesday through Sunday, April to mid-December. The house is in an area known as Square 13. A pamphlet describing the nineteen historic buildings in the area is available from the Fairfield Heritage Association (105 East Wheeling St.).

The Georgian (105 East Wheeling St.; 614/654-9923). An 1833 two-story brick house, reflecting both the Federal and the Regency styles, now is the Headquarters of the Fairfield Heritage Assn. Open Tuesday through Sunday, April to mid-December.

LEBANON

Fort Ancient State Memorial (7 miles southeast on OH 350; 513/932-4421). This is one of the largest and most important earthworks of its kind in the country. Built by the Hopewell Indians between 100 B.C. and A.D. 500 on an elevated plateau overlooking the Little Miami River Valley, the massive earthen walls, more than twenty-three feet high in places, enclose 100 acres. Inside are earth mounds used as a calendar of events. Museum with interpretive exhibits. Open Wednesday through Sunday, June through September and October weekends.

LOCUST GROVE

Serpent Mound State Memorial (4 miles northwest on OH 73; 513/587-2796). The largest and most unusual serpent-effigy earthwork in North America. Built between 800 B.C. and A.D. 100 of stone and yellow clay, it curls like an enormous snake for 1,335 feet. An oval earth wall forms the serpent's open mouth. Museum, observation tower. Site open daily; museum open Wednesday through Sunday, June through August; weekends only, September and October.

MARIETTA

General Rufus Putnam's New England Flotilla, arriving at the junction of the Muskingum and the Ohio to buy land, founded this town, the oldest settlement in Ohio.

Campus Martius, Museum of the Northwest Territory (601 2nd St. at Washington St.; 614/373-3750). On the premises is the 1788 Rufus Putnam home, part of the original Campus Martius Fort, and the 1788 Ohio Company Land Office, restored and authentically furnished. Open daily, May through September; Wednesday through Sunday, March–April and October–November.

MASSILLON

Spring Hill (1401 Spring Hill Lane NE; 216/833-6749). An 1821 house with a basement kitchen and dining room, a secret stairway, and original furnishings. Outbuildings include a springhouse, a smokehouse, a wool house, and a milkhouse. Picnicking. Open Wednesday through Sunday, June through August.

Canal Fulton and Museum (6 miles northwest on OH 21, then 1 mile northeast on OH 93; 216/854-3808, or 800-HELENA-3). The *St. Helena II,* a replica of a mule-drawn canal boat of the mid-19th century, takes forty-five-minute trips on the Ohio-Erie Canal from the Canal Fulton Park. Daily, June through August; weekends, late May and early September.

Accommodations: *The Buckley House* (332 Front St.; 614-373-3080). From the double verandah on this Greek Revival structure, guests can see the *Valley Gem,* a river steamboat. Three guest rooms. Breakfast, afternoon tea, and evening aperitifs. Inexpensive.

NEWARK

On July 4, 1825, construction on the Ohio-Erie Canal was begun here. The Ohio Canal was built north to Lake Erie and south to the Ohio River.

Newark Earthworks. Among the most extensive in the country, these constructions cover an area of more than four square miles. The Hopewell Indians used these geometric enclosures for social, religious, and ceremonial purposes. Three sites may be visited, and the Moundbuilders Museum nearby has an extensive collection of artifacts. *Moundbuilders State Memorial* (southwest on OH 79, at South 21st and Cooper streets; 614/344-1920). The Great Circle, encompassing sixty-six acres, has walls from eight to fourteen feet high, with burial mounds in the center. Open Wednesday through Sunday, June through August; weekends in September and October. *Wright Earthworks* (¼ mile northeast of Great Circle at James and Waldo streets). A one-acre area has a 100-foot wall remnant. Open daily. *Octagon Earthworks* (North 30th St.

and Parkview). This enclosure—octagonal in layout, as its name indicates—contains fifty acres that include small mounds joined by parallel walls to a circular embankment enclosing twenty acres. Open daily.

Licking County Historical Society Museum (6th St. at West Main; 614/345-4898). The restored circa-1815 Sherwood-Davidson House has period furnishings; the museum also includes the circa-1815 Buckingham Meeting House. Tours available. Open daily except Mondays, April through December.

Robbins Hunter Museum, Avery-Downer House (221 East Broadway; 614/587-0430). An 1842 Greek Revival house with period furnishings and decorative and fine arts. Tours available. Open Tuesday through Sunday, June through December.

Buckeye Central Scenic Railroad (U.S. 40; 614/928-3827). An hour-long trip through Licking County. Weekends and holidays, Memorial Day through October.

Accommodations: *Pitzer-Cooper House* (6019 Whitechapel Rd. SE; 614/323-2680 or 800/833-9536). This 1858 farmhouse, listed on the National Register, has a two-story verandah overlooking lawns and gardens. A common room overlooks the pond, and there is a music room with a baby grand piano. Two rooms with shared bath, full breakfast. Inexpensive.

NEW PHILADELPHIA

Zoar State Memorial (I-77 exit 93, 2½ miles southeast on OH 212; 216/874-3011). A German religious sect, the Separatists, found refuge here in 1817 and began an experiment in communal living that lasted for eighty years. A museum is in Number One House on Main Street Zoar Garden, in the center of the quaint village, constructed according to the description of New Jerusalem in the Bible. Restored buildings include a garden house, a blacksmith shop, a bakery, a tin shop, and a carpenter's shop. Open Wednesday through Sunday, June through August; weekends only, April–May and September–October.

Fort Laurens State Memorial (14 miles north via OH 39, I-77, and OH 212 to Bolivar, then ½ mile south; 216/874-2059). The site of the only American fort in Ohio during the Revolution, built in 1778 as a defense against the British and Indians and named in honor of Henry Laurens, president of the Continental Congress. Museum. Open Wednesday through Sunday, June through August; weekends only, September and October.

Schoenbrunn Village State Memorial (3 miles southeast off U.S. 250 on OH 259; 216/339-3636). The partial reconstruction of the first Ohio town built by Christian Indians under the leadership of Moravian missionaries. One of six such villages constructed between 1772 and 1798. Museum, picnicking. Open daily, May through August; weekends only, September and October.

OXFORD

McGuffey Museum (Spring and Oak streets; 513/529-2232). The restored home of William Holmes McGuffey, who compiled the *McGuffey Eclectic Readers* while a member of the Miami University faculty here. Memorabilia and a collection of his books. Phone for schedule.

Pioneer Farm and House Museum (Doty and Brown roads; 513/523-8005). An 1835 farmhouse with period furniture, toys, and clothing. The circa-1850 barn displays a collection of early tools and farm implements. Phone for schedule.

PIQUA

Piqua Historical Area (3½ miles northwest on OH 66; 513/773-2522). On 170 acres in the Great Miami River valley, near the crossroads used by Indians, French and English fur traders, and General "Mad Anthony" Wayne, are several historic attractions. The 1810 John Johnston Home is a restored Dutch Colonial farmhouse built by an Indian agent. Outbuildings include a double-pen log barn, a springhouse, a fruit kiln, and a cider house. Craft demonstrations. The Indian Museum has artifacts from the 17th to 19th centuries. Visitors ride the *Gen'l Harrison,* a replica of a mid-19th-century canal boat, on a section of the Miami and Erie Canal. Open Wednesday through Sunday, Memorial Day to Labor Day; weekends only, Labor Day through October.

PORTSMOUTH

The 1810 House (1926 Waller St.; 614/354-6344). The original homestead has nine rooms with period furniture. Tours available. Open weekends, May through December.

PUT-IN-BAY

Perry's Victory and International Peace Monument (2 Bay View Ave.; 419/285-2184). A 352-foot granite Doric column commemorates Commodore Oliver Hazard Perry's victory over the British Naval Squadron at the Battle of Lake Erie, near this town in 1813. The observation platform provides a view of the battle site and the neighboring islands. The monument also commemorates the 3,986-mile U.S.-Canadian boundary, the longest unfortified border in the world. Open daily, May through late October.

Accommodations: *Fether* (1539 Langram Rd.; 419/285-5511). Victorian gardens and views of Lake Erie are outstanding features of the three acres surrounding this stately Queen Anne. Wraparound porch with rocking chairs and a swing. Five guest rooms, four with shared bath. Full breakfast. Inexpensive.

We have met the enemy and they are ours.

—CAPTAIN OLIVER HAZARD PERRY, *AFTER HIS VICTORY ON LAKE ERIE, 1813*

SPRINGFIELD

Pennsylvania House (1311 West Main St.; 513/322-7668). Built in 1824 as a tavern and stagecoach stop on the National Pike, the building has period furnishings and displays of pioneer artifacts, as well as quilt and doll collections. Open the first Sunday of each month.

David Crabill House (818 North Fountain Ave. in Buck Creek State Park; 513/324-0657). Built by pioneer David Crabill in 1826, the restored house has period rooms, a log barn, and a smokehouse. Open Tuesday through Friday.

TOLEDO

The French explored the Toledo area, where the Maumee River flows into Lake Erie, in 1615. The city began as a cluster of small villages along the river. During 1835–36 it was claimed by Ohio and Michigan in the Toledo War, which resulted in Toledo becoming part of Ohio and the Northern Peninsula going to Michigan.

Fort Meigs State Memorial (I-475 exit 2, then north onto OH 65, on West River Rd.; 419/874-4121). A reconstruction of a fort built under the supervision of William Henry Harrison in 1813 and used during the War of 1812. Blockhouses contain exhibits and demonstrations of military life. Picnicking. Open Wednesday through Sunday, June through August; Wednesday through Sunday, September and October.

Wolcott Museum Complex (I-75, OH 475 to 1031 River Rd. SW; 419/893-9602). The complex contains an early-19th-century house, a log house, a Greek Revival house, a farmhouse, a saltbox house, and a depot, all furnished in the style of the period. Open Wednesday through Sunday, April through December.

WARREN

John Stark Edwards House (303 Monroe St. NW; 216/394-4653). Built in 1807, this is the oldest surviving house in the Western Reserve, now maintained by the Trumbull County Historic Society. Open Sundays.

YOUNGSTOWN

Five miles from the Pennsylvania line, Youngstown covers an area of thirty-five square miles in the eastern coal province, which provides nine tenths of the high-grade coal in the country. The city's steel industry started in 1803 with a crude iron smelter.

Mill Creek Park (southwest part of city; 216/743-7275). An 1821 Western Reserve pioneer woolen mill is now the Pioneer Pavilion here. Lanterman's Mill (circa 1846) is a working gristmill. Tours available. Open daily except Mondays, May through October; weekends in April and November.

ZANESVILLE

Ebenezer Zane, surveyor of Zane's Trace through the dense Ohio forests and great-great-grandfather of author Zane Grey, chose this site because it was the junction of the Muskingum and Licking rivers. Initially called Westbourne, it was the first state capital, from 1810 to 1812.

National Road–Zane Grey Museum (10 miles east via I-70 exit 164, on U.S. 22/40, near Norwich; 614/872-3143). A 136-foot diorama traces the history of the Old National Road (Cumberland, Maryland, to Vandalia, Illinois). Vehicles that once traveled the road are on display, along with memorabilia of Western writer Zane Grey. Craft shops. Open daily, May through September; Wednesday through Sunday, March–April and October–November.

APPENDIX
STATE TRAVEL OFFICES

NEW ENGLAND
Connecticut Department of Economic
Development
865 Brook Street
Rocky Hill, CT 06067; 800/282-6863

Massachusetts Office of Travel and
Tourism
100 Cambridge Street, 13th Floor
Boston, MA 02202; 617/727-3201

Rhode Island Tourism Division
7 Jackson Walkway
Providence, RI 02903; 401/277-2601 or
800/556-2484

Maine Publicity Bureau
P.O. Box 2300
Hallowell, ME 04347; 207/582-9300

New Hampshire Office of Travel &
Tourism
172 Pembroke Road, P.O. Box 856
Concord, NH 03302; 603/271-2666 or
800/944-1167

Vermont Department of Travel and
Tourism
134 State Street
Montpelier, VT 95602; 802/828-3236

THE MID-ATLANTIC
New York State Department of
Economic Development
Division of Tourism
One Commerce plaza
Albany, NY 12245; 518/474-4116 or
800/CALL-NYS

Pennsylvania Office of Travel
Marketing
Department of Commerce, P.O. Box 61
Warrendale, PA 15086; 800/VISIT-PA

Delaware Tourism Office
99 Kings Highway, P.O. Box 1401
Dover, DE 19903; 302/739-4271 or

800/441-8846
Maryland Office of Tourism
Development
217 East Redwood Street
Baltimore, MD 21202; 800/543-1036

New Jersey Division of Travel and
Tourism
CN-836
Trenton, NJ 08635; 609/292-2470 or
800/JERSEY-7

Washington D.C. Convention and
Visitor Association
1212 New York Avenue, NW
Washington, DC 20005; 202/789-7000

THE UPPER SOUTH
Kentucky Department of Travel
Development
Department MR, P.O. Box 2011
Frankfort, KY 40602; 800/255-8747
ext. 67

Tennessee Department of Tourist
Development
P.O. Box 23170
Nashville, TN 37202; 615/741-2158

North Carolina Travel and Tourism
Division
430 North Salisbury Street
Raleigh, NC 27603; 800/VISIT-NC

Virginia Division of Tourism
Bell Tower on Capitol Square
101 North 9th Street
Richmond, VA 23219; 804/786-2838

West Virginia Division of Tourism and
Parks
State Capitol Complex
Charleston, WV 25305; 304/746-2121

THE DEEP SOUTH
Florida Division of Tourism, Visitors
Inquiry
126 Van Buren Street

Tallahassee, FL 32399-2000; 904/487-
1462
Georgia Tourism Department
P.O. Box 1776
Atlanta, Ga 30301; 404/656-3590 or
800/VISIT-GA

South Carolina Department of Parks,
Recreation & Tourism
1205 Pendleton Street
Columbia, SC 29201; 803/734-0122

Alabama Bureau of Tourism & Travel
401 Adams Avenue, P.O. Box 4309
Montgomery, AL 36103-4309;
334/242-4169

Mississippi Department of Economic
and Community Development, Division
of Tourism
P.O. Box 22825
Jackson, MS 39205; 601/359-3297 or
800/647-2290

THE OLD
NORTHWEST
Illinois Bureau of Tourism
Springfield, IL 62703; 800/223-0121

Indiana Department of Commerce,
Tourism & Film Development Division
One North Capitol Street, Suite 700
Indianapolis, IN 46204; 317/232-8860
or 800/289-6646

Michigan Department of Commerce,
Travel Bureau
P.O. Box 30226
Lansing, MI 48909; 800/543-2YES

Ohio Division of Travel and Tourism
Columbus, OH 43211; 614/297-2300

Wisconsin Division of Tourism
P.O. Box 7606
Madison, WI 53707; 608/266-2161 or
800/432-TRIP

INDEX